YAHOO!
HACKS™

GW00566534

Other resources from O'Reilly

Related titles
Amazon Hacks
eBay Hacks
eBay: The Missing
Manual
Google Hacks
Google: The Missing
Manual

Spidering Hacks
PayPal Hacks
Firefox Hacks
Greasemonkey Hacks
Creating Web Sites:
The Missing Manual

Hacks Series Home
hacks.oreilly.com is a community site for developers and power users of all stripes. Readers learn from each other as they share their favorite tips and tools for Mac OS X, Linux, Google, Windows XP, and more.

oreilly.com
oreilly.com is more than a complete catalog of O'Reilly books. You'll also find links to news, events, articles, weblogs, sample chapters, and code examples.

oreillynet.com is the essential portal for developers interested in open and emerging technologies, including new platforms, programming languages, and operating systems.

Conferences
O'Reilly brings diverse innovators together to nurture the ideas that spark revolutionary industries. We specialize in documenting the latest tools and systems, translating the innovator's knowledge into useful skills for those in the trenches. Visit *conferences.oreilly.com* for our upcoming events.

Safari Bookshelf (*safari.oreilly.com*) is the premier online reference library for programmers and IT professionals. Conduct searches across more than 1,000 books. Subscribers can zero in on answers to time-critical questions in a matter of seconds. Read the books on your Bookshelf from cover to cover or simply flip to the page you need. Try it today for free.

YAHOO!
HACKS™

Paul Bausch

O'REILLY®

Beijing · Cambridge · Farnham · Köln · Paris · Sebastopol · Taipei · Tokyo

Yahoo! Hacks™
by Paul Bausch

Copyright © 2006 O'Reilly Media, Inc. All rights reserved.
Printed in the United States of America.

Published by O'Reilly Media, Inc., 1005 Gravenstein Highway North,
Sebastopol, CA 95472.

O'Reilly books may be purchased for educational, business, or sales promotional use. Online editions are also available for most titles (*safari.oreilly.com*). For more information, contact our corporate/institutional sales department: (800) 998-9938 or *corporate@oreilly.com*.

Editor:	Brian Sawyer	**Production Editor:**	A. J. Fox
Series Editor:	Rael Dornfest	**Cover Designer:**	Hanna Dyer
Executive Editor:	Dale Dougherty	**Interior Designer:**	David Futato

Printing History:

October 2005:	First Edition.

Nutshell Handbook, the Nutshell Handbook logo, and the O'Reilly logo are registered trademarks of O'Reilly Media, Inc. The *Hacks* series designations, *Yahoo! Hacks*, the image of boots and spurs, and related trade dress are trademarks of O'Reilly Media, Inc.

Many of the designations used by manufacturers and sellers to distinguish their products are claimed as trademarks. Where those designations appear in this book, and O'Reilly Media, Inc., was aware of a trademark claim, the designations have been printed in caps or initial caps.

While every precaution has been taken in the preparation of this book, the publisher and author assume no responsibility for errors or omissions, or for damages resulting from the use of the information contained herein.

Small print: The technologies discussed in this publication, the limitations on these technologies that technology and content owners seek to impose, and the laws actually limiting the use of these technologies are constantly changing. Thus, some of the hacks described in this publication may not work, may cause unintended harm to systems on which they are used, or may not be consistent with applicable user agreements. Your use of these hacks is at your own risk, and O'Reilly Media, Inc. disclaims responsibility for any damage or expense resulting from their use. In any event, you should take care that your use of these hacks does not violate any applicable laws, including copyright laws.

 This book uses RepKover™, a durable and flexible lay-flat binding.

ISBN: 0-596-00945-3
[C]

Contents

Credits ix

Preface xiii

Chapter 1. Search 1

  1. Fine-Tune Yahoo! Web Search Queries   5
  2. Save Time with Search Shortcuts   7
  3. Create a Yahoo! ID   10
  4. Set Persistent Yahoo! Search Preferences   14
  5. Assemble Advanced Search Queries   17
  6. Translate Any Page with Yahoo!   20
  7. Personalize, Track, and Share the Web   25
  8. Prefetch Yahoo! Search Results   31
  9. Compare Yahoo! and Google Search Results   34
  10. Find Content You Can Reuse Legally   37
  11. Find Video from Across the Web   41
  12. Streamline Browsing with the Yahoo! Toolbar   46
  13. Customize the Firefox Quick Search Box   53
  14. Spot Trends with Yahoo! Buzz   55
  15. Find Hot Technologies at the Buzz Game   58
  16. Tame Long Yahoo! URLs   62
  17. Opt Out of Advertiser Cookies   65
  18. Track News About Yahoo!   68
  19. Spider the Yahoo! Catalog   74
  20. Browse the Yahoo! Directory   81
  21. Track Additions to Yahoo!   83
  22. Yahoo! Directory Mindshare in Google   86

Chapter 2. Services 91

23. Track Your Investments	92
24. Build Your Own Stock Update Email	97
25. Download Financial Data Using Excel Web Queries	102
26. Convert Currencies with One Click	108
27. Do the Math with Yahoo! Calculators	112
28. Add a Yahoo! Bookmark with One Click	118
29. Import Existing Bookmarks into Yahoo! Bookmarks	122
30. Open Yahoo! Bookmarks in a Sidebar	124
31. Publish Your Yahoo! Bookmarks	128
32. Track the Media's Attention Span over Time	130
33. Monitor the News with RSS	135
34. Personalize My Yahoo!	137
35. Track Your Favorite Sites with RSS	143
36. Add a Feed to My Yahoo! with a Right-Click	149
37. Build Your Own News Crawler	151
38. Replace Your Phone Book with Yahoo!	155
39. Monitor Your Commute	160
40. Get the Facts at Yahoo! Reference	163
41. Find and Rate Movies	167
42. Subscribe to Movie Showtimes	174
43. View Movie Lists on Your Cell Phone	178
44. Plan Your TV Viewing	182
45. Create a TV Watch List	188
46. Develop and Share a Trip Itinerary	191
47. Shop Intelligently	196
48. Visualize Your Music Collection	201
49. Take Yahoo! on the Go	207
50. Stay Connected with Yahoo! Alerts	211

Chapter 3. Communicating 216

51. Navigate Yahoo! Mail	216
52. Manage Yahoo! Mail	220
53. Create Yahoo! Mail Macros	224
54. Read All Your Email in One Place	228

55. Read Yahoo! Mail in Your Preferred Email Client   233

56. Manage and Share Your Schedule   235

57. Add Contacts to Your Yahoo! Address Book   241

58. Map Yahoo! Address Book Contacts   247

59. Discuss, Share, and Collaborate with Others   252

60. Archive Yahoo! Groups Messages with yahoo2mbox   256

61. Explore Your Social Networks   258

62. Import an Existing Blogroll to Yahoo! 360   264

63. Add an API to Your Yahoo! 360 Blog   268

64. Create a Yahoo! Avatar   273

65. Add a Content Tab to Yahoo! Messenger   276

66. Send Instant Messages Beyond Yahoo!   282

67. Store, Sort, and Share Your Photos   285

Chapter 4. Web Services **294**

68. Program Yahoo! with Perl   300

69. Program Yahoo! with PHP 5   302

70. Program Yahoo! with Python   305

71. Program Yahoo! with VBScript   308

72. Program Yahoo! with ColdFusion   311

73. Program Yahoo! with XSLT   314

74. Program Yahoo! with Java   317

75. Program Yahoo! with Ruby   321

76. Program Yahoo! with REBOL   323

Chapter 5. Applications **327**

77. Visualize Yahoo! Web Search Results   327

78. Find Links to Any Web Site   332

79. Import Yahoo! Local Listings into Your Address Book   336

80. Create a Yahoo! Local MIDlet   343

81. Import Yahoo! Local Listings into Excel   348

82. Spell Words with Yahoo! Images   353

83. Randomize Your Windows Desktop Background   358

84. Randomize Your Mac Desktop Background   364

85. Mash Up Images from Around the Web   367

86. Illustrate Any Web Site   369

87. Add Links to a Block of Text Automatically   373

88. Visualize News Topics as Tags   379

89. Get Related Terms Instantly with Ajax   382

90. Compare the Popularity of Related Search Terms   387

91. Plot Multiple Points on Your Own Map   392

Chapter 6. Webmastering **398**

92. Get Your Site Listed at Yahoo!   398

93. Hide Part of Your Web Site from Yahoo!   402

94. Search Your Web Site with Yahoo!   406

95. Add Presence to Your Web Site   408

96. Syndicate Rich Media   411

97. Add Contextual Search to Your Blog   417

98. Post Photos to Your Blog   421

99. Feed Your Latest Photos to Your Web Site   428

100. Display Messages from a Yahoo! Group on Your Web Site   435

Index **441**

Credits

About the Author

Paul Bausch is an independent web developer living in Corvallis, Oregon. When he's not hacking together web applications, he's writing about hacking together web applications. He put together *Amazon Hacks* for O'Reilly in 2003. Paul also helped create the popular weblog application Blogger (*http://www.blogger.com*), cowrote a book about weblogs called *We Blog: Publishing Online with Weblogs* (Wiley), and maintains a directory of Oregon weblogs called ORblogs (*http://www.orblogs.com*). When he's not working on a book, Paul posts thoughts and photos to his personal weblog, *onfocus* (*http://www.onfocus.com*).

Contributors

The following people contributed their hacks, writing, and inspiration to this book:

- Jacek Artymiak (*http://www.artymiak.com*) is a freelance consultant, developer, and writer. He's been programming computers since 1986, starting with the Sinclair ZX Spectrum. His interests include network security, computer graphics and animation, and multimedia. Jacek lives in Lublin, Poland, with his wife, Gosia, and can be reached at *jacek@artymiak.com*.

- Bonnie Biafore is the author of several books about personal finance, investing, and project management. As an engineer, she's tenaciously attentive to detail and digests tantalizing morsels about every topic she approaches. Her sick sense of humor turns subjects that are drool-inducing in other books into entertaining, easy reading. Her book the *NAIC Stock Selection Handbook* won major awards from both the Society of Technical Communication and APEX Awards for Publication Excellence, but she cherishes the raves she's received from beginning investors most of all. She is also the author of *Online Investing Hacks* (O'Reilly) and *QuickBooks 2005: The Missing Manual* (O'Reilly). Bonnie writes a monthly column called WebWatch for *Better Investing* magazine and is a regular contributor to WomensWallStreet.com. As a consultant, she manages projects for clients and wins accolades for her ability to herd cats. When not chained to her computer, she hikes in the mountains with her dogs, cooks gourmet meals, and practices saying no to additional work assignments. You can learn more at Bonnie's web site, *http://www.bonniebiafore.com*, or email her at *bonnie.biafore@gmail.com*.

- Tara Calishain is the editor of *ResearchBuzz* (*http://www.researchbuzz.com*), a weekly newsletter on Internet searching and online information resources. She's also a regular columnist for Searcher magazine. She's been writing about search engines and searching since 1996; her recent books include *Google Hacks* (O'Reilly) and *Web Search Garage* (O'Reilly).

- Kevin Hemenway (*http://www.disobey.com*), better known as Morbus Iff, is the creator of Disobey.com, which bills itself as "content for the discontented." Publisher, developer, and writer of more home cooking than you could ever imagine (like the popular open sourced syndicated reader AmphetaDesk, the best-kept gaming secret Gamegrene.com, the popular Ghost Sites and Nonsense Network, the giggle-inducing articles at the O'Reilly Network, a few pieces at Apple's Internet Developer site, etc.), he's an ardent supporter of cloning, merely so he can get more work done. He cooks with a Fry Pan of Intellect +2 and lives in Concord, New Hampshire.

- Ryan Kennedy is a software engineer at Yahoo!, working on Yahoo! Mail. In his spare time, he maintains the Yahoo! Java Search SDK.

- Philipp Lenssen lives in Stuttgart, Germany, where he blogs about Google, works as a programmer on an automobile web site, and eats spicy Thai food with his girlfriend. He likes to ponder future technology and jump on any technology bandwagon that seems worthwhile, especially all the APIs that make a developer's life that much easier. Philipp's daily musings can be found at *http://blog.outer-court.com*.

- Mikel Maron is an independent software developer and ecologist. He has built several geographic-oriented projects around the worldKit mapping package, including World as a Blog and mapufacture. Previously, he led development of My Yahoo! in the pre-RSS days. Mikel was awarded a master's degree from the University of Sussex for building a simulation of the evolution of complexity in food webs. Originally from California, Mikel is presently based mostly in Brighton, United Kingdom, with his wife, Anna. Links to various things can be found at *http://brainoff.com*.

- Deepak Nadig is an entrepreneur and has helped build innovative and useful products for 14 years. He is currently taking a break after cofounding and selling Covigna, a pioneer in Contract Lifecycle Management.

- Todd Ogasawara focuses on Mobile Workforce and Mobile Lifestyle technology, paying special attention to the Microsoft Windows Mobile platform (Pocket PC and Smartphone). Microsoft has recognized his demonstrated practical expertise and willingness to share his experience by recognizing him as a Microsoft Most Valuable Professional (MVP) in the Mobile Devices category since 2000. His other technology focus is in the effort to bring commercial (especially Microsoft-related) products and GNU/Open Source software together in a synergistic and productive way. Todd has written several articles about mobile devices, digital cameras, and the Apple Mac Mini for the O'Reilly Network. He previously worked as a technology analyst for GTE/Verizon. He also served as the contracted forum manager for the MSN.com (and later ZDNet) Telephony Forum and Windows CE Forum. More recently, he has served as the eGovernment team leader for the State of Hawaii. You can find his Mobile Workforce and Lifestyle commentary at *http://www.MobileViews.com*. You can learn more about Eccentric Technology at *http://www.OgasaWalrus.com*. You can reach Todd by email at *Hacks@OgasaWalrus.com*.

- Mark Pilgrim is an accessibility architect by day. By night, he is a husband and father who lives in North Carolina with his wife, his son, and his dog. Mark spends his copious free time sunbathing, skydiving, and reading Immanuel Kant's *Critique of Pure Reason* in the original Klingon. He can be found stirring up trouble at *http://diveintomark.org*.

- Premshree Pillai is a geek working at Yahoo!. He loves Ruby, beer, and classic rock. He blogs at *http://www.livejournal.com/users/premshree*.

- Eric Ries is currently CTO of IMVU, a startup creating 3-D, avatar-based instant messaging. Eric also serves, in a volunteer capacity, as CTO of the Taproot Foundation. Previously, he was senior software engineer at There and cofounder and CTO of Catalyst Recruiting. He is author of several free software projects, most recently the peer-to-peer RPC system Kenosis, and coauthor of several books, including *The Black Art of Java Game Programming* and *Mastering Java*.

- Alan Taylor has been a web developer for over 10 years and has worked for Monster.com, MSNBC.com, and Amazon.com. He builds web projects (such as Amazon Light; *http://kokogiak.com/amazon*) and web hacks/toys on an irregular basis, most of which can be found at *http://kokogiak.com*. Alan believes that open APIs are your friends and are positively the best trend on the Internet in years.

Acknowledgments

To my wife, Shawnde, thanks for the continuous feedback and frontline editing, and for cheerfully discussing Yahoo! during breakfast, lunch, dinner, and every spare moment in between.

Many thanks go to Brian Sawyer for providing direction and encouragement, and for fine-tuning the text.

Thanks to tech editor Steve Champeon for testing code, double-checking facts, and adding important points to the technical details.

Thanks to Morbus Iff for taking my Perl to task and simplifying the confusing bits.

Finally, thanks to everyone at Yahoo! who contributed tips and hack ideas, including Vijay Anisetti, Stig Sæther Bakken, Dave Brown, Aurora Casanova, David Dueblin, Jennifer Dulski, Marcus Foster, David Hall, Jason B. Silverstein, Jeremy Zawodny, and many anonymous Yahoos. Thanks also to Chris Kalaboukis and Bernard Mangold at Yahoo! Research for lending a hand.

Preface

Yahoo! is an impressive example of what can happen when a hobby takes on a life of its own. In 1994, Jerry Yang and David Filo began publishing a personal list of sites they found interesting on the emerging World Wide Web. As "Jerry's Guide to the World Wide Web" grew larger, the two Stanford grad students began organizing the sites into categories, and the basic structure of today's Yahoo! Directory was born. By late 1994, they chose to rename their directory after the word *yahoo* because its original definition describing a crude, rude person appealed to the pair's subversive natures. (And as true computer geeks, they turned Yahoo! into an acronym for Yet Another Hierarchical Officious Oracle.) Figure P-1 is a look at the Yahoo! home page from December 1994.

Yahoo! looks very different today. Figure P-2 shows the more familiar Yahoo! home page of 2005.

Though the two Yahoo! home pages look radically different, the original idea of taming the chaos of the World Wide Web and making it accessible to a wider audience remains. According to their vision statement, Yahoo! wants "to enable people to find, use, share, and expand all human knowledge." The goal of furthering this vision, nicknamed FUSE (for "find, use, share, and expand"), can be found in every acquisition Yahoo! makes and every product Yahoo! releases. Yahoo! has localized versions of its offerings in dozens of countries, and the Yahoo! brand is recognized around the world. Over the past 10 years, Yahoo! has become much more than a guide to the Web; Yahoo! is a platform for visualizing and connecting with the world.

Many Yahoo! features are familiar to anyone who uses the Web. Millions of people use Yahoo! Search to find information on the Web. Millions more use Yahoo! Groups to share information and collaborate on projects. And still more use Yahoo! Mail every day to stay in touch with friends, family, and coworkers. And Yahoo! is continually adding products and features to realize its vision.

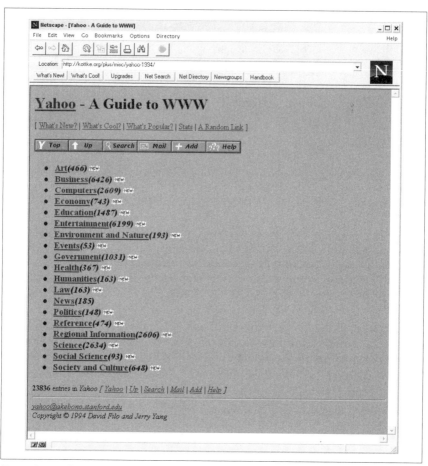

Figure P-1. Yahoo! in 1994

Over the past year, the FUSE philosophy has been a distinct feature of Yahoo!'s newest services. In February 2005, Yahoo! launched Yahoo! Web Services, allowing outside developers to use, share, and expand Yahoo! features. In March 2005, Yahoo! launched Yahoo! 360, a way for people to share thoughts and information with friends and family, while expanding a network of friends. In April 2005, Yahoo! introduced My Web, a way to save and share search results while creating your own personal categorized directory of the Web.

This book aims to help you FUSE Yahoo! features and services by introducing you to little-known corners of Yahoo!, by reintroducing you to familiar Yahoo! services, and by showing you examples of the many ways people are expanding Yahoo! on their own. Though the hacks might be crude and rude at times, they're written in the same spirit of sharing something interesting that inspired the creation of Yahoo! in the first place.

Figure P-2. Yahoo! in 2005

Why Yahoo! Hacks?

The term *hacking* has a bad reputation in the press. They use it to refer to someone who breaks into systems or wreaks havoc with computers as their weapon. Among people who write code, though, the term *hack* refers to a quick-and-dirty solution to a problem, or a clever way to get something done. And the term *hacker* is taken very much as a compliment, referring to someone as being *creative*, having the technical chops to get things done. The Hacks series is an attempt to reclaim the word, document the good ways people are hacking, and pass the hacker ethic of creative participation on to the uninitiated. Seeing how others approach systems and problems is often the quickest way to learn about a new technology.

While Yahoo! itself has been around for over 10 years, it is releasing new applications, web sites, and software at a blinding pace. This book isn't intended to catalog everything Yahoo! offers, but rather to introduce new technologies, such as Yahoo! Web Services, while showing novel ways to use perennial offerings like Yahoo! Search, Yahoo! Mail, and Yahoo! Groups. Through the years, developers have scraped, poked, and prodded every corner of Yahoo! for their own uses, and the release of Yahoo! Web Services is like a welcome mat being put out for a wider audience of would-be hackers. This book intends to show you what's possible when you view Yahoo! as a platform and inspire your inner hacker to take a new look at Yahoo!.

How to Use This Book

You can read this book from cover to cover if you like, but each hack stands on its own, so feel free to browse and jump to the different sections that interest you most. If there's a prerequisite you need to know about, a cross-reference will guide you to the right hack.

How to Run the Hacks

The programmatic hacks in this book run either on the command line (that's Terminal for Mac OS X folk, DOS command window for Windows users) or as CGI (that's "common gateway interface") scripts—dynamic pages living on your web site, accessed through your web browser.

Command-Line Scripts

Running a hack on the command line invariably involves the following steps:

1. Type the program into a garden-variety text editor: Notepad on Windows, TextEdit on Mac OS X, *vi* or Emacs on Unix/Linux, or anything else of the sort. Save the file as directed—usually as *scriptname.pl* (the *pl* bit stands for Perl, the predominant programming language used in *Yahoo! Hacks*).

   Alternately, you can download the code for all of the hacks online at *http://www.oreilly.com/catalog/yahoohks*, where there is a ZIP archive containing individual scripts saved as text files.

2. Get to the command line on your computer or remote server. In Mac OS X, launch the Terminal (Applications → Utilities → Terminal). In Windows, click the Start button, select Run..., type command, and hit the Enter/Return key on your keyboard. In Unix...well, we'll just assume you know how to get to the command line.

3. Navigate to where you saved the script at hand. This varies from operating system to operating system, but usually involves something like cd ~/Desktop (that's your Desktop on the Mac).

4. Invoke the script by running the programming language's interpreter (e.g., Perl) and feeding it the script (e.g., *scriptname.pl*) like so:

```
$ perl scriptname.pl
```

Most often, you'll also need to pass along some parameters—your search query, the number of results you'd like, and so forth. Simply drop them in after the script name, enclosing them in quotes if they're more than one word or if they include an odd character or three:

```
$ perl scriptname.pl '"much ado about nothing" script' 10
```

The results of your script are almost always sent straight back to the command-line window in which you're working, like so:

```
$ perl scriptname.pl '"much ado about nothing" script' 10
1. "Amazon.com: Books: Much Ado About Nothing: Screenplay ..." [http://
www.amazon.com/exec/obidos/tg/detail/-/0393311112?v=glance]
2. "Much Ado About Nothing Script" [http://www.signal42.com/much_ado_
about_nothing_script.asp]
...
```

 The elllpsis (...) bit signifies that we've cut off the output for brevity's sake.

To stop output scrolling off your screen faster than you can read it, on most systems you can *pipe* (read: redirect) the output to a little program called more:

```
$ perl scriptname.pl | more
```

Hit the Enter/Return key on your keyboard to scroll through line by line, or the space bar to leap through page by page.

You'll also sometimes want to direct output to a file for safekeeping, importing into your spreadsheet application, or displaying on your web site. This is as easy as:

```
$ perl scriptname.pl > output_filename.txt
```

And to pour some input into your script from a file, simply do the opposite:

```
$ perl scriptname.pl < input_filename.txt
```

Don't worry if you can't remember all of this; each command-line hack has a "Running the Hack" section that shows you just how it's done.

CGI Scripts

CGI scripts—programs that run on your web site and produce pages dynamically—are a little more complicated if you're not used to them. While fundamentally they're the same sorts of scripts as those run on the command line, they are more troublesome because setups vary so widely. You might be running your own server, your web site might be hosted on an Internet service provider's (ISP's) server, your content might live on a corporate intranet server—or anything in between.

Since going through every possibility is beyond the scope of this (or any) book, you should check your ISP's knowledge base, or call the ISP's technical support department, or ask your local system administrator for help.

Generally, though, the methodology is the same:

1. Type the program in to a garden-variety text editor: Notepad on Windows, TextEdit on Mac OS X, *vi* or Emacs on Unix/Linux, or anything else of the sort. Save the file as directed—usually as *scriptname.cgi* (the *cgi* bit reveals that you're dealing with a CGI script).

   Alternately, you can download the code for all of the hacks online at *http://www.oreilly.com/catalog/yahoohks*, where there is a ZIP archive containing individual scripts saved as text files.

2. Move the script over to wherever your web site lives. You should have some directory on a server somewhere in which all of your web pages (all those *.html* files) and images (ending in *.jpg*, *.gif*, etc.) live. Within this directory, you'll probably see something called a *cgi-bin* directory: this is where a CGI script must usually live in order for the server to run the script (rather than just displaying the script's text in your web browser) when you visit its URL.

3. You usually need to "bless" CGI scripts as executable—to be run rather than displayed. Just how you do this depends on the operating system of your server. If you're on a Unix/Linux or Mac OS X system, this usually entails typing the following on the command line:

   ```
   $ chmod 755 scriptname.cgi
   ```

4. Now you should be able to point your web browser at the script and have it run as expected, behaving in a manner similar to that described in the "Running the Hack" section of the hack at hand.

   Just what URL you use, once again, varies widely. It should, however, look something like *http://www.your_domain.com/cgi-bin/scriptname.cgi*, where *your_domain.com* is your web site domain, *cgi-bin* refers to the directory in which your CGI scripts live, and *scriptname.cgi* is the script itself.

If you don't have your own domain and are hosted at an ISP, the URL is more likely to look like *http://www.your_isp.com/~your_username/cgi-bin/scriptname.cgi*, where *your_isp.com* is your ISP's domain, *~your_username* is your username at the ISP, *cgi-bin* refers to the directory in which your CGI scripts live, and *scriptname.cgi* is the script itself.

If you come up with something called an "internal server error" or see the error code 500, something's gone wrong somewhere in the process. At this point you can take a crack at debugging (read: shaking the bugs out) yourself or ask your ISP or system administrator for help. Debugging—especially CGI debugging—can be a little more than the average newbie can bear, but there is help in the form of a famous frequently asked question (FAQ) archive: "The Idiot's Guide to Solving Perl CGI Problems." Search for it and step through as directed.

Learning to Code

Fancy trying your hand at a spot of programming? O'Reilly's best-selling *Learning Perl* (*http://www.oreilly.com/catalog/lperl3*), by Randal L. Schwartz and Tom Phoenix, provides a good start. Apply what you learn to understanding and using the hacks in this book, perhaps even taking on the "Hacking the Hack" sections to tweak and fiddle with the scripts. This is a useful way to get a little programming under your belt if you're a searching nut, since it's always a little easier to learn how to program when you have a task to accomplish and existing code to leaf through.

How This Book Is Organized

The book is divided into several chapters, organized by subject:

Chapter 1, *Search*
> This chapter shows you how to become a Yahoo! power searcher by taking advantage of meta keywords to return more relevant results. You'll also see how to use search shortcuts to find instant answers to some common questions. This chapter tells you how to find popular search phrases and technologies by analyzing Yahoo! Buzz, and we'll pit Yahoo! against Google to see which search engine returns the most relevant results.

Chapter 2, *Services*
> Yahoo! offers information about everything from stocks and bonds to movie and TV schedules. This chapter shows some unique ways to

use Yahoo! Web Services, including monitoring your commute for problems, watching TV schedules automatically for appearances by your favorite celebrities, and visualizing your music collection.

Chapter 3, *Communicating*

Use the hacks in this chapter to reach out and touch someone. You'll find hacks for managing your Yahoo! Mail, collaborating with Yahoo! Groups, and exploring your social networks with Yahoo! 360. This chapter also shows some ways to personalize Yahoo! Messenger and share your photos with the world.

Chapter 4, *Web Services*

This chapter introduces you to the back door that Yahoo! has opened for developers. You'll find bare-bones examples in several scripting languages that can give you a head start to creating your own Yahoo!-powered applications.

Chapter 5, *Applications*

See how people are using Yahoo! data in their own applications and have a bit of fun in the process. Find out how to randomize your desktop background with images from across the Web and how to integrate Yahoo! with Excel and Outlook.

Chapter 6, *Webmastering*

If you publish on the Web, you're well aware of the traffic Yahoo! can send to your site. This chapter shows how to get listed and introduces you to other Yahoo! components you can plug into your site.

Conventions Used in This Book

The following is a list of the typographical conventions used in this book:

Italics

Used to indicate URLs, filenames, filename extensions, and directory names. For example, a path in the filesystem will appear as */Developer/Applications*.

Constant width

Used to show code examples, the contents of files, and console output, as well as the names of variables, commands, and other code excerpts.

Constant width bold

Used to highlight portions of code, typically new additions to old code. Also used to show text you should type literally at a command-line prompt.

Constant width italic

Used in code examples and other excerpts to show sample text to be replaced with your own values.

Gray type

Used to indicate a cross-reference within the text.

↵

A carriage return (↵) at the end of a line of code is used to denote an unnatural line break; that is, you should not enter these as two lines of code, but as one continuous line. Multiple lines are used in these cases due to page-width constraints.

You should pay special attention to notes set apart from the text with the following icons:

This is a tip, suggestion, or general note. It contains useful supplementary information about the topic at hand.

This is a warning or note of caution, often indicating that your money or your privacy might be at risk.

The thermometer icons, found next to each hack, indicate the relative complexity of the hack:

 beginner   moderate   expert

Using Code Examples

This book is here to help you get your job done. In general, you may use the code in this book in your programs and documentation. You do not need to contact us for permission unless you're reproducing a significant portion of the code. For example, writing a program that uses several chunks of code from this book does not require permission. Selling or distributing a CD-ROM of examples from O'Reilly books *does* require permission. Answering a question by citing this book and quoting example code does not require permission. Incorporating a significant amount of example code from this book into your product's documentation *does* require permission.

We appreciate, but do not require, attribution. An attribution usually includes the title, author, publisher, and ISBN. For example: "*Yahoo! Hacks* by Paul Bausch. Copyright 2006 O'Reilly Media, Inc., 0-596-00945-3."

If you feel your use of code examples falls outside fair use or the permission given above, feel free to contact us at *permissions@oreilly.com*.

Safari Enabled

 When you see a Safari® Enabled icon on the cover of your favorite technology book, that means the book is available online through the O'Reilly Network Safari Bookshelf.

Safari offers a solution that's better than e-books. It's a virtual library that lets you easily search thousands of top tech books, cut and paste code samples, download chapters, and find quick answers when you need the most accurate, current information. Try it for free at *http://safari.oreilly.com*.

How to Contact Us

We have tested and verified the information in this book to the best of our ability, but you may find that features have changed (or even that we have made mistakes!). As a reader of this book, you can help us to improve future editions by sending us your feedback. Please let us know about any errors, inaccuracies, bugs, misleading or confusing statements, and typos that you find anywhere in this book.

Please also let us know what we can do to make this book more useful to you. We take your comments seriously and will try to incorporate reasonable suggestions into future editions. You can write to us at:

O'Reilly Media, Inc.
1005 Gravenstein Hwy N.
Sebastopol, CA 95472
(800) 998-9938 (in the U.S. or Canada)
(707) 829-0515 (international/local)
(707) 829-0104 (fax)

To ask technical questions or to comment on the book, send email to:

bookquestions@oreilly.com

The web site for *Yahoo! Hacks* lists examples, errata, and plans for future editions. You can find this page at:

http://www.oreilly.com/catalog/yahoohks

For more information about this book and others, see the O'Reilly web site:

http://www.oreilly.com

Got a Hack?

To explore Hacks books online or to contribute a hack for future titles, visit:

http://hacks.oreilly.com

## CHAPTER ONE

Search

Hacks 1–22

Many of us use search engines in the same way we we use street signs. We use them to navigate, to get our bearings, and to pinpoint our destination. We rarely stop to consider the signs themselves or look for more information they might be telling us. As with street signs, we'd be lost without search engines, and by taking a few minutes to contemplate the Yahoo! Web Search results page, you might find new ways to reach your destination.

Take a look at Figure 1-1, which shows a Yahoo! Web Search results page for the query ancient greece.

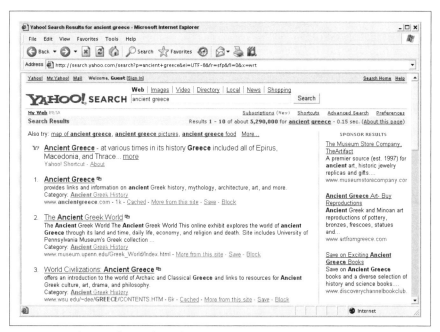

Figure 1-1. Yahoo! Web Search results

You can see the familiar numbered listing of search results, but there are a number of other bits of information on the page. Here's a look at what's available on a Yahoo! Search results page:

Navigation bar

You'll find the gray navigation bar at the top of the page on many pages at Yahoo! sites. The bar provides a consistent way to get to the main Yahoo! page (*http://www.yahoo.com*), the My Yahoo! portal [Hack #34], and Yahoo! Mail [Hack #52]. The bar also indicates your login status by displaying your Yahoo! ID [Hack #3] or *Guest*, along with links that let you sign in to Yahoo! or sign out. You can also click the Help link at the far right of the navigation bar to read documentation about the site.

Search links

Just above the search form, you'll find links to other Yahoo! searches, including Images, Video [Hack #11], the Yahoo! Directory [Hack #20], Yahoo! News [Hack #32], and Yahoo! Shopping [Hack #47]. You can click any of these search links to search with the exact query you used at one of the other Yahoo! Search properties so that you don't have to retype your search term.

Result count

Search results are returned as a number of pages, and you'll find your position within the results in the shaded blue bar. For instance, the first page of results will be labeled as Results 1–10, the second page will show Results 11–20, and so on. (You can adjust the number of results per page by setting your search preferences [Hack #4].) You'll also see the estimated total number of results for your query.

Query definition links

Just to the right of the result count, you'll see the words in the query as links. You can click the links to see dictionary definitions of the words at Yahoo! Reference [Hack #40].

Search speed

The shaded blue bar will also show you how long it took to fetch the results, usually less than a half-second.

Sponsor results

You'll find context-sensitive advertising along the right side of the page and in a shaded blue box above or below the Yahoo! Web Search results. Advertising is always clearly labeled Sponsor Results, and the type of ads will be triggered by the topic you're searching for.

Search suggestions

Search phrases similar to the one you entered are labeled with Also Try: at the top of the page. These suggestions show you what other Yahoo! users are searching for related to your topic and can help you refine your search. Yahoo! will display the top few suggestions, and if there are several suggestions you can click the More or Show All links to see a complete list of suggestions available.

Yahoo! shortcut info

If your query triggered a Yahoo! Shortcut [Hack #2], the shortcut info will be shown above the Web results and marked with the Y! logo. Shortcuts usually give you brief information about your query, with links to more information at other Yahoo! properties.

Web results

The Web Search results show the familiar list of documents from across the Web, which contain your query words or phrases. Each result is numbered and includes the document title, a brief excerpt with query words in bold, and the document location.

Results page

Below the Web Search results you can navigate between results pages by clicking a page number or the Prev and Next links.

Each Yahoo! Web Search result represents a document somewhere on the Web. The document will most likely be a web page written in HTML, but could be in another format such as Adobe PDF, Microsoft Word, or plain text. Figure 1-2 shows a typical Yahoo! Web Search result with all of the associated links and features.

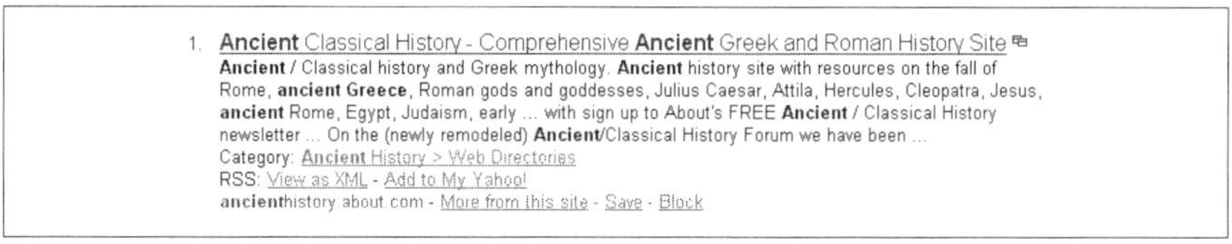

1. **Ancient** Classical History - Comprehensive **Ancient** Greek and Roman History Site
    Ancient / Classical history and Greek mythology. **Ancient** history site with resources on the fall of Rome, **ancient Greece**, Roman gods and goddesses, Julius Caesar, Attila, Hercules, Cleopatra, Jesus, **ancient** Rome, Egypt, Judaism, early ... with sign up to About's FREE **Ancient** / Classical History newsletter ... On the (newly remodeled) **Ancient**/Classical History Forum we have been ...
    Category: Ancient History > Web Directories
    RSS: View as XML - Add to My Yahoo!
    ancienthistory.about.com - More from this site - Save - Block

Figure 1-2. A single Yahoo! Web Search result

A closer look at a Web Search result shows that there's more listed than simply a document title and excerpt. Here's a look at what you'll find with each result:

Document title

The document title is pulled from the document itself, either from HTML `<title>` tags within the document or from the first few words in the document. Click the title to view the page or document.

New window link

To the right of the title is an icon showing two windows that you can click to open the document in a new browser window. This option is handy for keeping your search results in place while you read through pages of the results in different windows.

Document excerpt
> Just below the title, you'll find an excerpt of text from the document with words or phrases from your query in bold. This helps you determine the context of your search phrase and can tell you quickly whether the document is relevant.

Category
> If the document or page is listed in the Yahoo! Directory, you'll see the category that page is listed in. You can click the category title to see that category and view other sites that Yahoo! Editors have chosen to include in the directory.

RSS
> Many web publishers associate an RSS feed with their sites, which allows readers to subscribe to site updates in programs called Newsreaders or at sites such as My Yahoo! that pull content from other sources. When Yahoo! detects the presence of a site feed, you'll find a link to view that feed as raw XML or add the feed to My Yahoo! with a click.

URL
> On the last line of the listing, you'll see the document URL in green with any words from your query in bold. This tells you the domain the document is hosted under, and you can tell from the top-level domain (*.com*, *.edu*, *.gov*, etc.) whether the site is run by a business, a school, or the U.S. government.

Size in bytes
> Many results (such as those listed earlier in Figure 1-1) show the size of the document in bytes, which can give you a rough idea of how long the page will take to download. Web pages are usually fairly quick, but Microsoft Word documents or Adobe PDF files might vary widely in size.

Cache
> If Yahoo! has a copy of the document saved on its servers, you can click the Cached link to view the copy. This is particularly useful if the site isn't responding, as you can still get to an archived copy of the information.

Other pages
> The "More from this site" link will show you other pages at the domain that match your query.

My Web links
> Yahoo!'s My Web [Hack #7] lets you save sites that you want to remember, or block sites that you never want to see in results again. You can use the Save and Block links to add or remove documents.

Once you're aware of all the features of the Yahoo! Web Search results page, you can make decisions about the best path to the information you're after.

This chapter shows you how to take advantage of Yahoo! Web Search in a number of different ways—from using meta keywords for quick answers [Hack #1] to viewing results in a radically different way [Hack #77].

 HACK
#1 # Fine-Tune Yahoo! Web Search Queries

By understanding how to phrase your searches, you'll find more relevant search results.

Using Yahoo! Web Search (*http://search.yahoo.com*) is deceptively simple. You can type in any word or phrase and find matches in documents across the Web. The trade-off for this simplicity is having to look through hundreds, thousands, or millions of results to find the documents that are actually useful to you. By understanding how Yahoo! expects queries to be phrased, you can limit the results to include only those documents most relevant to you—saving you the time of looking through extraneous results.

Search Basics

To start building sophisticated queries, you need to know the basics. The following search basics will help you refine your Yahoo! searches:

Keyword

By default, Yahoo! searches for all of the words you type into a search form. If you type grammar into the search form, Yahoo! will return documents that contain the word *grammar*. A search for grammar school will return documents that contain both words somewhere within the document, but not necessarily together.

Complete phrase

To search for words in a specific order, enclose the words in quotation marks. A search for "grammar school" will return documents that contain the complete phrase *grammar school*. You can combine keyword and phrase searches. To find documents that contain the phrase *grammar school* and also have the word *Oregon* somewhere in the document, you could search for "grammar school" Oregon.

OR *keyword*

You can change the default behavior of keyword searches by using the capitalized keyword OR between words. A search for grammar OR primary will return documents that contain either *grammar* or *primary*, but not necessarily both words.

Exclude words or phrases

To find documents without a certain word, you can use the minus sign (-) along with the word you want to exclude. If a search for Oregon school returns too many pages for schools in the city of Portland, you could type Oregon school -Portland to exclude any pages with the word *Portland* from the results.

Once you have the basics down, you can start mixing and matching, and grouping queries together with parentheses. To find documents that contain the word *Oregon*, and the phrase *grammar school* or the phrase *elementary school*, you could type Oregon ("grammar school" OR "elementary school"). The parentheses are required to show where the OR should be used. Without the parentheses, Yahoo! would look for documents that contain both the word *Oregon* and the phrase *grammar school*, or documents that simply contain the phrase *elementary school*. Because the word *Oregon* is necessary across documents, the two secondary phrases need to be grouped into a single unit with parentheses.

Search Meta Words

In addition to the basic operators, there are keywords that Yahoo! calls *Search Meta Words* that you can use to refine your search:

site:
>   Use this keyword to limit search results to a single web site. You can search for the word *mars* across NASA sites by typing mars site:nasa. gov. All of the results will be from sites hosted at the *nasa.gov* domain. You also use this keyword to limit results to a single top-level domain, such as *.org*, *.com*, or *.edu*. To find mentions of the word *mars* across academic sites, type mars site:.edu.

hostname:
>   This keyword limits results to a specific host at a site. For example, NASA's Mars Exploration Program has a web site at *http://mars.jpl.nasa. gov*. If you want to search this specific section of the *nasa.gov* domain for the word *rover*, you could type rover hostname:mars.jpl.nasa.gov.

link:
>   You can use this keyword to find sites that link to a specific URL. This keyword works well if you want to judge the popularity of a specific page by finding the number of other sites linking to a particular page. You'll need to include the full URL, so to find pages that link to the *Amazon Hacks* page at the O'Reilly Hacks site, type link:http://www. oreilly.com/catalog/amazonhks/.

linkdomain:
>   Instead of a specific page, this keyword looks for any links to a specific domain. If you're interested in pages that link to *http://www.oreilly.com*, type linkdomain:oreilly.com.

url:

> This keyword lets you look up a single page at Yahoo! by specifying the URL. You can look up the O'Reilly Hacks home page by typing `url:http://hacks.oreilly.com`. You could use this keyword to see how pages at a site are displayed in Yahoo!'s Web, Images, and Video Search results.

inurl:

> Use this keyword to find sites that have a specific word within the URL. To find all sites that have the word *mars* in the URL, type `inurl:mars`.

intitle:

> Like `inurl:`, this keyword returns documents that have a specific word in the document title. To find documents with *mars* in the title, use `intitle:mars`.

You can also use the basic search operators in combination with the Search Meta Words to refine your search. Say you'd like to search for the word *mars* across documents, but you don't want pages from any *nasa.gov* site; type `mars -site:nasa.gov`. Because Yahoo! supports very long queries, you could specify a whole list of sites that you don't want information from: `mars -site:nasa.gov -site:mars.com -site:space.com`. But to search those sites exclusively, take away the minus symbol, group the site list together with parentheses, and use the `OR` keyword like this: `mars (site:nasa.gov OR site:mars.com OR site:space.com)`. Again, note that the use of the `OR` keyword requires the use of parentheses.

Some of these query combinations can also be accomplished with the advanced search form [Hack #5] available at *http://search.yahoo.com/web/advanced*.

HACK #2 Save Time with Search Shortcuts

By using a few specific keywords, you can have Yahoo! answer common questions within your search results, provide specific information, or point directly to your answer.

At its most basic, Yahoo! Search allows you to type in search terms, click the Search button, and receive documents that include that word or phrase from across the Web. This makes Yahoo! a *keyword* search engine, and knowing this can help you put together your queries.

Yahoo! Search accepts a number of key phrases that can provide quick answers to common questions. To illustrate, here's an example in which search shortcuts can give you a faster answer than keywords alone.

Imagine you're in California and you'd like to call a friend in London, England. You can't remember the time difference and you don't want to call at 3 a.m. London time, so you turn to Yahoo! for help. Browsing to *http://search.yahoo.com*, you find yourself in front of the search form, about to type. What's the best query? If you were asking a human being for the answer you might be tempted to type in a complete question: what is the time in London?.

Because Yahoo! Search looks for matching words or phrases, you've told Yahoo! to find documents that include the words in your phrase. So the top results will likely be the web site for the London newspaper *The Times* and other documents that contain the search terms *London* and *time*. You'll probably find your answer at sites that are in the results, but there's a much faster way to tell Yahoo! Search exactly what you're looking for. Understanding the time zone and other search shortcuts will give you quick answers to some common questions.

Yahoo! Search Shortcuts

When Yahoo! Search encounters a key phrase, Yahoo! tries to provide a direct answer, in addition to matching documents that include the terms in the phrase. For example, if you want to know the current time in London, you can type time in London and you'll find the current time in London above the search results, as shown in Figure 1-3.

> Y! Local time in London, United Kingdom is 8:24 PM, Tuesday, Jun 28,
> 2005
> Coordinated Universal Time (UTC) + 1:0 hours
> This city also exists in the US states of: TN - WI - WV - TX - View All
> This city also exists in these countries: Kiribati - Canada
> Yahoo! Shortcut - About

Figure 1-3. An answer using a Yahoo! Search shortcut

By using this shortcut, you'll have the answer without looking through the results or visiting other sites. Replace London with any city or with a city-and-state combination, and you'll never have to worry about calculating time zone differences again.

You'll know you've used a Yahoo! shortcut when you see a result at the top marked with the Yahoo! Y!, as shown in Figure 1-3. You can browse a complete, updated list of Yahoo! Search shortcuts at *http://tools.search.yahoo.com/shortcuts/*. Here are a few of the shortcuts available:

Definitions
　　Type define *word*, and Yahoo! will provide a brief dictionary definition for the word and a link to the full dictionary entry for that word at Yahoo! Reference [Hack #40].

Encyclopedia entries
　　Search for *word* facts, and Yahoo! will display an excerpt of the Columbia Encyclopedia entry for that word and a link to the full entry.

Airport information

Yahoo! provides quick links to maps, flight information, and local weather if you type *airport code* airport. For example, the shortcut for San Francisco International Airport is SFO airport.

Hotels

Type *city* hotels to get a quick list of hotels in that city, along with the Yahoo! Local rating, the base rate, and a link to check availability. You can also look for a specific hotel chain by typing *city chain*—for example, San Francisco Ramada.

Stock quotes

Type quote *stock symbol* to get the current trading price for a stock (delayed 15 minutes). You can keep tabs on Yahoo! by typing quote yhoo.

Sports scores

Find out how your favorite pro team is doing by typing *team-mascot* scores. You'll get a quick look at recent games, and sometimes you can see who they're playing in the next game. The query 49ers scores will give you information about the San Francisco 49ers football team.

Movie showtimes

To see when movies are playing in your area, type showtimes *Zip Code* and you'll get links to local theater showtimes and a few showtimes for current movies.

Zip Codes

You can find all of the Zip Codes for a city by typing zip code *city*.

Area codes

If you're not sure where someone is calling from, try typing the three-digit area code into Yahoo! Search. Yahoo! will return a list of cities in that area code.

Weather

For a quick look at the current weather for any city, type *city* weather. Yahoo! will give you the current conditions and the expected high and low temperatures.

Once you learn how to speak the Yahoo! Search shortcut language, you'll save time answering some basic questions.

Yahoo! Properties Shortcuts

Another set of shortcuts available via Yahoo! Search forms are shortcuts to Yahoo! properties. Say you want to get to Yahoo! Movies but can't remember the URL. You can simply type movies! into any search form, and you'll automatically be redirected to Yahoo! Movies (*http://movies.yahoo.com*).

The exclamation point at the end lets Yahoo! know you're looking for a Yahoo! property.

There are hundreds of Yahoo! properties, and most of the shortcuts are intuitive. Here's a list of a few Yahoo! properties, along with their URLs and shortcuts:

Property	URL	Shortcut
Yahoo! Mail	*http://mail.yahoo.com*	`mail!`
Yahoo! Games	*http://games.yahoo.com*	`games!`
Yahoo! News	*http://news.yahoo.com*	`news!`
Yahoo! Sports	*http://sports.yahoo.com*	`sports!`
Yahoo! Finance	*http://finance.yahoo.com*	`finance!`
Yahoo! Address Book	*http://address.yahoo.com*	`address!`
Yahoo! Calendar	*http://calendar.yahoo.com*	`calendar!`
Yahoo! Education	*http://education.yahoo.com*	`education!`
Yahoo! Next	*http://next.yahoo.com*	`next!`

Keep in mind that you can use these Yahoo! properties shortcuts from any Yahoo! Search form, including the Yahoo! Toolbar form and the Firefox quick search box.

HACK #3   Create a Yahoo! ID

The key to many of the services at Yahoo! is a unique Yahoo! ID, and understanding how IDs work is key to keeping your Yahoo! ID private.

A Yahoo! ID is what distinguishes you from the crowd and what lets Yahoo! remember you across browsing sessions and across computers. If you've been using the Web for any amount of time, chances are good that you already have a Yahoo! ID. In November 2004, Nielsen/Netratings estimated that 55 million people around the world use Yahoo! Mail, and all of them sign in with a Yahoo! ID.

Signing Up

If you don't already have a Yahoo! ID, you can create one in less than five minutes. Browse to *http://login.yahoo.com* and click Sign Up Now for the new account form.

The most important decision to make as you fill out the new account form is what your Yahoo! ID will be. You'll use your ID anytime you want to access your personalized Yahoo! data, and your ID will determine what your Yahoo! Mail email address will be. If your Yahoo! ID is *j0d00d*, your email address is *j0d00d@yahoo.com*. The hardest part is finding an ID that is different from the 55 million Yahoo! IDs that already exist. The next hardest part is keeping the ID short and memorable. Keep in mind that you'll use this ID anytime you want to log in to Yahoo!. A short ID will save your fingers some work if you plan to log in to Yahoo! from your cell phone. And friends might want to contact you with Yahoo! Instant Messenger via your Yahoo! ID, so a short ID that is similar to your name will help them remember it.

Before filling out the form, go straight to the Yahoo! ID field and start trying potential IDs. Click the Check Availability of This ID button until you find something that's not taken. If you can get something with your initials or first and last name, consider yourself lucky.

When it's time to choose your password, it's tempting to recycle a password that you use in other places. Your Yahoo! ID and password is the only thing protecting your email from unauthorized readers, so it's a good idea to make the password unique and somewhat complex. Yahoo! requires at least six characters, but you can do better than that. A complex password should include upper- and lowercase letters, as well as symbols or numbers. A good trick for creating long, memorable passwords that are hard for hackers to guess is to think of the first line of your favorite poem or song and choose the first letter of each word as your password. So "Mary had a little lamb, its fleece was white as snow" would translate into the password *Mhallifwwas*. Add a memorable number, such as the year you were born, to the end and you'll have something like *Mhallifwwas1973*, which looks completely random but has meaning for you.

> If you find yourself keeping track of several dozen unique passwords, you might want to consider using a password manager to store them securely in one place. You can download the freely available Password Safe program for Windows at *http://passwordsafe.sourceforge.net*—just be sure not to forget the master password! Mac and Linux users may want to try Password Gorilla, available at *http://www.fpx.de/ fp/Software/Gorilla/*.

If you ever forget your Yahoo! password, you can always reset it later, in a couple of different ways. If you provide an alternate email address during this process, you'll be able to verify that address and have the ability to reset your password at any time. But if you want a bit more anonymity and don't want to provide an alternate email, be sure to remember the answer you give to the security question when you sign up. Your answer will be your only key to recovering your password and any information associated with your account if you ever forget your password.

As you're finishing up the registration process, you'll notice an image with wavy numbers and letters, like the one in Figure 1-4.

Figure 1-4. Yahoo! Registration captcha equal to "6z3e"

The image is called a *captcha*, and Yahoo! uses them to keep spammers from automatically creating Yahoo! accounts. If you can discern the numbers and letters in the graphic, you will prove to Yahoo! that you are a human rather than an automated program. The captcha can be difficult to read sometimes, and if you can't make out the letters and numbers, it doesn't mean you're not a human. Simply reload the page to get a different—and hopefully more readable—captcha.

Signing In

If you just created your account, you'll be logged in and ready to use any of Yahoo!'s applications. But from time to time, you'll need to sign in. Again, your Yahoo! ID and password are your keys to security, so you should do what you can to protect these. Before you log in, you can protect this information by switching to a secure connection, as follows.

Underneath the login form, you'll find a text link labeled MODE:, which you can use to switch to a secure connection. Clicking the link, you'll find that the URL in the address bar begins with https: instead of the standard http: and you'll see a padlock icon in the lower status bar, as shown in Figure 1-5.

Firefox users will have the added indication of a yellow address bar when browsing a secure page.

The default login form uses a standard connection, and making this small switch to the secure SSL connection will ensure that your Yahoo! ID and password combination are hidden from prying eyes. But it's important to note that the rest of your Yahoo! activities will not be encrypted, even if you log in securely. Yahoo! uses a standard connection for most of its services, including email. If you're ever wondering whether the current page you're

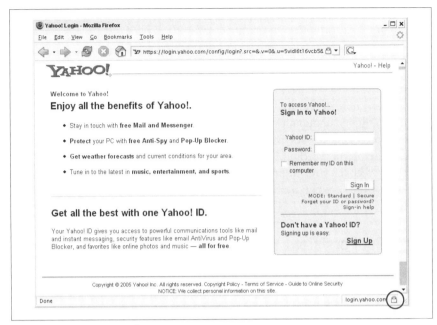

Figure 1-5. Yahoo! secure login page

visiting is secure, check for the padlock icon in the lower-right corner of your browser.

Checking the "Remember my ID on this computer" box sets a cookie in your browser that lets Yahoo! remember your ID between browsing sessions. Even with this option checked, Yahoo! will occasionally ask you to verify your password, so keep it handy if you don't have your password memorized. If you change your mind and no longer want Yahoo! to remember your ID on your computer, you can simply sign out.

Signing Out

At the top of most pages at Yahoo!, you'll find a welcome message that includes your Yahoo! ID, as shown in Figure 1-6.

Figure 1-6. Welcome message with Sign Out link

Under your ID, you'll find a Sign Out link that you can click anytime to sign out of Yahoo! If you share your computer with others or visit Yahoo! from a public computer, it's always a good idea to sign out when you're done using

Yahoo!. Signing out will help ensure that your personal data—everything from financial information to private email—stays personal.

Removing Your Account

If you ever want to part ways with Yahoo!, you can visit *https://edit.yahoo.com/ config/delete_user* to remove your account completely. You'll permanently lose access to any personal data you may have assembled (such as email) and any personal preferences (such as news sources at My Yahoo!). Weigh this option carefully before proceeding, because it's a permanent change, and you won't be able to recover your unique Yahoo! ID in the future. You'll need to enter your password a final time on this page and then click "Terminate this account."

Set Persistent Yahoo! Search Preferences

#4 Tweak your Yahoo! preferences to get the most out of your searching.

If you already have a Yahoo! ID, you can set some preferences that will affect the appearance and content of your Yahoo! searches. To set your preferences, first make sure you're logged in to Yahoo! by visiting *http://login.yahoo.com* and entering your Yahoo! ID and password. From there, browse to *http:// www.yahoo.com* or *http://search.yahoo.com* and look for the Preferences link to the right of the search form, like the one highlighted in Figure 1-7.

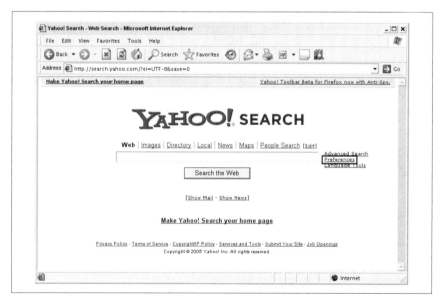

Figure 1-7. Yahoo! Search Preferences link

If you don't see the preferences link, you can browse directly to *http://search.yahoo.com/preferences*. From the Preferences page, you can set a number of options that Yahoo! will remember and apply to any search results in the future.

New Window

When searching a particular topic, it's easy to click on a search result, get lost in reading, and find yourself several clicks away from your original page of search results. If you find yourself clicking your browser's Back button again and again to get back to your Yahoo! search results, you might want to open links from the search results page in a new browser window. You can set this preference by checking the New Window box on the Preferences page. This is handy for keeping your search results page in place, allowing you to browse other sites without fear of losing your search results.

Number of Results

By default, Yahoo! shows 20 results on each page. You can change this setting on the Preferences page to 10, 15, 20, 30, 40, or 100 results. Setting it to display fewer results per page will keep your scrolling to a minimum, but if you have a large screen you might appreciate seeing up to a hundred results without clicking through several pages.

Adult Content Filtering

As in other media, the Web is filled with material that isn't appropriate for children or the workplace. Yahoo! indexes the entire Web—including the seamier sections—and Yahoo!'s answer to this dilemma is the *SafeSearch Filter*. With SafeSearch enabled, Yahoo! will do its best to exclude any adult material from search results. There are three different settings you can apply to your Yahoo! ID:

Filter out adult Web, video, and image search results
> This enables SafeSearch across every type of Yahoo! Search that has adult content.

Filter out adult video and image search results only
> This enables SafeSearch for video and image searches at Yahoo!, but Web searches might still contain adult material.

Do not filter results
> This setting completely disables SafeSearch, and adult material will be included in Yahoo! Search results.

The default setting is "Filter video and image search," so even if you never visit your Yahoo! Preferences page, SafeSearch is working behind the scenes.

In addition to choosing a filter level, you can lock a SafeSearch setting for a specific browser. When you check the SafeSearch Lock checkbox and update your preferences, Yahoo! sets a cookie for your browser that will keep your SafeSearch setting for every Yahoo! ID that uses that browser. If you have children in the house and they share your web browser, this is a way to keep adult material from them.

Because the SafeSearch Lock is tied to a particular browser rather than a particular Yahoo! ID, it functions a bit differently from the other settings. If another user logs in with a different Yahoo! ID using the same browser, she'll be able to change the SafeSearch Lock setting. However, if the particular Yahoo! ID has an age set and the user is listed as under 18, the SafeSearch Lock option will be hidden from view.

Language

Yahoo! keeps track of files and web pages on servers across the world and notes the language of each page in its index. You can specify that you'd like to receive results in all, one, or a custom combination of the many available languages. You've probably stumbled across pages in a language you don't understand before, and you can save some time by excluding these from your search results. Figure 1-8 shows the current list of languages that Yahoo! lets you choose from, and you can select one or more from the list.

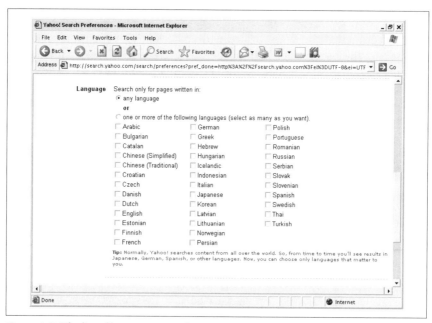

Figure 1-8. The list of languages at Yahoo!

By default, Yahoo! displays results in any language. Of course, English search terms generally return web pages in English, but without setting this preference, you'll probably run into pages in other languages from time to time. For example, my last name is a common German last name, so a search for "Paul Bausch" yields both English and German pages.

Assemble Advanced Search Queries
HACK #5
By understanding how Yahoo! Advanced Search URLs are structured, you can create your own Advanced Search queries on the fly.

In addition to the simple search form you'll find at *http://search.yahoo.com*, Yahoo! offers an Advanced Web Search form at *http://search.yahoo.com/web/advanced*. This form lets you refine your search in a number of ways, so you can narrow the results to a more useful list.

For example, if you'd like to find information about a generic topic, such as astronomy, you could go to Yahoo!, type astronomy into the search form, and find hundreds of sites related to the word. But if you want only a segment of those results, you can browse over to the Advanced Web Search form, type astronomy, and limit the results by top-level domain, as shown in Figure 1-9.

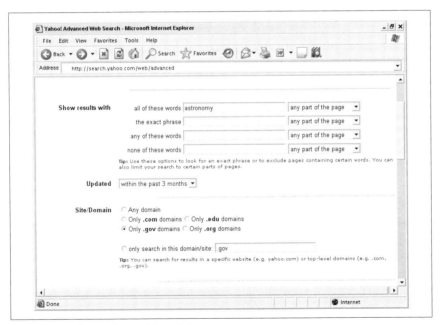

Figure 1-9. Yahoo! Advanced Search form

A search for astronomy across *.gov* sites returns only pages at NASA's web site. The same search limited to *.edu* sites results in astronomy programs at various universities, and limiting to *.com* gives you astronomy magazines at the top of the results.

You can further refine your search by limiting it to a specific file format, such as PDF files, Excel spreadsheets, or XML files. For any given search, you can also override your global preferences settings for language, number of results, and adult content filtering.

Anatomy of an Advanced Search URL

To get started with hacking URLs, type a term into the Advanced Web Search form and click the Yahoo! Search button, which will take you to the results page. Once there, note the insanely long URL in the address of your browser. It will look something like this:

```
http://search.yahoo.com/search?_adv_prop=web&x=op&ei=UTF-8&va=astronomy&va_↵
vt=any&vp_vt=any&vo_vt=any&ve_vt=any&vd=all&vst=.gov&vs=.gov&vf=all&vm=p&↵
fl=0&n=20
```

For any given search URL, some of the variables you'll find in the URL are redundant or not necessary. The web form basically acts as a URL-building tool that has assembled this URL for you, and it isn't picky about which variables it includes. By understanding the pieces of the URL, you can construct your own queries using shorter URLs without the form.

Note that the domain is followed by /search?, followed by a series of variable/value pairs separated by ampersands. Not all of these variables will affect the search results, but there are some that are useful to play with. The variables are a bit cryptic (to keep the URLs as short as possible), so here's a list of the relevant variables and what they represent.

The v* variables represent the way you'd like Yahoo! to handle the phrase. You can choose from the following variables:

va   Use this variable when you're looking for all of the words in a particular query. A query with the value astronomy magazine finds pages that contain both *astronomy* and *magazine*.

vp   This variable holds the search query when you want to match a specific phrase, so a query with the value astronomy magazine finds pages that contain the exact phrase *astronomy magazine*.

vo   This variable indicates a search for any of the words in a particular query. So a query with the value astronomy magazine returns documents that contain either *astronomy* or *magazine*.

ve   This variable indicates words that should not appear in any of the pages, and it must be used with one of the other variables. For example, combining one of the above queries with ve=NASA allows you to search for *astronomy magazine* on pages that don't include the term *NASA*.

Another group of similarly patterned variables lets you limit searching to a specific part of a document, such as the title or URL. The format for these variables is v*_vt, where the asterisk is replaced by the type of primary search query. The possible values include any, title, or url. For example, if you'd like to search for pages that have the exact phrase *astronomy magazine* in the title, use the vp and vp_vt variables together, like so:

    search?vp=astronomy+magazine&**vp_vt=title**

If you'd like to limit your results to pages that have been updated recently, you can use the vd variable. You can get all results, which is the default, or limit them to pages updated within the last three months, six months, or year. The respective values for these are all, m3, m6, or y. So finding all documents that contain the phrase *astronomy magazine* that have been updated within the last three months looks like this:

    search?vp=astronomy+magazine&vp_vt=any&**vd=m3**

The vs variable is useful for limiting searches to a top-level domain, such as *.com*. In addition to top-level searches, you can narrow things to a specific web site. If you want to find every mention of *astronomy magazine* at the specific web site *http://www.cnn.com*, you could use the variable like this:

    search?vp=astronomy+magazine&vp_vt=any&**vs=cnn.com**

The vf variable limits searches to a specific file type. Yahoo! supports a set number of file types, and here are the current values you can use with this variable:

all
    The default value; returns any type of document

html
    HTML documents

pdf
    Adobe PDF files

xl
    Microsoft Excel spreadsheets (note that this value is an abbreviation for the full file extension, *.xls*)

ppt
    Microsoft PowerPoint presentations

msword
    Microsoft Word files

rss
> Files formatted for syndication across web sites

text
> Plain text files, which typically end with .txt

To continue with the example, say you want to find the phrase *astronomy magazine* in only PowerPoint presentations. Append the vf variable, like so:

    search?vp=astronomy+magazine&vp_vt=any&**vf=ppt**

The number of results is controlled by the n variable, which can be set only to some predetermined values: 10, 15, 20, 30, 40, or 100. To return the first 40 results for the phrase *astronomy magazine*, add the n variable, like so:

    search?vp=astronomy+magazine&vp_vt=any&**n=40**

There are other variables in advanced search URLs, but these are a few that will affect the content of search results. Now that you know why the initial Advanced Web Search URL was so long, you can use some of the variables to create your own advanced Yahoo! searches on the fly.

HACK #6 Translate Any Page with Yahoo!

The World Wide Web has pages in every language, and Yahoo! can help you break through the language barrier.

Because the Web is a global space, we've all come across pages in different languages, especially among search results. If you're searching for information about a phrase like *hamburger recipe*, it's strange to come across a page about it in German. It's stranger still to find a mention of your name on a page in a foreign language. Imagine my surprise when I was searching Yahoo! for my name and found it at the Russian site shown in Figure 1-10.

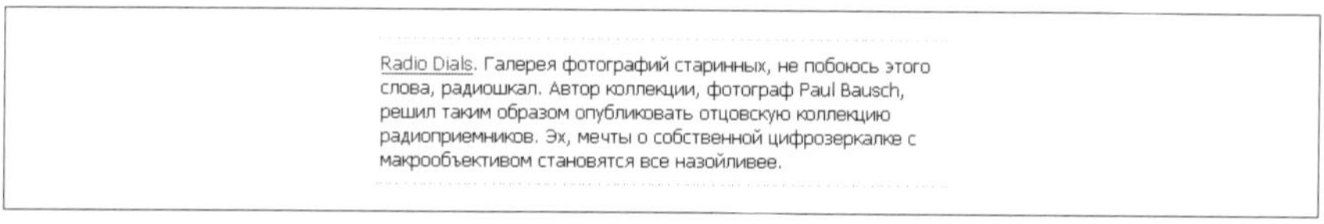

> Radio Dials. Галерея фотографий старинных, не побоюсь этого слова, радиюшкал. Автор коллекции, фотограф Paul Bausch, решил таким образом опубликовать отцовскую коллекцию радиоприемников. Эх, мечты о собственной цифрозеркалке с макрообъективом становятся все назойливее.

Figure 1-10. Russian text with my name (Paul Bausch)

I can't read Russian, so of course I had no idea what the text said. I had recently added a photo gallery of old radio dials to my web site; I could tell they were linking to it, but I wanted to know what they were saying.

Yahoo! Language Tools

Yahoo!'s Language Tools page (*http://tools.search.yahoo.com/language*) has some ways to help you work with other languages. Among them is a translation service that will translate any block of text to a different language. I copied the Russian text from Figure 1-10, pasted it into the text area labeled "Translate this web text," chose "From Russian to English" from the drop-down list of languages, and clicked Translate. Yahoo! responded with this:

Radio Dials. The gallery of the photographs of ancient, I will not be
afraid this word, radios-scale. The author of collection, photographer
Paul Bausch, decided thus to publish the paternal collection of radio
receivers. 3x, dreams about their own tsifrozerkalke with the
macro-objective become increasingly more importunately.

As you can see, the Yahoo! translation tool isn't perfect, but it's good enough to give a sense of what the page is talking about. The translated text refers to the "paternal collection" of photos, because the radios I photographed belonged to my father. I still have no idea what the last sentence of the translation means, but I'm closer to understanding now than when it was in Russian.

> If you'd like to limit the search results that Yahoo! returns to
> one language or a handful of languages, you can set your
> preferred languages in your search preferences. By default,
> Yahoo! returns the best search results from any language.

A faster way to translate any page you find in Yahoo! Search results is via the "Translate this page" link included within the results for non-English pages. Figure 1-11 highlights the link in the search results.

Figure 1-11. The "Translate this page" link in Yahoo! Search results

Clicking the "Translate this page" link takes you to a translated version of the page, rather than the page in its original language.

If you find yourself translating pages frequently, there are some ways to speed up the process. You can translate an entire web page by copying and pasting the URL into the field labeled "Translate this web page" on the Yahoo! Language Tools page, choosing the language from the drop-down menu, and clicking Translate. Yahoo! will display the page with all of the text translated.

Another quick way to translate entire pages is with the Yahoo! Toolbar [Hack #12]. If you've already installed the Yahoo! Toolbar, choose Add/Edit Buttons... from the Toolbar Settings button to bring up the Customize Yahoo! Toolbar page. Check the box next to Translate Current Page under Search & Navigation and then click Finished. You should now see a small yellow fish button, like the one shown in Figure 1-12, on your toolbar.

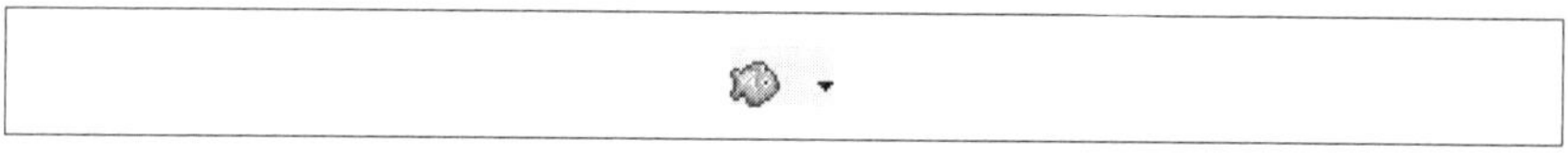

Figure 1-12. The Translate button on the Yahoo! Toolbar

From any web page, you can click the Translate button and Yahoo! will display a version in English. Yahoo! will also automatically detect the source language, so you don't need to choose a language from a menu. This is also handy if you can't tell what language the page is in. If you just want to translate a block of text instead of the entire page, you can click the arrow next to the fish and choose Language and Translation Tools from the menu; you'll go to the Yahoo! Language Tools page, where you can paste the text you want to translate into the translation form.

If the Yahoo! Toolbar isn't your style and copying and pasting into the Language Tools isn't fast enough, you can create your own Translate button with an understanding of Yahoo! Translation URLs and a JavaScript bookmarklet.

A Translation Bookmarklet

If you visit the Yahoo! Language Tools page and translate a page by URL, you'll end up at a Yahoo! page that uses frames. The top frame includes the Yahoo! Search logo and several links: View Original, Print Translation, Language Tools, and so on. The bottom frame is the original web page, with all of the text translated into a different language. Figure 1-13 shows such a translated page, with the O'Reilly Hacks page in Spanish in the bottom frame.

Figure 1-13. The Hacks site translated into Spanish

Looking at the URL in the address bar, you'll see that you're at a Yahoo! page with some parameters passed to it in the querystring, including the URL of the page to be translated. The whole URL looks like this:

```
http://tools.search.yahoo.com/language/translation/translatedPage.⏎
php?tt=url&urltext=http%3A%2F%2Fhacks.oreilly.com%2F&lp=en_es
```

Here are the three variables passed in the URL:

tt

    The type of translation to perform

urltext

    The URL of the page to translate

lp

    A code that represents the language to translate from and to

Knowing how to build Yahoo! Translate URLs, you can create a bookmarklet to fetch the current page URL, construct the proper Yahoo! Translate URL, and open it in a new window.

The code. As with other Yahoo! bookmarklets throughout this book, this JavaScript is not very readable, but is condensed to work within the confines of a browser bookmark. Create a new bookmark in your browser and then bring it up for editing. Put the following code into the location field of

the bookmark and be sure to give the bookmarklet a descriptive name, such
as Yahoo! Translate:

```
javascript:d=document;void(window.open('http://tools.search.yahoo.com/⏎
language/translation/translatedPage.php?tt=url&urltext='+escape(d.location.⏎
href)+'&lp=xx_en','_blank','width=640,height=480,status=yes,resizable=yes,⏎
scrollbars=yes'))
```

The value of the lp variable in this code is important to note. The value xx_en
tells Yahoo! to determine the language of the page you've sent it to translate.
Of course, you could make this a language-specific bookmarklet by replacing
xx_en with es_en (Spanish to English), fr_de (French to German), or any one
of the other codes for the translations that Yahoo! supports. To view a full list
of translation codes, simply view the source of the Language Tools page and
look at the value attribute in the <option> tags that display the language
choices. There are a few option lists on the page, so look for the list that contains values in the *xx_yy* format.

Running the hack. To run the code, browse to a foreign-language page and
click Yahoo! Translate from your bookmarks. A new browser window will
open, showing a translated version of the original page. Figure 1-14 shows a
Japanese page in the background that has been translated into English in the
foreground.

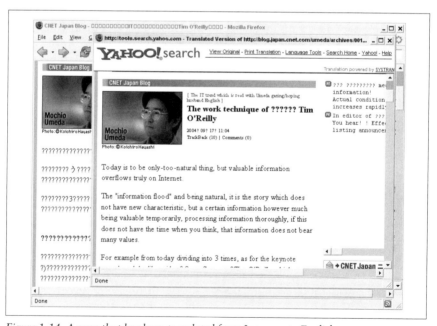

Figure 1-14. A page that has been translated from Japanese to English

The automatic translation might provide less-than-fluid English, but if you ever find your name on a page in a language you don't speak, you can find out why with a single click.

Personalize, Track, and Share the Web

A free Yahoo! service called My Web remembers your searches, saves copies of web pages, and shares your saved pages with others.

The Yahoo! My Web beta gives you a powerful set of tools to collect web pages, annotate them, and share them with others. In My Web, you can save links to your favorite web sites (much like bookmarks) and organize them in custom folders. But there are several features available at My Web beyond collecting links:

Site Notes
> You can add notes to any saved web site in My Web. You can use these notes to provide a site description, personal comments about the site, or any other bits of text.

Copies of Web Pages
> Instead of saving just a link to a web site, My Web saves a copy of a page as it looked when you added it My Web. So even if a web page changes between when you added the site to My Web and when you want to reference it later, you can be sure you'll see the original information.

Search History
> If you enable Search History, Yahoo! will remember which sites you click on in any Yahoo! search results and save them to your My Web History folder. If you have trouble remembering what search term you used to find a particular site, this might be a useful feature for you.

Blocked Sites
> Some sites that show up in search results simply aren't relevant and won't be relevant to any search you make. Clicking Block tells Yahoo! not to show that particular site in your future search results. Blocked sites show up in your My Web Blocked folder, so you can periodically review the sites you've blocked.

Shared Folders
> By default, folders with links and copied pages are private, but you can also choose to share any particular folder with the world. My Web also makes RSS feeds available for shared folders so others can subscribe to them and keep up with your changes.

To get started with My Web you just need a free Yahoo! ID. Browse to *http:// myweb.search.yahoo.com/myweb* and log in with your Yahoo! ID. As you activate My Web, you'll have the option to import any existing Yahoo! Bookmarks (*http://bookmarks.yahoo.com*) and the option to download the latest Yahoo! Toolbar (*http://toolbar.yahoo.com*), which is a quick way to add links to My Web as you browse other sites.

Using My Web

Once you've enabled My Web, you'll see some extra options as you search with Yahoo!. Make sure you're logged into Yahoo! and then browse to *http://search.yahoo.com*. The first change you'll notice is a My Web link under the Yahoo! logo, and the status of your Search History feature, as shown in Figure 1-15.

Yahoo! My Yahoo! Mail Welcome, yhoohacks [Sign Out, My Account]
Search Home Help
YAHOO! SEARCH
Web | Images | Video | Directory | Local | News | Shopping
hacks
Search the Web
My Web (beta)
My Web BETA
My Search History ON | Off
Subscriptions (New) Shortcuts Advanced Search Preferences
Search Results
Results 1 - 20 of about 13,000,000 for hacks - 0.18 sec. (About this page)

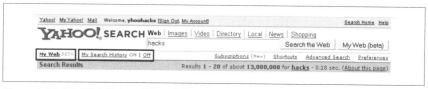

Figure 1-15. My Web link and Search History status at Yahoo! Search

Click Off or On at any time to enable or disable the Search History feature, respectively.

Each search result on the page will also have two links—Save and Block—as shown in Figure 1-16.

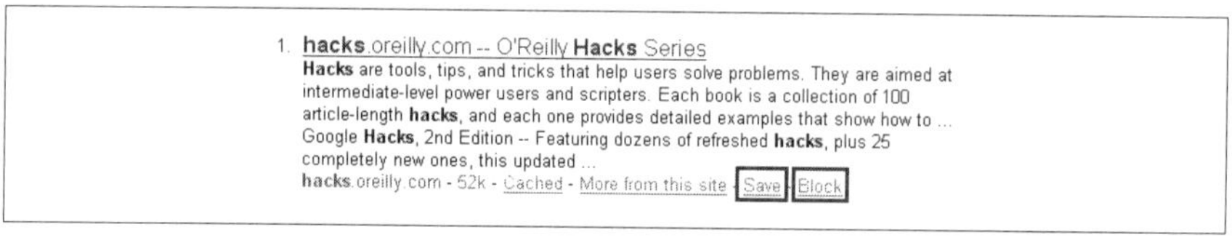
1. hacks.oreilly.com -- O'Reilly Hacks Series
Hacks are tools, tips, and tricks that help users solve problems. They are aimed at intermediate-level power users and scripters. Each book is a collection of 100 article-length hacks, and each one provides detailed examples that show how to ... Google Hacks, 2nd Edition -- Featuring dozens of refreshed hacks, plus 25 completely new ones, this updated ...
hacks.oreilly.com - 52k - Cached - More from this site - Save - Block

Figure 1-16. The Save and Block links on a search result

Clicking Save brings up a form on the page that will allow you to choose a folder to save the site in, and a text field for adding notes to the site. Figure 1-17 shows the Save form.

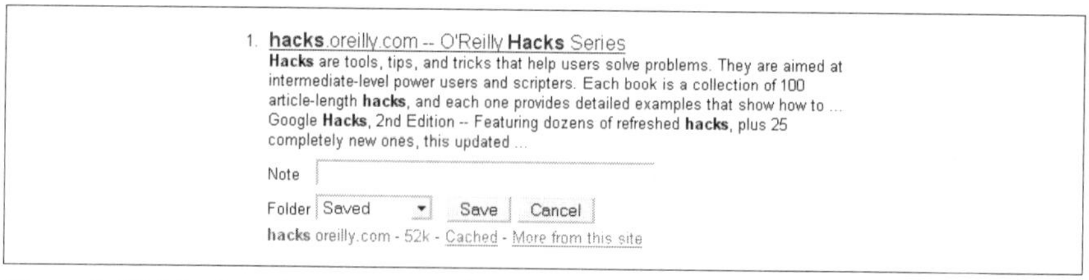
1. hacks.oreilly.com -- O'Reilly Hacks Series
Hacks are tools, tips, and tricks that help users solve problems. They are aimed at intermediate-level power users and scripters. Each book is a collection of 100 article-length hacks, and each one provides detailed examples that show how to ... Google Hacks, 2nd Edition -- Featuring dozens of refreshed hacks, plus 25 completely new ones, this updated ...
Note
Folder Saved
Save
Cancel
hacks.oreilly.com - 52k - Cached - More from this site

Figure 1-17. The Save form on a search result

Clicking Block produces the message shown in Figure 1-18, notifying you that the site will be blocked from future searches.

1. **hacks.oreilly.com** will be blocked in future searches - Unblock Site

Figure 1-18. Notification that a site has been blocked

You can click Unblock Site to restore the site in the current search results, or you can visit your Blocked folder to put the site back into view on future searches.

If you want to take the features of My Web with you to other web sites, you can use the Yahoo! Toolbar [Hack #12]. If you don't see the My Web button represented by a yellow folder on your toolbar, be sure you have the latest version of the toolbar (available at *http://toolbar.yahoo.com*). You can also choose Add/Edit Buttons from the toolbar settings button, check the box next to My Web under Personal Tools, and click the Finished button. Once the My Web button is installed, you should see it with its related pull-down menu, as shown in Figure 1-19.

Search Web ▾ ➕ ▾ | 🖸 ▾ 🔏 🌐 ▾ ⊠ ▾ 🖉 ▾

Go to My Web
Search My Web
≈≈ [Sign Out, My Account
Email this Page…
IM this page…
Import Bookmarks…   ures]
Browsing items 1

Figure 1-19. Yahoo! Toolbar My Web menu

If you want to save a particular web page, click on the yellow folder icon with the green plus (+) sign. The pop-up window—like the one shown in Figure 1-20—lets you modify the saved title, add a note about the page, save it to a specific My Web folder, and store the actual contents of the page just as if you'd clicked the Save button next to a Yahoo! Search result.

Sharing My Web

As you browse through your saved sites at *http://myweb.search.yahoo.com/ myweb*, you have the option to make folders full of sites public (they're private by default). Simply click the radio button next to Public in the My Web folder publishing options (see Figure 1-21).

Once your My Web folder is public, anyone will be able to view the sites you've saved to that folder in a number of ways. You can share the collection of web pages in a My Web folder directly via a predictable URL. Public folder URLs follow this pattern:

```
http://myweb.search.yahoo.com/myweb/user/hashed account/folder name
```

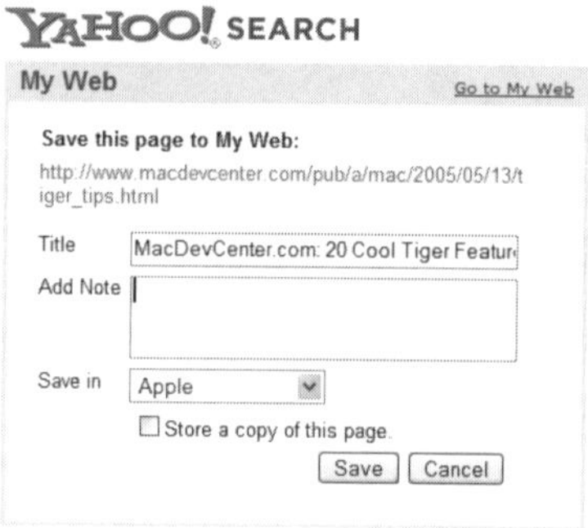
YAHOO! SEARCH
My Web
Go to My Web
Save this page to My Web:
http://www.macdevcenter.com/pub/a/mac/2005/05/13/tiger_tips.html
Title
MacDevCenter.com: 20 Cool Tiger Featur
Add Note
Save in
Apple
Store a copy of this page.
Save
Cancel

Figure 1-20. Yahoo! My Web "Save this page" pop-up window

Folder: ToddTechFinds
(?)
Private
Public
[Preview]
Subscribe to this folder:
MY YAHOO!
XML
Share on Yahoo! 360
(coming soon)

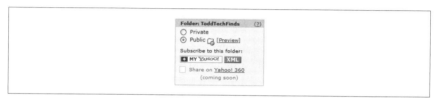

Figure 1-21. Yahoo! My Web folder publishing options

The *hashed account* in the URL is a text string that is an encrypted version of your account name. To find your particular hashed account text, click the Preview link in your folder publishing options and take a look at the URL. You should see a seemingly random string of characters in the URL, something like this:

```
YZWDcbcIupRv2bLnSax_Qg-
```

This is your hashed account name, and you can use it to build URLs to shared folders. The folder name in the URL pattern is, predictably, the name of the public folder. So if your folder is named *ToddTechFinds*, the final URL would look like this:

```
http://myweb.search.yahoo.com/myweb/user/YZWDcbcIupRv2bLnSax_Qg-/↵
ToddTechFinds
```

You could then pass this URL along to friends or coworkers so that they can see the sites you've gathered together. If you frequently update the folder, there are a couple of options that let others subscribe to any public My Web folder.

People viewing your site with a My Yahoo! account can choose to add your page to their My Yahoo! RSS feed list. This lets them get updates about content in your shared folder. And Yahoo! also provides a direct link to the syndicated RSS 2.0 format XML. The RSS feeds also have a predictable URL that follows this pattern:

```
http://myweb.search.yahoo.com/myweb/user/hashedaccount/foldername/rss.xml
```

Of course, this RSS 2.0 feed URL can be found by clicking on the familiar XML button.

Programming My Web

In addition to the web and RSS options available for sharing My Web sites, you can access your public folders via Yahoo! Web Services. The documentation for the My Web API is found at *http://developer.yahoo.net/myweb*.

There are two public My Web functions. The `listFolders` function lists the public folders for a Yahoo! My Web account. You can call it like so:

```
http://api.search.yahoo.com/MyWebService/V1/listFolders?appid=insert ⏎
appID&yahooid=insert Yahoo! ID&results=10
```

Replace *insert appID* with your own Yahoo Application ID and use someone else's Yahoo! ID for *insert Yahoo! ID*. The URL returns an XML page that contains a list of that user's public folders, along with the number of sites in that folder. You can parse the XML with any programming environment.

The `listUrls` function returns information about a specific public folder. You can call it with a URL like this:

```
http://api.search.yahoo.com/MyWebService/V1/listUrls?appid=insert ⏎
appID&yahooid=insert Yahoo! ID&folder=insert public folder&results=10
```

This function is handy for browsing the contents of folders you found with the `listFolders` function.

A basic example of using My Web data programmatically is to display the sites in a public folder on a remote web site—a perfect job for PHP.

The code. The PHP 5 integrated `SimpleXML` module makes parsing and displaying the XML easy. The `simplexml_load_file( )` function retrieves the My Web web services–generated XML for easy parsing. The `foreach` loop iterates through the list of saved web pages and lets you extract individual items. Note that the tag names are case-sensitive. For example, `$result->Url` succeeds, but `$result->URL` fails.

The following simple PHP 5 script, *showMyWebFolder.php*, displays the contents of a public My Web folder:

```php
<?php
$myweb = simplexml_load_file('http://api.search.yahoo.com/MyWebService/V1/⏎
listUrls?appid=insert appID&yahooid=insert Yahoo! ID&folder=insert public ⏎
folder&results=10');
```

```
print "<h2>Shared Links</h2>";
foreach ($myweb->Result as $result)
{
    $date_text      = $result->StoreDate;
    $summary_text    = $result->Summary;
    $title_text      = $result->Title;
    $url_text      = $result->Url;
    $note_text      = $result->Note;

    print "<h3>" . date("M d, Y", $date_text) . "</h3>\n";
    print "<a href=\"$url_text\">";
    print $title_text;
    print "</a>" . "<br />";
    print "<div>$summary_text</div><br />";
    print "<div style=\"background:#eee;\"><b>Notes:</b>
            $note_text</div>";
}
```

Be sure to create and include a unique application ID and insert your own
Yahoo! ID and public folder name.

Running the hack. Upload *showMyWebFolder.php* to your server and bring it
up in a browser. You should see a simple HTML page, like the one shown in
Figure 1-22. This page shows the links, notes, and date each site was added
to the public folder.

Figure 1-22. The contents of a My Web folder on a remote site

At the time of this writing, My Web is still in beta testing, but with its powerful abilities to annotate, share, and shape search results, My Web will likely be a standard part of Yahoo! in the future.

—Todd Ogasawara and Paul Bausch

HACK #8   Prefetch Yahoo! Search Results

Automatically prefetch and cache the first search result on Yahoo! Web Search.

If you know how to use them properly, search engines are pretty darn good at finding exactly the page you're looking for. Google is so confident in its algorithm that it includes a hidden attribute in the search results page that tells Firefox to prefetch the first search result and cache it. You're probably going to click on the first result anyway, and when you do, it will load almost instantaneously because your browser has already been there.

Yahoo! Web Search is pretty good too, but it doesn't yet have this particular feature. So let's add it.

> This hack relies on the Greasemonkey extension and thus works only in Firefox. If you're interested in doing much more with Greasemonkey, see Mark Pilgrim's forthcoming *Greasemonkey Hacks*, from which this hack is excerpted.

To begin, you'll need to install the Greasemonkey plug-in for Firefox. If you don't already have it, browse to *http://greasemonkey.mozdev.org* and click the Install Greasemonkey link. Follow the Software Installation prompts and then restart your browser. You'll know the plug-in is working if you see a small monkey icon in the lower-right corner of Firefox. Once installed, you can move on to analyzing Yahoo! and building the Greasemonkey script.

There are two important things about Yahoo! Search results that you can discover by viewing source on the search results page. First, the links of the search results each have a class yschttl. Yahoo uses this for styling the links with CSS, but you can use it to find the links in the first place. A single XPath query can extract a list of all the links with the class yschttl, and the first one of those is the one we want to prefetch and cache.

The second thing you need to know is that the search results Yahoo! provides are actually redirects through a tracking script on *rds.yahoo.com* that records which link you clicked on. A sample link looks like this:

```
http://rds.yahoo.com/S=2766679/K=gpl+compatible/v=2/SID=e/TID=F510_112/⏎
l=WS1/R=2/IPC=us/SHE=O/H=1/SIG=11sgv1lum/EXP=1116517280/*-http%3A//⏎
www.gnu.org/licenses/gpl-faq.html
```

To save time and bandwidth, and to avoid skewing Yahoo's tracking statistics, this user script will extract the target URL out of the first search result link before requesting it. The target URL is always at the end of the tracking URL, after the *-, with characters such as colons (:) escaped into their hexadecimal equivalents. Here's the target URL in the previous example:

```
http://www.gnu.org/licenses/gpl-faq.html
```

When I say "prefetch and cache," there is really only one step: prefetch. By default, Firefox automatically caches pages according to HTTP's caching directives and your browser preferences. For this script to have the desired effect, make sure your browser preferences are set to enable caching pages. Open a new window or tab, go to *about:config*, and double-check the following preferences:

```
* browser.cache.disk.enable          /* should be "true" */
* browser.cache.check_doc_frequency /* should be 0, 2, or 3 */
```

about:config shows you all your browser preferences, even ones that are not normally configurable through the Options dialog. Type part of a preference name (such as `browser.cache`) in the Filter box to narrow the list of displayed preferences.

The Code

Save the following user script as *yahooprefetch.user.js*:

```
// ==UserScript==
// @name         Yahoo! Prefetcher
// @namespace    http://www.oreilly.com/catalog/greasemonkeyhks/
// @description  prefetch first link on Yahoo! web search results
// @include      http://search.yahoo.com/search*
// ==/UserScript==

var elmFirstResult = document.evaluate("//a[@class='yschttl']", document,
    null, XPathResult.FIRST_ORDERED_NODE_TYPE, null).singleNodeValue;
if (!elmFirstResult) return;
var urlFirstResult = unescape(elmFirstResult.href.replace(/^.*\*-/, ''));
var oRequest = {
    method: 'GET',
    url: urlFirstResult,
    headers: {'X-Moz': 'prefetch',
        'Referer': location.href}};
GM_log('prefetching ' + urlFirstResult);
GM_xmlhttpRequest(oRequest);
```

Running the Hack

To verify that the script is working properly, you'll need to clear your browser cache. You don't need to do this every time, just once to prove to yourself that the script is doing something. To clear your cache, go to the

Tools menu and select Options; then go to the Privacy tab and click the Clear button next to Cache.

Now, install the user script from Tools → Install User Script, and then go to *http://search.yahoo.com* and search for gpl compatible. The prefetching happens in the background after the page is fully loaded, so wait for a second or two after the search results come up. There won't be any visible indication on screen that Firefox is prefetching the link. You might see some additional activity on your modem or network card, but it's hard to separate this from the activity of loading the rest of the Yahoo! Search results page.

Open a new browser window or tab and go to *about:cache*. This displays information about Firefox's browser cache. Under "Disk cache device," click List Cache Entries. You should see a key for *http://www.gnu.org/philosophy/license-list.html*. This is the result of Firefox prefetching and caching the first Yahoo! Search result. Click that URL to see specific information about the cache entry, as shown in Figure 1-23.

Figure 1-23. Information about a prefetched page

Hacking the Hack

By now you should realize that this prefetching technique can be used anywhere, with any links. Do you use some other search engine, perhaps a site-specific search engine such as Microsoft Developer's Network (MSDN)? You can apply the same technique to those search results.

For example, going to *http://msdn.microsoft.com* and searching for active accessibility takes you to a search results page at this URL:

```
http://search.microsoft.com/search/results.aspx?qu=active+accessibility&↵
View=msdn&st=b&c=0&s=1&swc=0
```

If you view source on this page, you will see that the result links are contained within a `<div class="results">` tag. This means that the first result can be found with this XPath query:

```
var elmFirstResult = document.evaluate("//div[@class='results']//↵
a[@href]",
    document, null, XPathResult.FIRST_ORDERED_NODE_TYPE, null).↵
singleNodeValue;
```

Unlike with Yahoo! Search results, these search result links are not redirected through a tracking script, so you will need to change this line:

```
var urlFirstResult = unescape(elmFirstResult.href.replace(/^.*\*-/, ''));
```

to this:

```
var urlFirstResult = elmFirstResult.href;
```

The rest of the script will work unchanged.

—Mark Pilgrim

Compare Yahoo! and Google Search Results

HACK #9

Pit Yahoo! and Google against each other and find more search results in the process.

If you've ever searched for the same phrase at both Yahoo! and Google, you've probably noticed that the results can be surprisingly different. That's because Yahoo! and Google have different ways of determining which sites are relevant for a particular phrase. Though both companies keep the exact way that they determine the rank of results a secret—to thwart people who would take advantage of it—both Yahoo! and Google provide some clues about what goes into their respective ranking systems.

Here's the official word from Yahoo!:

> Yahoo! Search ranks results according to their relevance to a particular query by analyzing the web page text, title, and description accuracy as well as its source, associated links, and other unique document characteristics.

At the heart of Google's ranking system is a proprietary method called PageRank, and Google doesn't give detailed information about it. But Google does say this:

> Google's order of results is automatically determined by more than 100 factors, including our PageRank algorithm.

Though we might never know exactly *why* results are different between the two search engines, at least we can have some fun spotting the differences—and end up with more search results than either one of the sites would have offered on its own.

One way to compare results is to simply open each site in a separate browser window and manually scan for differences. If you search for your favorite dog breed—say, australian shepherd—you'll find that the top few sites are the same across both Yahoo! and Google, but the two search engines quickly diverge into different results. At the time of this writing, both sites estimate exactly 1,030,000 total results for this particular query, but estimated result counts are sometimes a way to spot differences between the sites.

Viewing both sets of results in different windows is a bit tedious, and a clever Norwegian developer named Asgeir S. Nilsen has made the task easier at a site called Twingine.

Twingine

The Twingine site (*http://twingine.com*) contains a blank search form into which you can type any search query. When you click Search, the site brings up the results pages for that query from both Yahoo! and Google, side by side. For fairness, Twingine randomly changes the sides that Google and Yahoo! come up on, so people who prefer one side of the screen over the other won't be biased. Plugging australian shepherd into Twingine yields a page like the one shown in Figure 1-24.

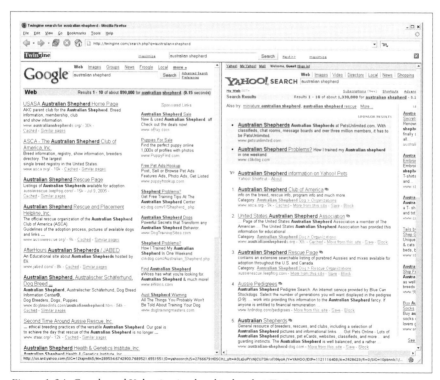

Figure 1-24. Google and Yahoo! going head to head at Twingine

Clicking Next or Previous in the top frame at Twingine takes you to the next or previous page in the search results at both sites.

Surfing the pages in the search results at Twingine at can be a bit tricky. You'll probably want to open linked search results in a new window or tab, so that you can keep your place in the search results at both Yahoo! and Google. You can open links in a new window by right-clicking the link (Ctrl-click on a Mac) and choosing "Open Link in New Window" from the menu. You can also set your Yahoo! Search preference to automatically open links in a new window when you're clicking a Yahoo! Search result.

Yahoo! Versus Google Diagram

Another site, developed by Christian Langreiter, adds a bit of analysis to the differing sets of search results between Yahoo! and Google. If you have Flash installed, you can type a search query into the form at *http://www.langreiter.com/exec/yahoo-vs-google.html* and the site fetches the search results from both engines in the background using their open APIs. The site delivers the results in a chart like the one shown in Figure 1-25.

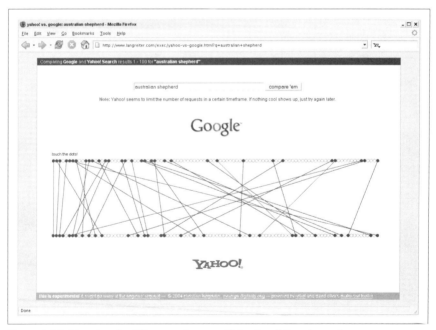

Figure 1-25. Mapping the differences between Yahoo! and Google results

Each blue or white dot in the diagram represents a search result URL, and the position of the dot represents the ranking. The dots on the far left are the top search results, and the further right you go, the further down you go in the search results. The blue lines represent the same URL, so you can see exactly where Google and Yahoo! line up. In Figure 1-25, you can see that the top search result for australian shepherd is the same URL, but the lines aren't as evenly matched further down in the results. As you hover over each dot, you'll see the URL, which you can click to visit that particular search result.

The white dots in the diagram represent a URL that one search has in the results that the other does not. And as this diagram demonstrates, neither search engine has a monopoly on matching pages, nor does each engine's index have every page on a particular topic.

HACK #10 Find Content You Can Reuse Legally

Use the Yahoo! Creative Commons Search to find text and images with special licenses.

Most of the text, images, and audio you find through a Yahoo! Search are copyrighted materials. In fact, even if the author of a page or image doesn't specify that her work is copyrighted, a copyright still exists; by default, all works are copyrighted. This means you can never be sure how a particular author will react if you use part or all of her work in your own project.

Say you're preparing a public presentation and you'd like to use a photo of the Statue of Liberty. Unless you specifically pay for an image, you can't be sure the photographer of a photo you find on the Web won't sue you for copyright violation. Without contacting the photographer (or owner of the copyright), there's no way to know what he'll consider a fair use of his materials. While there is a legal concept called *fair use* that protects some use of copyrighted materials—especially for educational use—it's hard to know exactly which uses fall under this legal definition, because the concept of fair use is only vaguely defined.

This legal ambiguity is one of the reasons the nonprofit group Creative Commons (CC) has made several alternative licenses available to artists who want to license their work in a more specific way than a general copyright provides. For example, an artist can make her work available to anyone who wants to use his photo or text on the condition that it's used for noncommercial purposes, but the artist can still require payment for any commercial use. This means you could use a photo licensed in this way for a school report, but you'd need to pay the photographer if you were compiling a book you intended to sell. With a CC license, you know exactly how the artist would like her work to be used—or not used.

Another compelling aspect is that as long as you're following the conditions set forth in the license, you don't need to pay the artist to use the work—or even contact her asking to use the work. If for any reason you'd like to use the work in a way that's not covered by the license, however, you'll need to contact the artist. Basically, you just need to know how the Creative Commons licenses work to make sure you're playing by the rules.

Understanding CC Licenses

There are four primary conditions that Creative Commons offers in its licenses, in different combinations:

Attribution
No matter how you use the work, you must give the author credit. All licenses include this condition.

NoDerivs (No Derivatives)
You can use only exact copies of the work in its entirety, not pieces of the work arranged in a different way.

NonCommercial
The work can only be used for a noncommercial project.

ShareAlike
You can use the work as long as your work is licensed in the same way.

And here are the six licenses offered with these uses in combination:

- Attribution
- Attribution-NoDerivs
- Attribution-NonCommerical-NoDerivs
- Attribution-NonCommercial
- Attribution-NonCommercial-ShareAlike
- Attribution-ShareAlike

So if you spot a photograph of the Statue of Liberty on the Web with an Attribution-NoDerivs CC license, you know that the author has made his photo available to anyone who wants to use it for any purpose. In exchange, the author wants credit for the photo and wants you to use the photo in its entirety, rather than cropping the photo or blending it with other photos. The other licenses work in a similar way. Once you know the four conditions, you can quickly determine how the author would like you to use the work by looking at combinations in the license.

Finding CC-Licensed Content

Yahoo! has created a special search form (in beta testing at the time of this writing) for finding content with CC licenses. The Yahoo! Creative Commons Search is available at *http://search.yahoo.com/cc* and provides a few options for filtering results, as shown in Figure 1-26.

Figure 1-26. Yahoo! Creative Commons Search form

You can leave both checkboxes under the search form blank to find all types of CC licenses. Alternately, you can find content that doesn't have the NonCommercial condition, content that doesn't have the NoDerivs condition, or both, by checking the boxes accordingly.

The search results look exactly like standard Yahoo! Search results but take you to pages with CC-licensed material. Once you visit the site, you'll need to find out which license the author has chosen for her work. Look around the page for a Creative Commons logo like the one shown in Figure 1-27.

Figure 1-27. Creative Commons logo and license link

Click the logo or link, and you'll see exactly which license the work is under. Figure 1-28 shows the license page at Creative Commons that explains an Attribution-NonCommerical-ShareAlike license.

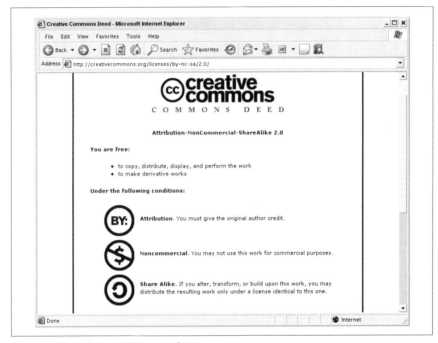

Figure 1-28. A Creative Commons license page

Note that the URL for the license page includes an indication of which license type you're looking at. In this example, the URL is:

http://creativecommons.org/licenses/**by-nc-sa**/2.0/

The combination of two-letter codes after licenses/ shows the type of license that you'll find at that URL. Here's the shorthand for the conditions:

by   Attribution

nd   NoDerivs

nc   NonCommericial

sa   ShareAlike

Just by looking at the URL, you can tell that by-nc-sa represents an Attribution-NonCommerical-ShareAlike license. As you work with Creative Commons–licensed material, you can spot the license quickly this way, by hovering your mouse over a CC logo and noting the URL in the status bar of your browser—without having to visit the license page.

So the next time you're looking for supporting text or photographs, you can use the Yahoo! Creative Commons Search to find something appropriate, such as Sheila Morris's photograph of the Statue of Liberty in Figure 1-29.

Figure 1-29. CC-licensed image of the Statue of Liberty

Sheila Morris published the photo under an Attribution license, which means she simply wants credit in exchange for use of the photo. Paying attention to CC-licensed material takes the ambiguity out of the standard copyright system and lets you know how you can use some materials you find on the Web.

HACK #11 Find Video from Across the Web

The Yahoo! Video Search can help you find video clips that have been posted to the Web.

As Yahoo! Search scours the Web, it indexes not only the documents, text, and images it finds, but also video clips. Video files don't show up in a standard Yahoo! Web Search, but you can visit the Yahoo! Video Search to find clips from every corner of the Web.

Simple Video Searching

To start finding videos, browse to *http://video.yahoo.com* (or type `video search!` into any Yahoo! Search form), enter a word or phrase, and click Search Video. Say you're interested in learning more about NASA's robotic vehicle for exploring Mars and you'd like to see the rover in action. You can

find thumbnails of videos from across the Web by searching with the phrase
mars rover, as shown in Figure 1-30.

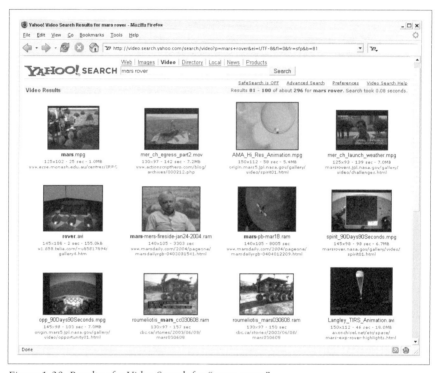

Figure 1-30. Results of a Video Search for "mars rover"

Among the hundreds of results are clips from professional television news
stories about the Mars rover, clips from NASA itself with video from the
Mars rover, and amateur videos about the Mars rover. Yahoo! displays a single frame from the video, the name of the file, the video's dimensions, and
the URL that contains a link to the video clip. To view a video, just click the
thumbnail. The video will open from its original site within a Yahoo! frame,
like the clip shown in Figure 1-31.

The top frame of a search result detail contains the video thumbnail, a link
to play the video within your browser, and a link to send an email with a
link to the clip. The bottom frame shows the page where the video was
found, so you can see the video in its original context.

> The videos you find through Yahoo! Video Search might be
> protected by copyright laws, so you'll need to be mindful of
> how you use any materials you find.

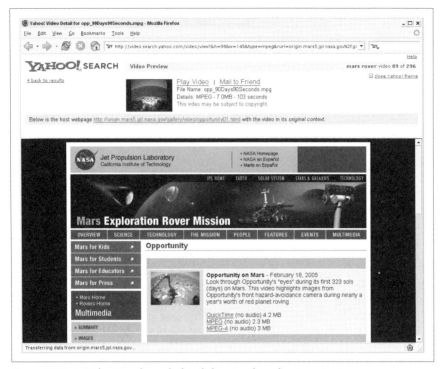

Figure 1-31. A Video Search result detail showing the video in context

Advanced Video Searching

As with a Yahoo! Web Search, there's an advanced video search form (*http://video.search.yahoo.com/video/advanced*). You can use the advanced search form to limit results to specific video formats, one of three sizes of videos—small, medium, or large—and videos that are longer or shorter than one minute. As with the Web Search, you can also limit your search to a specific site or adjust the SafeSearch features for the search.

As an example of a specific search, you could still use the phrase mars rover, but limit the search to MPEG and Quicktime files that are shorter than a minute long, small in size, and found on a government domain. Instead of hundreds of results to sort through in a broad mars rover search, you'll find five clips from a NASA site with the narrowly defined advanced search.

If the advanced search controls still don't provide enough control over your query, there are several special search keywords you can use to refine your video searches further.

At the time of this writing, these video keywords aren't documented on Yahoo!, so thanks go to Stig Sæther Bakken and David Hall from Yahoo! for sharing the syntax elements listed here.

Here's a look at each of the special syntax keywords and how they'll refine a search. Note that a keyword is followed by a colon and a value with no space in between.

filesize

Limits search results to files of a specific size, in bytes. You can use this in combination with a greater-than sign (>) or less-than sign (<) to find files that are larger or smaller than the specified amount, respectively. For example, `filesize:<1073741824` limits results to video files that are smaller than one gigabyte.

date

Limits results to videos that have been last modified on, before, or after a certain date. You need to use a Unix-style date, which is the time in seconds since January 1, 1970. So a query that includes `date:>1107803581` returns results with videos that have been modified after February 7, 2005.

width

Finds videos of a specific width in pixels. A query with `width:640` finds videos that are 640 pixels wide.

height

Finds videos of a specific height in pixels. So `height:480` finds videos that are 480 pixels tall.

duration

Finds clips of a certain length in seconds. As you'd expect, `duration:>30` limits results to videos longer than 30 seconds, and `duration:<30` limits results to videos that are shorter than 30 seconds.

tld

Finds videos that are hosted on a specific *top-level domain* (a phrase for which the keyword `tld` is an abbreviation), such as *.org*, *.com*, *.gov*, *.edu*, or a specific county top-level domain, such as *.jp* for Japan.

fromtld

Narrows results to videos that have been referenced on a page at a specific top-level domain, because some sites can link to videos on other domains. So even though a particular video might reside at *.com* address, Yahoo! might have indexed the video via a page at an *.edu* domain that linked to the video. The syntax `fromtld:edu` finds videos that have been referenced in pages at *.edu* domains.

site

> Searches for videos at a specific site. The syntax `site:nasa.gov` limits results to videos hosted at *http://www.nasa.gov*.

fromsite

> Limits search results to pages that reference videos at the specified site. While the site specified might not host videos, this special syntax still ensures that pages with links to videos from the site are included.

title

> Limits search results to video clips with specific words in the video's filename. A search with `title:rover` returns only videos with *rover* in the filename or link text.

fromtitle

> Limits results to words in a referring document's title. The syntax `fromtitle:rover` finds videos that have been referenced on pages with *rover* in the filename, even though the word *rover* might not appear in the name of the video file.

A final special keyword, aspect, lets you limit search results to video files with a specific *aspect ratio*. The aspect ratio refers to a video's display width divided by its height. A standard television screen is almost square, but its width is a bit longer than its height. The aspect ratio of a standard television screen is noted as 4:3. The newer high-definition television screens are much longer than they are wide, and their aspect ratio is noted as 16:9. Naturally, the video for each of these devices matches the proper aspect ratio.

The aspect keyword expects a standard single integer to represent an aspect ratio, so you'll need to do a little math before you use it. The formula is the video width multiplied by 100, then divided by the height and rounded down if necessary. To make things easy, here are the most common aspect ratios, along with the computed value you'd use with the aspect keyword:

Aspect ratio	Computed value
Television (4:3)	133
Computer monitors (5:4)	125
Widescreen movies and HDTV (16:9)	177

For example, using `aspect:177` in a video search query limits the results to files that are in a widescreen format.

 You can also use the special video syntax with the Yahoo! Video Web Services if you want programmatic access to video search results. Read the full documentation for the service at *http://developer.yahoo.net/video/V1/videoSearch.html*.

You can use these special syntax elements in combination to build some fairly sophisticated queries. Yahoo! Movies (*http://movies.yahoo.com*) hosts hundreds of movie previews and clips, and you can find a full listing at *http://movies.yahoo.com/trailers*. The site doesn't offer thumbnail browsing of its archive, but you can easily see thumbnails of the clips available with an advanced Yahoo! Video Search. Search for `site:yahoo.com matrix` to see thumbnails of video clips and trailers from the three *Matrix* movies.

Streamline Browsing with the Yahoo! Toolbar

#12   The Yahoo! Toolbar integrates Yahoo! with your web browser, letting you search, customize features, and access your mail from the browser at all times.

The Yahoo! Toolbar is a browser extension offered by Yahoo! that integrates many of Yahoo!'s features with your web browser. After installing the toolbar, you'll find an extra row of buttons in your browser, as shown in Figure 1-32.

Figure 1-32. The Yahoo! Toolbar

The toolbar contains buttons that perform Yahoo!-specific functions and a search form for quick access to Yahoo! searching. The toolbar can provide one-click access to all of your pages at Yahoo!, including your mail, groups, calendars, address book, and stock quotes. The toolbar is completely customizable, and you can choose which buttons and Yahoo! features are available on the toolbar. Because Yahoo! makes most of its features available via the toolbar, you can tailor your toolbar to suit the way you use Yahoo!.

Installation

To install the Yahoo! Toolbar, point your browser to *http://toolbar.yahoo.com* and click the orange Download button. From there, you'll find a page with instructions about downloading and installing the toolbar. At the time of this writing, the toolbar is available only for Internet Explorer, but there is a *beta* (i.e., testing) version available for Mozilla Firefox. Because the program is a browser extension rather than a traditional application, the download and installation will happen within the browser window. You'll need to approve some security requests along the way, and Yahoo! has laid out all of the steps to take on its site. Firefox requires you to restart the browser to see the toolbar, but Internet Explorer doesn't.

 You can uninstall the Yahoo! Toolbar at any time by choosing Uninstall from the Toolbar Settings button.

Once the toolbar is installed, it will try to log in with your Yahoo! ID. If you are currently logged into Yahoo!, or if you have asked Yahoo! to "remember you," the toolbar should display the introductory Choose Buttons and Welcome Tour buttons. Otherwise, click the Sign In button and enter your Yahoo! ID and password.

The Welcome Tour is a quick Flash demo that shows how you can use the toolbar. Select Choose Buttons to pick which buttons you'd like to see. If you don't see the Choose Buttons option, click the Toolbar Settings button shown in Figure 1-33 and choose Add/Edit Buttons... from Personal Options.

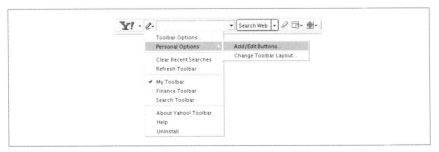

Figure 1-33. The options under the Yahoo! Toolbar Settings button

Once you click Choose Buttons or Add/Edit Buttons..., you'll find a page in your browser like the one shown in Figure 1-34, which will let you check off the features you'd like to have in the toolbar.

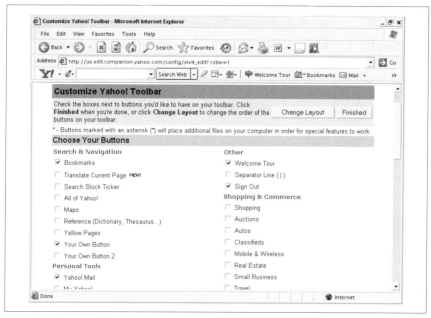

Figure 1-34. The Customize Yahoo! Toolbar page

There are over 60 different buttons you can choose from, and your choices should depend on which parts of Yahoo! you use the most.

Features

You can think of the Yahoo! Toolbar as a portal to everything Yahoo! offers. In fact, looking at the various buttons you can add to the Yahoo! Toolbar is a great way to get an overview of all the features that Yahoo! offers. Many of the buttons simply provide a link to a particular section of Yahoo!, but here are a few that offer some features particularly suited for the toolbar.

Get notification of new email. The Yahoo! Mail button listed under Personal Tools on the Customize Yahoo! Toolbar page lets you quickly compose mail, access your address book, and send the current page to someone via email. Figure 1-35 shows the list of options with the Yahoo! Mail button.

Even without the mail button enabled, you'll receive an alert when you have new mail at your Yahoo! Mail address. A button like the one shown in Figure 1-36 will appear, letting you know how many messages you have waiting for you. You can click the message count to go directly to Yahoo! Mail.

Figure 1-35. The Yahoo! Mail button options

Figure 1-36. The Yahoo! Toolbar Mail Alert

Manage bookmarks. If you've already discovered the convenience of storing bookmarks at Yahoo!, you'll appreciate the convenience that the Bookmarks button provides. You can enable the Bookmarks button by checking Internet Explorer Bookmarks under Search & Navigation on the Customize Yahoo! Toolbar page. The Yahoo! Toolbar lets you add the current page in the browser to your Yahoo! bookmarks with one click. In addition, you'll have one-click access to all of your Yahoo! bookmarks, as shown in Figure 1-37.

Figure 1-37. Yahoo! Toolbar bookmarks

The nice feature of using Yahoo! bookmarks instead of browser bookmarks is that they'll be available on any browser and across multiple computers. If you install the Yahoo! Toolbar on your home computer as well as your computer at work, you'll have the same bookmarks in both places.

Add content to My Yahoo!. If you enable the My Yahoo! button by choosing it on the Customize Yahoo! Toolbar page, found under Personal Tools, you'll have one-click access to your personalized news portal. Yahoo! will also analyze every page you visit, looking for the ability to subscribe to its related RSS or Atom feed. If the page offers a feed, you'll find a blue plus symbol next to the My Yahoo! button on the toolbar (see Figure 1-38).

Figure 1-38. The Yahoo! Toolbar Subscribe to RSS button

Clicking the Subscribe to RSS button takes you to a page at Yahoo! that asks you to confirm the addition of the news source to your personalized My Yahoo! page. From then on, you'll see headlines from the site when something new is added.

Block pop-up windows. The Yahoo! Toolbar includes options for taking care of some common annoyances. The Internet Explorer version of the Toolbar includes a button that stops *pop-up windows*: those annoying ads that open in new browser windows.

> The Firefox browser stops pop-ups by default, so the pop-up blocker is not included with the Yahoo! Toolbar for Firefox.

Figure 1-39 shows the options for the pop-up-blocking button.

Figure 1-39. The Yahoo! Toolbar pop-up blocker

If you ever want to allow pop-ups from a domain that is using them for a good cause, you can choose Always Allow Pop-Ups From... and enable them for the current site.

The pop-up blocker is enabled by default, but you can always disable it by choosing Toolbar Settings → Toolbar Options... and unchecking Pop-Up Blocker.

Enable quick searches. The most prominent feature of the toolbar is the search form. From any web page, you can type some text into the form, click enter, and go to the Yahoo! Search results for that phrase. You can also choose one of the many search options in the drop-down list shown in Figure 1-40.

Figure 1-40. The Yahoo! Toolbar search form

Another nice feature of the search form lets you highlight some text on the page, drag it to the form, and release the mouse button. This will add the highlighted text to the form so you can search with it, saving you some typing.

 If you use Firefox, you're probably already familiar with the search box in the upper-right corner, which is similar to the Yahoo! Toolbar search form. The default search engine is Google, but you can easily select Yahoo! by clicking the Google icon and choosing the Yahoo! icon from the drop-down menu.

Privacy

It's important to keep in mind that the Yahoo! Toolbar—like the Yahoo! web site—holds some of your personal information. The Yahoo! Toolbar provides instant access to your mail, personalized news sources, and book-marks. If you're the only person with access to your browser, this probably isn't a problem. But if you're in a shared computing environment, there are some steps you can take to keep your information private.

First, always click the Sign Out button (see Figure 1-41) when you're finished using the browser.

Figure 1-41. The Yahoo! Toolbar Sign Out button

If you don't see a Sign Out button, you might already be signed out. You can also enable the Sign Out button by checking Sign Out under Other on the Customize Yahoo! Toolbar page. Adding this button and using it when you're finished browsing will ensure that your personal information is not available to others using the computer. For good measure, you can click the Refresh Toolbar option under the Toolbar Settings button to make sure all traces of your Yahoo! ID have been removed for the next user. Refreshing the toolbar manually updates the status of all buttons for the current user. Once you have logged out and refreshed the toolbar, your personal button choices will not appear on the toolbar.

The Yahoo! Toolbar also tracks recent searches to keep them handy for references. You might not want all other users to know that you searched for athlete's foot earlier in the day, so you can either clear searches or completely disable the feature. To get rid of the stored searches, click the Toolbar Settings button and choose Clear Recent Searches. To disable the feature, choose the Toolbar Settings → Toolbar Options... and you'll see the form shown in Figure 1-42.

Figure 1-42. The Yahoo! Toolbar Options dialog

Under Search Box, uncheck the Remember Recent Searches option, and the Yahoo! Toolbar will lose its memory. Optionally, you could check the Auto-clear option to remove recent searches anytime you close the browser. At the time of this writing, the Yahoo! Toolbar Options form is available only with the Internet Explorer toolbar, so Firefox users have to get by with the Clear Recent Searches option.

This hack just scratches the surface of what's available through the Yahoo! Toolbar. With quick access to Yahoo! features as you browse other sites, you will find efficient ways to share information and take advantage of more of Yahoo!'s applications.

Customize the Firefox Quick Search Box

#13 Though Yahoo! Web Search is a default option in the Firefox search box, with some quick coding you can add many other Yahoo! Search types.

If you use the Firefox web browser (available at *http://www.mozilla.org/ products/firefox*), you're probably already aware of the useful search box in the upper-right corner. From any page, at any time, you can simply type a query into the box and press Enter to bring the search page up in the browser. Though Google is the default search engine, you can click the arrow to choose another search engine, as shown in Figure 1-43.

Figure 1-43. Firefox search box options

Yahoo! Web Search is a default option, and once you choose Yahoo! from the drop-down list, it will stay your top choice until you change it again.

The nice thing about this list of potential search engines is that you can add any search engine of your choice. In fact, Firefox offers an Add Engines... option that takes you to a page with more search choices you can install with a few clicks. The New Search Engines section contains a page (*http://mycroft. mozdev.org/quick/yahoo.html*) full of over 30 different Yahoo!-related searches you can add to the Firefox search box. These are searches that others have found useful and decided to share with the larger Mozilla community (Mozilla is the technology behind Firefox). The specialty Yahoo! searches include everything from searching Yahoo! Auctions and searching Yahoo! in different countries, to the Yahoo! Oxford Shakespeare reference. If you find yourself constantly looking for pithy quotes from *The Tempest*, adding this option to the Firefox search box could be the stuff dreams are made of.

To add a search engine from this Mozilla page, simply click the name of the search engine you'd like to add. A pop-up box will ask you to confirm your choice; click OK, and the new choice will be available in the Firefox search box menu. Behind the scenes, Firefox has copied a small *.src* file and icon to the *searchplugins* directory of the Firefox installation. This text file defines how the search works.

If you don't find the search of your dreams at the Mozilla page, it's fairly easy to build your own specialty Yahoo! search and add it to your list of available search engines. You just need a simple text editor to create the search engine text file, and an eye for spotting patterns in search URLs.

The Code

Maybe you're a fan of the Yahoo! Image Search (*http://images.yahoo.com*) and you'd like to be able to search for images quickly from Firefox. The first step in creating a custom entry is to perform a search and take a look at the URL. For this example, browse to *http://images.yahoo.com*, type Shakespeare into the search form, and click Search Images. You should receive a page full of various pictures of Shakespeare, but take a look at the URL in the address bar. The relevant pieces of the URL include the *images.search.yahoo.com* domain, the *images* file, and the p variable, which is set to the search query:

```
http://images.search.yahoo.com/search/images?p=shakespeare
```

Now that you know how Yahoo! Image Search URLs are constructed, you can write the file that will tell Firefox where to send search requests. Create a file called *yahoo_image.src* in a plain-text editor such as Notepad, and add the following code:

```
# Yahoo! Image Search
#
# Created April 16, 2005

<SEARCH
    version="7.1"
    name="Yahoo! Image Search"
    description="Search for images at Yahoo!"
    method="GET"
    action="http://images.search.yahoo.com/search/images" >

<input name="p" user>

</search>
```

As you can see, this quick file begins with an opening <SEARCH> tag that holds the name of the search, and a brief description. Everything before the question mark in the search results URL becomes the value of the action attribute. The input tag lets Firefox know the value should come from user input and that it should be named p, as in the Yahoo! Image URL.

Running the Hack

Save the file and add it to the Firefox *searchplugins* directory, usually located at *C:\Program Files\Mozilla Firefox\searchplugins* on Windows and at */Applications/Mozilla.app/Contents/MacOS/searchplugins* on Mac OS X. You'll also need an icon for the search, and because Firefox comes with a Yahoo! search option, you can simply copy the existing *yahoo.gif* file from the *searchplugins* directory and name it with the same prefix as your new Yahoo! Image Search text file—*yahoo_image.gif*, in this example.

Once you restart Firefox, you'll find a new option in the search list called Yahoo! Image Search. Choose this option and type the original Shakespeare query in the search box. If all goes well, you should see a page of Shakespeare images like the one shown in Figure 1-44.

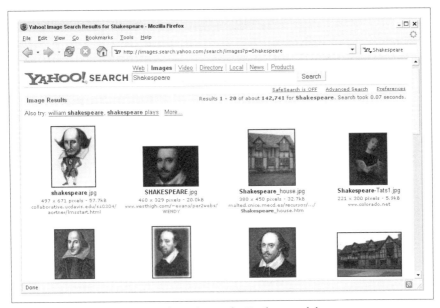

Figure 1-44. Yahoo! Image Search results via the Firefox search box

If you find yourself using a particular Yahoo! search time and again, you might be able to speed up your access to the search with an eye for search URLs and some quick text editing.

Spot Trends with Yahoo! Buzz
HACK #14

Find out which pop culture phenomenon is on the way in or out by looking at trends in search queries.

Everywhere we look in the media, there are lists of bestsellers that can tell us what's hot at the moment. People watch the top-grossing movies like they'd watch the stock market, and best-selling books are always a topic of conversation. Yahoo! has its own way of tracking what's hot: by looking at the most common phrases people search for. If Yahoo! users are suddenly searching for singer Gwen Stefani more often than for Britney Spears, that shows a shift in interest or popularity.

Determining Current Leaders and Movers

Yahoo! tracks exactly these kinds of trends at the Yahoo! Buzz Index (*http://buzz.yahoo.com*). When you browse the Buzz Index, you'll find several Top Movers Charts, separated into categories such as TV, Music, Sports, Movies, Actors, Video Games, and overall queries. Each chart has the top 15 search queries with the greatest percentage increase for that particular day. These charts are a quick snapshot of which queries are gaining the most ground.

At the bottom of each chart, you'll find a "View complete chart..." link, which you can click to compare the top Movers with the Leaders. Instead of tracking the greatest change in terms of percentage, the Leaders chart shows you the top search queries for that category. Figure 1-45 shows the Leaders and Movers lists, side by side. The current champs (Leaders) are on the left, and the challengers (Movers) are on the right.

Figure 1-45. The overall Leaders and Movers at Yahoo! Buzz Index

Each entry on the Leaders chart shows the rank, whether the term is gaining or losing ground, how many points the term has moved in the last day, the number of days the term has been on the chart, and the overall *buzz score*. According to Yahoo!, a single buzz point is what 0.001% of Yahoo! users were searching for on a particular day. So the buzz score of 370 for the top entry in Figure 1-45 means that 0.37% of all Yahoo! users searched for American Idol on that day. With millions of users, that small percentage means thousands of people.

From the left side of the page, you can click the Decliners link under Overall to list terms that have dropped over the last day. Many of the entries are related to news stories that were on top of people's minds the previous week.

The terms are placed into categories like TV, Music, and Sports by Yahoo! Buzz Index editors, and general terms like *television* or *football* are filtered out of the results. The editors also exclude terms that aren't appropriate for children.

If you don't plan on visiting the Yahoo! Buzz Index every day to see the movers and shakers, you might want to subscribe to the Buzz Index Weekly Report by browsing to *http://subscribe.yahoo.com/subscribe?.optin=ybz&.src=ybz*. Once subscribed, you'll receive an email every Sunday with the hottest search trends from the previous week. The report is compiled by Yahoo! editors and sometimes contains a slice of reporting that doesn't show up on the leader boards. For example, the April 3, 2005, report included a look at the most popular diet searches and found that Weight Watchers was beating out South Beach Diet and Atkins Diet, even though these terms weren't high enough to be in the overall search. You can also stay on top of the Yahoo! Buzz Log—a frequently updated look at what's hot by Yahoo! Editors—by subscribing to the Buzz Log RSS feed (*http://buzz.yahoo.com/feeds/buzzlog.xml*) in your favorite newsreader.

Going Back in Time

If you're interested in what was popular at some point in the past, you can take a stroll through the Yahoo! Buzz Log archives. At the time of this writing, Yahoo!'s archives go back to June 20, 2004. To find the page, enter this search query at *http://search.yahoo.com*:

```
site:buzz.yahoo.com "June 20, 2004"
```

The Yahoo! Buzz Log archives are based on Sundays, so you can change the date to any Sunday you'd like to see between June 20, 2004, and the present.

Your Yahoo! Calendar at *http://calendar.yahoo.com* in monthly view works well for finding any given Sunday.

So if you'd like to find out what was on people's minds in mid July of 2004, you could search like this:

```
site:buzz.yahoo.com "July 11, 2004"
```

Or you could create the archive URL yourself in this format:

```
http://buzz.yahoo.com/buzz_log/yyyymmdd/
```

So the URL for the Buzz Log archive for July 11, 2004, would be:

```
http://buzz.yahoo.com/buzz_log/20040711/
```

Unfortunately, Yahoo! doesn't provide access to past charts, but you can get the Yahoo! Editors' takes on what was happening by visiting these archives.

HACK #15 Find Hot Technologies at the Buzz Game

The Buzz Game lets tech geeks speculate about where their industries are headed, and you can use their insider knowledge to spot tech trends.

If you follow technology trends like some people follow the stock market, you can put your knowledge to work by placing your bets on where technology is headed at the Yahoo! Buzz Game (*http://buzz.research.yahoo.com*). But even if you can't tell an iPod from a Typepad, the Yahoo! Buzz Game can help you make sense of the technology landscape.

A joint venture between Yahoo! Research and O'Reilly Media, Inc., the Yahoo! Buzz Game is a fantasy stock market for technology terms. The market attempts to predict what's going to be hot, by letting tech enthusiasts "buy" and "sell" technology terms. If the value of a particular tech term goes up, the score of players holding that term goes up. The players with the best scores can win prizes.

The Buzz Game is split into around 50 different markets, ranging from specific types of hardware and software, such as Portable Media Devices and Operating Systems, to less tangible ideas, such as Annoyances (which lets people bet on pop-up advertising or email spam).

Spotting Trends

Beyond letting you place bets and play the game, the Yahoo! Buzz Game site gives you a great snapshot of the current state of technology in a particular industry. For example, click Markets at the top of the home page and browse the categories for Portable Media Devices. At a glance, you can see the top contenders in the portable media gadget space. Figure 1-46 shows the relative market prices for various MP3 players in April 2005, with the iPod clearly ahead of the pack.

Clicking through each entry in a particular market, you can get a sense of how game players feel about each product's chances for success. If you browse through the items listed under Rumor Mill, you'll see products that don't exist yet and what tech-heads are predicting about their chances at existence.

Each company or product has a detail page, similar to a stock-tracking page, with the current price, its history, and overall *buzz score* (see Figure 1-47).

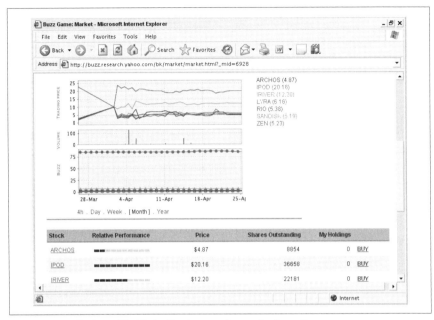

Figure 1-46. The Portable Media Devices market at the Buzz Game

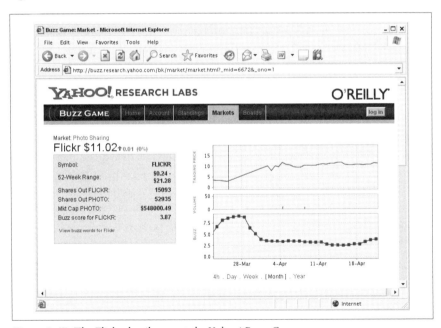

Figure 1-47. The Flickr detail page at the Yahoo! Buzz Game

The buzz score is derived via the same methodology used for the Yahoo! Buzz Index [Hack #14] scores, and it represents the number of searches for that particular term. The detail page includes related news about a particular technology, thanks to Yahoo! News, and, if you're playing along, a form that lets you buy or sell shares.

Buzz Game API

If you'd like to do a bit of your own fantasy market analysis, Yahoo! offers all of the Buzz Game data as XML. There are several ways to access the data, including two files that offer most of the information in one place:

All Buzz Game data in one file
Available at *http://buzz.research.yahoo.com/bk/rest/allinfo.xml*, this file includes data for every market and stock. Each stock entry includes the stock's internal ID, price, buzz score, and number of shares, and every market includes the market capitalization.

All stock prices in one file
This is a simplified version of the above file, and it includes prices of each stock organized by market. This file is at *http://buzz.research.yahoo.com/bk/rest/prices.xml*.

Another way to find data about individual stocks is to create request URLs that contain the stock symbol and the symbol for the market that stock belongs to. Here's the URL format for looking up individual stocks:

```
http://buzz.research.yahoo.com/bk/rest/info.xml?marketsymbol=insert market ⏎
symbol&stocksymbol=insert stock symbol
```

So if you'd like to find out what the iPod is trading at, you can visit the Portable Media Devices market detail page (*http://buzz.research.yahoo.com/bk/market/market.html?_mid=6928*) and find the symbol for that market (PORTMEDIA) at the top of the page. A bit further down the page, you'll see that the symbol for the individual iPod stock is, appropriately, IPOD. Knowing these two symbols, you can get an XML representation of the price, buzz score, and number of shares available with the following URL:

```
http://buzz.research.yahoo.com/bk/rest/info.xml?marketsymbol=PORTMEDIA&⏎
stocksymbol=IPOD
```

Finally, you can also access individual stocks via their internal ID number with the following URL format:

```
http://buzz.research.yahoo.com/bk/rest/info.xml?stockid=insert stock ID
```

To find a stock ID for any particular stock, you'll first need to look up the ID via one of the XML files.

Graphing Markets

One potential use of the Buzz Game API is to create your own charts and graphs to spot trends in the fantasy market. Using a bit of Perl to move the Buzz Game data into Excel, you can don your green visor and start doing your own analysis about where to place your bets.

The code. To use this code, you'll need a copy of LWP::Simple, for fetching the Buzz Game page. This script accepts a market symbol, fetches the *prices.xml* file, and loops through the file looking for the specific market. Once the script finds the market, it prints the stock names and prints a comma-separated value list suitable for opening in Excel. To get started, save the following code to a file called *buzz_excel.pl*:

```
#!/usr/bin/perl
# buzz_excel.pl
# Accepts a Buzz Game Market Symbol and returns a CSV
# list of stock prices you can open in Excel.
# Usage: buzz_excel.pl <market symbol>
#
# You can find market IDs, and read more about the Buzz Game
# at http://buzz.rsearch.yahoo.com/

use strict;
use LWP::Simple;
use Data::Dumper;

# Grab the incoming market ID
my $msym = join(' ', @ARGV) or die "Usage: buzz_excel.pl <market symbol>\n";

# Set the request URL
my $buzz_url = "http://buzz.research.yahoo.com/bk/rest/prices.xml";

# Make the request
my $prices = get($buzz_url);

# Find the market
while ($prices =~ m!<Market.*?symbol="$msym" name="(.*?)".*?>(.*?)
                    </Market>!mgis) {
    my $market_name = $1;
    print "\"$market_name\"\n\n";
    my $stocks = $2;
    while ($stocks =~ m!<Stock.*?symbol="(.*?)" name="(.*?)">\n<Price>(.⏎
*?)</Price>\n</Stock>!mgis) {
        my $stock_symbol = $1;
        my $stock_name = $2;
        my $stock_price = $3;
        print "\"$stock_name\",$stock_symbol,$stock_price\n";
    }
}
```

Running the hack. To run the code, simply call the script from the command line, adding your relevant market ID and choosing an output file:

```
perl buzz_excel.pl RUMOR > rumors.csv
```

If you have a spreadsheet program, you should be able to double-click *rumors.csv* to take a look at the data. If you'd like to whip up a snazzy pie chart, highlight the block of data and start the chart wizard by selecting Insert → Chart..., choosing the pie chart type, and following the rest of the wizard's steps. You'll end up with a quick visualization of the market, as shown in Figure 1-48.

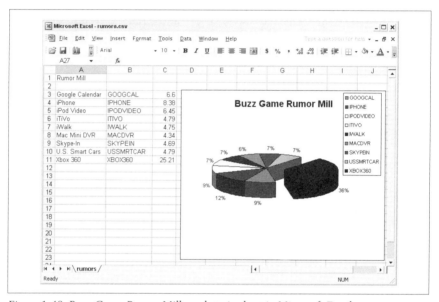

Figure 1-48. Buzz Game Rumor Mill market pie chart in Microsoft Excel

At a glance, you can see that the Xbox 360 rumor has the biggest slice of the pie at the time of this writing (May 2005). This particular analysis won't tell you where to place your bets in the game, but hopefully it shows how you can start to play with the data this fantasy market is generating.

The Yahoo! Buzz Game won't replace traditional market research for spotting trends, but it's a fun way take the pulse of tech geeks and see what they're predicting.

H A C K   **Tame Long Yahoo! URLs**
#16
With an eye for URLs and the right tools, you can shorten long Yahoo! URLs when you need to send them via email.

Most of the time, we're all surfing the Web in virtual isolation. It's just you and the computer, and the last thing on your mind is the length of a URL at a page you're visiting. But as soon as you want to share the piece of the Web you're viewing with someone else, the length of a URL becomes important.

Because email programs wrap text at 72 characters (for easy reading), any URL that's longer could be broken. A broken URL means someone on the other end of the message won't be able to see the page you've sent them—or that they will have to spend a minute or two pasting the URL together in Notepad. And imagine trying to handwrite a note to someone that includes some of the URLs you stumble across!

Trimming Yahoo! URLs

Yahoo! has a lot of great content to share with others, but some of the URLs are definitely too long to send via email. Here's a Yahoo! Local URL for a page that shows a list of coffee shops in Sebastopol, CA:

```
http://local.yahoo.com/results;_ylt=AvyPaCOwOiCme6J1PYb56tSHNcIF;_↵
ylu=X3oDMTBtbGZ2dXFpBF9zAzk2NjEzNzY3BHNlYwNzZWFyY2g-.?stx=coffee&↵
csz=Sebastopol%2C+CA&fr=
```

Those 154 characters in the URL are definitely past the 72-character safe zone. If you take a look at the URL, you can see some variable/value pairs that contain the relevant information. The string ?stx=coffee looks important, as does csz=Sebastopol%2C+CA. But the rest of the URL looks like gibberish.

> It's important to note that what looks like gibberish is actually useful information to Yahoo!, but it's not useful to you when you're trying to share links, so you can cut it out.

Cutting the garbage characters out of the URL will give you something more manageable:

```
http://local.yahoo.com/results?stx=coffee&csz=Sebastopol%2C+CA
```

If the area you want to search is small enough, you can even use a Zip Code instead of the city and state combination:

```
http://local.yahoo.com/results?stx=coffee&csz=95472
```

The 51 characters in this URL are well within the safe zone, and the URL points to exactly the same page. If you frequently find yourself sharing pages from Yahoo! Local, you might want to pick up a bookmarklet by Brian Cantoni (available at *http://www.cantoni.org/2005/06/06/ylocal*) that automates the process of removing the garbage characters. Drag the bookmarklet link to your toolbar, and click it anytime you want to share a link to Yahoo! Local. The bookmarklet opens a new email message with a shortened URL as the text of the message. From there, you can compose your message and share the link without fear of a broken URL.

Even URLs that seem short enough can be just over the limit. Here's a page of Yahoo! Search results for Brevity is the soul of wit:

```
http://search.yahoo.com/search?ei=UTF-8&fr=sfp&p=Brevity+is+the+soul+of+wit
```

The 75 characters in this URL are barely over the limit. But you can do some trimming here to bring it back under 72 characters. By cutting the URL to its bare essentials, you can get the same search results page down to 59 characters:

```
http://search.yahoo.com/search?p=Brevity+is+the+soul+of+wit
```

When you're ready to share a URL, keep an eye out for ways to trim the URL down to size. But there will be times when the only option you have is a URL-trimming service.

URL-Trimming Services

The scourge of long URLs is so rampant on the Web that several free services have appeared to help you share even the most insanely long URLs with others. To see how these services can help, here's an example of a Yahoo! Maps URL that points to a page with driving directions from San Francisco, CA, to the O'Reilly offices in Sebastopol, California:

```
http://maps.yahoo.com/dd_result?newaddr=&taddr=1005+Gravenstein+Hwy+N&↵
csz=San+Francisco%2C+CA&country=us&tcsz=Sebastopol+CA&tcountry=us
```

As you can see, this 135-character URL is dense with information. There's nothing extraneous we can strip out to get the same information. This is where TinyURL.com can help. Copy any long URL you'd like to abbreviate and paste it into the form on the front page at *http://tinyurl.com*. Click the Make TinyURL! button, and the next page will give you an abbreviated URL, like this:

```
http://tinyurl.com/b356b
```

These 24 characters are well within the safe zone and definitely won't break in an email. Another service, available at *http://shorl.com*, produces the following URL:

```
http://shorl.com/disaprigrohegi
```

Each of these services stores the long URL on its server, assigns the URL a random character string, and redirects to that long URL when someone visits the short address. Shorl.com even provides some usage statistics, so you can see how many people have used the shortened URL.

There are some drawbacks to using these third-party services. The person you're sharing the link with won't know what site they're actually going to visit. This might make for some fun practical jokes, but it's always better to be as direct as possible when sharing URLs with people. Also, the longevity of the link isn't guaranteed. If TinyURL.com or Shorl.com goes out of business tomorrow, your link will fail. Using redirection services like these isn't the best choice if you're going to print a URL in a book, for example. But for casual use, these services are a good way to share long URLs without annoying the person on the other end.

HACK #17 Opt Out of Advertiser Cookies

Advertisers on Yahoo! might set browser cookies to track patterns, but you can tell them you'd rather not be tracked.

Browser cookies are an important piece of web technology that sites like Yahoo! rely on to give you a personalized experience at their site. Without cookies, Yahoo! wouldn't be able to let you choose your own news sources at My Yahoo!, watch your favorite stocks at Yahoo! Finance, or even send email with Yahoo! Mail. The *cookie* itself is simply a small bit of text that resides on your computer. When the cookie is set by a site such as Yahoo!, only that site can access the cookie's text in the future. The cookie lets Yahoo! know that a particular user is browsing its site, and Yahoo! can bring up saved preferences and settings for that particular user for future visits.

Cookies at Yahoo!

Cookies aren't inherently good or bad; such a judgment just depends on how they're used. You should be aware of how cookies are used, so that you can decide for yourself whether you want them to be set on your computer. You can view Yahoo!'s privacy policy regarding its use of cookies at *http:// privacy.yahoo.com*.

In addition to the cookies that Yahoo! sets in order to remember your settings, Yahoo! allows other companies to set cookies through its web site. One of the ways Yahoo! makes money is through advertising, and Yahoo! sells sections of its pages to other companies. These other companies (called *third parties*) might set cookies that are in no way related to your Yahoo! account. In addition, these cookies do not have to follow the guidelines in Yahoo!'s privacy policy. This means that any advertiser or advertising network on Yahoo! might have its own privacy policy you should be aware of. Yahoo! lists more information about this practice on their Third Party and Affiliate Cookies on Yahoo! page (*http://privacy.yahoo.com/privacy/us/adservers/details.html*).

Most of these third-party cookies are probably being used to track patterns in Yahoo! usage. If a company has an advertisement on Yahoo! Finance, it might also want to know if those users are visiting Yahoo! Mail. These broad usage patterns help companies refine and target their campaigns without tracking any one person specifically. However, if you aren't thrilled with the idea of being tracked—even in a general way—across the sites you use, most of these advertising companies give you a way out.

Opting Out

Many advertising networks offer the ability to *opt out* of cookie-related monitoring. By visiting a special page on the advertiser's site, you allow the advertiser to set a cookie on your machine. Instead of tracking your movements, this opt-out cookie tells the advertiser that you don't want to participate. The next step is simply finding this page on all of Yahoo!'s third-party advertisers and setting it.

Luckily, Yahoo! keeps a list of its advertisers at *http://privacy.yahoo.com/ privacy/us/adservers/details.html*. When you bring the page up in your browser and scroll down to the section labeled Opting Out of Third Party Cookies, you'll find a list of companies that are currently advertising at Yahoo! Unfortunately, Yahoo! doesn't go the next step and provide a link to each company's opt-out page, but why not use Yahoo! Web Search to help you find them?

At the time of this writing, the top company on the list is 24/7 Media, Inc. and their URL is *http://www.247realmedia.com/*. With the URL in hand, you can construct a special query to search their site for the special opt-out page. The site: meta keyword will limit a Yahoo! Search to a particular domain, and the phrase "opt out" will probably appear on the page I'm looking for. So the particular query for this company is:

```
site:www.247realmedia.com opt-out
```

Note that I've removed the http:// prefix from the URL because the site: meta keyword only works with the domain. And, sure enough, plugging that query into the form at *http://search.yahoo.com* returns the 24/7 Media, Inc. Opt-Out page that will set the opt-out cookie in your browser.

You can repeat this process for every company in the list, until you've opted out of every one of Yahoo!'s advertising partners. Or, if you have an amazing amount of time to kill, you could use a similar query to find each company's privacy policy to make sure its cookie-setting policy is something you agree with, like so:

```
site:www.247realmedia.com Privacy Policy
```

If this process seems too time-consuming to follow, there are some ways to change your browser settings so that it accepts cookies only from Yahoo! if your browser supports controlling cookies.

 Yahoo! tracks its own advertising efforts both on and off Yahoo! sites through a technology called Web Beacons. These are invisible images that load in a browser and set cookies. You can find out more about Yahoo!'s Web Beacons and opt out at *http://privacy.yahoo.com/privacy/us/ beacons/details.html*.

Browser Settings

Cookies are handled by web browsers, and you can change how your browser handles them. The default setting on most browsers simply accepts all cookies in the background, without any user intervention. This allows a seamless browser experience, taking advantage of all of the personalization options that sites like Yahoo! offer.

To get a sense of just how many cookies are flying around behind the scenes, try changing your browser settings so that you have to approve every cookie that's set. In Firefox, choose Tools → Options... → Privacy and select Ask Me Every Time from the Keep Cookies drop-down menu. Internet Explorer (IE) users can choose Tools → Internet Options → Privacy → Advanced → Override and then choose Prompt for both First-party Cookies and Third-party Cookies. With these settings enabled, you'll be asked to approve every cookie that comes your way with the prompt shown in Figure 1-49.

Figure 1-49. Cookie prompt in Internet Explorer

As you browse around different sections of Yahoo!, you'll see the cookie prompt window with both *yahoo.com* and third-party cookies being set in various places and you'll have the option to allow or block the cookies. Keep in mind that blocking cookies set by *yahoo.com* will negatively affect your ability to use Yahoo!'s features. Seeing all of these cookie prompts is an interesting to get a sense of the cookies being set on your computer, but surfing around with this setting will get tiresome quickly.

Another available option is to allow first-party cookies while blocking third-party cookies. *First party* means the cookies are set by the site you're visiting. For example, if you're at *http://mail.yahoo.com* and you get a request to set a cookie from *yahoo.com*, that is a first-party cookie from the domain you're browsing. But if you're at *http://movies.yahoo.com* and you get a request to set a cookie from *questionmarket.com*, that's a third-party cookie. Both Internet Explorer and Firefox allow you to accept first-party cookies without question, while blocking all third-party cookies without question.

To apply this setting in Internet Explorer, go to Tools → Internet Options → Privacy and click Advanced. Set the browser to accept first-party cookies but block third-party cookies, as shown in Figure 1-50.

Figure 1-50. Internet Explorer Advanced Privacy Settings

Click OK to save your settings.

In Firefox, go to Tools → Options... → Privacy and check the box that says "for the originating web site only."

 ## HACK #18   Track News About Yahoo!

Yahoo! is a big company, and there are many ways to watch Yahoo! in action.

Whether you're a potential employee, investor, competitor, or just a fan of the site, you'll want to keep tabs on what Yahoo! is doing and where it may be headed. The news sources in this hack should give you a starting point for watching the company, and you can add the RSS feeds for the sources directly to My Yahoo! or your favorite newsreader. Once you subscribe to a few Yahoo!-related feeds, you won't have any trouble keeping up with the latest news.

Yahoo! Sources

You can use Yahoo! to find information about anything in the world, even Yahoo! itself:

Yahoo! News Search
    Search over 7,000 news sources to find mentions of Yahoo! in news stories:
    Web
        http://search.news.yahoo.com/search/news/?p=Yahoo%21
    RSS
        http://news.search.yahoo.com/news/rss?ei=UTF-8&p=Yahoo%21

Yahoo! Finance Search
>Track the progress of Yahoo!'s stock and find financial news and analysis at Yahoo! Finance:

Stock
>*http://finance.yahoo.com/q?s=YHOO*

News
>*http://finance.yahoo.com/q/h?s=YHOO*

News RSS
>*http://finance.yahoo.com/rss/headline?s=YHOO*

Yahoo! Search Blog
>This official weblog from Yahoo!, written by Yahoo! employees and special guest bloggers, gives you the inside scoop on what's new at Yahoo!:

Web
>*http://www.ysearchblog.com*

RSS
>*http://www.ysearchblog.com/index.xml*

Yahoo! Web Services Blog
>Find out what's happening with Yahoo! Search Web Services at this official weblog:

Web
>*http://developer.yahoo.net/blog*

RSS
>*http://developer.yahoo.net/blog/index.xml*

Yahoo! 360 Product Blog
>The Yahoo! 360 development team keeps a weblog with the latest updates and offerings at Yahoo! 360:

Web
>*http://blog.360.yahoo.com/product_360*

RSS
>*http://blog.360.yahoo.com/rss-1qCkw2Ehaak.hdNZkEAzDrpa4Q--*

Yahoo! Jobs
>Discover where Yahoo! is hiring with Yahoo! HotJobs:

Web
>*http://hotjobs.yahoo.com/jobseeker/jobsearch/search_results.html?keywords_all=Yahoo*

RSS
>*http://hotjobs.yahoo.com/rss/0/USA/-/-/-/Yahoo*

Yahoo! Next
Yahoo! promotes their latest projects at this site, and you can be sure the latest and greatest Yahoo! offerings will show up here:
Web
http://next.yahoo.com
RSS
http://next.yahoo.com/index.rss

Yahoo! Research
Yahoo! Research is a group within Yahoo! that works on pushing the technology envelope. This site covers who they are and what they're working on:
Web
http://research.yahoo.com

Everything Yahoo!
This page points to virtually every Yahoo! site, and it's worth visiting periodically to get a general overview of Yahoo! offerings:
Web
http://docs.yahoo.com/docs/family/more

Outside News Sources

Not everything is available at Yahoo! Here are a few other news sources that frequently have information about Yahoo!:

CNET News.blog: Yahoo
CNET has a special weblog devoted to Yahoo!-related news:
Web
http://ecoustics-cnet.com.com/2060-65243_3-0.html
RSS
http://news.com.com/2063-65243_3-0.xml

The Unofficial Yahoo! Weblog
This is a Weblogs, Inc., production that focuses on Yahoo!:
Web
http://yahoo.weblogsinc.com
RSS
http://yahoo.weblogsinc.com/rss.xml

Wired News
Wired News keeps tabs on the entire tech industry, and a search for Yahoo! will yield many articles:

Web

> *http://search.wired.com/wnews/default.asp?query=Yahoo*

RSS

> *http://search.wired.com/wnews/default.asp?query=Yahoo&format=rss*

John Battelle's Searchblog

John writes about search engines and follows Yahoo! closely:

Web

> *http://battellemedia.com*

RSS

> *http://feeds.feedburner.com/JohnBattellesSearchblog*

Search Engine Watch Blog

This is a Jupitermedia weblog that follows all major search engines, including Yahoo!:

Web

> *http://blog.searchenginewatch.com*

RSS

> *http://blog.searchengi newatch.com/blog/blog.xml*

ResearchBuzz: Yahoo

Tara Calishain covers all aspects of Internet research, and her Yahoo! category is continually updated:

Web

> *http://www.researchbuzz.org/search_enginesyahoo.shtml*

RSS

> *http://www.researchbuzz.org/rss_search_enginesyahoo.xml*

Google News

A search for Yahoo! at Google will yield news across hundreds of sources:

Web

> *http://news.google.com/news?q=Yahoo!*

Yahoo! Employee Weblogs

Yahoo! has over 7,600 employees, so it makes sense that some keep personal journals via weblogs. Most employee weblogs aren't connected with the company in any way, and you might not learn much about Yahoo! from them. But tune in to a few for a while and you'll definitely see the company in a new way.

Yahoo! provides official blogging guidelines to their employees. You can read them at *http://jeremy.zawodny.com/yahoo/
yahoo-blog-guidelines.pdf*.

Here are a few employees with weblogs:

Jeremy Zawodny
Jeremy is probably the most outspoken Yahoo! employee in the blogosphere, and he frequently discusses Yahoo! on his weblog:

Web
http://jeremy.zawodny.com/blog

RSS
http://jeremy.zawodny.com/blog/rss2.xml

Russell Beattie Notebook
If you're interested in Yahoo! Mobile—and mobile products in general—
be sure to tune into Russell's weblog:

Web
http://www.russellbeattie.com/notebook

RSS
http://www.russellbeattie.com/notebook/index.rss

Jeffrey McManus
Jeffery works on *developer.yahoo.net*, and this is his personal weblog:

Web
http://mcmanus.typepad.com

RSS:
http://mcmanus.typepad.com/grind/index.rdf

Little. Yellow. Different.
Ernie Hsiung has been writing his weblog for years, and at the time of
this writing he's working on the weblog features of Yahoo! 360:

Web
http://www.littleyellowdifferent.com

RSS
http://www.littleyellowdifferent.com/index.xml

Ravi's Blog
Ravi Donamraju is a Yahoo! Search engineer:

Web
http://www.dronamraju.com/journal/index.html

RSS
http://www.dronamraju.com/journal/rss.xml

Premshree's Personal Weblog
Premshree is a self-described hacker and is a contributor to this book:
Web
http://www.livejournal.com/users/premshree
RSS
http://feeds.feedburner.com/premshree

Ian C. Roger's Y! blog
Ian works for Yahoo! Music and writes about web technology on his Yahoo! 360 blog:
Web
http://blog.360.yahoo.com/blog-FDuiCSg4eqinB8z.GGJ7TmAz
RSS
http://blog.360.yahoo.com/rss-FDuiCSg4eqinB8z.GGJ7TmAz

You can probably spot many more employee weblogs by browsing to Yahoo! Search (*http://search.yahoo.com*) and typing in the phrase "I work at Yahoo" weblog or "I work for Yahoo" weblog.

Grassroots Sources

Even though these sources don't pass through an editor, and the content isn't produced by professionals, these sources can provide a unique perspective on the company, point to interesting personal opinions, or refer you to obscure bits of information about Yahoo!:

Flickr Photos
Public photos tagged with Yahoo! at Flickr are often photos by employees, pictures from Yahoo! campuses, or pictures from Yahoo! events:
Web
http://www.flickr.com/photos/tags/yahoo
RSS:
http://www.flickr.com/services/feeds/photos_public.gne?tags=yahoo&format=rss_200

del.icio.us
The social bookmarks service del.icio.us has hundreds of people swapping links, and every day there are several dozen tagged with Yahoo!:
Web
http://del.icio.us/tag/yahoo
RSS
http://del.icio.us/rss/tag/yahoo

Furl

Like del.icio.us, Furl is a way to share links, and you can tune into the Yahoo! headlines:

Web

http://www.furl.net/furled.jsp?topic=yahoo

RSS

http://www.furl.net/members/rss.xml?topic=yahoo

Technorati

Use Technorati to find weblog posts that mention Yahoo!. Technorati's Yahoo! tag page also pulls in content from Flickr, del.icio.us, and Furl:

Web

http://www.technorati.com/tag/Yahoo

Daypop

Daypop is another weblog search that can point out mentions of Yahoo! across the blogosphere:

Web

http://www.daypop.com/search?q=yahoo&t=w

RSS

*http://www.daypop.com/search?q=yahoo&s=1&c=10&ext
=true&t=w&o=rss*

Yahoo!-related Yahoo! Groups

Check out the Yahoo! category on Yahoo! Groups to see what Yahoo!-related topics people are discussing:

Web

http://dir.groups.yahoo.com/dir/1600653854

It would be impossible to track everything Yahoo! is doing on a daily basis, but subscribing to a combination of these sources should help keep you in the Yahoo! loop.

HACK
#19   Spider the Yahoo! Catalog

Writing a spider to spider an existing spider's site may seem convoluted, but it can prove useful when you're looking for location-based services. This hack walks through creating a framework for full-site spidering, including additional filters to lessen your load.

In this hack, you'll learn how to write a spider that crawls the Yahoo! group of portals. The choice of Yahoo! was obvious; because it is one of the largest Internet portals in existence, it can serve as an ideal example of how one goes about writing a portal spider.

But before we get to the gory details of code, let's define what exactly a portal spider is. While many may argue with such a classification, I maintain that a *portal spider* is a script that automatically downloads all documents from a preselected range of URLs found on the portal's site or a group of sites, as is the case with Yahoo!. A portal spider's main job is to walk from one document to another, extract URLs from downloaded HTML, process said URLs, and go to another document, repeating the cycle until it runs out of URLs to visit. Once you create code that describes such basic behavior, you can add additional functionality, turning your general portal spider into a specialized one.

Although writing a script that walks from one Yahoo! page to another sounds simple, it isn't, because there is no general pattern followed by all Yahoo! sites or sections within those sites. Furthermore, Yahoo! is not a single site with a nice link layout that can be described using a simple algorithm and a classic data structure. Instead, it is a collection of well over 30 thematic sites, each with its own document layout, naming conventions, and peculiarities in page design and URL patterns. For example, if you check links to the same directory section on different Yahoo! sites, you will find that some of them begin with *http://www.yahoo.com/r*, some begin with *http://uk.yahoo.com/r/hp/dr*, and others begin with *http://kr.yahoo.com*.

If you try to look for patterns, you will soon find yourself writing long if/ elsif/else sections that are hard to maintain and need to be rewritten every time Yahoo! makes a small change to one of its sites. If you follow that route, you will soon discover that you need to write hundreds of lines of code to describe every kind of behavior you want to build into your spider.

This is particularly frustrating to programmers who expect to write code that uses elegant algorithms and nicely structured data. The hard truth about portals is that you cannot expect elegance and ease of spidering. Instead, prepare yourself for a lot of detective work and writing (and throwing away) chunks of code in a hit-and-miss fashion. Portal spiders are written in an organic, unstructured way, and the only rule you should follow is to keep things simple and add specific functionality only once you have the general behavior working.

Okay—with taxonomy and general advice behind us, we can get to the gist of the matter. The spider in this hack is a relatively simple tool for crawling Yahoo! sites. It makes no assumptions about the layout of the sites; in fact, it makes almost no assumptions whatsoever and can easily be adapted to other portals or even groups of portals. You can use it as a framework for writing specialized spiders.

The Code

Save the following code to a file called *yspider.pl*:

```perl
#!/usr/bin/perl -w
#
# yspider.pl
#
# Yahoo! Spider--crawls Yahoo! sites, collects links from each downloaded HTML
# page, searches each downloaded page and prints a list of results when done.
# http://www.artymiak.com/software/ or contact jacek@artymiak.com
#
# This code is free software; you can redistribute it and/or
# modify it under the same terms as Perl itself.

use strict;
use Getopt::Std;          # parse command line options.
use LWP::UserAgent;       # download data from the net.
use HTML::LinkExtor;      # get links inside an HTML document.
use URI::URL;             # turn relative links into absolutes.

my $help = <<"EOH";
----------------------------------------------------------------------------
Yahoo! Spider.

Options: -s    list of sites you want to crawl,
               e.g. -s 'us china denmark'
         -h    print this help

Allowed values of -s are:

   argentina, asia, australia, brazil, canada,
   catalan, china, denmark, france, germany, hongkong,
   india, ireland, italy, japan, korea, mexico,
   newzealand, norway, singapore, spain, sweden, taiwan,
   uk, us, us_chinese, us_spanish

Please, use this code responsibly. Flooding any site
with excessive queries is bad net citizenship.
----------------------------------------------------------------------------
EOH

# define our arguments and
# show the help if asked.
my %args; getopts("s:h", \%args);
die $help if exists $args{h};

# The list of code names, and
# URLs, for various Yahoo! sites.
my %ys = (
    argentina => "http://ar.yahoo.com", asia => "http://asia.yahoo.com",
    australia => "http://au.yahoo.com", newzealand => "http://au.yahoo.com",
    brazil    => "http://br.yahoo.com", canada   => "http://ca.yahoo.com",
    catalan   => "http://ct.yahoo.com", china    => "http://cn.yahoo.com",
```

```
denmark    => "http://dk.yahoo.com", france    => "http://fr.yahoo.com",
germany    => "http://de.yahoo.com", hongkong => "http://hk.yahoo.com",
india      => "http://in.yahoo.com", italy    -> "http://it.yahoo.com",
korea      => "http://kr.yahoo.com", mexico   => "http://mx.yahoo.com",
norway     => "http://no.yahoo.com", singapore => "http://sg.yahoo.com",
spain      => "http://es.yahoo.com", sweden   => "http://se.yahoo.com",
taiwan     => "http://tw.yahoo.com", uk       => "http://uk.yahoo.com",
ireland    => "http://uk.yahoo.com", us       => "http://www.yahoo.com",
japan      => "http://www.yahoo.co.jp",
us_chinese => "http://chinese.yahoo.com",
us_spanish => "http://espanol.yahoo.com"
);

# if the -s option was used, check to make
# sure it matches one of our existing codes
# above. if not, or no -s was passed, help.
my @sites; # which locales to spider.
if (exists $args{'s'}) {
    @sites = split(/ /, lc($args{'s'}));
    foreach my $site (@sites) {
        die "UNKNOWN: $site\n\n$help" unless $ys{$site};
    }
} else { die $help; }

# Defines global and local profiles for URLs extracted from the
# downloaded pages. These profiles are used to determine if the
# URLs extracted from each new document should be placed on the
# TODO list (%todo) or rejected (%rejects). Profiles are lists
# made of chunks of text, which are matched against found URLs.
# Any special characters, like slash (/) or dot (.) must be properly
# escaped. Remember that globals have precedence over locals.
my %rules = (
    global     => { allow => [], deny => [ 'search', '\*' ] },
    argentina  => { allow => [ 'http:\/\/ar\.' ], deny => [] },
    asia       => { allow => [ 'http:\/\/(aa|asia)\.' ], deny => [] },
    australia  => { allow => [ 'http:\/\/au\.' ], deny => [] },
    brazil     => { allow => [ 'http:\/\/br\.' ], deny => [] },
    canada     => { allow => [ 'http:\/\/ca\.' ], deny => [] },
    catalan    => { allow => [ 'http:\/\/ct\.' ], deny => [] },
    china      => { allow => [ 'http:\/\/cn\.' ], deny => [] },
    denmark    => { allow => [ 'http:\/\/dk\.' ], deny => [] },
    france     => { allow => [ 'http:\/\/fr\.' ], deny => [] },
    germany    => { allow => [ 'http:\/\/de\.' ], deny => [] },
    hongkong   => { allow => [ 'http:\/\/hk\.' ], deny => [] },
    india      => { allow => [ 'http:\/\/in\.' ], deny => [] },
    ireland    => { allow => [ 'http:\/\/uk\.' ], deny => [] },
    italy      => { allow => [ 'http:\/\/it\.' ], deny => [] },
    japan      => { allow => [ 'yahoo\.co\.jp' ], deny => [] },
    korea      => { allow => [ 'http:\/\/kr\.' ], deny => [] },
    mexico     => { allow -> [ 'http:\/\/mx\.' ], deny => [] },
    norway     => { allow => [ 'http:\/\/no\.' ], deny => [] },
    singapore  => { allow => [ 'http:\/\/sg\.' ], deny => [] },
    spain      => { allow => [ 'http:\/\/es\.' ], deny => [] },
    sweden     => { allow => [ 'http:\/\/se\.' ], deny => [] },
```

```
taiwan     => { allow => [ 'http:\/\/tw\.' ], deny => [] },
uk         => { allow => [ 'http:\/\/uk\.' ], deny => [] },
us         => { allow => [ 'http:\/\/(dir|www)\.' ], deny => [] },
us_chinese => { allow => [ 'http:\/\/chinese\.' ], deny => [] },
us_spanish => { allow => [ 'http:\/\/espanol\.' ], deny => [] },
);

my %todo = ();      # URLs to parse
my %done = ();      # parsed/finished URLs
my %errors = ();    # broken URLs with errors.
my %rejects = ();   # URLs rejected by the script

# print out a "we're off!" line, then
# begin walking the site we've been told to.
print "=" x 80 . "\nStarted Yahoo! spider...\n" . "=" x 80 . "\n";
our $site; foreach $site (@sites) {

    # for each of the sites that have been passed on the
    # command line, we make a title for them, add them to
    # the TODO list for downloading, then call walksite(),
    # which downloads the URL, looks for more URLs, etc.
    my $title = "Yahoo! " . ucfirst($site) . " front page";
    $todo{$ys{$site}} = $title; walksite(); # process.

}

# once we're all done with all the URLs, we print a
# report about all the information we've gone through.
print "=" x 80 . "\nURLs downloaded and parsed:\n" . "=" x 80 . "\n";
foreach my $url (keys %done) { print "$url => $done{$url}\n"; }
print "=" x 80 . "\nURLs that couldn't be downloaded:\n" . "=" x 80 . "\n";
foreach my $url (keys %errors) { print "$url => $errors{$url}\n"; }
print "=" x 80 . "\nURLs that got rejected:\n" . "=" x 80 . "\n";
foreach my $url (keys %rejects) { print "$url => $rejects{$url}\n"; }

# this routine grabs the first entry in our todo
# list, downloads the content, and looks for more URLs.
# we stay in walksite until there are no more URLs
# in our to do list, which could be a good long time.
sub walksite {

    do {
        # get first URL to do.
        my $url = (keys %todo)[0];

        # download this URL
        print "-> trying $url ...\n";
        my $browser = LWP::UserAgent->new;
        my $resp = $browser->get( $url, 'User-Agent' => 'Y!SpiderHack/1.0' );

        # check the results.
        if ($resp->is_success) {
            my $base = $resp->base || '';
            print "-> base URL: $base\n";
```

```
            my $data = $resp->content; # get the data.
            print "-> downloaded: " . length($data) . " bytes of $url\n";

            # find URLs using a link extorter. relevant ones
            # will be added to our to do list of downloadables.
            # this passes all the found links to findurls()
            # below, which determines if we should add the link
            # to our to do list, or ignore it due to filtering.
            HTML::LinkExtor->new(\&findurls, $base)->parse($data);

            ############################################################
            # add your own processing here. perhaps you'd like to add #
            # a keyword search for the downloaded content in $data?    #
            ############################################################

        } else {
            $errors{$url} = $resp->message();
            print "-> error: couldn't download URL: $url\n";
            delete $todo{$url};
        }

        # we're finished with this URL, so move it from
        # the to do list to the done list, and print a report.
        $done{$url} = $todo{$url}; delete $todo{$url};
        print "-> processed legal URLs: " . (scalar keys %done) . "\n";
        print "-> remaining URLs: " . (scalar keys %todo) . "\n";
        print "-" x 80 . "\n";
    } until ((scalar keys %todo) == 0);
}

# callback routine for HTML::LinkExtor. For every
# link we find in our downloaded content, we check
# to see if we've processed it before, then run it
# through a bevy of regexp rules (see the top of
# this script) to see if it belongs in the to do.
sub findurls {
    my($tag, %links) = @_;
    return if $tag ne 'a';
    return unless $links{href};
    print "-> found URL: $links{href}\n";

    # already seen this URL, so move on.
    if (exists $done{$links{href}} ||
        exists $errors{$links{href}} ||
        exists $rejects{$links{href}}) {
        print "--> I've seen this before: $links{href}\n"; return;
    }

    # now, run through our filters.
    unless (exists($todo{$links{href}})) {
        my ($ga, $gd, $la, $ld); # counters.
        foreach (@{$rules{global}{'allow'}}) { $ga++ if $links{href} =~ ⏎
/$_/i; }
        foreach (@{$rules{global}{'deny'}}) { $gd++ if $links{href} =~ ⏎
```

```
/$_/i; }
        foreach (@{$rules{$site}{'allow'}}) { $la++ if $links{href} =~ ⏎
/$_/i; }
        foreach (@{$rules{$site}{'deny'}}) { $ld++ if $links{href} =~ /$_/i; }

        # if there were denials or NO allowances, we move on.
        if ($gd or $ld) { print "-> rejected URL: $links{href}\n"; return; }
        unless ($ga or $la) { print "-> rejected URL: $links{href}\n"; ⏎
    return; }

        # we passed our filters, so add it on the barby.
        print "-> added $links{href} to my TODO list\n";
        $todo{$links{href}} = $links{href};
    }
}
```

Running the Hack

Before sending the spider off, you'll need to make a decision regarding which part of the Yahoo! directory you want to crawl. If you're mainly interested in the United States and United Kingdom, inform the spider of that by using the -s option on the command line, like so:

```
% perl yspider.pl -s "us uk"
============================================================================
Started Yahoo! spider...
============================================================================
-> trying http://www.yahoo.com ...
-> base URL: http://www.yahoo.com/
-> downloaded: 28376 bytes of http://www.yahoo.com
-> found URL: http://www.yahoo.com/s/92802
-> added http://www.yahoo.com/s/92802 to my TODO list
-> found URL: http://www.yahoo.com/s/92803
... etc ...
-> added http://www.yahoo.com/r/pv to my TODO list
-> processed legal URLs: 1
-> remaining URLs: 244
----------------------------------------------------------------------------
-> trying http://www.yahoo.com/r/fr ...
-> base URL: http://fr.yahoo.com/r/
-> downloaded: 32619 bytes of http://www.yahoo.com/r/fr
-> found URL: http://fr.yahoo.com/r/t/mu00
-> rejected URL: http://fr.yahoo.com/r/t/mu00
...
```

You can see a full list of locations available to you by asking for help:

```
% perl yspider.pl -h
...
Allowed values of -s are:

    argentina, asia, australia, brazil, canada, catalan, china,
    denmark, france, germany, hongkong, india, ireland, italy, japan,
    korea, mexico, newzealand, norway, singapore, spain, sweden,
    taiwan, uk, us, us_chinese, us_spanish
```

Hacking the Hack

The section you'll want to modify most contains the filters that determine how far the spider will go; by tweaking the allow and deny rules at the beginning of the script, you'll be able to better grab just the content you're interested in. If you want to make this spider even more generic, consider rewriting the configuration code so that it'll instead read a plain-text list of code names, start URLs, and allow and deny patterns. This can turn a Yahoo! spider into a general Internet spider.

Whenever you want to add code that extends the functionality of this spider (such as searching for keywords in a document, adding the downloaded content to a database, or otherwise repurposing it for your needs), include your own logic where specified by the hashed-out comment block.

See Also

- If you're spidering Yahoo! because you want to start your own directory, you might want to consider Google's Open Directory Project (*http://dmoz.org/about.html*). Downloading the project's freely available directory data, all several hundred megs of it, will give you plenty of information to play with.

— Jacek Artymiak

HACK

#20

Browse the Yahoo! Directory
When you don't know exactly what you're looking for, the Yahoo! Directory might be able to help you find it.

Yahoo! started in 1994 as Jerry Yang and David Filo's organized list of favorite sites they'd found on the Web. Yahoo! has grown into much, much more, and many people think of Yahoo! as strictly a *search* company. Searching is great when you have a fairly good idea of what you're looking for, but the Yahoo! Directory is a great place when you'd rather browse.

Searching Versus Browsing

There are two different kinds of shoppers, and they illustrate the difference between *searching* and *browsing*. Some shoppers know exactly what they're after and they want to find a store that carries that item, locate it in the store, and purchase it as quickly as possible. As with a web search, it helps to know a bit about what you're looking for if this is your style. Other shoppers want to explore a particular store, see what the store offers, and choose an item if the right one comes along. This style of browsing is suited to people who want to get a larger survey of items in a particular category before they necessarily decide what they're looking for.

Search forms are obviously built for searching. *Directories* are built for browsing. Unlike Yahoo! Search results, the Yahoo! Directory doesn't try to include every page it can find from across the Web. Instead, the sites listed in the directory are hand picked and reviewed by paid Yahoo! editors.

If you were interested in looking at a sampling of weblogs about politics, you might try a search at *http://search.yahoo.com* with the query political weblog. You would find political weblogs in the search results, along with news articles about political weblogs, college papers about political weblogs, and even pages that just mention the terms *political* and *weblogs*. But browsing the Political Weblogs category in the Yahoo! Directory (*http://dir.yahoo.com/ Computers_and_Internet/Internet/World_Wide_Web/Weblogs/Politics*) will give you hundreds of links that have been selected by Yahoo! employees as being political weblogs.

The editors leave it as an exercise to the reader to determine which side of the political spectrum any given weblog is on.

In addition to a less noisy list of sites to browse, you'll find other evidence of the editors in the directory. Some sites will have a PICK! icon after them, along with a review of the site, like the last entry shown in Figure 1-51.

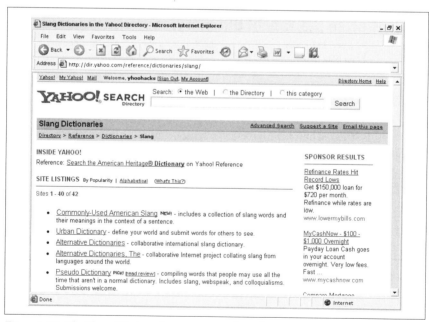

Figure 1-51. The Slang Dictionaries category in the Yahoo! Directory

Click the "read review" link after any PICK! icon to see a brief description of the site, written by a Yahoo! editor. Other sites that have been chosen as *cool* by Yahoo! editors have an icon of sunglasses next to their listing.

> If you spot a site in the directory that you'd like to see chosen and reviewed as a Yahoo! pick, you can email your suggestion to *suggest-picks@yahoo-inc.com*. You can read new picks at *http://picks.yahoo.com*.

Adding a Site

Unlike the Yahoo! Search index, which is constantly looking for and adding new sites automatically, the Yahoo! Directory considers sites for inclusion only from user suggestions. You can suggest a site for the Yahoo! Directory by browsing to the category you'd like to see the site listed in and clicking the "Suggest a Site" link at the top of the page. From there, you'll be asked to choose a paid or free listing (paying users get preferential treatment, including faster listing times). If you choose the free option, you'll be asked to confirm the category and enter the site information.

Because there are hundreds of requests, it's not possible for Yahoo! to include all of the suggested sites. But if you've found that your site isn't included within a few weeks of submitting it, you can submit your site again.

> Multiple submissions in a short period are considered abuse by Yahoo! and the request won't be considered.

If your site is accepted, it will appear at the top of the list with a NEW! icon next to it for two weeks. The Yahoo! for Webmasters chapter has even more details about adding a site to Yahoo! **[Hack #92]**.

Keeping up with recent additions to categories you're interested in is a great way to find new sites. You can subscribe to new additions in a particular category via RSS, or add the category's feed to your list of My Yahoo! news sources. To get started, browse to the Yahoo! Directory RSS Feeds page at *http://dir.yahoo.com/rss/dir/index.php* and choose from the categories listed.

Track Additions to Yahoo!
#21

Keep track of the number of sites added to your favorite Yahoo! categories.

Every day, a squad of surfers at Yahoo! adds new sites to the Yahoo! index. These changes are reflected in the Yahoo! What's New page (*http://dir.yahoo.com/new*), along with the Picks of the Day.

If you're a casual surfer, you might not care about the number of new sites added to Yahoo!. But there are several scenarios when you might have an interest:

You regularly glean information about new sites from Yahoo!
Knowing which categories are growing and which categories are stagnant will tell you where to direct your attention.

You want to submit sites to Yahoo!
Are you going to spend your hard-earned money adding a site to a category where new sites are added constantly (meaning your submitted site might quickly get buried)? Or will you be paying to add to a category that sees few additions (meaning your site might have a better chance of standing out)?

You're interested in trend tracking
Which categories are consistently busy? Which are all but dead? By watching how Yahoo! adds sites to categories, over time you'll get a sense of the rhythms and trends and detect when unusual activity occurs in a category.

This hack scrapes the recent counts of additions to Yahoo! categories and prints them out, providing an at-a-glance look at additions to various categories. You'll also get a tab-delimited table of how many sites have been added to each category for each day. A tab-delimited file is excellent for importing into a spreadsheet, where you can turn the count numbers into a chart.

The Code

Save the following code to a file called *hoocount.pl*:

```
#!/usr/bin/perl -w

use strict;
use Date::Manip;
use LWP::Simple;
use Getopt::Long;

$ENV{TZ} - "GMT" if $^O eq "MSWin32";

# the homepage for Yahoo!'s "What's New".
my $new_url = "http://dir.yahoo.com/new/";

# the major categories at Yahoo!. hash'd because
# we'll use them to hold our counts string.
my @categories = ("Arts & Humanities",   "Business & Economy",
                  "Computers & Internet", "Education",
                  "Entertainment",        "Government",
```

```
                 "Health",              "News & Media",
                 "Recreation & Sports", "Reference",
                 "Regional",            "Science",
                 "Social Science",      "Society & Culture");
my %final_counts; # where we save our final readouts.

# load in our options from the command line.
my %opts; GetOptions(\%opts, "c|count=i");
die unless $opts{c}; # count sites from past $i days.

# if we've been told to count the number of new sites,
# then we'll go through each of our main categories
# for the last $i days and collate a result.

# begin the header
# for our import file.
my $header = "Category";

# from today, going backwards, get $i days.
for (my $i=1; $i <= $opts{c}; $i++) {

    # create a Data::Manip time that will
    # be used to construct the last $i days
    my $day; # query for Yahoo! retrieval.
    if ($i == 1) { $day = "yesterday"; }
    else { $day = "$i days ago"; }
    my $date = UnixDate($day, "%Y%m%d");

    # and this date to
    # our import file.
    $header .= "\t$date";

    # and download the day.
    my $url = "$new_url$date.html";
    my $data = get($url) or die $!;

    # and loop through each of our categories.
    my $day_count; foreach my $category (sort @categories) {
        $data =~ /$category.*?(\d+)/; my $count = $1 || 0;
        $final_counts{$category} .= "\t$count"; # building our string.
    }
}

# with all our counts finished,
# print out our final file.
print $header . "\n";
foreach my $category (@categories) {
    print $category, $final_counts{$category}, "\n";
}
```

Running the Hack

The only argument you need to provide to the script is the number of days back you'd like it to travel in search of new additions. Since Yahoo! doesn't archive its "new pages added" indefinitely, a safe upper limit is around two weeks. Here, we're looking at the past two days:

```
% perl hoocount.pl --count 2
Category          20050711      20050710
Arts & Humanities       32      9
Business & Economy      44      2
Computers & Internet    30      0
Education      0      0
Entertainment    77      0
Government      2      0
Health  11      0
News & Media    0      0
Recreation & Sports     48      1
Reference      0      0
Regional        81      3
Science 6       9
Social Science  0      0
Society & Culture       12      0
```

Hacking the Hack

If you're not only a researcher but also a Yahoo! observer, you might be interested in how the number of sites added changes over time. To that end, you could run this script under cron or the Windows Scheduler and output the results to a file. After three months or so, you'd have a pretty interesting set of counts to manipulate with a spreadsheet program.

—Kevin Hemenway and Tara Calishain

Yahoo! Directory Mindshare in Google

HACK #22

How does link popularity compare in Yahoo!'s searchable subject index versus Google's full-text index? Find out by calculating mindshare!

Yahoo! and Google are two very different animals. Yahoo! indexes only a site's main URL, title, and description, while Google builds full-text indexes of entire sites. Surely there's some interesting cross-pollination when you combine results from the two.

This hack scrapes all the URLs in a specified subcategory of the Yahoo! directory. It then takes each URL and gets its link count from Google. Each link count provides a nice snapshot of how a particular Yahoo! category and its listed sites stack up on the popularity scale.

What's a *link count*? It's simply the total number of pages in Google's index that link to a specific URL.

There are a couple of ways you can use your knowledge of a subcategory's link count. If you find a subcategory whose URLs have only a few links each in Google, you may have found a subcategory that isn't getting a lot of attention from Yahoo!'s editors. Consider going elsewhere for your research. If you're a webmaster and you're considering paying to have Yahoo! add you to its directory, run this hack on the category in which you want to be listed. Are most of the links really popular? If they are, are you sure your site will stand out and get clicks? Maybe you should choose a different category.

We got this idea from a similar experiment done by Jon Udell (*http://weblog.infoworld.com/udell*) in 2001. He used AltaVista instead of Google; see *http://udell.roninhouse.com/download/mindshare-script.txt*. We appreciate the inspiration, Jon!

The Code

You will need a Google API account (*http://api.google.com*) as well as the Perl modules SOAP::Lite (*http://www.soaplite.com*) and HTML::LinkExtor (*http://search.cpan.org/author/GAAS/HTML-Parser/lib/HTML/LinkExtor.pm*) to run the following code. You'll also need a copy of the Google WSDL file in the same directory as the script (*http://api.google.com/GoogleSearch.wsdl*). Save the following code to a file called *mindshare.pl*:

```perl
#!/usr/bin/perl -w

use strict;
use LWP::Simple;
use HTML::LinkExtor;
use SOAP::Lite;

my $google_key  = "your API key goes here";
my $google_wdsl = "GoogleSearch.wsdl";
my $yahoo_dir   = shift || "/Computers_and_Internet/Data_Formats/XML__".
                  "eXtensible_Markup_Language_/RSS/Aggregators/";

# download the Yahoo! directory.
my $data = get("http://dir.yahoo.com" . $yahoo_dir) or die $!;

# create our Google object.
my $google_search = SOAP::Lite->service("file:$google_wdsl");
my %urls; # where we keep our counts and titles.
```

```
# extract all the links and parse 'em.
HTML::LinkExtor->new(\&mindshare)->parse($data);
sub mindshare { # for each link we find...

    my ($tag, %attr) = @_;

    # only continue on if the tag was a link,
    # and the URL matches Yahoo!'s redirectory,
    return if $tag ne 'a';
    return if $attr{href} =~ /us.rd.yahoo/;
    return unless $attr{href} =~ /^http/;

    # and process each URL through Google.
    my $results = $google_search->doGoogleSearch(
                    $google_key, "link:$attr{href}", 0, 1,
                    "true", "", "false", "", "", ""
                ); # wheee, that was easy, guvner.
    $urls{$attr{href}} = $results->{estimatedTotalResultsCount};
}

# now sort and display.
my @sorted_urls = sort { $urls{$b} <=> $urls{$a} } keys %urls;
foreach my $url (@sorted_urls) { print "$urls{$url}: $url\n"; }
```

Running the Hack

The hack has its only configuration—the Yahoo! directory you're interested in—passed as a single argument (in quotes) on the command line (if you don't pass one of your own, a default directory will be used instead):

```
% perl mindshare.pl "/Entertainment/Humor/Procrastination/"
```

Your results show the URLs in those directories, sorted by total Google links:

```
554: http://www.p45.net/
339: http://www.ishouldbeworking.com/
124: http://www.india.com/
45: http://www.geocities.com/SouthBeach/1915/
15: http://www.eskimo.com/~spban/creed.html
15: http://www.jlc.net/~useless/
5: http://www.black-schaffer.org/scp/
2: http://www.angelfire.com/mi/psociety
1: http://www.geocities.com/wastingslatetime/
```

Hacking the Hack

Yahoo! isn't the only searchable subject index out there, of course; there's also the Open Directory Project (DMOZ, *http://www.dmoz.org*), which is the product of thousands of volunteers busily cataloging and categorizing sites on the Web—the web community's Yahoo!, if you will. This hack works just as well on DMOZ as it does on Yahoo!; they're very similar in structure.

Replace the default Yahoo! directory with its DMOZ equivalent:

```
my $dmoz_dir = shift || "/Reference/Libraries/Library_and_Information_↵
Science/".
                  "Technical_Services/Cataloguing/Metadata/RDF/".
                  "Applications/RSS/News_Readers/";
```

You'll also need to change the download instructions:

```
# download the Dmoz.org! directory.
my $data = get("http://dmoz.org" . $dmoz_dir) or die $!;
```

Next, replace the lines that check whether a URL should be measured for mindshare. When we were scraping Yahoo! in our original script, we skipped over Yahoo! links and those that weren't web sites:

```
return if $attr{href} =~ /us.rd.yahoo/;
return unless $attr{href} =~ /^http/;
```

Since DMOZ is an entirely different site, we'll make sure it's a full-blooded location (i.e., it starts with *http://* as before and that it doesn't match any of DMOZ's internal page links. Likewise, we'll ignore searches on other engines:

```
return unless $attr{href} =~ /^http/;
return if $attr{href} =~ /dmoz|google|altavista|lycos|yahoo|alltheweb/;
```

Can you go even further with this? Sure! You might want to search a more specialized directory, such as the FishHoo! fishing search engine (*http://www.fishhoo.com*).

You might want to return only the most linked-to URL from the directory, which is quite easy by piping the results to head, another common Unix utility:

```
% perl mindshare.pl | head 1
```

Alternatively, you might want to go ahead and grab the top 10 Google matches for the URL that has the most mindshare. To do so, add the following code to the bottom of the script:

```
print "\nMost popular URLs for the strongest mindshare:\n";
my $most_popular = shift @sorted_urls;
my $results = $google_search->doGoogleSearch(
                  $google_key, "$most_popular", 0, 10,
                  "true", "", "false", "", "", "" );

foreach my $element (@{$results->{resultElements}}) {
    next if $element->{URL} eq $most_popular;
    print " * $element->{URL}\n";
    print "   \"$element->{title}\"\n\n";
}
```

Then run the script as usual (the output here uses the default hardcoded directory):

```
% perl mindshare.pl
24600: http://www.newsburst.com/
22700: http://www.bloglines.com/
9640: http://radio.userland.com/
6890: http://www.feedreader.com/
4770: http://www.sharpreader.net/
4660: http://www.newsgator.com/
3580: http://www.newsisfree.com/
2680: http://www.pubsub.com/
2090: http://www.disobey.com/amphetadesk/
1740: http://www.serence.com/site.php?page=prod_klipfolio
1690: http://www.pluck.com/
1610: http://www.rssbandit.org/
1160: http://www.allheadlinenews.com/
1140: http://www.newzcrawler.com/
961: http://www.rojo.com/

...

Most popular URLs for the strongest mindshare:
 * http://www.newsburst.com/Source/?add=PUTyourFEEDurlHERE
   ""

 * http://deeplinking.net/xmlsrv/rss.php?blog=4
   "Deeplinking"

 * http://www.bloglines.com/citations?url=http://www.newsburst.com
   "Bloglines | Citations"

 * http://www.feedforall.com/forum/posting.php?mode=quote&amp;p=624
   "FeedForAll :: Post a reply"
...
```

—Kevin Hemenway and Tara Calishain

## CHAPTER TWO

Services
Hacks 23–50

In addition to pointing people to documents and resources across the Web through Yahoo! Search and the Yahoo! Directory, Yahoo! has become a destination itself. By gathering information from many sources under a single roof, Yahoo! has made following the financial markets [Hack #23], the daily news [Hack #33], or even the products available online [Hack #47] a breeze.

Yahoo! also allows you to personalize the information you find at the sites so the information is more meaningful to you. This means you can gather and track your favorite news sources together at My Yahoo! [Hack #34] or even visualize your personal music collection [Hack #48] in a new way. And once your personal preferences are stored at Yahoo!., they're accessible from any computer connected to the Internet. This is especially useful for storing bookmarks [Hack #28] or keeping tabs on movies you'd like to see [Hack #43].

Yahoo! also has several methods of routing your personalized information to you when and where you need it. Yahoo! Alerts [Hack #50] can send updated information to you via email, instant messenger, or cell phone. And Yahoo! Mobile [Hack #49] can give you access to your settings on a mobile device when you're out and about.

The hacks in this chapter are about personalizing and working with the data you'll find across Yahoo! properties. The hacks here represent only a portion of Yahoo! Here are some additional Yahoo! properties that didn't make it into the book:

Ask Yahoo!
  http://ask.yahoo.com

Banking
  http://banking.yahoo.com

Cars
  http://autos.yahoo.com

Classifieds
  http://classifieds.yahoo.com

Health
    http://health.yahoo.com
Horoscopes
    http://astrology.yahoo.com
Insurance
    http://insurance.yahoo.com
Jobs
    http://hotjobs.yahoo.com
Loans
    http://loans.yahoo.com
Lottery
    http://lottery.yahoo.com
Pets
    http://pets.yahoo.com
Real Estate
    http://realestate.yahoo.com
Small Business
    http://smallbusiness.yahoo.com
Sports
    http://sports.yahoo.com
Tax Info
    http://taxes.yahoo.com
Tickets
    http://tickets.yahoo.com
Weather
    http://weather.yahoo.com
Yellow Pages
    http://yp.yahoo.com

As you can see, Yahoo! is home to an impressive amount of information, and knowing how to tap into what's available can help you make your data more accessible to you.

HACK #23 Track Your Investments

Yahoo! Finance can help you track the performance of your stocks, bonds, or mutual funds.

Financial information that was once available only to brokers and Wall Street insiders is now available to anyone in the world with an Internet connection. Yahoo! Finance collects much of the information available about stocks, bonds, and mutual funds into a single site, and it's a fantastic resource for do-it-yourself investors. As financial guru Andrew Tobias put it, "You should manage your own money. No one is going to care about it as much as you." Managing your own investments means there's more work for you, but the online tools at Yahoo! Finance can help you get a picture of where your investments stand.

Get Quotes and News

Yahoo! Finance is well known for providing stock quotes and business news. (Even Yahoo! competitor Google sends people to Yahoo! Finance for more detailed information when they look up a ticker symbol.) Simply type a ticker symbol into the form at the top of the page at Yahoo! Finance (*http://finance.yahoo.com*) to see a detailed page with the current trading price (delayed 20 minutes) and information about the stock's activity for the day. Figure 2-1 shows the stock detail page for Yahoo's symbol (YHOO).

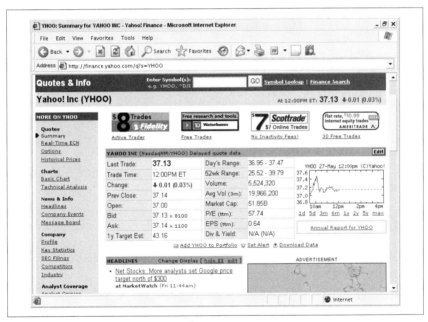

Figure 2-1. Details about YHOO at Yahoo! Finance

Running down the left side of the page, you'll find links to detailed information about the stock, including a message board for discussing the stock with other Yahoo! users, lists of company insiders who have sold stock recently, opinions on the stock from dozens of industry analysts, SEC filings, and a history of the stock performance.

> Feeling lost in all of the financial technical jargon? Yahoo!
> Finance provides a detailed glossary of financial terms at
> *http://biz.yahoo.com/f/g.*

Just below the numbers is a list of any current headlines about the company
from about 50 different news sources, and they're all enabled by default.
You can click the Edit link in the headlines title to add or remove news
sources from the headlines.

Yahoo! Finance also offers RSS feeds for company news, so you can monitor media mentions of your favorite companies in My Yahoo! or your preferred newsreader. To put together an RSS feed, visit the feed generator at
http://biz.yahoo.com/rss.html. From there, you can enter one or more stock
symbols, and Yahoo! will assemble the proper URL. If you're a do-it-yourself URL builder, you can assemble a URL in this format:

```
http://finance.yahoo.com/rss/headline?s=insert stock symbol(s)
```

To watch more than one company, separate the stock symbols with commas. So an RSS feed combining news for Yahoo!, Amazon, Microsoft, and
eBay looks like this:

```
http://finance.yahoo.com/rss/headline?s=yhoo,amzn,msft,ebay
```

In addition to the daily charts and numbers for U.S. stocks, Yahoo! Finance
offers some other interesting information:

After-hours quotes
> Even when the markets close for the day, Yahoo! gathers information
> about after-hours trading and displays it on the stock's detail page.

Stock options
> Yahoo! offers information about stock options that you can look up via
> the company's stock symbol. Click Options on the left side of a stock's
> detail page. You can also add options to your portfolio by using the
> symbols on the options page.

International stock exchanges
> You can access markets around the world at *http://biz.yahoo.com/ifc.*
> The Yahoo! International Finance Center includes links to localized
> Yahoo! Finance pages and financial facts about hundreds of countries.

Build a Portfolio

At its most basic, a *portfolio* is a way to watch a group of your favorite
stocks, bonds, or mutual funds. Say you have an employee 401(k) plan
invested in some mutual funds, a personal retirement account, and maybe
some stocks at a brokerage. All of these would have their own statements at

various web sites, with numerous logins to remember. If you wanted to track their progress on a regular basis, you'd need to visit all of the sites. With Yahoo! Finance, you can pull financial data together from various sources and turn it into a one-stop site for tracking your net worth.

You can set up a portfolio by clicking the Create link next to the Portfolios heading in the upper-left corner of the Yahoo! Finance page (*http://finance.yahoo.com*). Or you can browse to *http://edit.finance.yahoo.com/eh* and click the "Track a symbol watch list" link. Give your group of stocks a name, choose the currency you'd like to see the stocks in (U.S. Dollar is the default), and then add stock ticker symbols to the form, separated by spaces.

> If you don't know the symbol for a company or mutual fund you'd like to track, look it up at *http://finance.yahoo.com/l*.

For example, you could add YHOO AMZN MSFT EBAY to the form to track the stock prices of Yahoo!, Amazon, Microsoft, and EBay.

Click Finished, and you can view your portfolio at any time by clicking the Quotes link in the upper-right corner of the Yahoo! Finance home page. The basic view of your portfolio includes the ticker symbol, last trade, change, and volume, as shown in Figure 2-2.

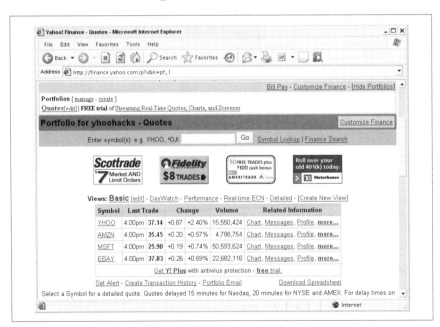

Figure 2-2. A simple stock portfolio at Yahoo! Finance

If you use My Yahoo! to track information, you can also watch your portfolios there. Click Add Content at the top of the page at *http://my.yahoo.com* and then click Yahoo! Services on the list of choices. Find Stock Portfolios on the list and click the Add button. You should find your stock watch list as a content box on your My Yahoo! page, as shown in Figure 2-3.

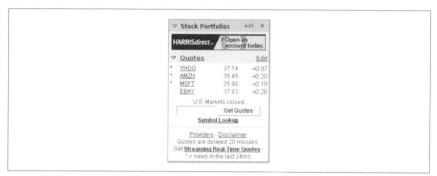

Figure 2-3. A stock portfolio on My Yahoo!

You can also track your portfolio via a cell phone with a web connection. Point your phone to *http://mobile.yahoo.com* and choose Finance → My Portfolios. You'll see a list of your stocks, just like you'd find on the web site. Figure 2-4 shows the example portfolio on Yahoo! Mobile.

Figure 2-4. A stock portfolio on Yahoo! Mobile

As you browse the web site, you'll see Set Alert links in various places. Click the link to set an alert for a particular stock that can be sent to an email address, Yahoo! Instant Messenger, or a cell phone. With an alert set [Hack #50], you can be sure you'll be notified if there are any wild swings in the stocks you're watching.

To take your saved portfolios a step further, you can also add information such as the number of shares you own of each stock and the price you purchased them at. Click the Edit link next to the Quotes heading on the Yahoo! Finance page and scroll down to Advanced Features. From here, you can choose which personalized information you'd like to add.

Yahoo! Finance pages are not encrypted and could be subject to eavesdropping. If you consider your personal financial holdings confidential, do not add the number of shares, purchase price, or any personally identifiable information to your Yahoo! portfolios.

Once you've added the number of shares you own, you can click the Performance link above the basic view of your portfolio to see the value of your holdings. If you included your purchase price, the performance page will also tell you how much you've gained or lost since buying each stock in the portfolio.

Yahoo! doesn't offer brokerage services such as buying and selling stocks, so you'll always need to update your portfolio by hand after you've made any trades.

Build Your Own Stock Update Email
HACK #24
Receive simple stock price updates via email—on your own schedule—with a bit of Perl scripting.

If you have money in stocks, bonds, or mutual funds, you know how addictive it can be to check the current value of your investments. Some people enjoy the roller-coaster ride of watching their money ebb and flow throughout the day, while others take the long view and just want an occasional look at how their portfolio is progressing. Somewhere in the middle of these extremes lie daily stock updates. They can let you keep tabs on your portfolio on a regular basis without the ulcers caused by minute-to-minute checks.

Yahoo! Finance offers a daily update email that is easy to set up. Log in to Yahoo!, go to *http://finance.yahoo.com*, and look for the Portfolios box at the top of the page. On the right side of the box, click the Customize Finance link, and then click Daily Update from the following page. From there, you can sign up for the email and set some preferences, including how often you want to receive the email: every market day or weekly.

The email itself is HTML-formatted like a web page and includes top finance stories from the day, any changes in your portfolios (if you have them set up), and announcements related to Yahoo! Finance. It's a good way to get a snapshot of the market from the day and looks like the email in Figure 2-5.

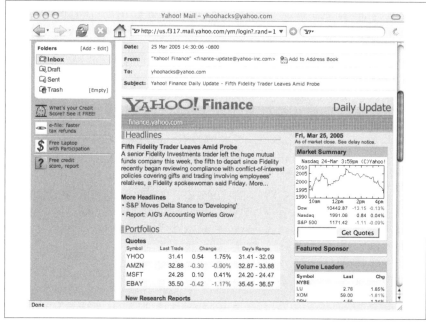

Figure 2-5. Yahoo! Finance Daily Update email

If you'd like to just get down to your stock prices, or have a bit more control over when the email is sent, you'll have to do a bit of scripting. Luckily, Yahoo! Finance gives you all of the information you need to make it happen; you just need to tie it together into a single email with a bit of Perl.

This example relies on the fact that you can look up any ticker symbol via a Yahoo! Finance URL. For example, all of the day's stock information about YHOO (the ticker symbol for Yahoo!, Inc.) is here: *http://finance.yahoo.com/ q?s=YHOO*. On each stock detail page like this one, you'll find a tiny Download Data link under the quote data. This gives you a text-only file with the relevant information for that stock in a format suitable for importing into a spreadsheet. The raw data itself is a series of comma-separated values that looks like this:

```
"YHOO",31.57,"3/24/2005","3:17pm",+0.70,31.91,32.09,31.49,20544748
```

Though the intended destination for this data is a spreadsheet, you can use the same file to build your own email containing only the stock information you want to see.

The Code

This example has a few nonstandard Perl modules that you'll need to have installed before you can run it. The script uses LWP::Simple to fetch the stock data, Number::Format to make the stock prices look nice, and NET::SMTP to send the email.

You'll also need to replace a few values in the script with your own data. Set $smtp_server to your email server, $from_email to an address with permissions to send email on that server, and $to_email to the email address where you'd like to receive the stock update. And most importantly, set the list of stocks you'd like to track by adding their ticker symbols on this line:

```
my @stocks = qw(insert ticker symbols separated by spaces);
```

So if you want to track Yahoo!, Amazon, eBay, and Microsoft as this example script does, you'll want this line to look like this:

```
my @stocks = qw(YHOO AMZN EBAY MSFT);
```

Save the following code to a file called *stock_update.pl*:

```perl
#!/usr/bin/perl
# stock_update.pl
# A script to download Yahoo! Finance info about stocks
# and send it via email
# Usage: stock_update.pl

use LWP::Simple;
use Number::Format;
use Net::SMTP;
use strict;

# Set your stocks
my @stocks = qw(YHOO AMZN EBAY MSFT);

# Set output file
my $file = "quick_stock_update.txt";
open(FILE, ">$file")||die "Can't open $file";

# Set email info
my $subject = "Quick Stock Update";
my $smtp_server = "insert your SMTP server";
my $from_email = 'insert your from email';
my $to_email = 'insert your to email';

# Define some variables
my $stock_symbol;
my $last_trade_f;
my $trade_date;
my $change;

# Define the file header
```

```
format FILE_TOP=
       Quick Stock Update
-------------------------------------
Symbol   Price     Date        Change
-------------------------------------
.

# Define the line-item details
format FILE=
@<<<<<   @>>>>  @|||||||||||   @>>>>>
$stock_symbol, $last_trade_f, $trade_date, $change
.

# Loop through stocks
foreach my $stock (@stocks) {
    my $stock_request = "http://finance.yahoo.com/d/quotes.csv?s=".
                        "$stock&f=sl1d1t1c1ohgv&e=.csv";
    my $stock_data = get($stock_request);

    ($stock_symbol, my $last_trade, $trade_date, my $trade_time,
        $change, my $open, my $high, my $low, my $volume)
        = split(/,/, $stock_data);

    my $x = new Number::Format(-int_curr_symbol => '');
    $last_trade_f = $x->format_number($last_trade,2,2);
    $trade_date =~ s/"//g; $trade_time =~ s/"//g;
    $stock_symbol =~ s/"//g;
    write FILE;
}

# Close output file
 close(FILE);

# Open output file for reading
 open(FILE, "$file")||die "Can't open $file";

# Send the file in email
my $smtp = Net::SMTP->new($smtp_server);
$smtp->mail($from_email);
$smtp->to($to_email);
$smtp->data();
$smtp->datasend("From: $from_email\n");
$smtp->datasend("To: $to_email\n");
$smtp->datasend("Subject: $subject\n");
$smtp->datasend('Content-Type: text/plain; charset="iso-8859-1"');
$smtp->datasend("\n\n");
while(<FILE>) {
    $smtp->datasend("$_");
}
$smtp->dataend();
$smtp->quit;

# Close output file
close(FILE);
```

As you can see in the section labeled Loop through stocks, there's quite a bit more data in the Yahoo! Download Data file than this script makes use of for the email. The email sent by this script displays the ticker symbol, latest price, date of the last trade, and the change in price for the day. But you'll also find good tidbits in the data file, such as the opening price, high and low for the day, and the volume of the stock traded. This data is available for use, so if it's something you're interested it, you can tweak this script to show more.

> Email is not a secure way to communicate, so be careful about what information you expose in your email messages. Think of email as a postcard that others might be able to read rather than a sealed envelope that only its intended recipient opens. An individual email can pass through several servers on the way to its destination, and there are plenty of opportunities for others to eavesdrop, so email is not the place for any sensitive financial information.

Running the Hack

To run this script once, you can just call it from the command line:

```
perl stock_update.pl
```

But the value of the script is in running it on a schedule you're comfortable with. Using Windows Scheduler, you can set it to run every weekday after the market closes, once a week, or once a quarter. If you really want to feel the bumps of the market, you could set this to run every hour.

The email itself is plain text, so you should see something like the message shown in Figure 2-6 in your inbox.

```
⊞  Subject:  Quick Stock Update                    From:

            Quick Stock Update
      -----------------------------------
      Symbol   Price      Date       Change
      -----------------------------------
      YHOO      31.50   3/24/2005     +0.63
      AMZN      33.14   3/24/2005     -0.04
      EBAY      35.75   3/24/2005     -0.17
      MSFT      24.37   3/24/2005     +0.19
```

Figure 2-6. Custom stock update email

While not nearly as aesthetically pleasing and packed with information as the standard Yahoo! Daily Update, this quick email has a certain minimalist charm. And this bit of scripting can get you exactly the information you want, when you want it.

Download Financial Data Using Excel Web Queries

#25   When a web site doesn't offer a downloadable file of the data you want, avoid manual data entry by using Microsoft Excel's web query feature.

These days, you can find most of the data you need to analyze investments on the Web, and much of it for little or no cost. However, putting that data into a spreadsheet where you can use it is another matter. Some web sites include links to download spreadsheets, text files of prices, or other financial data to your computer. Other sites offer subscriptions to downloadable data. However, if you can accept with equanimity the inevitable web page changes and the subsequent rework of your Excel spreadsheets that those changes require, you can create your own tools to download data from the Web. Excel *web queries* are easy to use and capture data by taking advantage of tables in a web page's HTML source. You can use web queries to feed your financial formulas and produce new investment studies or update portfolio management tables in a matter of seconds.

> Web queries are available in Excel for Windows 2000 and later, or in Excel X for Macintosh.

Creating an Excel Web Query

Web queries are pretty slick. The only information a web query needs is the address (URL) of the web page and the tables on that page that contain the data that you want. When you specify a URL in the New Web Query dialog box, the web page appears in the dialog box. In Excel XP and 2003, arrows point to each table on the page. After you select the tables to query, Excel extracts the labels and values from those tables and adds them to cells in a worksheet. With one shortcut command, you can refresh the data from the Web. To illustrate a web query, let's use an easy example—the price quote for a stock or mutual fund from Yahoo! Finance.

> Web queries are tailored to the configuration of a specific web page. If the web site changes its URL or reformats data into different tables, you must recreate your web queries.

To add a web query to an existing worksheet in an Excel workbook, open the workbook and select the tab for the worksheet you want. To create a new web query in Excel XP, follow these steps:

1. Choose Data → Import External Data → New Web Query. The New Web Query dialog box opens, displaying the home page you use in Internet Explorer. The toolbar in the New Web Query dialog box includes an Address drop-down list, which is automatically populated with your

URL History list from Internet Explorer. The toolbar has other frequently used browser commands, such as Back, Forward, and Refresh.

2. If you've recently accessed the web page you want to query, click the
Address arrow to display your URL History list and select the desired
web page. Otherwise, you can type the URL for the web page in the
Address box and click Go. For example, to use Yahoo! Finance, type
http://finance.yahoo.com in the Address box.

You can browse in the New Web Query dialog box, so you don't have
to enter the URL for a specific page. For example, after you navigate to
the Yahoo! Finance home page, you can type the ticker symbol for the
stock you want in the Enter Symbol(s) box and click Go—all on the
Yahoo! Finance web page in the dialog box browser. The browser in the
dialog box displays the quote page for the stock ticker you typed.

> Make sure you click the Go button on the Yahoo! Finance
> web page, not the Go button in the New Web Query toolbar.

3. In the New Web Query dialog box, the browser positions a yellow box
with a black arrow next to every table on the web page. To select a
table, position the mouse pointer over the yellow box to the left of the
data you want. Excel outlines the table with a thick line so you can verify the data that the query will return. If you picked the correct table,
click the yellow box. It changes to a green box with a checkmark, as
shown in Figure 2-7. Continue to click tables until you've selected all
the ones you want.

> If you don't see yellow boxes in the browser, click the Show
> Icons button on the New Web Query toolbar.

4. Click Import. The Import Data dialog box appears.

5. To insert the results of the query into the current worksheet, select the
Existing Worksheet option. By default, the address for the currently
selected cell appears in the box. Type another cell address to specify
where you want to import the data on the worksheet.

To create a new worksheet for the query, select the New Worksheet
option.

6. Click OK to import the data into the worksheet.

Although the cells don't look like they have superpowers, they are associated with your web query. You can refresh the data from the associated web
page by right-clicking any cell in the web query and choosing Refresh Data
from the shortcut menu, as illustrated in Figure 2-8.

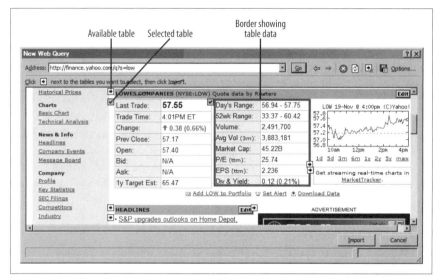

Figure 2-7. Visual feedback helps you select tables for a web query

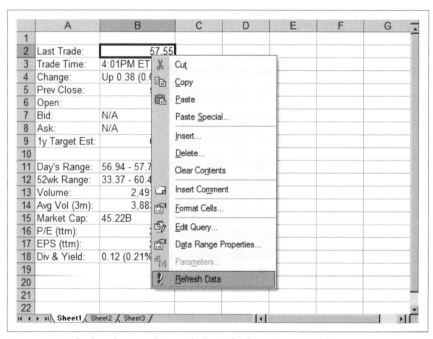

Figure 2-8. Refresh web query data with the Refresh Data command

Making a Web Query Work for Any Ticker Symbol

The web query you just created is pretty handy. You can update the quote for a stock you own or watch by refreshing its data. However, as you manage your investment portfolio, you must constantly evaluate new stocks and mutual funds. Creating a new web query for each investment prospect would become downright tiresome. Wouldn't it be cool if you could make this query download data for a new prospect simply by typing its ticker symbol into a worksheet cell? Well, you can, and it's easy when you follow these steps:

1. To customize a web query, first save it as a file. Right-click any cell for the web query in the worksheet and choose Edit Query from the shortcut menu. In the Edit Web Query dialog box, make sure that the tables you want show green boxes with checkmarks, and then click the Save As icon on the toolbar (see Figure 2-9). In the Save As dialog box, navigate to the folder in which you want to store the web query, type a name for the file (such as Yahoo_Price_Quote) in the File Name box and click Save.

Figure 2-9. Click the Save As icon to save a web query to a file

2. Next, add the ticker symbol as a parameter to the saved web query file. Navigate to the saved web query file in Windows Explorer (*Yahoo_Price_Quote.iqy* in this example), right-click it, and choose "Edit with Notepad" from the shortcut menu. The third line in the file specifies the URL for the web page. The URL for a Yahoo! Finance quote page, like most web pages with data for a specific investment, includes the ticker symbol of the stock or mutual fund quoted. In Example 2-1, the ticker symbol low represents Lowe's.

Example 2-1. The URL for a web page with financial data often includes the investment's ticker symbol

```
http://finance.yahoo.com/q?s=low
```

3. To make the web query download the data for the ticker symbol you specify, replace the ticker symbol in the URL with ["symbol", "Enter Symbol"]. The URL in the web query should look like the line in Example 2-2.

Example 2-2. Modifying the URL in a web query to prompt for the ticker symbol

```
http://finance.yahoo.com/q?s=["symbol", "Enter ticker symbol"]
```

4. To save the web query, choose File → Save.

Now, use this new web query in a spreadsheet to retrieve data based on the ticker symbol you specify:

1. Type a ticker symbol in a worksheet cell—for example, use cell A2 on Sheet1.

2. To use the web query to import data, choose Data → Import External Data → Import Data.

3. In the Select Data Source dialog box, navigate to the folder that contains your saved web query file and double-click it.

4. In the Import Data dialog box, select an option to specify whether to use the current worksheet or create a new one. If you select the Existing Worksheet option, type the cell address that denotes the upper-left corner of the cell range where you want the data imported in the Existing Worksheet box.

5. Click Parameters. In the Parameters dialog box, select the "Get the value from the following cell" option, click the box immediately below the option, and then select the worksheet cell that contains the ticker symbol (in this example, A2).

> The "Get the value from the following cell" option does not accept named cells. You must either select the cell that contains the parameter value in the worksheet or type the cell address using column and row references, such as A2.

6. If you want the web query to retrieve new values automatically from the Web when you enter a new ticker symbol, check the "Refresh automatically when cell value changes" checkbox.

7. Click OK twice to import the data. In this example, when you type a new ticker symbol in cell A2 and press Enter or an arrow key to navigate away from the ticker symbol cell, the web query refreshes the web query cells with values for the new ticker symbol.

> When a web query uses parameters, you can use the same web query text file to import data for multiple companies into different areas of a worksheet. To reuse a web query text file, select the cell in the upper-left corner of the cell range into which you want to import data, and then repeat steps 1–7.

Hacking the Hack

After your web query successfully grabs the data you want from the Web, you can feed those values into a data summary worksheet or into formulas on other worksheets. You could name the cells within the web query cell range, but that could throw your calculations off if the query returns values in a different order. By using a function such as VLOOKUP instead, you can find the text label that identifies the value you want, regardless of the cell. For example, suppose you want to use values from a price query to compare the current price to the 52-week high and low prices. In Figure 2-10, the Current Price and 52-week range cells use VLOOKUP to find values based on labels, as the formula bar shows.

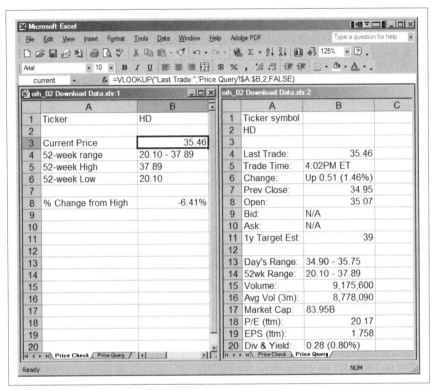

Figure 2-10. The VLOOKUP function finds values based on labels, not cell addresses

Take a look at the worksheets in Figure 2-10 to see how this works. To obtain the current price from the Yahoo! price web query, find the row that has the label Last Trade: in column A on the Price Query worksheet. Then, retrieve the value in that row from column B. The formula to perform these tasks is in cell B3 on the Price Check worksheet and is also shown in Example 2-3.

Example 2-3. Using VLOOKUP to find a value in one column based on the label in another column

```
Current Price = VLOOKUP("Last Trade:",'Price Query'!$A:$B,2,FALSE)
```

In Example 2-3 and other examples of Excel formulas throughout the book, the text to the left of the equals sign (=) identifies the information being calculated or retrieved by the Excel formula. To enter the formula in a cell in a spreadsheet, enter the formula beginning with the equals sign.

To find the 52-week price range, use 52wk Range: as the lookup_value, as shown in Example 2-4.

Example 2-4. Another example of VLOOKUP

```
Price Range = VLOOKUP("52wk Range:",'Price Query'!$A:$B,2,FALSE)
```

Web queries come with a built-in name that represents the cell range that contains the result of the web query. To view or modify this name, right-click within the web query results and choose Data Range Properties from the shortcut menu. If you specify the web query name as the table_array parameter of the VLOOKUP function, the cell range adjusts automatically to match the web query results.

Finally, you can use some nested text functions to extract the high and low values out of the 52-week price range, as shown in Example 2-5—for instance, to calculate the percentage change from the stock's high price to its current value. You can use functions such as RIGHT, LEFT, LEN, and FIND to parse the prices out of the price range. The VALUE function converts the text to a numeric value.

Example 2-5. Using text functions to extract information from text strings

```
High Price = VALUE(RIGHT(price_range,LEN(price_range)-FIND("- ",price_range)-1))
Low Price = VALUE(LEFT(price_range,FIND("- ",price_range)-1))
Percent Change = (Current Price - High Price)/High Price
```

—*Bonnie Biafore*

Convert Currencies with One Click

#26   Yahoo! Finance can tell you how many euros there are in a U.S. dollar, and a little JavaScript can speed up the answer.

While browsing the Web, you might find yourself in some unusual places. You're potentially just a click away from any site that exists, including online stores large and small, across the globe. The next time you're reading about a bleeding-edge European cell phone from your home in the United States, you might want to find out just how much that £500 would be in U.S. dollars.

Yahoo! Finance's Currency Converter (*http://finance.yahoo.com/currency*) can give you the answer. From this page, you can select a currency to convert from, a currency to convert to, and the amount of currency you'd like to convert.

This is a fairly painless process, but it still involves leaving your review site, opening a new browser window, and generally losing focus from all of those cutting-edge features of that smart phone you're really interested in.

Because Yahoo!'s Currency Converter handles everything in the URL query-string, you can write some JavaScript to automate this process and find out what you would need to pay, with just one click. For example, the following URL goes directly to the Yahoo! page that converts £500 into U.S. dollars:

```
http://finance.yahoo.com/currency/convert?amt=500&from=GBP&to=USD
```

The querystring variables are fairly self-explanatory:

amt
  The amount of currency to convert

from
  The three-letter abbreviation for the currency you're converting from

to
  The three-letter abbreviation for the currency you're converting to

By changing these values in the URL, you can change the results page. Here's the URL for converting 100 U.S. dollars into British pounds:

```
http://finance.yahoo.com/currency/convert?amt=100&from=USD&to=GBP
```

Here's just a handful of the 157 currencies Yahoo! currently supports:

USD
  U.S. dollar

EUR
  Euro

CAD
  Canadian dollar

AUD
  Australian dollar

JPY
  Japanese yen

INR
  Indian rupee

NZD
  New Zealand dollar

CHF
  Swiss franc

ZAR
  South African rand

You can find a list of all the currencies and abbreviations that Yahoo! supports in the drop-down list at the Currency Converter page.

The Code

This hack will let you highlight a currency amount on a web page and con-vert it from British pounds to U.S. dollars. It's a piece of JavaScript that resides in a browser bookmark, otherwise known as a *bookmarklet*. Book-marklets run when you click the bookmark, and they can get information from the current page you're browsing. In this case, the information the bookmarklet gets is the currency amount you've highlighted.

The code for bookmarklets isn't very pretty to look at, so here's some nicely formatted JavaScript that approximates the bookmarklet functions:

```
// Dissected JavaScript bookmarklet for one-click Currency Conversion

// Set d to the document object as a shortcut
var d = document;

// Set t to the currently selected text, if available
var t = w.selection?w.selection.createRange().text:w.getSelection();

// Test to make sure t is a number
t = parseFloat(t);
If (t != parseFloat(t)) {
    // If not, warn that the value isn't numeric
    alert('Please highlight a numeric value.');
} else {
    // Build the URL
    var url = http://finance.yahoo.com/currency/convert?';
    url += 'amt='+escape(t)+'&';
    url += 'from=GBP&';
    url += 'to=USD';

    // And open in a new window
    window.open(url,
    '_blank',
    'width=480,height=440,status=yes,resizable=yes,scrollbars=yes');
}
```

Because bookmarklets are compact, this is the actual code you'll need to use:

```
javascript:d=document;t=d.selection?d.selection.createRange().text:d.↵
getSelection();t=parseFloat(t);if(t!=parseFloat(t)){alert('Please ↵
highlighta numeric value.')}else{url='http://finance.yahoo.com/↵
currency/convert?amt='+escape(t)+'&from=GBP&to=USD';void(window.open(url,↵
'_blank','width=480,height=440,status=yes,resizable=yes,scrollbars=yes'))}
```

Running the Hack

Running the code is just a matter of adding a bookmark to your preferred browser. Once a new bookmark exists, replace the URL with the JavaScript. Also, give the bookmarklet a descriptive name, such as *GBP to USD*. Once the bookmarklet is set, when you want to perform a currency conversion, you can highlight a numeric value on any page and click the bookmark. For example, Figure 2-11 shows a mobile phone site that mentions a price of £500.

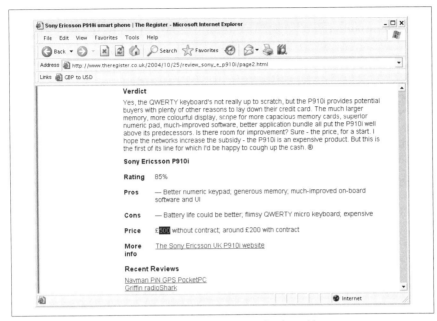

Figure 2-11. A browser with the currency conversion bookmarklet

Highlighting the amount and clicking the GBD to USD bookmark opens a new window with the conversion at Yahoo! Finance, as shown in Figure 2-12.

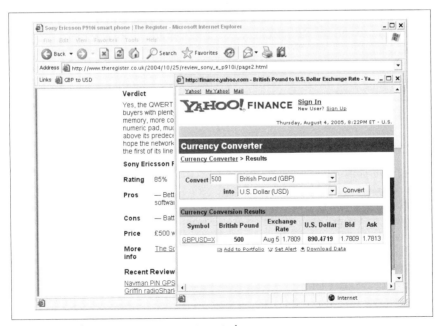

Figure 2-12. The new currency conversion window

Now you know that (at the time of this writing) £500 equals US$890.47. But more importantly, you'll have this information a click away the next time you're browsing exotic locales across the Web.

Do the Math with Yahoo! Calculators

#27 The next time someone tells you to "do the math," try a Yahoo! Calculator.

Every computer has a simple calculator application, which you probably use to do addition and subtraction. Yahoo! can take the place of this calculator, and Yahoo! Calculators can give you answers to complex financial questions.

For the simplest types of calculations, you can use any Yahoo! Search form. Type 237 + 13 into a Yahoo! Search form and you'll find the answer at the top of the search results. You can also group together more complex functions with parentheses, as shown in Figure 2-13.

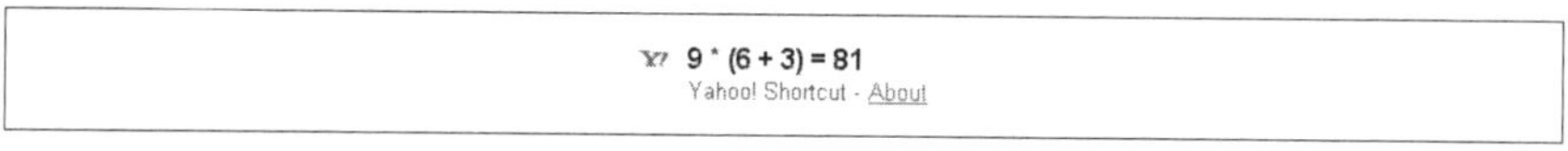

Y! **9 * (6 + 3) = 81**
Yahoo! Shortcut · About

Figure 2-13. Simple math in a Yahoo! Search result

Yahoo! Search forms can also handle unit conversion with the convert shortcut. Type convert 25 miles to kilometers into a Yahoo! Search form, and the top result will tell you the answer is 40.234 kilometers. And the time in shortcut will do some quick time zone math. Type time in London, and you'll know whether it's too late or too early to call someone there.

In addition to the simple calculators built in to Yahoo! Search, there are more sophisticated ones that help you answer everything from how to pay down your debt to which stock to invest in, providing charts and detailed explanations to help you make sound financial decisions. Computers are calculators, but they don't necessarily tell you what to calculate when you want answers to complex financial questions. That's where Yahoo! Calculators can help.

Anatomy of a Yahoo! Calculator

Before you start calculating how much credit you can receive based on the value of your house, take a minute to orient yourself to the basic Yahoo! Calculator format. Instead of a traditional calculator with a keypad and numbers, a Yahoo! Calculator is a questionnaire that you fill in with relevant values. Filling out a calculator can take some time—especially when you have to gather all of the information required—but the end result will give you a sharper picture of your financial situation, which should help you make informed decisions.

Within each calculator section of a Yahoo! site, you'll find a series of questions like the ones shown in Figure 2-14, organized by subject.

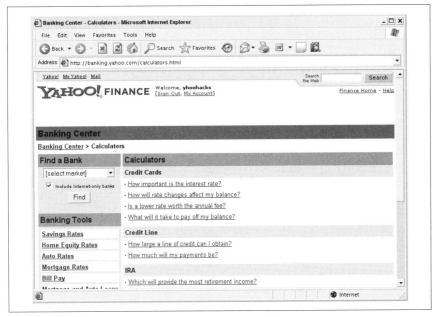

Figure 2-14. A listing of banking calculators at Yahoo!

Click any question to bring up a calculator that's designed to help you answer that particular question.

You can navigate within many Yahoo! calculators by clicking tabs running across the top of the page, as shown in Figure 2-15.

Here's a look at what you'll find behind each tab, but keep in mind that some calculators will have only some (or none) of these options:

Inputs

This is the web form where you enter your personal data. Many calculators have sample numbers in the fields already, but you can highlight the values and enter your own figures.

Results

Once you've entered your personal data, this is where you'll find the results of the calculations. The results can be displayed as a series of tables, charts, or sometimes a few paragraphs.

Graphs

In addition to the standard results, many calculators offer additional graphs that display your calculations in a visual format.

Explanation (or help)

The page behind this tab summarizes the results you've seen in a general way and explains how you should be using the calculator.

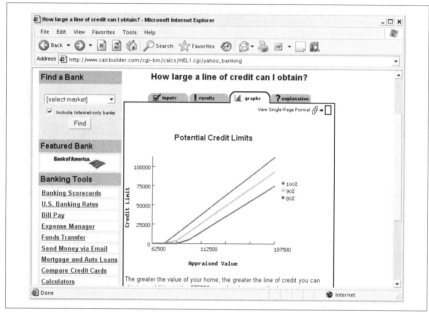

Figure 2-15. The graphs tab on a Yahoo! calculator

There are over a hundred different calculators available at Yahoo!, in a number of different categories. Here's a look at some of the main subject areas you can run numbers for and where you can find the calculators.

Saving and Investing

Whether you're fine-tuning your retirement plans or trying to pay off your credit cards, there are a number of calculators to help you project and strategize.

Banking. You'll find calculators that deal with credit cards, home equity, individual retirement accounts, and general savings at *http://banking.yahoo.com/ calculators.html*. This page contains links to answers on questions in the following topics:

Credit Cards
See how changes in interest rates, annual fees, and paying off balances affect your credit card debt.

Credit Line
Find out the difference between a home equity loan and a home equity line of credit in real numbers.

IRA
Compare different types of retirement accounts and analyze when to begin saving for retirement.

Savings
Calculate how much you'll need for retirement and review the benefits or drawbacks to paying off debt compared with saving.

Mutual funds. You can analyze your current mutual funds or compare potential investments at *http://biz.yahoo.com/edu/fundcalc.html*. You'll find the following topics:

Compare Funds
Compare growth versus income funds, or compare two different funds side by side.

Determine When to Sell
Look at the financial impact of different selling scenarios: selling today, waiting one year, and working to achieve a specific return.

Analyze Fee Structures
Look at load versus no-load funds, front versus back-end loads, and the impact of fees on your return.

Miscellaneous
See the impact of exchange rates on foreign funds and see how fees and taxes affect when fund costs will be recovered.

Bonds. Much like mutual fund calculators are bond calculators, which you can find at *http://bonds.yahoo.com/calculator.html*. Topics include:

Compare Bonds
Look at tax-exempt versus taxable bonds, zero coupon bonds, discount or high coupon rate, and compare two bonds side by side.

Purchasing & Selling
Take a look at pricing and returns, including which selling price yields the desired return, selling before or after one year, and yield to maturity. You can also see the impact of rate changes on current bond values.

Home, Auto, and Education

Your home, car, and college education are some of the biggest purchases you'll make in your life, and you can find several calculators to help you plan them.

Mortgage. In the Mortgage section of Yahoo! Finance, you'll find a series of questions designed to help you learn about mortgage options. Point your browser to *http://loan.yahoo.com/m/mortcalc.html* and you'll find the following topics:

Starting a Loan
Calculate the benefits of renting versus owning, look at the range of houses you can afford, and determine how much you'll need to borrow. Compare loans side by side to see which is better.

Calculating Rates and Payments
Compare fixed and adjustable loans, payment schedules, and see how paying points to lower the rate will affect your loan.

Refinancing
Find out how much refinancing your home would cost.

More Home Financing Calculators
Calculate tax savings from a home purchase, reduce mortgage insurance costs, and review the long-term financial savings by making extra payments.

Auto. The auto calculators at *http://loan.yahoo.com/a/autocalc.html* are divided into three concepts:

Type of Purchase
Compare loaning and leasing, and see estimated payments for each. You can also compare buying new and used cars.

Financial Impact
Calculate monthly payments associated with a car loan, how much money to put down, and the costs of depreciation.

Loan Specifics
Review the terms of loans, financing versus paying cash, home equity versus auto loan, and rebates versus special dealer financing.

School financing. You can plan for the costs associated with college at *http://education.yahoo.com/college/financial_aid/articles/loan_calculators.html*. You'll find calculators to help with monthly budgets, expected family contribution (EFC) for some loans, and repayment plans.

Death and Taxes

They're both inevitable, so you may as well get a handle on the numbers.

Life insurance. You can find calculators dealing with life insurance at *http://insurance.yahoo.com/lh/lhcalc.html*. The questions there will help you understand how life insurance works and what the differences are between plans. General topics covered include:

Coverage
How much life insurance do you need?

Returns
Find returns for whole life policies, universal policies, and variable universal policies.

Analysis of the Different Types
Compare term life insurance with whole life, universal life, and variable universal life.

Taxes. Get a jump on tax time at *http://taxes.yahoo.com/calculators/*. Yahoo! keeps all of the calculators up-to-date for the current tax season, unless otherwise specified. You'll find help with the following:

Filing Tools
Using TurboTax, these tools help you find deductions, estimate your refund, and calculate your average tax rate.

Income/Employment Tax Tools
Using TurboTax, find out if you are withholding the right amount from your paycheck, estimate your take-home pay after deductions, and estimate your self-employment tax.

Family Life Tools
Use TurboTax to find out how much of a benefit or penalty you'll get from education expenses, your marital status, and selling a home.

Retirement Tax Planning
Yahoo! calculators look at the impact of potential tax changes and inflation in the future for your savings and IRAs. Also, calculate how much you can invest before taxes each year to save some money.

Calculators Beyond Yahoo!

If you can't find the right calculator at Yahoo!, you might be able to use Yahoo! to find what you need elsewhere. There are several online calculator categories in the Yahoo! Directory; just browse to *http://dir.yahoo.com* and type calculator into the search form. Or go directly to *http://search.yahoo.com/search/dir?p=calculator* for a list of related categories.

Add a Yahoo! Bookmark with One Click

HACK #28

Speed up the process of adding sites to your Yahoo! Bookmarks with a browser bookmark and a bit of JavaScript.

Yahoo! Bookmarks are an easy way to share a list of web sites across several computers. If you have a set of sites you like to visit from home, the office, a friend's house, or any other place you might find yourself in front of a computer, they'll always be just a few clicks away at your Yahoo! account, instead of trapped inside your browser at home.

Unfortunately, setting up this list of sites for the first time can be time-consuming. After logging into My Yahoo!, you must find your bookmarks (usually in the upper-right corner); click Add; copy and paste the site URL, name, and any comments into the form; and click the Save button. This might not sound too labor intensive, but it amounts to quite a few steps if you're adding more than a few sites.

If you've installed the Yahoo! Toolbar, you might have already experienced the joy of one-click Yahoo! Bookmarks. On any web page, you can click the Add Bookmark button to add a site. From then on, the site will be available at your Yahoo! Bookmarks. If you don't want to install the Yahoo! Toolbar (to save browser real estate) but still want the convenience of adding bookmarks, you can build your own JavaScript bookmarklet and add it to your browser's bookmarks toolbar to get the same one-click effect.

The Magic of Bookmarklets

A *bookmarklet* is a bit of JavaScript code stored in a web browser bookmark. Bookmarklets give you a way to run code that can interact with the current page in the browser. For example, bookmarklets can change the size and colors of fonts on a page, open new browser windows, or extract information about the current page. With bookmarklets, you're in control of the script, because it runs when you click the bookmark.

In order to implement this hack, the only thing you'll need is a browser that has bookmarks and understands JavaScript. Don't worry, that covers just about every web browser!

The Code

Here's a look at some nicely formatted JavaScript that gets the title, URL, and selected text from the current web page at the time the bookmarklet is clicked. It then builds the proper URL for adding a Yahoo! Bookmark and opens it in a new browser window. Keep in mind that this code is nicely formatted so you can see how it operates; the functioning bookmarklet code will be formatted without linebreaks or spaces.

```
// Dissected JavaScript bookmarklet for one-click Yahoo! Bookmarks

// Set d to the document object as a shortcut
var d = document;

// Set t to the currently selected text, if available
var t = d.selection?d.selection.createRange().text:d.getSelection();

// Build the URL that will add a bookmark to Yahoo! Bookmarks
var url = 'http://e.my.yahoo.com/config/edit_bookmark?';
url += '.src=bookmarks&';
url += '.done=http%253a%2F%2Fe.my.yahoo.com/config/set_bookmark&';
url += '.folder=1&';
url += '.action=ab&';
url += '.display=1&';
url += '.protocol=http%3A%2F%2F&';

// include the URL of the current page
url += '.url='+escape(d.location.href)+'&';

// include the title of the current page
url += '.name='+escape(d.title)+'&';

// include any selected text of the current page as a comment
url += '.comment='+escape(t)+'&';
url += '.save=+Save+';

// open a new window to add the bookmark and show the results
window.open(url,
            '_blank',
            'width=640,height=440,status=yes,resizable=yes,scrollbars=yes');
```

Take a look at the bold querystring variables in the code. These are the primary elements of the Yahoo! URL we're concerned with. Here's a quick look at what each variable represents:

.done
The URL to display after the action is completed.

.folder
The ID of the folder in which you'd like the bookmark to be included. If you don't have multiple folders, use 1, which is the default.

.url
The URL of the site you're adding as a bookmark.

.name
The name of the site you're adding as a bookmark.

.comment
Some arbitrary text that is associated with the bookmark.

Note also that values for these querystring variables have been escaped for use in a URL—either by hand, as in the case of .done, or with the JavaScript escape( ) function. This ensures that any characters that are illegal in URLs have been converted to their hexadecimal equivalent.

Unfortunately, a bookmarklet is no place for readable code with comments and line breaks. Instead, the code needs to be smashed into its most compact form. Here's a look at the code reformatted for use in a bookmarklet:

```
javascript:d=document;t=d.selection?d.selection.createRange( ).text:d.↵
getSelection( );void(window.open('http://e.my.yahoo.com/config/edit_↵
bookmark?.src=bookmarks&&.done=http%253a%2F%2Fe.my.yahoo.com/config/set_↵
bookmark&.folder=1&.action=ab&.display=1&.protocol=http%3A%2F%2F&.↵
url='+escape(d.location.href)+'&.name='+escape(d.title)+'&.comment=↵
'+escape(t)+'&.save=+Save+','blank','width=640,height=440,status=yes,↵
resizable=yes,scrollbars=yes'))
```

As you can see, it looks similar to the preceding code, but with some important changes. The javascript: at the beginning tells the browser to execute what follows as a bookmarklet rather than a standard bookmark with a URL. Also, the void( ) operator often comes in handy in bookmarklets, because it stops the expression it surrounds from returning a value. In this case, we don't really care what value is returned when the window opens; we just want the window to open, and void( ) does the trick.

Running the Hack

The installation process for the bookmarklet will be unique to the browser you'd like to use it with. If you know how to create and edit a bookmark, you know how to install a bookmarklet. Simply create a new bookmark and add the code in place of a URL. Some browsers will warn you that javascript: is not a valid protocol, but you can ignore that message. You'll also want to give your bookmarklet a snappy, short name, such as Add Y!Bookmark, as shown in the links bar in Figure 2-16.

Once the bookmark is in place, browse to any page, highlight some text on the page, and click away! Once you click, a new window will let you know the bookmark has been added to your list, as shown in Figure 2-17.

From here, you can edit the newly added bookmark by clicking on the pencil icon. Simply close the window when you're finished.

Yahoo! removes any apostrophes from Bookmark Comments, so you'll have to put up with misspellings here and there, especially if you're adding text that was highlighted on a web page.

Figure 2-16. The Add Y!Bookmark bookmarklet in the browser toolbar

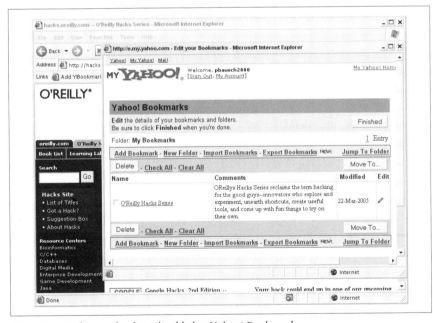

Figure 2-17. The new bookmark added to Yahoo! Bookmarks

The best part of keeping your bookmarks at Yahoo! is that the next time people are gathered around someone else's laptop trying to remember the location of some cool site you visited last week, you can save the day by saying, "I have that site bookmarked at Yahoo!"

H A C K #29 Import Existing Bookmarks into Yahoo! Bookmarks

To consolidate or build a Bookmark library quickly, you can import existing bookmarks from applications such as Firefox, Internet Explorer, or web applications that support OPML.

Yahoo! lets you store up to 1,000 bookmarks on their server, making them easily accessible from any computer. But transferring or creating 1,000 bookmarks by hand could take you a few months of concentrated effort and some vacation time from work. Even with one-click adding [Hack #28], you're looking at a few hours of solid clicking to even approach the limit.

Luckily, you can take advantage of the bookmarks you already have by importing them. Yahoo! provides some tools to make the process of importing bookmarks take a few minutes rather than a few months. Also, if you use other bookmark-like applications on the Web (such as Blogrolling, Bloglines, or Kinja) you can probably find a way to import them into Yahoo! Bookmarks by using exporting features those applications provide.

Each of these hacks relies on the Import Bookmarks feature that you'll find at your Yahoo! Bookmarks (at *http://bookmarks.yahoo.com*, toward the top of the page).

Internet Explorer Bookmarks

Importing your Internet Explorer bookmarks is a fairly painless process, thanks to an ActiveX Control Yahoo! has put together that's appropriately called Yahoo! Favorites Importer. To get to the import page, click Import Bookmarks from the Yahoo! Bookmarks page and choose the Internet Explorer for Windows link.

An *ActiveX Control* is a bit of code that runs in your browser and that can interact with your desktop applications. As you might guess, there are some security concerns with this type of code, so you might see a warning in your browser like the one shown in Figure 2-18.

Go ahead and click on the yellow-highlighted area, and then choose Install ActiveX Control.... Once it's installed, click the Import Favorites button, and all of your folders and bookmarks will be added to your Yahoo! Bookmarks.

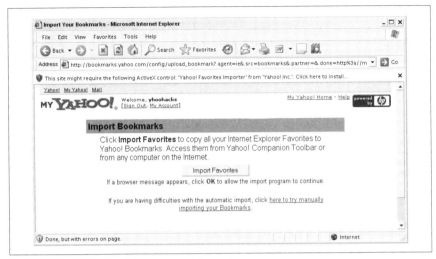

Figure 2-18. Import Bookmarks ActiveX warning

Firefox Bookmarks

Importing Firefox or Netscape bookmarks is a two-step process. First, you need to export your Firefox bookmarks to an HTML file. From any browser window, choose Bookmarks → Manage Bookmarks to bring up the Firefox bookmark manager. From there, choose File → Export. The default name for the file is *bookmarks.html*; be sure to save it in a location you'll remember.

Next, back at Yahoo! Bookmarks, click the Import Bookmarks link and then click Netscape (the label is a relic from the Netscape browser that Firefox grew out of). Click the Browse button at the bottom of the page, and find *bookmarks.html* on your local computer. Finally, click Import Bookmarks, and Yahoo! will do the heavy lifting from there. You should now find all of your bookmarks and bookmark folders in your Yahoo! Bookmarks.

OPML Applications

Browsers aren't the only place you'll find lists of sites. With the rising popularity of web-based RSS readers and link-sharing services, many people have lists of favorite links in many different formats across the Web. Fortunately for us, an emerging standard of exchanging links between applications exists. This standard is an XML format called Outline Processor Markup Language (OPML). OPML is used for making lists of just about anything, but it's used primarily for trading lists of links.

Yahoo! doesn't import OPML files, so the trick to importing bookmarks stored in OPML is to convert an existing OPML file into the Firefox/Netscape bookmark format. Rogers Cadenhead ran into this same problem and created a program called the OPML Link Publisher (*http://www.cadenhead.org/workbench/code/opmlLinkPublisher*). The OPML Link Publisher takes an OPML file and converts it into the proper HTML for bookmarks. With these tools, you can import bookmarks from just about anywhere.

For example, I use the RSS reader Bloglines (*http://www.bloglines.com*). This application lets me assemble a list of sites I read on a regular basis and alerts me when something new has been posted. To get an OPML list of your Bloglines sites, go to your feeds and click Edit from the top menu. Scroll past your list of feeds and choose Export Subscriptions. You'll find a list of all of your subscriptions in OPML format. Save it somewhere handy, such as your C: drive, and give it a name you'll remember, such as *bloglines_export.xml*.

Because OPML is an evolving standard, you might need to massage the file a bit to turn it into a format that OPML Link Publisher expects. Though most implementations of OPML for bookmarks are similar, there are enough differences to make them seem incompatible. For example, OPML Link Publisher looks for text and url attributes in the XML, while Bloglines gives you title and htmlUrl attributes. A quick fix is to open the file in Notepad and do a global search and replace for these terms. It's a bit of a hassle, but it's far faster than building your own bookmarks file.

Once the OPML file is ready to go, download a copy of Cadenhead's OPML Link Publisher and create the required *olp.properties* file in the same directory as the application. Then, edit the new file to contain the location of your OPML file to be converted and the location of the resulting *bookmarks.html* file. The *olp.properties* file should look something like this:

```
olp.mozillaUserFolder=C:/
olp.bookmarkSource=C:/bloglines_export.xml
```

With these pieces in place, you can run OPML Link Publisher from a Windows command prompt, like so:

```
java -jar OPMLLinkPublisher.jar
```

If everything goes as expected, you should have a shiny new *bookmarks.html* file you can use to import your links at Yahoo! Bookmarks. Yahoo! never has to know the file wasn't generated by Firefox, and you get to have instant access to all of your favorite sites.

H A C K   #30   Open Yahoo! Bookmarks in a Sidebar

The easiest way to take your Yahoo! Bookmarks out for a surfing binge is by tacking them up in a browser sidebar.

Once you've invested the time and energy into building your Yahoo! Bookmarks collection, you'll be ready to take them for a spin. Of course, you can view them in My Yahoo!, where they're meant to be displayed, but it's also useful to bring them up in a browser sidebar for quick surfing. This saves you the trouble of opening the sites in a new window and losing your place, and it lets you focus on seeing what's new at your favorite sites.

One problem with this plan is that you can't isolate your Yahoo! Bookmarks to their own page. They're fully integrated with the My Yahoo! page. Fortunately, Jason B. Silverstein at Yahoo! pointed out a little-known page that does isolate your Yahoo! Bookmarks into their own space: *http://my.yahoo.com/tearoff/sites.html*. This page is used to display bookmarks inside Yahoo! Messenger, but there's no reason you can't use it to build your own sidebar.

To use the sidebar, you'll need to be logged in at My Yahoo!. But once that's taken care of, your new isolated Yahoo! Bookmarks will be ready to go.

A Firefox Sidebar

The Firefox browser makes quick work of opening web pages in a sidebar. Simply navigate to the Yahoo! Bookmarks URL and choose Bookmarks → Bookmark This Page... from the Firefox menu (or Ctrl-D if you're a fan of keyboard shortcuts). Then give the bookmark a descriptive name, such as Y!Bookmarks Sidebar.

Now find your newly added bookmark, right-click, and choose Properties to bring up the bookmark's properties, as shown in Figure 2-19.

Figure 2-19. Bookmark properties dialog

Check the "Load this bookmark in the sidebar" option, and you'll be set. Whenever you click the bookmark in the future, your Yahoo! Bookmarks will open in a sidebar. From there, you can click down the list, and the sidebar will stay put while your bookmark opens in the main window (see Figure 2-20).

An Internet Explorer Sidebar

Setting up a custom Internet Explorer sidebar isn't quite as easy, but it is possible to customize the built-in *search bar*. Internet Explorer's search bar is a window that opens in a sidebar. You can activate the search bar by clicking the Search button in your main toolbar, as shown in Figure 2-21.

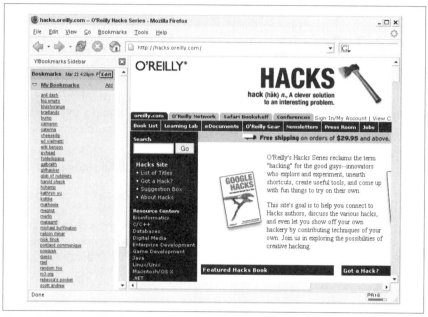

Figure 2-20. Yahoo! Bookmarks in a Firefox sidebar

Figure 2-21. Internet Explorer's Search button

This brings up one of several search forms from some of the big search engines on the Web, including Yahoo!. However, you can put your isolated Yahoo! Bookmarks in this window by changing some values in the Windows Registry.

 The Windows Registry is a database that stores important application information. Be aware that hand-editing the Windows Registry could cause serious problems that would require you to reinstall Windows.

The code. To keep things simple, you can edit the relevant Windows Registry settings with a *.reg* file. Create a new file on your desktop called *Y!Bookmarks.reg* and add the following text:

```
REGEDIT4


[HKEY_CURRENT_USER\Software\Microsoft\Internet Explorer\Main]
"Use Search Asst"="no"
"Search Bar"="http://my.yahoo.com/tearoff/sites.html"
```

Running the hack. Save the file, double-click it, confirm the changes, and you're all set. This file will disable the default search pane and instead load your Yahoo! Bookmarks. You'll need to restart Internet Explorer if it's running. After that, clicking the Search button from now on will give you something similar to the page shown in Figure 2-22.

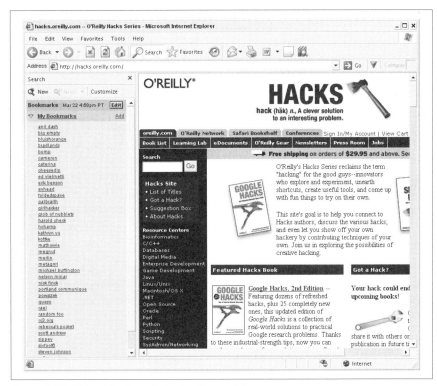

Figure 2-22. Yahoo! Bookmarks in the IE search bar

Hacking the hack. If you'd ever like to go back to the default search behavior, it's just another *.reg* file. You could call this one *search_restore.reg* and add the following text:

```
REGEDIT4


[HKEY_CURRENT_USER\Software\Microsoft\Internet Explorer\Main]
"Use Search Asst"="yes"
"Search Page"="http://home.microsoft.com/access/allinone.asp"
"Search Bar"="http://home.microsoft.com/search/lobby/search.asp"
```

Save the file, double-click it, and Internet Explorer should go back to the way it was.

Publish Your Yahoo! Bookmarks

HACK #31

Give the gift of your accumulated links to the world by publishing your Yahoo!
Bookmarks to the Web.

Part of the fun of using the Web is being able to share where you've been with
others. The fact that any web site can be connected to any other web site via a
link is one of its defining features. On weblogs, a list of links to other weblogs is
called a *blogroll*, and there's even a web service called Blogrolling.com that
helps people organize and publish these lists of links. Since Yahoo! Bookmarks
is basically one big link repository, you're already using it to store and organize
your favorite links. The only piece missing from rolling your own blogroll or
link directory is publishing your Yahoo! Bookmarks for the world to see.

If you log in and view your Yahoo! Bookmarks at *http://bookmarks.yahoo.com*,
you'll notice an Export Bookmarks link toward the top of the page. This feature is primarily used for transferring bookmarks between Yahoo! and your
browser. But because the Netscape bookmark format is an extension of standard HTML, you can use the export file to publish your links. To get the file,
choose Export Bookmarks → Netscape (for Windows) → "Click here" to export
it. Once you have the *bookmarks.html* file on your desktop, you can upload it
to a web server, where anyone can view it.

This process takes only a minute or two, but you wouldn't want to do this
each time you added a bookmark, changed a bookmark, or reorganized your
links. With a bit of Perl, you can automate this whole process and write
some cleaner HTML in the process.

To run this hack, you'll need a couple of nonstandard Perl modules
installed: WWW::Yahoo::Login and WWW::Mechanize for logging into Yahoo! and
fetching the *bookmarks.html* export, respectively.

The Code

This script logs into Yahoo! and fetches your exported bookmarks. From
there, it goes through the bookmarks line by line, adding folder names and
links to a filename you specify in $file. Be sure to replace the $user and
$pass values with your Yahoo! username and password so that the script can
log in on your behalf. Create a file called *getBookmarks.pl* and add the following code:

```
#!/usr/bin/perl
# getBookmarks.pl
# A script to download Yahoo! Bookmarks and format them as HTML
# Usage: getBookmarks.pl

use WWW::Yahoo::Login qw( login logout );
```

```perl
use WWW::Mechanize;
use strict;

# Set some user variables
my $user = "insert Yahoo! ID";
my $pass = "insert Yahoo! Password";
my $file = "links.html";
my $bookmarkurl = "http://bookmarks.yahoo.com/config/";
$bookmarkurl .= "export_bookmark?.commit=1";

my $mech = WWW::Mechanize->new( );

# Log into Yahoo!
my $resp = login(
    mech    =>  $mech,
    uri     =>  $bookmarkurl,
    user    =>  $user,
    pass    =>  $pass,
);

# If login succeeded, loop through the HTML
if ($resp) {
    print "Login ok!\n";
    my $bookmarks = $mech->content;
    my @bookmarks = split(/\n/, $bookmarks);

    # Open the output file
    open FILE, "> $file" or die "Can't open $file : $!";

    # Loop through the bookmarks, printing to file
    foreach my $line (@bookmarks) {

        # If the line is folder, print it
        if ($line =~ m!<H3[^>].*>(.*?)</H3>!gi) {
            print FILE "<div class=\"folder\">";
            print FILE $1;
            print FILE "</div>\n";
        }

        # If the line is a bookmark, print it
        if ($line =~ m!<A HREF="([^"]+)"[^>]+>(.*?)</A>!gi) {
            print FILE "<div class=\"link\">";
            print FILE "<a href=\"$1\">$2</a>";
            print FILE "</div>\n";
        }
    }

    # Close the output file
    close FILE;
} else {
    warn $WWW::Yahoo::Login::ERROR;
}
```

Running the Hack

To run the code, simply call the script from a command prompt:

```
perl getBookmarks.pl
```

After the script has run, you should find a new file called *links.html*, full of your Yahoo! Bookmarks. Each link should be on its own line, surrounded by HTML <div> tags. This lets you create your own look and feel for the links with an external stylesheet. The folders have a CSS class of folder, and links have a CSS class of link. The file is all set for you to drop it into an existing web site as a server-side include, or with a bit more formatting it could be its own page.

Now that this process is automated through a script, you can run it on a regular schedule to reap its benefits. Any changes you make at Yahoo! Bookmarks will be reflected on your remote site the next time this script runs; once every 24 hours should do it. In Windows, you can set it to run as a scheduled task from the Control Panel, calling Perl from the Run line, like this:

```
C:\Perl\bin\perl.exe "C:\insert your location\getBookmarks.pl"
```

And from Linux-based servers, you can set it as a cron job.

Now that you're able to use Yahoo! as a public links manager, the process of sharing resources should be much simpler.

 ## Track the Media's Attention Span over Time

#32 Visualize media trends by counting the total number of Yahoo! News mentions of a specific phrase over a series of dates.

The nature of news is that it reports about what's new in the world each day. But in the rush to bring the latest news to the public, news organizations often have a pack mentality. The news being covered by the top media outlets this week is different from what was covered last week. And sometimes, looking at what news organizations decide to cover can be more interesting than the news itself.

In that spirit, this hack is about tracking a topic's ebbs and flows through the news cycle. Because Yahoo! News brings together over 7,000 different news sources from around the world into one site, it's the perfect place to spot trends and track what the media is tracking. One drawback to tracking 7,000 news sources is that storage of that information becomes an issue. So Yahoo! News stores only the last 30 days' worth of articles. But in our 24-hour-a-day news world, 30 days ago can seem like ancient history.

This hack was inspired by "Tracking Result Counts over Time" **[Hack #63]** from the first edition of *Google Hacks*. If you'd like to see how to implement a similar hack for Google Search results, track down a copy of the first edition of *Google Hacks*.

The key to being able to track a keyword in news articles over time is being able to isolate articles by day. Luckily, the Yahoo! News advanced search interface (*http://news.search.yahoo.com/news/advanced*) gives the option to limit searches by time. So, if you want just the stories about Apple from March 1, 2005, the advanced search interface lets you bring them up by specifying March 1 as the start and end date. Another great feature of the advanced search interface is the ability to limit your search to a specific category. By selecting Technology in addition to specifying the date, you can be sure to weed out stories about the fruit that grows on trees and stick with stories about the company that makes computers.

Once you isolate stories to a particular day, you can find out how many stories contained the term you're interested in on that day. For example, there were 143 technology stories that mentioned Apple on March 1, 2005, but only 115 stories mentioned Apple on March 2. At the time of this writing, the news data available at Yahoo! Search Web Services doesn't include the ability to limit requests to a specific date, so this hack uses *screen scraping* to gather the data.

Screen scraping involves programmatically downloading the HTML for a web page and picking through the source to find the bits of information you're looking for. Screen scraping is a notoriously brittle process, because it relies on finding patterns within the HTML. If Yahoo! decides to change its HTML tomorrow, the code in this hack that picks up the total results for a query will fail. Even knowing this, we're interested in only one bit of data on Yahoo! News search results pages: the estimated total number of articles for our query. Figure 2-23 shows the bit we're looking for in a search for Apple stories from March 1, 2005.

Searching through the almost 250 lines of HTML in a results page, you can pick out the total results number from this line:

```
<em>Results <strong>1 - 10</strong> of about <strong>143</strong> for
<strong>apple</strong>.</em>
```

Armed with the pattern to find the total results, you can assemble the code.

Figure 2-23. Total results of a Yahoo! News search for "apple"

The Code

Though you can't limit search by date with the Yahoo! Search Web Services, this code relies on the fact that Yahoo! News search pages at the web site have stable, predictable URLs for date-specific searches. Sticking with our example, here are the relevant pieces from a URL for Apple articles from March 1:

```
http://news.search.yahoo.com/news/search?va=apple&smonth=3&↵
sday=1&emonth=3&eday=1
```

As you can see, the va variable holds the query, smonth and sday the start date, and emonth and eday the end date. Knowing this pattern, you can construct a query for any time period you'd like.

You'll need a couple of modules for this hack, including LWP::Simple to fetch the Yahoo! News page, and Date::Manip to work with dates. Add the following code to a file named *track_news.pl*:

```perl
#!/usr/bin/perl
# track_news.pl
# Builds a Yahoo! News URL for every day
# between the specified start and end dates, returning
# the date and estimated total results as a CSV list.
# usage: track_news.pl query="{query}" start={date} end={date}
# where dates are of the format: yyyy-mm-dd, e.g. 2005-03-30
```

```
use strict;
use Date::Manip;
use LWP::Simple qw(!head);
use CGI qw/:standard/;

# Set your unique Yahoo! Application ID
my $appID = "insert your app ID";

# Get the query
my $query = param('query');

# Set the News category to search tech articles
# Alternates: top, world, politics, entertainment, business
# more at: http://news.search.yahoo.com/news/advanced
my $category = "technology";

# Regular Expression to check date validity
my $date_regex = '(\d{4})-(\d{1,2})-(\d{1,2})';

# Make sure all arguments are passed correctly
( param('query') and param('start') =~ /^(?:$date_regex)?$/
  and param('end') =~ /^(?:$date_regex)?$/ ) or
  die qq{usage: track_news.pl query="{query}" start={date} end={date}\n};

# Set timezone, parse incoming dates
Date_Init("TZ=PST");
my $start_date = ParseDate(param('start'));
my $end_date = ParseDate(param('end'));

# Print the CSV column titles
print qq{"date","count"\n};

# Loop through the dates
while ($start_date <= $end_date) {
    my $month = int UnixDate($start_date, "%m");
    my $day = int UnixDate($start_date, "%d");
    my $date_f = UnixDate($start_date,"%y-%m-%d");
    my $total;

    # Construct a Yahoo! News URL
    my $news_url = "http://news.search.yahoo.com/news/search?";
        $news_url .= "ei=UTF-8";
        $news_url .= "&va=$query";
        $news_url .= "&cat=$category";
        $news_url .= "&catfilt=1";
        $news_url .= "&pub=1";
        $news_url .= "&smonth=$month";
        $news_url .= "&sday=$day";
        $news_url .= "&emonth=$month";
        $news_url .= "&eday=$day";

    # Make the request
    my $news_response = get($news_url);
```

```
    # Find the number of results
    if ($news_response =~ m!of about <strong>(.*?)</strong>!gi) {
        $total = $1;
    } else {
        $total = 0;
    }

    # Print out results
    print
    '"',
    $date_f,
    qq{","$total"\n};

    # Add a day, and continue the loop
    $start_date = DateCalc($start_date, " + 1 day");
}
```

Running the Hack

Run the script from a command line, specifying the query term and dates. Here's the query for Apple news between March 1 and March 10, 2005:

```
    track_news.pl query="apple" start=2005-03-01 end=2005-03-10
```

Of course, by the time you're reading this, these dates are out of the 30-day window, so you'll need to replace them with dates that fall into the range Yahoo! News can deliver.

If you'd like to pipe the script output to a text file, simply call it like so:

```
    track_news.pl query="apple" start=2005-03-01 end=2005-03-10 > apple.csv
```

The results will look like this:

```
    "date","count"
    "05-03-01","147"
    "05-03-02","111"
    "05-03-03","112"
    "05-03-04","173"
    "05-03-05","27"
    "05-03-06","51"
    "05-03-07","181"
    "05-03-08","171"
    "05-03-09","111"
    "05-03-10","130"
```

Just glancing at this list, you can see that Apple media coverage started off strong, tapered off a bit, and then came back with a vengeance on March 7. It's tough to pinpoint a reason for the differences, but it might be a way to spot changes that will affect the company.

Working with the Results

With a short list, it's easy to see where the spikes in media mentions are. But with longer lists, it might help to have a visual representation of the data. If you send the script output to a *.csv* file, you can simply double-click the file to open it with Excel. The chart wizard can give you a quick overview, such as the one for the entire month of March 2005 shown in Figure 2-24.

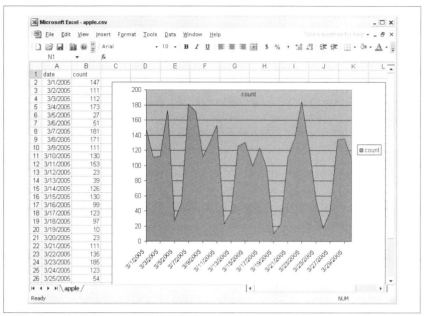

Figure 2-24. Excel graph tracking tech news mentioning "apple"

As you can see, the mentions of Apple across technology stories in the month of March dip and peak at the beginning and end of the work week.

H A C K #33 Monitor the News with RSS

Keep your finger on the pulse of your favorite news topics by adding Yahoo! News search results to your favorite RSS reader.

Trying to stay on top of all of the news on a specific topic can feel like a losing battle. Say you spend your time working with maps, so you're interested in cartography. Imagine you're interested in every aspect of cartography and want to keep up with any new mentions of the word *cartography* in the news. You'd like to hear about everything from new mapping applications for the Web to new geographic discoveries. This could take a lot of time and effort, subscriptions to all of the major newspapers, and the time to read every article looking for mentions of cartography. Of course, Yahoo! News pulls this information together into one web site and makes it searchable, but even that can be tedious to check on a regular basis.

Starting at Yahoo! News, you could type the word into the form and get back some stories from the past few days. You could visit the site every day to check for new stories, but keeping track of the changes between queries each day would be a tedious task by hand. You'd have to compare the current list of stories with yesterday's list, and see what sites show up in the results that weren't there the day before. Luckily, there's an easier, automated way to monitor search results with RSS.

Yahoo! offers RSS output of many of its features, including search results. The simple RSS format can be used to syndicate information across web sites (including services such as My Yahoo!). Web sites and programs that consume RSS are called *newsreaders*, and using one can dramatically increase the amount of information you can consume in a much shorter period of time. Instead of visiting a series of news sites looking for new information on topics you're interested in, you can simply subscribe to a news feed for the topic and any new information automatically appears in your newsreader.

Yahoo! has made it painfully easy to track information from Yahoo! News in My Yahoo!. If you do a Yahoo! News search at *http://news.search.yahoo.com*, you'll see an "Add to My Yahoo! / RSS" header to the right of the results, as shown in Figure 2-25.

Figure 2-25. "Add to My Yahoo! / RSS" box on News search results

This box gives you all of the information you need to start tracking a phrase in your own newsreader. If you use My Yahoo!, you can simply click the button with the blue plus sign and you'll be reading the latest stories about your favorite topic on a regular basis (see Figure 2-26).

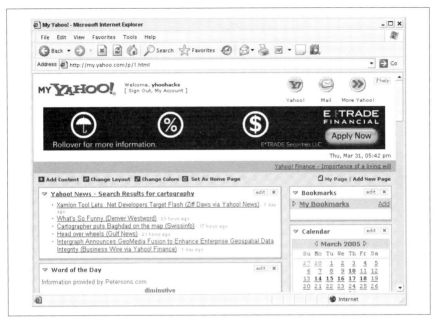

Figure 2-26. Yahoo News! search results in My Yahoo!

If you use a different newsreader, you'll need to follow some quick steps. First, right-click the white-on-orange XML icon (or Ctrl-click it on a Mac) and choose Copy Link Location or Copy Shortcut, depending on your browser. This will put the *feed URL* for the current search results onto your virtual clipboard. Then, open your newsreader and find the dialog for adding a subscription. Copy the feed URL, and you should find a new subscription for your search, such as the one highlighted in Figure 2-27.

Now, if any news articles that flow through one of the 7,000 sources at Yahoo News! contain the term *cartography*, you'll know about it as you browse your other news sources. Of course, this works just as well with other queries, and if mapping isn't your area, you can customize the feeds to track your own interests.

HACK #34 Personalize My Yahoo!

My Yahoo! can be your window to the world, if you take some time to specify what you want to see and how you want to see it.

My Yahoo! is designed to be a one-stop spot for information that's important to you. Putting together a My Yahoo! space is a bit like editing your own newspaper. You can decide which news sources you'd like to see headlines from, where each source is placed on the page, and how the page itself

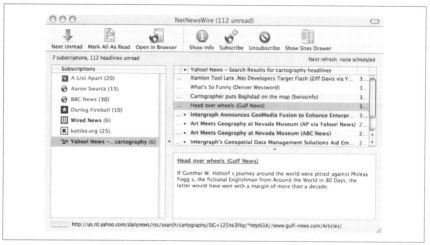

Figure 2-27. Yahoo News! search results in NetNewsWire

appears. Every good editor needs to know what's available, and this hack should provide you with the tools to build your own personalized information hub.

To get started, browse to My Yahoo! (*http://my.yahoo.com*) and note the controls across the top of the page, as shown in Figure 2-28.

Figure 2-28. My Yahoo! controls

Each of these controls lets you personalize My Yahoo! in some way. Add Content lets you add information sources, Change Layout adjusts where each module is located, and Change Colors lets you specify a look and feel. With these three options, you can create a source of news and information tailored specifically for you.

Yahoo! Modules

A My Yahoo! module is simply a box on a My Yahoo! page. Each module typically contains information from a single source, and you can specify some preferences for each module.

Adding a module to your My Yahoo! page is simply a matter of browsing through a list of modules and clicking the Add button. Start by clicking Add Content at the top of the My Yahoo! page. From here, you can search for a specific type of content or news source, or browse lists of modules arranged by topic.

In addition to news headlines from sources such as the *New York Times* or *USA Today*, there are a number of modules powered by Yahoo! that add extra features to the page. Some of the Yahoo! modules go beyond a list of headlines and let you tap into some features from across Yahoo! web sites. You can find them under the Yahoo! Services link, and here are just a few of the Yahoo!-powered modules available:

Best Fare Tracker
Choose a departure city and an arrival city and you can monitor low fare prices for the trip. You can add several trips to the module, so you can keep your eye on prices for different areas.

Lottery Results
Select your state and see winning lottery numbers from lotteries in your area.

Package Tracker
This module provides links to the package tracking services at Yahoo! Small Business (*http://smallbusiness.yahoo.com*). To track a package, click the link for Airborne Express, Federal Express, UPS, or the U.S. Postal Service and enter a tracking number. You can also quickly look up Zip Codes by address with this module.

HotJobs
View job openings in your city for a selected industry. If you use Yahoo! HotJobs (*http://hotjobs.yahoo.com*), you can also use this module to track your existing job searches and see how many people have viewed your resume.

Weather
Powered by Yahoo! Weather (*http://weather.yahoo.com*), this module tracks the daily high and low temperature in cities you specify, and it includes an icon that indicates whether it's a sunny, cloudy, or stormy day in that city.

Stock Portfolios
If you've created your own stock portfolios [Hack #23] at Yahoo! Finance (*http://finance.yahoo.com*), you can view them with this module.

Movie Showtimes
Based on your chosen cities and favorite theaters [Hack #41] at Yahoo! Movies (*http://movies.yahoo.com*), this module displays movies and their showtimes.

TV Schedule
This module shows what's on your channel lineup [Hack #44] at the time you specify. You can use the list of favorite channels that you set up at Yahoo! TV (*http://tv.yahoo.com*), or you can see a specified number of channels.

To add some visual interest to the page, try adding a few of the following modules that will show pictures:

Comics

This module is included by default and includes a daily comic strip or editorial cartoon. You can choose which comics you'd like to see each day by clicking the Edit link.

Photos

If you have personal photographs stored on Yahoo! Photos (*http://photos.yahoo.com*), you can add this module to see a random photo from your collection. You can choose which albums you want the module to draw from and how often you want the photo to change.

News Photos

You can choose from three different Yahoo! News (*http://news.yahoo.com*) photo modules: Lead Photo with a single photo and story, News Photos showing popular photos from Yahoo! News, or Entertainment Photos for celebrity watching.

Once you've added a module to My Yahoo!, you can change the settings at any time by clicking the Edit button and then clicking Edit Content. Each Yahoo! module has its own settings page. For example, Figure 2-29 shows the page that lets you add or remove cities from the Weather module.

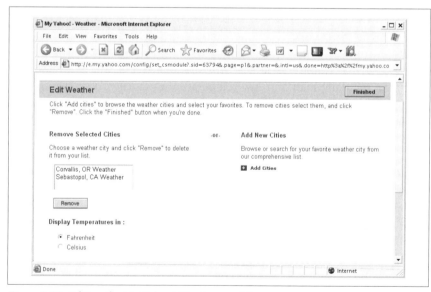

Figure 2-29. Editing the My Yahoo! Weather module

You can completely remove a module from the page by clicking the box with the × in the upper-right corner of the module.

Of course, there are many options for content beyond those powered by Yahoo!, and chances are very good that you can add modules from your favorite web sites [Hack #35] with My Yahoo!.

Layout

There are a couple of different ways to move modules around within the page. The simplest way to move a module is to click the Edit button and from the menu choose a direction in which to move the module. You can move a module up or down or to the top or bottom within a column. Figure 2-30 shows the Edit menu for the Weather module.

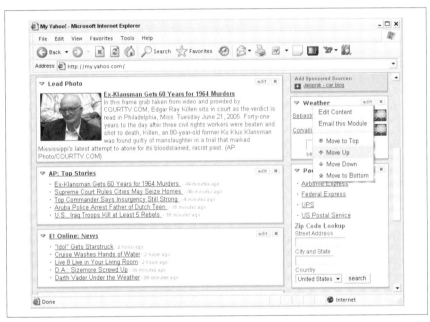

Figure 2-30. Moving the Weather module

For a more complex change in the layout, click the Change Layout link at the top of the page. From here, you can switch from the standard two-column layout to three columns and move modules up or down and between columns, as shown in Figure 2-31.

You can also have up to six My Yahoo! pages, if you have a lot of information to track. Click the Add New Page link in the upper-right corner of the page to create a new space to work with. You can name the pages anything

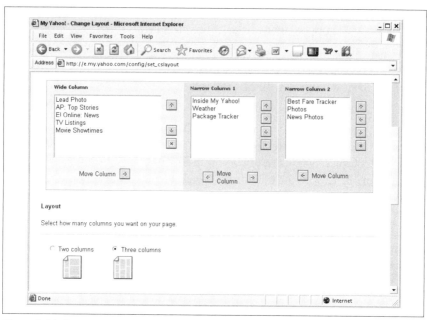

Figure 2-31. Layout settings page at My Yahoo!

you'd like. Once you've created your new page, you can choose a page to view by selecting it from the page menu as shown in Figure 2-32.

Choose Add/Delete Page from the menu to organize your pages. You can rename them, remove them, set a default page, or change the refresh rates for the pages.

Colors

With modules and the layout tailored to your taste, the only piece left is the look and feel. Click the Change Colors link at the top of the page to browse through existing themes for My Yahoo! pages. The themes range from subtle to gaudy, and you'll have to browse around to find one you like.

> If you ever change themes to something that makes your eyes bleed and you just want to get back to something readable, choose the Yahoo! category from the Theme Directory and look for My Yahoo! Basic. Click "Use this theme," and you'll go back to the default highly readable (though bland) theme.

If none of the themes quite fit the bill, you can always edit the theme colors by hand. On the left side of the page, you'll find a Customize Theme link that leads to the color editor. As you choose colors for parts of the My

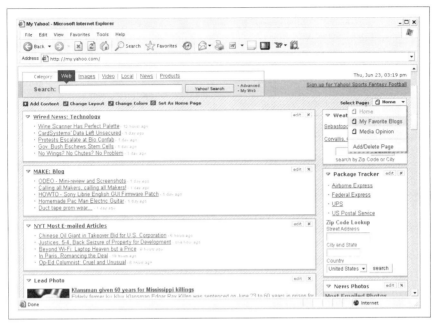

Figure 2-32. Choosing a My Yahoo! page

Yahoo! page, you can see the changes reflected in the preview in the bottom frame, as shown in Figure 2-33.

You can also choose between a half-dozen different fonts for the text on the page and increase or decrease the font size. You won't be able to add your own background graphics or logos to the page, but you can alter the colors for almost every element on the page.

Once you've taken the time to customize My Yahoo! by adding modules, adjusting the layout, and changing the colors, you'll find that it feels much more like your own space, with quick access to the information you want.

HACK #35 Track Your Favorite Sites with RSS

One of the most powerful features of My Yahoo! allows you to add RSS feeds from any online information source.

My Yahoo! offers easy access to national and international news. With a few clicks, you can add the top headlines from national news services, such as Reuters, the Associated Press, or USA Today. But the real power of My Yahoo! is not only that it gives you access to these great sources, but also that it lets you add any news source to your daily read. The key to this flexibility is My Yahoo!'s ability to read RSS.

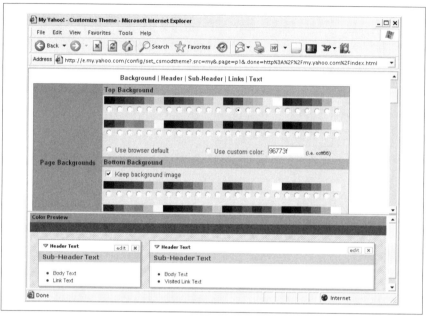

Figure 2-33. Editing theme colors at My Yahoo!

RSS stands for "really simple syndication" or "rich site summary," depending on who you ask. What's important is that RSS is a standard XML format for sharing headlines and news summaries across web sites. Just as a web page is formatted for display in a web browser, RSS feeds are formatted for display in newsreaders like My Yahoo!.

Everyone from an individual in his basement writing a weblog to a large media giant like the *New York Times* can publish RSS to be used with services such as My Yahoo! Knowing this allows you to bring in more news sources than the standard choices Yahoo! provides automatically.

Finding RSS Feeds

Keep in mind that not every news source out there has an RSS feed. And those that do don't always make the RSS feed easy to find. Part of the skill of adding content to My Yahoo! is being able to find the RSS feeds you care about. The key to the process is finding the *feed URL* so you can copy and paste it into a form at My Yahoo!. Like an address on a house, a feed URL tells services like My Yahoo! where to find updated information. Here are some tips for spotting feed URLs.

Go to the source. The first place to look for feed URLs is at your favorite web sites. Most sites that offer an RSS feed will have an orange image with white letters that say "XML" or "Finding RSS Feeds." Figure 2-34 shows a number of variations you might see on the front page of a web site.

Figure 2-34. Variations on the white-on-orange XML theme

Nine times out of ten, this image will link to the site's feed URL.

 Remember that RSS is an XML format, which is why the terms are used interchangeably in the images.

To copy the feed URL, right-click the icon and choose Copy Link Location (or Copy Shortcut in Internet Explorer) from the menu. At this point, the feed URL will be available on your virtual clipboard, ready to paste into My Yahoo!

Look for auto-discovery. Even sites that don't include an orange-and-white XML icon might leave clues about the RSS feed URL in their source HTML. To solve the problem of finding feeds, a standard called *RSS auto-discovery* has emerged. Sites that want to make it easy for people to find their feed URL can include a special HTML tag in the source of their pages to let applications such as web browsers find their feed URL. Once browsers are "aware" of auto-discovery and looking for the auto-discovery tag, they can let the user know when they've spotted an RSS feed URL in a web page. Firefox lets users know by displaying an orange icon in the lower-right corner of the browser window, as shown in Figure 2-35.

Even though SFgate.com doesn't have an orange XML icon or a link to its RSS feed on the home page, once you spot this orange RSS feed indicator, you can use Firefox's View Source feature to find the auto-discovery HTML tag that holds the feed URL. To view the source of any web page, choose View → Page Source from the browser's top menu. Finding the tag can be tricky, but it is always located toward the top of the HTML page, between the opening <head> and closing </head> tags. For example, the SFGate.com page in Figure 2-35 has the following auto-discovery tag in its HTML source:

```
<link href="http://www.sfgate.com/rss/feeds/news.xml" rel="alternate"
type="application/rss+xml" title="SFGate: Top News Stories" />
```

Note the URL contained in the href element. This is the site's RSS feed URL, ready for copying and pasting into My Yahoo!.

Like Firefox, the Yahoo! Toolbar is also smart enough to recognize this tag in pages you visit. If you have the toolbar installed and browse a site with the RSS auto-discovery tag, you'll find that a blue "Add to My Yahoo!" button with a plus sign—like the one shown in Figure 2-36—will appear on the toolbar.

Instead of rooting around in a site's HTML to find the URL, you'll be able to simply click the button to add the site to your list of news sources.

Figure 2-35. Firefox with the orange RSS feed indicator in the lower-right corner

Figure 2-36. The Yahoo! toolbar with a blue "Add to My Yahoo!" button

Adding to My Yahoo!

Once you have the feed URL of the news source copied to your virtual clip-board, head to My Yahoo! and log in. From there, click the Add Content link toward the top of the page. On the Add Content page, click the "Add RSS by URL" link shown in Figure 2-37.

The RSS Add page contains a single form field, where you can paste the feed URL you've been saving in your clipboard with Ctrl-V. Clicking Add will let you preview the feed so that you can make sure it's what you want. Figure 2-38 shows the SFGate.com feed preview.

If you compare the preview in Figure 2-38 with the web page in Figure 2-35, you'll see that the headlines are the same. And finally, the Add button with the blue plus sign will finish the work of adding the feed. From that point on, you'll find the news source on your My Yahoo! page, as shown in Figure 2-39.

Figure 2-37. "Add RSS by URL" link at My Yahoo!

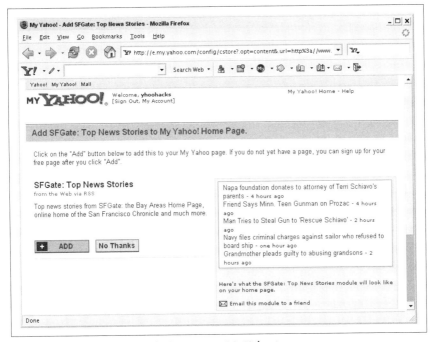

Figure 2-38. SFGate.com RSS feed preview at My Yahoo!

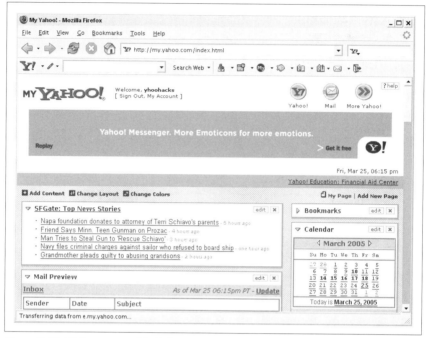

Figure 2-39. SFGate.com in My Yahoo!

Now that you know the complex way to add outside sources to My Yahoo!, you'll be happy to know there's an easier way. The entire copy and paste process can be shortened to one click at sites that support the "Add to My Yahoo!" button shown in Figure 2-40.

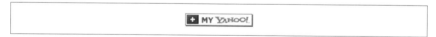

Figure 2-40. The "Add to My Yahoo!" button found at some sites

Not every site with an RSS feed includes the "Add to My Yahoo!" button, but as RSS feeds become more and more popular—and as My Yahoo! becomes known as a place to consume RSS—you might see it popping up at more of the sites you visit. When you spot one, click it, and you'll go directly to the preview page for that feed at My Yahoo!

Taking the time to add your favorite sites to My Yahoo! will let you keep up with many more sites than you'd be able to by visiting each site individually. Not only will you be reading information that's more relevant to you, you'll be reading it more efficiently—when it's updated, and alongside the rest of your favorites.

Add a Feed to My Yahoo! with a Right-Click

Speed up the time it takes to add RSS feeds to My Yahoo! with Internet Explorer.

Adding an RSS feed to My Yahoo! isn't a complex process, but it does involve some copying, pasting, clicking, and generally breaking out of the flow of reading a site. With a bit of browser hacking, you can reduce the friction of adding sites to My Yahoo! by adding a *context menu* entry.

A context menu is the menu that pops up when you right-click an element on a web page (or Ctrl-click it on a Mac). The *context* part of its name refers to the fact that different choices appear in different situations. For example, when you right-click a link, you have the options to "Open Link in New Window," Copy Link Location, Bookmark This Link, and others. In another context, such as when clicking an image or clicking highlighted text, you have different choices in the menu.

If you've been reading personal weblogs for a while, you've probably seen many variations of the white-on-orange XML buttons that indicate a link to an RSS feed, and if not you can find some examples [Hack #35] in this book.

Wouldn't it be great if you could right-click one of these buttons and have the option to "Add to My Yahoo!"? That would save you quite a few steps, and you wouldn't have to break from the site you're currently reading to add the feed. This hack shows how to add this context menu entry in Internet Explorer.

The Code

Much like a bookmarklet [Hack #28], any JavaScript that runs via a context menu entry has access to the page currently loaded in the browser. That means that when you click the context menu entry you've added, the browser executes a script that takes some action using information from the current page.

In this case, the action is grabbing the URL linked from the currently clicked image, constructing a special My Yahoo! URL that includes the feed URL, and opening the new URL in a new browser window.

Save the following code to a file called *AddToMyYahoo.html*:

```
<script language="JavaScript">
var addURL = new String("http://add.my.yahoo.com/rss?url=");

var w = window.external.menuArguments
var url = w.event.srcElement.parentElement.href;

window.open(addURL + url,null,
    "height=455,width=788,status=yes,scrollbars=yes,resizable=yes");
</script>
```

The external.menuArguments object holds information about the current document, and the event.srcElement is the document item the user clicked. Grabbing the href attribute of the element's parent will give you the link URL that is around the image tag. Save the file in a spot you'll remember. For simplicity in this hack, save it to a directory called *c:\scripts*.

Now that the script is ready to go, you just need to add the context menu entry to Internet Explorer and tell it to run this particular script when you click the entry. You'll accomplish this through the Windows Registry. The Registry is a system database that holds information about applications, including Internet Explorer. You can safely make additions to the Registry via *.reg* files. Create a new text file called *AddYahooContext.reg* and add the following code:

```
Windows Registry Editor Version 5.00

[HKEY_CURRENT_USER\Software\Microsoft\Internet Explorer\MenuExt\Add to My ⏎
Yahoo!]

@="c:\\scripts\\AddToMyYahoo.html"
"contexts"=dword:00000002
```

> Backslashes, such as those in filesystem paths, must be escaped as double slashes (\\) in Registry entry files.

Note that the contexts entry here ends with 2, which means the entry will appear only when the user has clicked an image. Other values you could use here include 1 (for anywhere), 20 (for text links), or 10 (for text selections).

Save the file, double-click it, and confirm that you want to add the new Registry information. You'll now have a right-click menu entry called "Add to My Yahoo!" whenever you right-click an image.

Running the Hack

Once the code and Registry settings are in place, restart Internet Explorer. Browse to a site with a feed URL link and take the new context menu entry for a spin. When you right-click an image, you should see "Add to My Yahoo!," as shown in Figure 2-41.

When you click the "Add to My Yahoo!" menu entry, a window like the one shown in Figure 2-42 should appear with the My Yahoo! feed preview page.

Keep in mind that the "Add to My Yahoo!" context menu entry will be available for *every* image on a web page, regardless of whether or not it links to an RSS feed. So you'll have to use your best judgment about when to use the

---

Figure 2-41. "Add to My Yahoo!" context menu entry

feature. If the image turns out not to be linked to an RSS feed, the Yahoo! feed preview page will let you know quickly. If you don't see posts in the preview box on the right side of the page, you'll know that a feed won't be added to My Yahoo! if you click the Add button.

Once you're finished adding the feed, you can simply close the pop-up window and go back to reading the site.

HACK #37 Build Your Own News Crawler

The My Yahoo! Ticker can provide a nonstop stream of news, weather, and stock quotes in your Windows toolbar.

When you watch any of the 24-hour news channels such as CNN or MSNBC, you see the ever-present crawling news ticker running along the bottom of the screen. While the news anchor reads a story about the latest celebrity court case or natural disaster, you can read completely unrelated information in the news crawler about other stories that are breaking. On

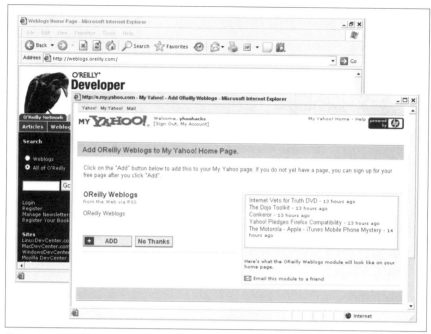

Figure 2-42. "Add to My Yahoo!" preview page in new window

the financial news channels, the news crawler across the bottom gives stock quote information that lets you keep up with how the market is faring.

Thanks to the My Yahoo! Ticker (in beta testing at the time of this writing), you can create your own endlessly crawling news ticker in your Windows taskbar that will keep you up to date with headlines, stock quotes, and weather while you're working.

Installing the Ticker

To use the ticker, you'll need Windows 98 or higher and a recent version of Internet Explorer. If you meet these requirements, browse to *http://ticker.yahoo.com* and click the Download button. Follow the installation instructions and enable the toolbar by clicking an empty area in your Windows taskbar and choosing Toolbars → My Yahoo! Ticker Beta, as shown in Figure 2-43.

Once enabled, the ticker will add a scrolling list of stock quotes, weather, and news headlines on the right side of your Windows taskbar, similar to those shown in Figure 2-44.

Figure 2-43. Enabling the My Yahoo! Ticker toolbar

Figure 2-44. My Yahoo! Ticker showing news headlines

You could use the ticker like this without changing any of the settings, but making the ticker your own means you'll get more relevant news and stock quotes.

Personalizing the Ticker

To edit your ticker preferences, click the small down arrow at the far right of the ticker and then click the top choice, My Yahoo! Ticker Beta Preferences. You should see a preferences window like the one shown in Figure 2-45.

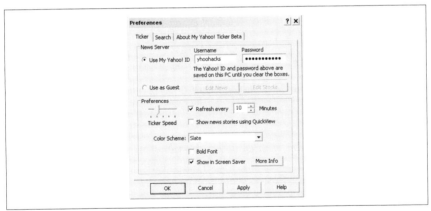

Figure 2-45. My Yahoo! Ticker preferences

If you already have a set of customized news sources set up at My Yahoo! [Hack #34], you can enter your Yahoo! ID and password to show your My Yahoo! news sources in the ticker. Once you are logged in, any Yahoo! modules or RSS feeds you've added to My Yahoo! will scroll through the ticker.

Alternately, you can choose the "Use as Guest" option and click the Edit News and Edit Stocks buttons to set up your ticker information. Even if you have a My Yahoo! page, you might want to see different news sources scrolling by, and the Guest account will do the trick.

Clicking the Edit News button will give you the preferences window, as shown in Figure 2-46.

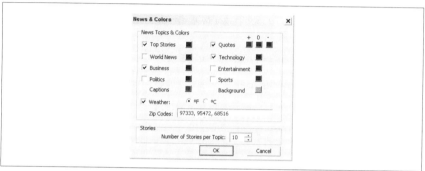

Figure 2-46. My Yahoo! Ticker Guest News preferences

You can choose from a number of news categories and set specific colors for each. You can also set some specific Zip Codes for weather information. Clicking Edit Stocks will take you to a similar preferences window, where you can enter a number of stock symbols to watch throughout the day. They'll scroll by in your ticker, as shown in Figure 2-47.

Figure 2-47. Stock symbols in My Yahoo! Ticker

Using the Ticker

As information crawls by, you can stop the ticker or move it backward and forward by clicking and dragging with your mouse. You can also click any headline to read the full story in your web browser, or click any stock quote to see that stock's detail page at Yahoo! Finance.

Clicking the Y! icon on the right side of the ticker turns the ticker into a Yahoo! search form. You can enter any search query into the field, click Enter, and the results for the query will appear in a special browser window. If you'd rather see queries and links in your default web browser, you can check the Default Browser option in the Search tab of the ticker preferences. To get back to the crawling ticker at any point, click the newspaper icon on the left side of the taskbar.

If you ever feel you're cramped for space in your Windows taskbar, right-click the newspaper icon to minimize the My Yahoo! Ticker. And if you want more space for the ticker, grab the bar to the left of the newspaper icon and pull down. This will put the My Yahoo! Ticker on its own row of your taskbar, stretching the full width of your screen.

You can also navigate to a number of different Yahoo! properties with the ticker by clicking the arrow at the far right to bring up a menu like the one shown in Figure 2-48.

My Yahoo! Ticker Beta Preferences	
Refresh My Yahoo! Ticker Beta Now	
Help	
Submit Feedback	
Yahoo!	
My Yahoo!	
Yahoo! Mail	
Search Web	
Search Images	Ctrl+I
Search Directory	Ctrl+D
Search Yellow Pages	Ctrl+Y
Search News	Ctrl+N
Search Products	Ctrl+P
Maps	Ctrl+M
Dictionary	Ctrl+T
Stock Quotes (ticker symbol)	Ctrl+Q
Movie Showtimes (city or zip)	Ctrl+S
Address Book	Ctrl+A

Figure 2-48. My Yahoo! Ticker menu

The menu has links to a dozen different Yahoo! properties, including Yahoo! Maps, a dictionary at Yahoo! Reference, and showtimes from Yahoo! Movies. You can also click Refresh My Yahoo! Ticker Beta Now to get the latest news and headlines.

The My Yahoo! Ticker is simple to set up and customize, and with a little work, you can create a news crawler to rival CNN's.

HACK #38 Replace Your Phone Book with Yahoo!

Throw out the giant book of numbers, and find everything from business information to personal phone numbers by searching at Yahoo!.

In the days before the Web, the local telephone directory was probably the most used book in the house. Getting in touch with friends, finding a place for dinner, and reaching local government agencies was accomplished by flipping through the pages of your phone book. Even the maps printed in the book could help you locate hard-to-find addresses.

Now, every home that has an Internet connection can get the same local information with Yahoo!. And with Yahoo!, you not only have access to local listings and business, but you are also able to browse virtually every phone book from every city across the United States.

Finding Businesses

Finding a business address and phone number on Yahoo! is similar to finding the information in a traditional phone book. Say you want to get a haircut in Sebastopol, California. You'd find a local directory, flip through the Yellow Pages until you find the Barbers category—or maybe Salon, Hairdresser, or Hair Stylist—and look through the listings.

On the Web, you can browse to *http://local.yahoo.com* and type in barbers and a location—in this case, 1005 Gravenstein Hwy N Sebastopol, CA. Yahoo! will come back with a list of phone numbers and addresses, as shown in Figure 2-49.

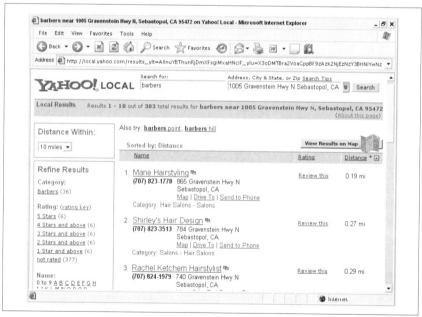

Figure 2-49. Yahoo! Local results for "barbers" near a Sebastopol, California, address

The listing of phone numbers and addresses is where the similarity with the phone book ends. In addition to the standard listings, Yahoo! offers many improvements that the phone book can't compete with.

Mapping and directions. Depending on how specific your initial query is, Yahoo! can know something about you the phone book could never know: your exact location. Then along with the phone and address, Yahoo! provides a distance to your location. And if you provide an exact address with your query—say, 1005 Gravenstein Highway North, Sebastopol, CA—Yahoo! can sort the entries by how far away they are, giving you a good guess at how long it would take you to get there.

This knowledge of geography also lets Yahoo! show the results of any search on a map. Click the View Results on Map button at the top of any search results page to see each entry in relation to your current location and in relation to the other entries, as shown with the barbershops in Figure 2-50.

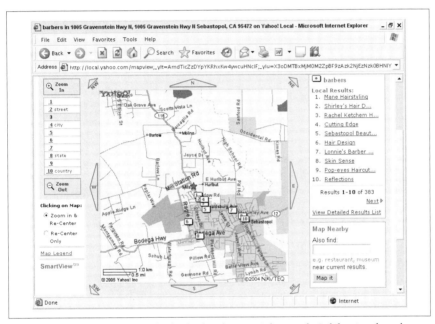

Figure 2-50. Yahoo! Local results for barbershops in Sebastopol, California, plotted on a map

The star in the center of the map represents your current location, and each numbered square is an entry from the results page. You can click any of the squares or the titles on the right side of the page to see more information about that particular business.

Yahoo! can also give you detailed directions to any business in the results. Click Drive To next to any entry on the results page, and you'll be asked to verify the start address and destination. From here, click Get Directions to display a map like the one shown in Figure 2-51, with a highlighted route and detailed information about where to turn along the way.

Replace Your Phone Book with Yahoo!

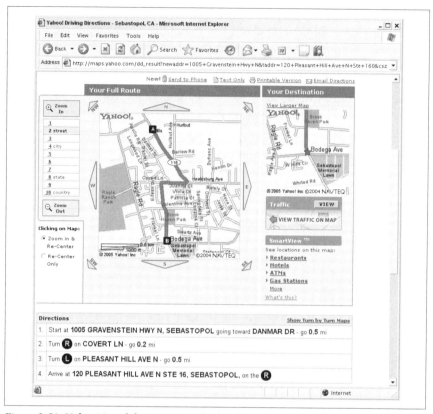

Figure 2-51. Yahoo! Local directions to a barbershop in Sebastopol, California

From here, you have the option to print the directions so you can take them with you, email them to someone else, or send them to your cell phone.

Sending to cell phone. Where a pencil and paper might have once been used to jot down an address from the phone book, you can now use the multimillion-dollar wireless networks all around us to send detailed information from Yahoo! Local to a mobile device. When you click "Send to Phone" next to any entry on a Yahoo! Local search results page, you'll see a form into which you can type a cell phone number. You can also check the "Add link to map and driving directions" option. When you click Send, Yahoo! sends an SMS (Short Message Service) message to the number. SMS is a protocol cell phones use to send and receive text messages.

The SMS message will contain the name, address, and phone number of the business. Many phones let users highlight the number so they can simply click a button to call the business. Optionally, the SMS message can include a link to a map or driving directions to the business. As with phone numbers, many phones allow you to highlight the link and bring up a smaller version of the map you'd see on the Yahoo! web site.

Ratings. Another insight the standard phone book can't provide is how other users of the phone book feel about a particular business. Yahoo! lets any user rate any business in its listing on a scale from one to five stars. If you feel like you need to voice more than a rating, you can also add a review of the business. You can browse ratings and reviews for any business by clicking the business name in the search results. The business detail page contains the average rating by Yahoo! users and links to any reviews that have been added.

Finding People

Yahoo! provides a service called Yahoo! People Search (*http://people.yahoo.com*) for finding residential phone numbers. You can search for phone numbers by name and city, or for email addresses by name. The difference between the Yahoo! People Search and your local phone book is scale: you can use Yahoo! to search across the United States. Try searching for just your last name, leaving the city blank and Entire USA (the default) selected for the state. The list might include some long-lost relatives.

In addition to the name, address, and telephone number, each entry includes shortcuts to add the address to your Yahoo! Address Book or show the address on a map.

> Look carefully on results pages for boxes or columns labeled ADVERTISEMENT or Sponsored Results. Even though you might see what look like official Yahoo! links, be aware that any site within one of these boxes or columns will take you to another domain that Yahoo! doesn't control.

If you find your own information listed in Yahoo! People Search and you'd rather not be included, you can request to be removed. To remove your email address, go to *http://people.yahoo.com/py/psEmailSupp.py* and enter your name and email address. Yahoo! will remove the listing within five days. To remove your address and phone listing, go to *http://people.yahoo.com/py/psPhoneSupp.py* and enter your information.

Keep in mind that filling out these forms removes your information only from the Yahoo! People Search database; you'll need to contact your phone company and any other services to keep your information out of other directories. The data for the Yahoo! People Search is supplied by a company called Acxiom, and you might want to read their privacy policy and opt-out provisions at *http://www.acxiom.com/default.aspx?ID=1671&DisplayID=18*.

While you won't be able to use Yahoo! Local or Yahoo! People Search as a booster seat for your toddler, the added features and convenience will let you finally say goodbye to your old phone book.

HACK #39   Monitor Your Commute

Let Yahoo! Local point out construction, accidents, and other potential slow spots on your route.

If you've ever been stuck in an inexplicable traffic jam, you know how important information can be. Just knowing the reason behind a slowdown can help you estimate how much longer you'll be stuck and make some sense of the sea of cars surrounding you. With a little planning and research, you might be able to avoid those trouble spots entirely.

Scout Your Route

To get a general sense of traffic in your area before you leave the house, try looking up your city at Yahoo! Maps. Browse to *http://maps.yahoo.com/ traffic* and plug in your city. You'll see a map that includes any known construction areas and traffic incidents, along with the general speed of the routes. Figure 2-52 shows the traffic around San Francisco and southern Marin County.

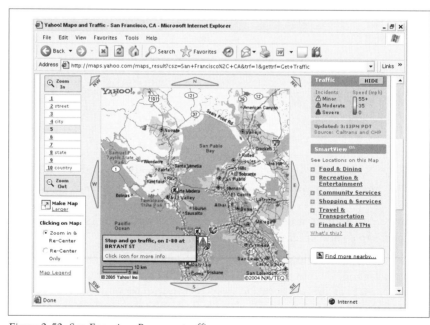

Figure 2-52. San Francisco Bay area traffic

The squares on the map indicate areas with construction and triangles with exclamation points indicate a traffic incident. You can get more detail by hovering over these icons. Clicking the icon gives you even more information, as shown in Figure 2-53.

Figure 2-53. Traffic incident detail

As you can see from Figure 2-53, the information won't always tell you when an incident will be over, but at least you'll know that the route could be slow.

In addition to the general overview of your city, you can look for problems along a specific route. Any driving directions provided by Yahoo! Maps also include traffic information. Point your browser to *http://maps.yahoo.com*, click Driving Directions (toward the top of the page), and enter a starting and ending location. The map you get by clicking Get Directions will show you traffic incidents along the route. This is great for routes you might not be familiar with, but if you have a regular commute, there are a few other ways to work this information into your daily routine.

Add Incidents to Your Dashboard

If you're a commuter, you probably know your route by heart and won't need the map. Instead, you'll want the traffic incident information in a handy spot, such as your *dashboard*—that is, your Mac OS X Dashboard. In Mac OS X Tiger (Version 10.4), Apple introduced a feature called Dashboard, which contains a series of *widgets* that can provide information or control applications.

The Yahoo! Local Traffic widget for Dashboard lets you specify a city, state, or Zip Code and receive traffic incidents within a radius of 4, 10, or 40 miles from the center of the area. You can also set the severity threshold to Minor, Moderate, or Major to filter out smaller incidents. Figure 2-54 shows the widget with traffic data for San Francisco.

Clicking on any of these incidents will open a web browser to a page that shows the incident on a map at Yahoo! Maps. You can change the location or other settings by clicking the *i* icon in the upper-right corner. You can also run multiple instances of the widget to track several locations.

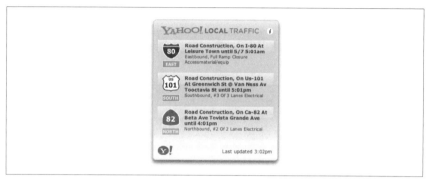

Figure 2-54. Yahoo! Local Traffic widget for Mac OS X

To install the Yahoo! Local Traffic widget, go to *http://www.apple.com/ downloads/dashboard/transportation/yahoolocaltraffic.html* and click Download. Double-click the *.zip* file to decompress it and then open the file *YahooTraffic.wdgt* to add the widget to your Dashboard.

Subscribe to Your Commute

Dashboard is great for Tiger users, but if you're on Windows (or if you're a Mac user who simply hasn't upgraded yet), there's still a way to subscribe to information about your commute with RSS.

Studying the data behind the Yahoo! Local Traffic widget, intrepid developer John Resig found that the widget was getting its data from Yahoo! in the popular RSS format; he posted his findings to his web site: *http://ejohn.org/blog/ traffic-conditions-data*. This means you can create your own specially formatted URL to create an RSS feed of traffic incidents in your area.

Here's a look at the format of the URL:

```
http://maps.yahoo.com/traffic.rss?csz=94101&mag=4&minsev=2
```

The three variables correspond to the preferences you can set in the dashboard widget:

csz

>The Zip Code, city, or state.

mag

>The *magnification* of the area—that is, the radius of traffic data from the center of the specified location. Possible values are 3, 4, or 5, which correspond to 4 miles, 10 miles, and 40 miles respectively.

minsev

>The minimum severity that should be shown in the feed. A value of 1 sets the minimum to Minor, 2 is Moderate, and 3 is Major.

So, putting all of the variables together, you can set a feed of moderate traffic incidents within 40 miles of San Francisco, like so:

```
http://maps.yahoo.com/traffic.rss?csz=94101&mag=5&minsev=2
```

Now you can add this URL to your favorite RSS newsreader to keep up with any traffic problems in the area. This also means you can add the data to My Yahoo! by visiting *http://my.yahoo.com* and choosing Add Content from the top of the page. Then click "Add RSS by URL" and plug in your newly created traffic feed. You'll find the new module on your My Yahoo! page, as shown in Figure 2-55.

Figure 2-55. Yahoo! Traffic data in My Yahoo!

Another nice feature is that once this traffic data is available in My Yahoo!, you can view these incidents with your cell phone's browser. So, not only will you be able to check your commute from home or office, but you'll also have something to check when you're stuck in your car dealing with one of these incidents!

Get the Facts at Yahoo! Reference
HACK
#40

Yahoo! has collected several reference books into one site for easy research and fact-checking.

The Yahoo! Education site (*http://education.yahoo.com*) contains information about schools of every level across the United States. You can look up local elementary and high schools, read reviews by parents and students, or find degree programs at universities. As part of the mix, Yahoo! has put together a collection of publicly available reference sources called Yahoo! Research to help students with their own research.

Yahoo! Reference is available directly at *http://reference.yahoo.com*, or by typing reference! into any Yahoo! search form. At this site, you'll find a collection of reference books, from a dictionary and thesaurus to classics such as *Bartlett's Familiar Quotations* and *The Columbia Encyclopedia*. Yahoo! makes these books available online for free, saving you the cost of purchasing each of these books yourself. But be aware that Yahoo! includes advertising on each page. Luckily, the advertising is clearly marked with the word *Advertising*, so you won't confuse a Shakespeare sonnet with an ad for The Gap.

The Collection

Yahoo! Reference provides a single entry point for a collection of publicly available resources. Here's a look at the reference sources available:

The American Heritage® Dictionary, Fourth Edition
The dictionary gives you more than just a definition. It also provides an audio (WAV file) pronunciation guide and a link to a thesaurus entry for the defined word.

The American Heritage® Spanish Dictionary, Second Edition
The Spanish dictionary lets you type in either English or Spanish words and returns the appropriate translation. It does not, however, provide an audio pronunciation guide.

Roget's II: The New Thesaurus
The thesaurus provides a list of related words. But, since this is a web thesaurus, it also links each related word to that word's own thesaurus entry, letting you drill deeply in the population of related terms.

Columbia Encyclopedia
The encyclopedia is based on the single-volume reference book that was once the staple for many students, who used it for quick fact lookups. Although it does not have the depth or breadth of for-fee products such as MSN Encarta, it is a good starting point for research.

Bartlett's Familiar Quotations
The quotes are from the 10th edition, published in 1919. It has indexes alphabetized by authors and quotations, and searchable by keyword.

Gray's Anatomy of the Human Body
This electronic version is based on the 1918 edition. It provides descriptions of anatomical structures and 1,247 illustrations.

The Oxford Shakespeare
This electronic version of the complete works of William Shakespeare is based on the edition published in 1914. A complete text search of the works is available and returns the location of the search text, down to the line number of a specific play, sonnet, or other work.

World Factbook
The *World Factbook* is maintained by the U.S. Government and placed in the public domain. The Factbook provides facts about the countries of the world as well as flag drawings and 267 color maps. The audio pronunciation guide requires the Apple Quicktime plugin.

Conversion Calculator
This easy-to-use unit conversion tool lets you quickly convert values for area, length, volume, and mass.

By combining these sources into one site, Yahoo! has made it easy to search all of these sources at once. If you're putting together a paper about the planet Saturn, for instance, you can browse to *http://reference.yahoo.com*, type Saturn into the search form, choose All Reference from the drop-down menu, and click Search. You'll find a page of search results from these specific sources, as shown in Figure 2-56.

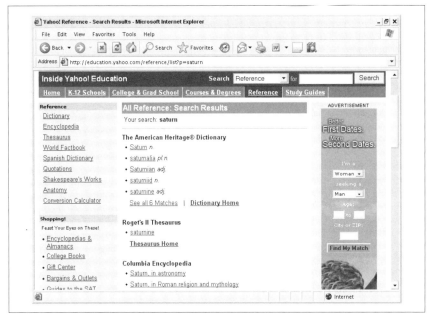

Figure 2-56. Search Results for "Saturn" at Yahoo! Reference

If you're doing academic work, these results can be more manageable than what you get from typing Saturn into the web search form at Yahoo!, and you'll know the information you find is from established reference books that have been used in the classroom for decades.

Programmatic Access

Yahoo! doesn't provide access to these reference books through its web services API, but with some attention to URLs and a look at the HTML, you can *screen scrape* any information you need from one of these sources. For example, searching the Yahoo! Bartlett's Familiar Quotations returns a list of quotes with the search word or phrase in a bulleted list. And a simple Python script can take advantage of the fixed web presentation style to create a quick list of results.

The code. This script lets you retrieve a list of encyclopedia entries related to a search word argument passed to the script. The script builds a Yahoo! Research URL with the incoming term, downloads the HTML, separates the contents by HTML tag, and then prints out the results. The results can be collected in a text file to provide you with a number of quotations with a specific word or phrase.

Save the following code to a file called *YahooQuotations.py*:

```python
#!/usr/bin/python

import sys
import urllib

def processline(quoteline):
    tagstart = "<"      # start of an HTML tag
    tagend = ">"        # end of an HTML tag
    tagon = STOP
    stringcollect = ""

    for yahoochar in quoteline:
        if (yahoochar == tagstart):
            tagon = START
        elif (yahoochar == tagend):
            tagon = STOP
            continue    # Do not print the > character itself

        if (tagon == STOP):     # get everything between HTML tags
            stringcollect += yahoochar

    return stringcollect.strip()

myword = str(sys.argv[1])    # word to search for in quotations
quotationurl = "http://education.yahoo.com/search/bfq?p="
searchword = quotationurl + myword

START = 1
STOP = 0
quoteon = STOP

f = urllib.urlopen(searchword)

for line in f.readlines():
    if (line.find("<li>") > -1):    # display quotation search results
        quoteon = START
    elif (line.find("</li>") > -1):
        quoteon = STOP
        print "===================="
    elif (line.find("-end search") > -1): # ignore bullet points after ↵
results
        break

    if (quoteon == START):
        print processline(line)     # print quotation without HTML tags
```

Running the hack. To run the script, type the following at the command line:

```
YahooQuotations.py insert keyword
```

You should see a list of quotes matching the term you used. And by piping the results of the program to a text file, you can build a text file filled with quotes. If you're interested in finding famous historic quotations related to planets, you might run the script like this:

```
YahooQuotations.py planets > planets_quotes.txt
```

Figure 2-57 shows the text file that was built with this command.

Figure 2-57. A text file filled with quotes from Yahoo! Reference

Even if you're not looking to automatically add quotes to a text file, you might find that the Yahoo! Reference web site will help you get a jumpstart on a school paper, teach you more about the world, or settle a bet between friends.

—Todd Ogasawara

HACK #41 Find and Rate Movies

You can find showtimes, review movies, and get recommendations at Yahoo! Movies.

You can streamline your movie-viewing habits by using *http://movies.yahoo.com* or by typing movies! into any Yahoo! search form. Yahoo! Movies is designed to help you find what movies are out, which movies are hot, and where you can see them. Here's a quick look at some of the features you'll find on the site:

Movie Showtimes

Enter a Zip Code or City and State into the form on the front page to find a list of theaters in your area, with a complete list of movies and times they're playing.

New Releases

Click Coming Soon on the front page to see a list of movies that will be in theaters soon. Be sure to browse the Further Out column on the right side of the page to see movies opening in the more distant future.

Movie Trailers

Click Trailers on the front page or browse to *http://movies.yahoo.com/trailers* to view video clips and previews of movies. The archive includes movies from the past several years.

Entertainment News

Click News on the front page to view film-related news from the entertainment industry. For an overview of news from the entire entertainment business, point your browser to *http://entertainment.yahoo.com*.

Box Office Charts

Click Box Office to find out which movies are making the most money. You can view the rankings by day or week, or view the top-grossing movies of all time. You can also choose archived charts from the past few months to see how recent movies have done at the box office.

Movie Details

Click the title of any movie to find a detailed *movie info page* that includes cast and credits, photos, reviews from critics and other Yahoo! users, and a message board for discussing the movie.

Find Movie Showtimes

Yahoo! Movies gathers showtimes from every theater and makes them available in one place. Instead of scanning through a newspaper or looking up theater phone numbers and listening through their menus, you can quickly find showtimes via the Web, email, or even cell phone.

Showtimes page. The most direct way to look up showtimes for your area is through the Showtimes page at Yahoo! Movies. You can type your Zip Code into the form on the front page or you can use predictable URLs to bookmark your theaters. Here's the format for the Showtimes page URL:

```
http://movies.yahoo.com/showtimes/showtimes.html?z=insert zip code
```

Add your Zip Code and bookmark the page to have your local theater schedules one click away. If you don't know the Zip Code for a particular area, you can also use a city and state combination in place of the Zip Code, using a plus sign instead of spaces. So, you could bring up a list of theaters and showtimes in Sebastopol, California, with either of the following URLs:

```
http://movies.yahoo.com/showtimes/showtimes.html?z=95472
http://movies.yahoo.com/showtimes/showtimes.html?z=Sebastopol+CA
```

You'll see that some showtimes at some listed theaters are also links. You can click the link to buy tickets to that showing at Yahoo! partner Fandango, and you won't have to stand in line when you get to the theater!

If you'd rather just see a list of all the movies playing in your area, you can click the View By: Movie Title link on the Showtimes page or use the following URL format:

```
http://movies.yahoo.com/showtimes/allmovies?z=insert zip code
```

The Movie Titles page lists all of the movies playing in your area, along with the rating and total running time for each movie. You can click the movie title to see the theaters where the movie is playing and the showtimes.

If you're logged in to Yahoo!, you can customize the Showtimes page with your favorite theaters. Next to any theater listed, click the "Add to My Favorite Theaters" link. To add several theaters at once, click Edit next to the Favorite Theaters title (customized with your own Yahoo! ID) at the top of the page. Once your favorites are set, you can limit lists of movies and showtimes by theater location.

Email newsletter. To receive a weekly email with showtimes at theaters in your area, scroll to the bottom of any page at Yahoo! Movies and click the "Get Yahoo! Movies in Your Mailbox" link. The sign-up form requires your Zip Code and will ask a few optional questions about your movie-going habits. The email itself is a scaled-down version of the Yahoo! Movies web site, and you'll get movie news and info about new releases.

Cell phone schedule. For the ultimate in convenience, you can look up movie showtimes on any cell phone with a web browser. The path to Yahoo! Mobile will vary by cell phone provider, but you can always manually type in the URL *http://mobile.yahoo.com* if you don't see a link to Yahoo! when you start your phone's browser.

Once you're at the mobile site, you can either log in with your Yahoo! ID to see the times at your favorite theaters, or you can scroll to the Movies link and enter a Zip Code. You should see a list of theaters you can click on, as shown in Figure 2-58.

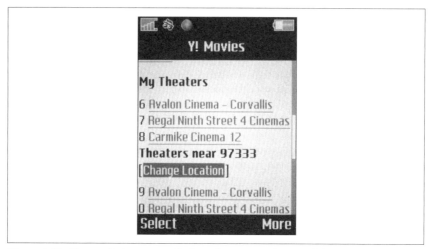

Figure 2-58. Theater listings on a cell phone browsing Yahoo! Mobile

Entering or changing your preferred Zip Code is particularly handy if you're on the road and aren't familiar with the local theaters.

Click on a theater to see a list of the movies and showtimes like the one shown in Figure 2-59.

Clicking a movie title will show you all of the theaters in the area that are playing the movie, along with an image of the movie poster, as shown in Figure 2-60, if your phone supports images.

Carrying Yahoo! Movies around in your pocket means you can be a bit more spontaneous with your movie choices, and you won't have to plan your viewing in front of your computer before you leave the house.

Connect with Movie Fans

In addition to the official information available about movies, Yahoo! Movies lets you read reviews, add your own reviews, and find out what other movie fans think, in a number of different ways.

Create your profile. To get started, click the My Movies tab on the Yahoo! Movies front page. Click the Edit links next to different elements of the page

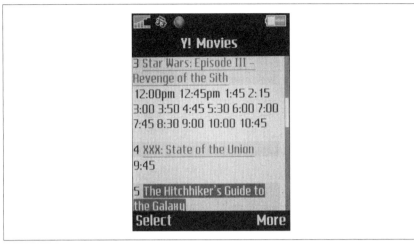

Figure 2-59. Movie listings on a cell phone browsing Yahoo! Mobile

Figure 2-60. An individual movie listing on a cell phone browsing Yahoo! Mobile

to add your Real Name, Location, a bit about you, and your favorite movie genres. When you're done, you should see a completed profile page like the one shown in Figure 2-61.

Your profile page collects some of your Yahoo! Movies contributions into one place. As you review movies or create lists of movies, they'll be listed on your profile page. That way, someone who enjoys a list or review you've added can browse other contributions you've made.

Movie lists let you bring some order to the universe of movies by gathering them together into groups. You can put lists together based on any criteria you see fit—anything from your personal favorites, to an obscure category that you might be familiar with. Figure 2-62 shows a custom list open for editing.

Figure 2-61. Yahoo! Movies profile page

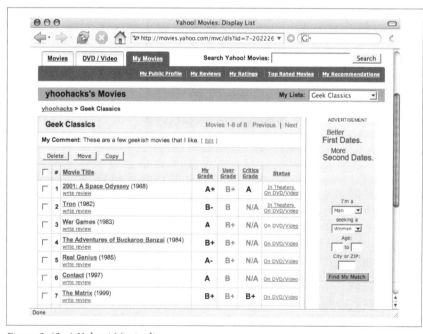

Figure 2-62. A Yahoo! Movies list

To add movies to a list, you can search by title and choose from the search results. You can also look for an "Add to My Movies" link as you're browsing movies at the site. Clicking the link will let you add the movie to one or more of your existing lists.

You can also add your own review of any movie past or present, and Yahoo! has a great set of guidelines to keep in mind while you're writing. You can read their guidelines at *http://help.yahoo.com/help/us/movies/movies-13.html*.

Get recommendations. As you browse the movies at Yahoo! Movies, you can assign letter grades with a plus or minus to any movie, if you're logged in with your Yahoo! ID. If you hate the latest *Star Wars*, you can give it an F. If you're lukewarm on the latest romantic comedy but thought it was good for a laugh, you could give it a C+. After you've rated a few movies, Yahoo! will start to know what types of movies you prefer and will offer recommendations in four areas:

- Movies in Theaters
- Movies on TV
- New releases on DVD/VHS
- Movie fans like you

Figure 2-63 shows a personalized recommendations page.

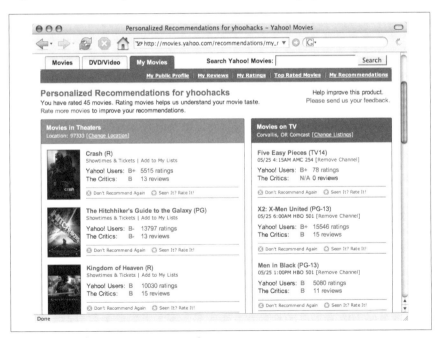

Figure 2-63. Yahoo! Movies recommendations

If you're ever stumped about what movies to see or rent, a trip to the Yahoo! Movies recommendations page could clue you in to some movies you don't already know about. As Alfred Hitchcock said, "A good film is when the price of the dinner, the theater admission, and the babysitter were worth it." And with a little time and effort at Yahoo! Movies, you can make sure the films you watch are good and worth the cost.

H A C K   Subscribe to Movie Showtimes
#42
With some quick scripting, subscribe to your favorite theaters to keep up with the movies they're playing.

Even though there are a number of ways to keep up with ever-changing movie schedules at Yahoo! Movies [Hack #41], if you already use an RSS newsreader, you can start watching your favorite theaters with just a bit of scripting.

RSS is an XML syndication format that's great for keeping up with changing information—typically news stories—and Yahoo! offers RSS for many features of its site. You can add any data that's available as RSS to a newsreader and see any changes or additions on a regular basis. Unfortunately, at the time of this writing, Yahoo! doesn't provide movie schedules via RSS, so if you want to see showtimes in your newsreader, you'll need to build a feed yourself.

Finding Your Theaters

Yahoo! doesn't offer movie schedules through their web services API, so this hack relies on *screen scraping* to gather the information. Screen scraping refers to downloading the HTML on the web site with a script and processing it to find relevant pieces of information. Keep in mind that screen scraping is a very brittle process, and if Yahoo! changes the HTML used to display movie times even slightly, the code in this hack will have to be modified to keep up with the changes.

To download the schedule page, you first need to know how to get there. Each theater listed at Yahoo! Movies has a unique internal ID number. But it's fairly easy to find this number, because it's exposed in the URL. Simply browse to Yahoo! Movies (*http://movies.yahoo.com*) and enter your Zip Code into the form labeled Get Showtimes and Tickets.

You should see a list of theaters in your area, along with movie showtimes. Under each theater title is link for Theater Info. Click the link and note the URL in your browser address bar, which will include the theater ID. As you'd expect, the four- to five-digit number following the variable named id in the URL is the theater ID for that theater. Jot down the IDs of your favorite theaters, because you'll need them to generate RSS feeds later.

Once you know the internal ID of a specific theater, you can link directly to the theater detail page on Yahoo! Movies with the following URL format:

```
http://movies.yahoo.com/showtimes/theater?id=insert theater ID
```

The theater detail page contains the theater's address and phone number, a list of services available, and the current schedule of movies. For this hack, the only relevant pieces of data are the theater title and the list of movies. Some Perl can isolate those elements and turn them into an RSS feed you can subscribe to.

The Code

This code relies on a single Perl module: XML::RSS::SimpleGen by Sean Burke. This module makes it easy to create an RSS feed with screen scraping, and it keeps the tough work of formatting the feed properly in the background.

Save the following code to a file called *theater_rss.pl*:

```
#!/usr/bin/perl
# theater_rss.pl
# Accepts a Yahoo! Movies theater ID and prints
# an RSS feed of currently playing movies.
# Usage: theater_rss.pl <theater_ID>
#
# You can find theater IDs at Yahoo! Movies
# at http://movies.yahoo.com/

use strict;
use XML::RSS::SimpleGen;

# Grab the incoming theater ID
my $tid = join(' ', @ARGV) or die "Usage: theater_rss.pl <theater_ID>\n";
my $theater_title = "My favorite theater";

# Set the theater schedule URL
my $url = "http://acid1.oa.yahoo.com/mbl/mov/tdet?tid=$tid";

# Download the schedule page
my $content = get_url($url);

# Find the theater name
if ($content =~ m!<dl><dt>(.*?)</dt>!sg) {
    $theater_title = $1;
}

# Start the RSS Feed
rss_new($url, "$theater_title Schedule");
rss_language('en');
rss_webmaster('insert your email address');
```

```
rss_daily();

# Set the regular expression to find data
my $regex = '<table.*?>.*?mid=(.*?)">(.*?)</a></td>.*?';
   $regex .= '<td>(.*?)</td>.*?</table>';

# Loop through the HTML, grabbing elements
while ($content =~ m!$regex!sg) {
   # rss_item accepts url, title, description.
   my $url = "http://movies.yahoo.com/shop?d=hv&cf=info&id=$1";
   rss_item($url, $2, $3);
}

# Warn if nothing was found
die "No items in this content?! {{\n$_\n}}\nAborting"
 unless rss_item_count();

# Save the rss file as <theater_ID>.rss
rss_save("$tid.rss");
exit;
```

This code accepts a theater ID, builds the appropriate Yahoo! Movies URL, downloads the HTML, and picks through the HTML with some regular expressions to find theater and movie information. The code uses the functions that are a part of XML::RSS::SimpleGen to create and save an RSS file based on the movie information.

The name of the RSS file this script generates is based on the incoming ID and will be *theater_ID*.rss. If you'd rather save the file to another location, just append the path to the filename where the script calls the rss_save function. Be sure that the file this script creates is in a location that's accessible via the Web.

Running the Hack

You can run the script once by passing in a theater ID on the command line, like this:

```
perl theater_rss.pl insert theater ID
```

But the real value of the script is that you can run it on a regular schedule on a web server to keep up with changes to the theater's schedule. Once per day should be enough to keep up with changes, and you can set the script to run regularly with Windows Scheduler or the Unix cron command.

On Windows servers, you can find the scheduler at Start → Settings → Control Panel → Scheduled Tasks. Click Add Scheduled Task at the top of the list to start the task wizard and set the program to run like this:

```
C:\perl\bin\perl.exe "C:\path\to\theater_rss.pl insert theater ID"
```

You might need to adjust the location of the Perl executable, depending on where it's installed on your server. You'll also need to include the full path to *theater_rss.pl*.

On Unix-based systems, you can run the script once per day by adding an entry like the following to your crontab file:

```
52 23 * * * ~/theater_rss.pl insert theater ID
```

If you want to subscribe to more than one theater in your area, set up a separate recurring task for each theater, using its unique theater ID.

Finally, add the new RSS feed to your favorite newsreader and you'll find out about any new movies playing at that theater. Figure 2-64 shows a subscription to theater 8193—Carmike Cinema 12 in Corvallis, Oregon—in the latest version of the Safari browser (which doubles nicely as an RSS newsreader).

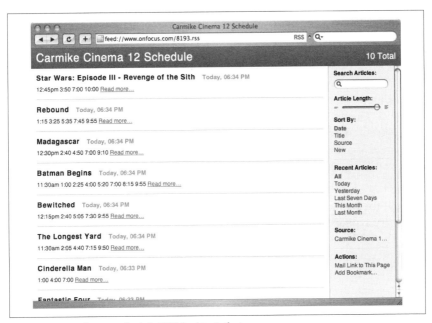

Figure 2-64. A theater schedule RSS feed in Safari

Clicking "Read more..."—or the movie title in some newsreaders—will take you to the movie detail page at Yahoo! Movies, where you can find out more about that particular movie. And by subscribing to your favorite local theaters' schedules, you'll always be on top of new additions to their lineups.

View Movie Lists on Your Cell Phone

HACK #43 Next time you go to the video store, take a Yahoo! Movies list with you on your cell phone.

Imagine you find yourself in a video store, searching for the perfect movie among the thousands of choices and drawing a blank. Even though you might have a mental list of several movies you've been meaning to see, it always seems those crucial bits of information aren't available when you need them. If you have a cell phone with web access, Yahoo! Movies and some Perl scripting can get you out of this jam.

This hack takes advantage of the Lists feature at Yahoo! Movies [Hack #41], which is designed to put movies together into a group. By creating a list of movies you'd like to see, you'll have the movies in a convenient format for scripting. From there, the hack uses some Perl to convert the Yahoo! Movies list into Wireless Markup Language (WML) that you can view on your phone.

Creating Your List

To get started, you need to turn your mental list of movies you'd like to see into something more tangible. Browse to *http://movies.yahoo.com/profiles* and click Create New List. If you don't already have a Yahoo! ID [Hack #3], you'll need to create one in order to use the movie list feature. Choose "Movies I Want to See" from the suggestions list or create your own title. Now you'll have a blank list waiting for some entries.

At the top of the page, you should see a form titled Search Yahoo! Movies. Type in the name of a movie you'd like to see. If you don't have anything in mind, try typing Buckaroo Banzai. Click Search and you should see a result with the 1984 cult classic *The Adventures of Buckaroo Banzai*. Click the "Add to My Movies" link next to the title, and you'll see a list of your movie lists. Click the checkbox next to the list you just created and then click "Add to List." The movie will be on your list, and you can repeat the process as many times as you need to until your movie list is filled with films you'd like to see, as shown in Figure 2-65.

Once your movie list is ready to go, you just need to jot down its URL. Head back to your profile page by clicking the My Movies tab or browsing to *http://movies.yahoo.com/profiles*. Click the title of your movie list and copy the URL from your browser's address bar. The URL should look something like this:

```
http://movies.yahoo.com/mvc/dls?iid=7-2022263&lid=7-150274
```

With the movie list URL in hand, you're ready to build the script that will convert that list into a cell phone–friendly format.

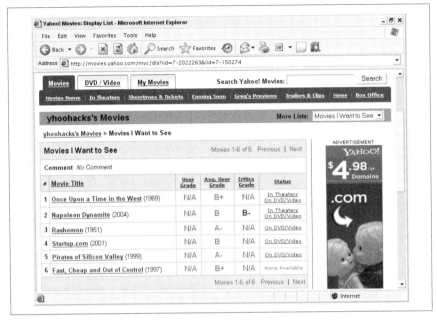

Figure 2-65. A Yahoo! Movies list

The Code

This script needs to run on a publicly available web server that can execute Perl scripts. You'll need the nonstandard Perl module LWP::Simple, which will fetch the movie list from Yahoo! Movies. You'll also need HTML:: TableExtract, which will do the tough work of deconstructing the HTML for you.

This script relies on screen scraping to gather the movies in a list, which means it's picking through the HTML to find relevant information. This also means that if Yahoo! changes their movie list HTML, even slightly, this script will likely fail. Keep in mind that you might need to tinker with the script to keep up with changes to Yahoo! Movies.

To keep your fingers from doing too much work when you're ready to bring it up your phone, you'll want to keep the name of this script short. Save the following code to a file called *m.cgi* and be sure to include your unique movie list URL as the value of $listURL at the top of the script:

```
#!/usr/bin/perl
# m.pl
# Convert a Yahoo! Movies list into WML for cell phones
# Usage: m.cgi

use strict;
```

```perl
use HTML::TableExtract;
use LWP::Simple;

# Set your Yahoo! Movie list URL
my $listURL = "insert your movie list URL";

# Set the base movie URL
my $movieURL = "http://acid1.oa.yahoo.com/mbl/mov/mdet?mid=";

# Set the titles of the Yahoo! Movies table you're parsing. note
# that if the title contains HTML, so too must these headers.
my @tehs = ["#", "Movie Title", "User<br>Grade",
            "Avg. User<br>Grade", "Critics<br>Grade","Status"];
my $te = HTML::TableExtract->new(headers=>@tehs, keep_html=>1);

# Fetch the HTML
my $content = get($listURL);

my ($wml,@moviedata);

# Parse the table that matches the headers above.
$te->parse($content);
foreach my $ts ($te->table_states) {
  foreach my $r ($ts->rows) {
    next if @$r[0] =~ /grayText/; # final table footer.
    my ($title, $mid); # parse ID and title from "Movie Title" field.
    if (@$r[1] =~ m!.*?id=(.*?)"><b>(.*?)</b>.*?!gis) {
        $mid = $1; $title = $2;
    }

    my $thisMovie = {
        title   => $title,
        mid     => $mid,
        grade   => &clean_text(@$r[2]),
        avg     => &clean_text(@$r[3]),
        critics => &clean_text(@$r[4]),
        status  => &clean_text(@$r[5]),
    };
    push @moviedata, $thisMovie;
  }
}

# Assemble the WML by looping through the array of hashes
for my $i ( 0 .. scalar(@moviedata)-1) {
    $wml .= "<anchor>$moviedata[$i]{title} ";
    $wml .= "<go href=\"$movieURL$moviedata[$i]{mid}\"/>";
    $wml .= "</anchor><br />\n";
    $wml .= "<b>Status:</b> $moviedata[$i]{status}<br />\n";
    $wml .= "<b>Critics:</b> $moviedata[$i]{critics}<br />\n";
    $wml .= "<b>Users:</b> $moviedata[$i]{avg}\n";
    $wml .= "<br /><br />\n";
}

# Send final WML to the client
print "Content-Type: text/vnd.wap.wml\n\n";
```

```
print "<?xml version=\"1.0\" encoding=\"UTF-8\" ?>\n";
print "<!DOCTYPE wml PUBLIC \"-//WAPFORUM//DTD WML 1.1//EN\"";
print "\"http://www.wapforum.org/DTD/wml_1.1.xml\">\n";
print "<wml><card id=\"Menu\" title=\"Movie Wishlist\">\n";
print "<p><b>Movie Wishlist</b><br/><br />\n";
print $wml;
print "</p></card></wml>\n";

# This function removes HTML, space entities,
# linebreaks, and leading/trailing spaces from strings
sub clean_text( ) {
    my $text = shift(@_);
    $text =~ s!<.*?>!!g;
    $text =~ s! !!g;
    $text =~ s!\n!!g;
    $text =~ s!^\s+!!;
    $text =~ s!\s+$!!;
    $text =~ s!\s{16}!, !;
    return $text;
}
```

This script downloads the HTML from the URL you supply and picks relevant information from the HTML. When the script runs into a movie title, it also grabs the internal Yahoo! ID for that movie. Then, using the $movieURL as a base, the script assembles a link to that movie's detail page at Yahoo! Mobile. This means that if you're ever browsing your list on your phone and can't quite remember what that particular movie is about, you can simply click through to Yahoo!'s mobile site to get a summary of the movie.

In addition to the titles in the list, the script includes whether the movie is in theaters or on DVD, the critics' grade, and the average grade assigned by Yahoo! users.

Notice that at the end of the script, when it's printing out the WML, the content type is set as text/vnd.wap.wml. Setting this content type ensures that the device viewing the page will know how to render it. Web browsers won't be able to view the page, so you can either test it exclusively on your cell phone, or temporarily change the content type to text/xml in order to test it in a web browser.

Running the Hack

Upload *m.cgi* to a publicly available web server and bring it up in your cell phone's browser as you would any URL:

```
http://example.com/m.cgi
```

You'll have to key in the URL by hand on your phone. But most phone browsers can set bookmarks, so you can add this to your favorite mobile sites for one-click access in the future. On your phone, you should see your movie list, as shown in Figure 2-66.

Figure 2-66. A Yahoo! Movies list on a cell phone

Of course, you'll have to do the work of keeping your to-see list up-to-date. You'll need to revisit your list frequently to add movies you'd like to see or remove those you've seen. With an active list and your cell phone in your pocket, you'll never be faced with drawing a blank as you browse movies!

HACK #44 Plan Your TV Viewing

Yahoo! TV can help you plan what to watch and when to watch it.

Television is a big part of our lives; according to the Bureau of Labor Statistics, people spend about half of their leisure time watching TV. If you've ever started a long channel-surfing binge, you know that you can feel you've wasted that leisure time by the time you're done. Even though we now have hundreds of channels to choose from, it can still be hard to find something to watch.

It shouldn't be a surprise that *TV Guide* is one of the top-selling magazines in the country. It takes a bit of energy to really find what you're interested in, and Yahoo! TV can help you plan so you won't be wasting your time scanning. To get to Yahoo! TV, browse to *http://tv.yahoo.com* or type tv! into any Yahoo! Search form. Here's a look at what you'll find at the site:

TV Listings
> Enter your Zip Code at *http://tv.yahoo.com/grid*, and you'll find what shows are on each of your channels, whether you have cable, satellite, or rabbit ears. You can view shows by time and date, limit listings to certain categories, or create a custom lineup of your favorite channels.

Picks from Yahoo! Editors
> Yahoo! TV editors offer their take on the best bets for viewing, as well as brief synopses of the shows at *http://tv.yahoo.com/picks*. You can take a look at editors' choices for that day or move back or forward a few days.

TV News and Gossip
Find out what's happening in the television industry and what TV celebrities are up to. You can even read about celebrities at their worst from several different supermarket tabloids at *http://tv.yahoo.com/entgossip.*

Nielsen Ratings
Find out which shows had the highest numbers of viewers for the week, as calculated by Nielsen. You'll find the Top 20 at *http://tv.yahoo.com/nielsen.*

TV Show Database
You can look up television shows to read a brief synopsis, see photographs of the actors, and review descriptions of upcoming episodes. Browse to *http://tv.yahoo.com/db* and search alphabetically or by genre. The database contains listings for shows from the late 1980s through today.

Soap Opera Synopses
Miss an episode of your favorite soap? Browse to *http://tv.yahoo.com/soaps* and you'll be caught up on who was sleeping with whom and whether their amnesia has worn off.

Message Boards
Discuss shows with other Yahoo! users at the Yahoo! Message Boards by browsing to *http://messages.yahoo.com* and clicking the TV link under Hot Topics on the left side of the page. You can also find many Yahoo! Groups devoted to specific programs or general TV discussion at *http://tv.dir.groups.yahoo.com.*

Personalize Your Listings

One of the most useful features is personalized TV listings. To personalize your listings, bring up the Yahoo! TV site (*http://tv.yahoo.com*) and sign in with your Yahoo! ID [Hack #3] by clicking the Sign In link on the right side of the page. If you don't have a Yahoo! ID, you can still temporarily personalize the TV listings by clicking the My Listings link, but keep in mind that your listings won't be available across different browsers and computers you use without signing in, and you won't be able to save your favorite channels.

You'll need to enter your Zip Code, which will narrow your choices down to cable, broadcast, and satellite listings for your area. Choose your provider from those listed and click Go!. You should see listings for all of the channels you receive. Click the Create Personalized Listings link at the top of the page to create a list of your favorite channels. Highlight a channel on the left and click the Add button; the channel will appear in the Your Choices box on the right.

You can also set your display preferences and a preferred start time. You can either display the first 15, 30, or 45 channels, or just display your favorite channels. You can also set the start time as 7:00 or 8:00 p.m. to display prime-time shows as your default display. Setting these preferences lets Yahoo! know which listings to show in My Yahoo!.

Click Finished and you should see a list of what's currently playing on your favorite channels, as shown in Figure 2-67.

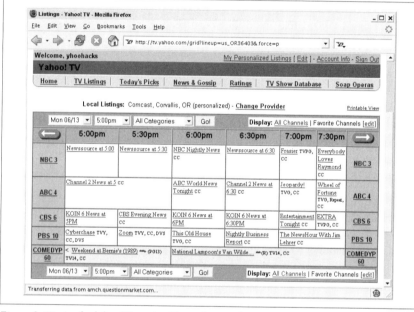

Figure 2-67. A schedule of Favorite Channels at Yahoo! TV

Once your favorites are set, you can also keep tabs on the schedule at My Yahoo! (*http://my.yahoo.com*). Figure 2-68 shows listings on My Yahoo!, with favorite channels set to begin at 8:00 p.m.

If you'd rather not visit a Yahoo! web site to view your schedule, Yahoo! doesn't offer any options for you yet. But with some Perl scripting, you can create your own options.

Email Your Listings

If you're more of an email person than a web person and prefer to read information in your inbox instead of a browser, some quick scripting can take care of that for you. This hack relies on screen scraping to gather data,

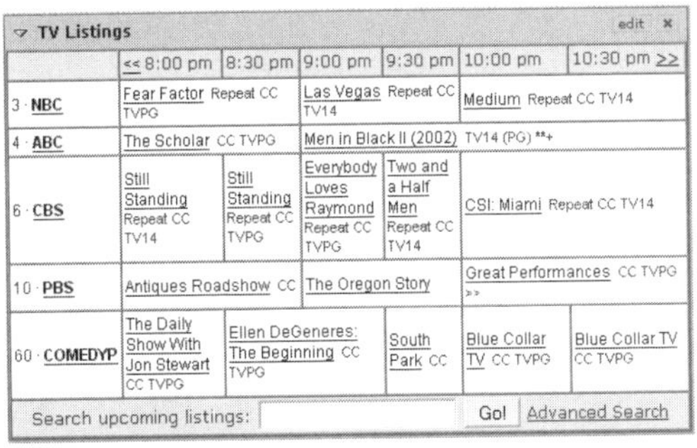

Figure 2-68. The TV Listings module at My Yahoo!

and the usual caveats apply, because any change to the HTML that Yahoo! uses to display TV listings could break this script. Be aware that you might need to tweak this code from time to time.

To run this hack, you'll need your Yahoo! TV personalized listings URL and a computer that can run Perl scripts. If you haven't already personalized your listings, you'll need to back up and set your location and TV provider. Once it's set up, browse to the Yahoo! TV front page (*http://tv.yahoo.com*) and click on the My Personalized Listings link at the top of the page. Note the URL in your browser's address bar. It should look something like this:

```
http://tv.yahoo.com/grid?lineup=us_OR36403&zip=97333
```

You'll need to add this URL to the code so the script knows where to get your listings.

The code. This code uses three modules that you might need to install. LWP::Simple handles fetching the TV listings and Net::SMTP sends the email the script builds. As you'd expect, Date::Format handles some simple date formatting.

> This script doesn't actually log in to your Yahoo! account, so you won't see your favorite channels in the email. Instead, you'll see all of the channels from your cable, satellite, or broadcast listings.

Save the following code to a file called *whats_on.pl* and include your personalized listings URL, your mail server, and your email address. You can also change the value of $starthour to get listings for another time of day. It's set to 20, which is 8:00 p.m. on a 24-hour clock, and this will give you listings for prime-time shows.

```perl
#!/usr/bin/perl
# whats_on.pl
# A script to download a Yahoo! TV schedule
# and send it via email
# Usage: whats_on.pl

use strict;
use LWP::Simple;
use Net::SMTP;
use Date::Format;

# Set your start time in 24-hour hh format
my $starthour = 20;

# Set the Yahoo! TV URL
my $url = "insert your personalized listings URL";
    $url .= "&starthour=$starthour&prt=1";

# Set email info
my $subject = "On TV Tonight";
my $smtp_server = "insert your mail server";
my $from_email = 'insert your email address';
my $to_email = 'insert your email address';

# Grab the Yahoo! TV listings page and
my $body = get($url);
my ($lastchannel,$out);

# Build the email by looping through the HTML
# and picking out the important stuff
my $regex = '<td.*?>.*?<a href=".*?chname=(.*?)&.*?progutn=(.*?)&';
    $regex .= '.*?">(.*?)</a>.*?</td>';
my $out = "On TV tonight--";
while ($body =~ m!$regex!gis) {
    my $channel = $1;
    my $channel_f = $1;
    my $time = $2;
    my $title = $3;
    if ($lastchannel ne $channel) {
        $channel_f =~ s!\+(\d{1,2})! \($1\)!;
        $out .= "\n\n$channel_f\n\n";
    }
    my $airtime = time2str("%l:%M", $time);
    $out .= "  $airtime $title\n";
    $lastchannel = $channel;
}

# Send the schedule via email
my $dtm = time2str("%m%d%Y%T", time);
my $smtp = Net::SMTP->new($smtp_server);
$smtp->hello($smtp_server);
$smtp->mail($from_email);
$smtp->to($to_email);
$smtp->data();
$smtp->datasend("From: $from_email\n");
```

```
$smtp->datasend("To: $to_email\n");
$smtp->datasend("Subject: $subject\n");
$smtp->datasend("Message-Id: tv.yahoo.com-sched-$dtm\@$smtp_server\n");
$smtp->datasend('Content-Type: text/plain;');
$smtp->datasend("\n\n");
$smtp->datasend($out);
$smtp->dataend();
$smtp->quit;

# Close output file
close(FILE);
```

Notice that $url holds your personalized listings URL and adds a couple of querystring variables and values, including starthour and prt=1, which sets the page to the Printable View on Yahoo!, which is easier to scrape.

The $regex variable holds the patterns the script uses to find the relevant bits of information in the HTML, and you might need to adjust this regular expression if Yahoo! modifies their HTML.

Running the hack. To run this script once, you can just call it from the command line, like this:

```
perl whats_on.pl
```

To really take advantage of the script, set it to run daily with the Windows Scheduler or by adding a cron job on Unix-based machines. Once set, you'll receive daily emails like the one shown in Figure 2-69, with the prime-time TV schedule listed by channel.

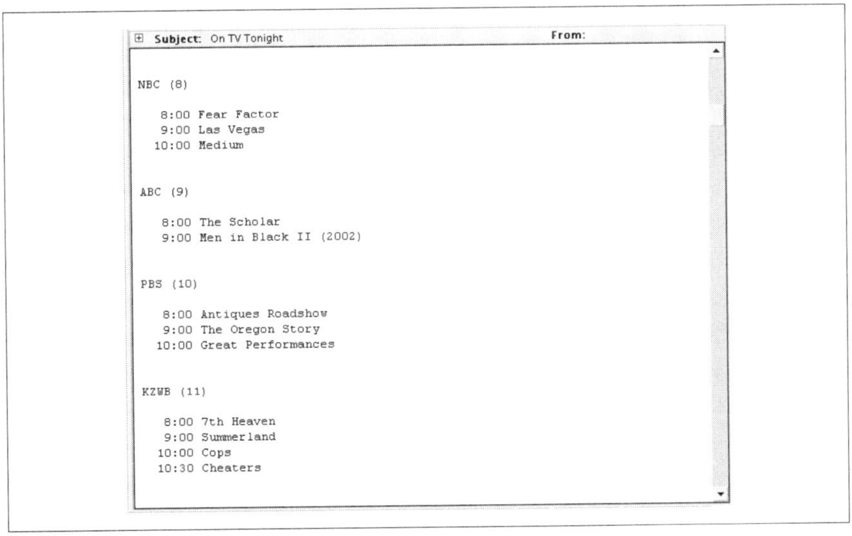

Figure 2-69. TV listings email

The text listing in the email is simple and includes only the channel, time, and program name. If you like to read information in your inbox, though, it's a no-frills way to find out what's going to be on TV.

HACK #45 Create a TV Watch List
Combine Yahoo! TV with Yahoo! Calendar to build a custom TV schedule.

You can find lots of information about upcoming television shows at Yahoo! TV [Hack #44]. By clicking on a program title in your personalized listings, you can find a brief synopsis of the show, members of the cast, and even directors and producers. And, of course, Yahoo! lets you search this information. Browse to Yahoo! TV (*http://tv.yahoo.com*) and you'll see the search form labeled "Search listings by Keyword."

Imagine you're a Tom Hanks fan and you'd like to find out when a show or movie he's been in will be on. Type "Tom Hanks" into the form, and click Go!. Note that the quotes are important when you're looking for a full phrase. You'll see a list of shows that Tom Hanks appears in within the next 14 days, as shown in Figure 2-70.

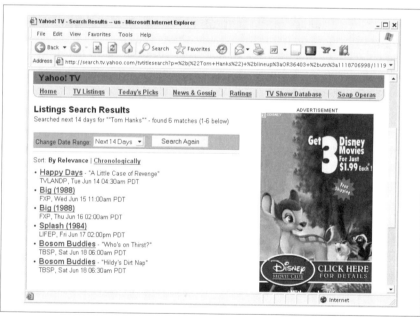

Figure 2-70. Yahoo! TV listings search results for "Tom Hanks"

Who knew he was in old episodes of *Happy Days*? Click a title in the results and you'll find the detail page for the program. Alongside the channel and air time, you'll see an "Add to My Calendar" link. This link lets you add the show as an event on your Yahoo! Calendar so that you can track the shows you'd like to watch. And once a show is an event on your calendar, you'll receive reminders about the event in your email, which can help you remember to catch the show when it airs.

You could run the search for Tom Hanks yourself every couple of weeks at Yahoo! TV and add any programs that look interesting. But this hack shows you how to be lazy, letting a script do the work for you. In fact, this hack will run a Yahoo! TV search for any keyword and add *every* result to your Yahoo! Calendar. Then you can visit your Yahoo! Calendar periodically to see what Yahoo! has suggested that you view based on your favorite keyword.

The Code

This hack relies on the web automation module WWW::Mechanize (called Mech) and the WWW::Yahoo::Login module. This code logs in to Yahoo! TV with your Yahoo! ID and password, searches for the provided keyword, and adds all of the results to your Yahoo! Calendar. To get started, add the following code to a file called *tv_watchlist.pl* and include your Yahoo! ID and password in the code:

```perl
#!/usr/bin/perl
# tv_watchlist.pl
# A script to gather programs from a Yahoo! TV search
# and add them to a Yahoo! Calendar
# Usage: tv_watchlist.pl <query>

use strict;
use WWW::Yahoo::Login qw( login logout );
use WWW::Mechanize;

# Set your account info
my $user = "insert Yahoo! ID";
my $pass = "insert Yahoo! Password";
my $count = 0;

# Grab the incoming query
my $query = join(' ', @ARGV) or die "Usage: tv_watchlist.pl <query>\n";

# Set login URL
my $url = 'http://e.my.yahoo.com/config/login?';
   $url .= '.intl=us&.src=tv&.done=http%3a//tv.yahoo.com/';
   $url .= 'grid%3f.force=p%26setlineupcookie=true';

# Log into Yahoo! TV
my $mech = WWW::Mechanize->new( );
my $login = login(
      mech    => $mech,
      uri     => $url,
```

```
        user    => $user,
        pass    => $pass,
    );

    # If login succeeded, add each program to calendar
    if ($login) {
        my $form = $mech->form_number(3);
        $mech->field("title", "\"$query\"");
        $mech->click();
        my $response = $mech->response()->content;
        while ($response =~ m!<a href="(http://tv.*?tvpdb.*?)">.*?</a>!gis) {
            my $showlink = $1;
            $showlink =~ s!\n!!gs;
            $mech->get( $showlink );
            $mech->follow_link( url_regex => qr/calendar/ );
            $mech->follow_link( text_regex => qr/Add to/ );
            my $result = $mech->response()->content;
            if ($result =~ m!<div class="alertbox">(.*?)</div>!gis) {
                $count++;
                my $msg = $1;
                $msg =~ s!<.*?>!!gs;
                $msg =~ s!\n!!gs;
                print "$msg\n";
            }
        }
    } else {
            warn $WWW::Yahoo::Login::ERROR;
    }

    if ($count == 0) {
        print "No shows added.";
    }
```

Because adding shows from Yahoo! TV search results to a Yahoo! Calendar
can be accomplished by clicking a predictable series of links, the Mech function `follow_link` does most of the work in this script. A simple regular
expression for either the URL or text of a link on the page tells Mech which
links to follow.

Running the Hack

To run the hack, call it from the command line and pass in a search term.
Remember to enclose complete phrases in quotes, like this:

```
perl tv_watchlist.pl "Tom Hanks"
```

As the script runs, it will print a message with any shows added to your calendar, or—if no shows were found—the message "No shows added." You
can pipe the output of the script to another file if you'd like to keep a log of
the script's activities. Simply call the script, like so:

```
perl tv_watchlist.pl "Tom Hanks" > tv_watchlist.log
```

Figure 2-71 shows a Yahoo! Calendar with Tom Hanks shows automatically added. Each listing includes the time of the show and the channel it's on. You can even hover over a program title to see a brief synopsis of the show. And, of course, you can click the title to alter or delete the event.

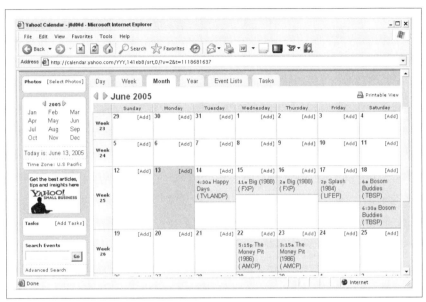

Figure 2-71. TV shows with Tom Hanks on a Yahoo! Calendar

If you set the script to run every 14 days in Windows Scheduler or as a cron job, you can simply visit your Yahoo! Calendar to keep up with the watch list, or let the Yahoo! Calendar autoreminders send email messages that include program times.

HACK

Develop and Share a Trip Itinerary
#46

Yahoo! Trip Planner can help you organize an excursion and let you share your travel plans with others.

Type travel! into any Yahoo! Search form and you'll find yourself at Yahoo! Travel (*http://travel.yahoo.com*): a one-stop shop for planning vacations or business trips. You can find flights, hotels, and rental cars. You can read reviews from other Yahoo! users and look for special travel deals.

Yahoo! Travel includes a feature called Trip Planner (*http://travel.yahoo.com/ trip*) that can help you create a personalized travel guide that you can access at any time or share with others. Imagine you find yourself in charge of organizing a group trip for students; you could enter your itinerary into the Trip Planner and share it with students, parents, and teachers. Instead of printing and distributing pages of information, you can add everything at Yahoo! and pass around a URL for the itinerary. Even a smaller group going on a family vacation could benefit from having hotel, restaurant, and sightseeing details in one place.

Create a Trip

To start a custom trip, browse to *http://travel.yahoo.com/trip* and click the "Create your first trip" link. You can add a name, description, and dates for the trip into the form, as shown in Figure 2-72.

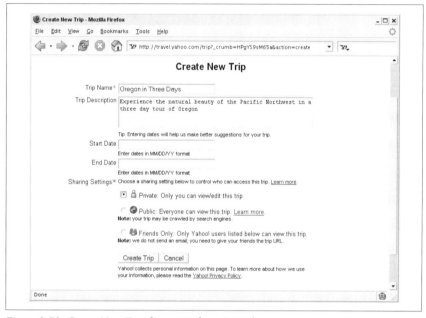

Figure 2-72. Create New Trip form at Yahoo! Trip Planner

You'll need to choose how you want to share your trip. Each trip can be Public, Private, or for a list of specific Yahoo! IDs. As you're building the trip, you might want to leave this setting as Private. You can change the sharing settings for a trip at any point in the future.

> Be aware that setting a trip as Public means anyone can view the details of the trip. If your trip includes notes with personally identifiable information and the dates you'll be traveling, you could be letting the world know when you won't be home!

Your new trip is a container that can hold all of your trip plans. You can add just about anything you find at Yahoo! Travel to a trip, such as restaurants, hotels, and tourist attractions. Keep an eye out for the "Save to Trip" link as you browse or search Yahoo! Travel, and click the link to add anything you find interesting to an existing trip. Figure 2-73 shows a list of things to do around Newport, Oregon, and each listing includes the "Save to Trip" link.

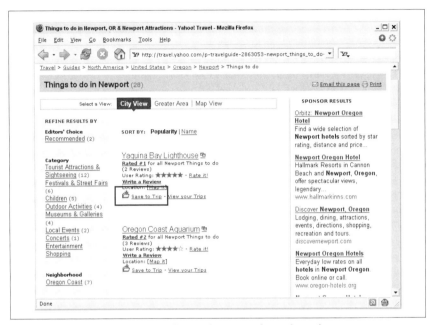

Figure 2-73. The "Save to Trip" link on Yahoo! Travel search results

If you can't find a particular location or event in Yahoo! Travel, you can add it as a custom item to your itinerary. For example, a stop at a relative's house for tea isn't going to appear in Yahoo! Travel, but there's no reason you can't add it yourself.

To add a custom trip item, browse to the Trip Planner and click the title of your trip to view the trip page. On the right side of the trip page, you'll find a box labeled "Add Items to Your Trip." Click the "Add your own custom items" link, and you'll see a form like the one in Figure 2-74.

Select the trip the item should be included with and then choose a category for the item. You can choose from Entertainment, Hotel, Restaurant, Shopping, "Things to do," or Other. Once you've chosen a name for the item, you can include as few or as many details as you'd like, including URL, phone number, and address.

Yahoo! Travel also provides a bookmarklet for adding custom items to your trip. You can find the bookmarklet on the right side of your trip page. To install, drag the bookmarklet link to your bookmarks. Then, when you're

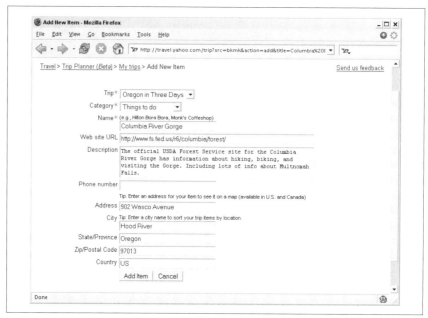

Figure 2-74. Adding a custom item to an itinerary

browsing a site and would like to add it as an item to your trip, click the bookmarklet and the item name and the URL will be filled in for you.

Personalize the Trip

Once you have the hotels, restaurants, and any custom stops listed in your trip, you can take some time to personalize them by adding a schedule, categorizing the items, or adding custom notes.

To personalize the trip, browse to the trip page and review the items. Each item should have three links directly under the listing: "Edit notes," "Edit tags," and "Add dates." As you click any of these links, a window will pop up to let you add personal information. For example, click the "Add dates" link under a restaurant to choose the day of the trip you'll be visiting and whether it's for Breakfast, Brunch, Lunch, Dinner, or Other, as shown in Figure 2-75.

Click Update when you're finished, and the item will be scheduled. You can schedule other items in a similarly intuitive way. Hotels list the check-in and check-out dates, and attractions can be listed as Morning, Afternoon, All Day, or Other. You can't list precise times for each item in the itinerary, but then what trip ever goes exactly as planned?

If you want to add specific times to a particular item, you can add the times as part of a note. Notes are any arbitrary text you'd like to associate with an

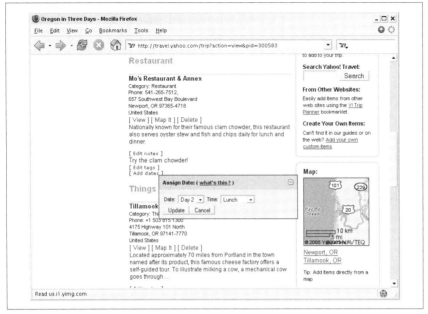

Figure 2-75. Assigning a date to a restaurant item

item. This can be anything from information that only you have about a particular location to warnings about a location that aren't included in the listing.

To add another layer of organization to the trip, you can give each item a set of arbitrary keywords called *tags*. For example, you might want to tag every item in a particular city with the name of that city. Or you might want to tag every activity planned for Friday with the word *Friday*. People viewing the itinerary can sort items by tag, so they can zoom in on one aspect of the trip.

You can also add custom map views to your trip. Browse to your trip page and click Map View at the top of the page. Adjust the map by zooming in or out and choosing attractions to list. Once you have a map view you'd like to share with the group, click the "Save this map" link above the map, as shown in Figure 2-76.

Once you add the map to your trip, it will be available to anyone viewing the trip. Plus, you can add notes and tags to the map to add detailed explanation or group the map with other items in your trip.

As you can see, the Yahoo! Travel Trip Planner provides a way for you to be your own travel agent and share detailed plans with others. Plus, each stop in the itinerary links to web sites with more information, giving your travel mates the ability to do their own research about areas they'll be visiting. And storing the travel plans on Yahoo! means the itinerary will be available anywhere there's an Internet connection.

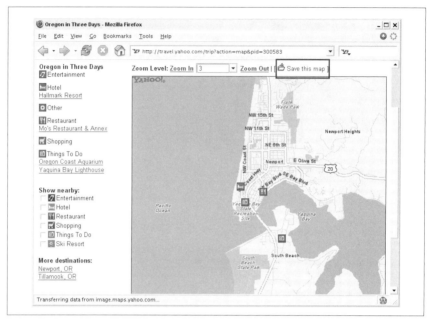

Figure 2-76. Yahoo! Trip Map View with the "Save this map" link

Shop Intelligently

H A C K
#47   Use Yahoo! Shopping to find and compare products across the Web.

Shopping is more of an art than a science. Finding the right item at the right price involves a bit of intuition and luck. But there's no reason you can't bring a bit of science into your shopping habits to help you find, compare, and buy. Imagine you're interested in purchasing a portable music player, but you're not sure which to buy or where to buy it. You could physically drive to your local electronics stores and browse, but you'd miss out on the benefit of choices beyond what they have in stock and you wouldn't have instant access to information about each of the products and their differences. You could browse to your favorite online stores, but you'd only find prices at each individual outlet.

Just as Yahoo! brings together thousands of news sources at Yahoo! News (*http://news.yahoo.com*) and millions of web pages at Yahoo! Search (*http://search.yahoo.com*), Yahoo! Shopping (*http://shopping.yahoo.com*) indexes merchants across the Web to find prices for thousands of products. Instead of typing portable music player into Yahoo! Search and sifting through hundreds of results to find online stores, you can search or browse Yahoo! Shopping and see prices at merchants that Yahoo! has approved. In addition to finding and comparing prices, you can add items from multiple merchants to a wish list and compare product features side by side.

Find

There are several ways to find products at Yahoo! Shopping, whether you know exactly what you're looking for, want to browse from products available, or want suggestions for special occasions.

Searching. Type portable music player into the search form at *http://shopping.yahoo.com*, and each result will be a specific product. You can click each result to see more product details and compare prices across different merchants, or you can select several results and compare differences in the product features. The search form is also handy if you already know the product you're looking for.

> You can click the Advanced Search link next to the search form (or point your browser to *http://shopping.yahoo.com/search/advanced*) to narrow your search results to a specific product category or price range.

Browsing. If you don't know quite what you're looking for, you can use the categories on the left side of the Yahoo! Shopping home page to narrow your search. Or browse directly to *http://shopping.yahoo.com/directory.html* to see a list of all categories, as shown in Figure 2-77.

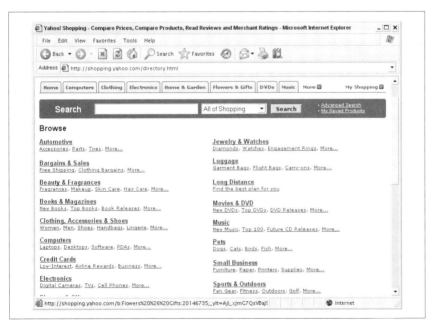

Figure 2-77. Browsing categories at Yahoo! Shopping

For example, you can browse to the category Electronics and select the subcategory MP3 Players to see links with more information about players, lists by brand, and a list of the top five players. Browsing for products gives you a few more options along the way than simply viewing a list of individual products.

Gift Finder. When you're shopping for someone else, it can be hard to come up with ideas. Yahoo! Gift Finder (*http://shopping.yahoo.com/giftfinder*) will give you product suggestions based on information you provide in a short questionnaire. Browse to the Gift Finder, choose an occasion (birthday, wedding, specific holiday, etc.), and then answer several questions about the gift recipient. The Gift Finder will give you a series of options to look through.

SmartSort. SmartSort (*http://shopping.yahoo.com/smartsort*) is a tool that lets you specify the importance of different product features and returns a list based on your criteria. At the time of this writing, SmartSort supports only electronic gadgets, but it can help you decide which gadgets to buy. Say you're interested in digital cameras and are most concerned about a compact size. You can specify that criteria in SmartSort and see a list of possibilities, as shown in Figure 2-78.

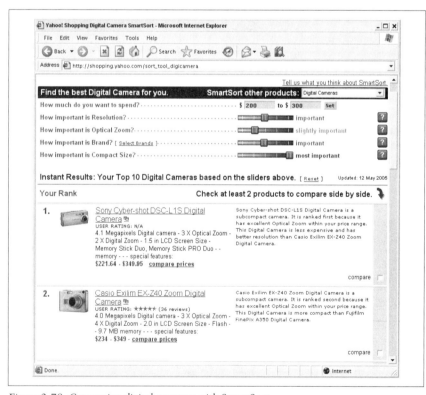

Figure 2-78. Comparing digital cameras with SmartSort

Internet Explorer users will see sliders at the top of the SmartSort page that they can adjust to affect the results, while users of other browsers will see a series of radio buttons.

Product feeds. Yahoo! also provides RSS for various product categories, and you can see a full list of feeds available at *http://shopping.yahoo.com/rss*. If you're not quite ready to buy a portable music player today but want to keep your eye on the market, you can subscribe to the MP3 Player feed and see new products in your newsreader or at My Yahoo!.

Compare

As you're browsing or searching products, you can check the Compare box next to many products and then click the "Compare side by side" button at the bottom of the page. This will show you the selected products together on one page, with a list of features compared. Figure 2-79 shows two digital cameras side by side.

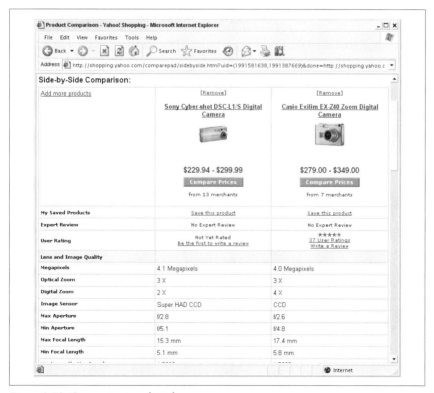

Figure 2-79. Comparing two digital cameras

Shop Intelligently

Once you've found a product you're interested in, you can click the product title to visit the product detail page. Figure 2-80 shows a product detail page for a 20GB iPod.

Figure 2-80. An iPod product detail page

The product detail page provides links to more information, such as specifications and reviews. But most importantly, it prices across different merchants. You can scan the page to find the lowest price and view merchant ratings.

 Merchant ratings at Yahoo! Shopping are based on the reviews of Yahoo! users. If you've had a positive or negative experience with a merchant listed at Yahoo! Shopping, you can click the "Write a review" link to add your own rating and comments for that merchant.

When you're ready to buy, click the Buying Info button to leave the Yahoo! Shopping site and visit the merchant's page for that product. From there, you can follow that merchant's procedure for buying the item.

Save and Share

Another unique feature of Yahoo! Shopping is the ability to save products from many different merchants to a single shopping list. Instead of maintaining multiple wish lists across different sites, you can store the items at Yahoo! Shopping by clicking the "Save and Share" link next to any product listing. Once an item is on your wish list, you can keep tabs on the price and add your own notes about the product, shown in Figure 2-81.

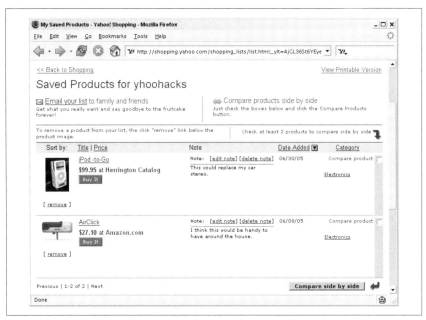

Figure 2-81. Saving products from different merchants to a wish list

And, of course, it wouldn't be a wish list if you couldn't share it with others. Click the "Email your listings" link at the top of the page to send an email like the one shown in Figure 2-82.

Sharing exactly what you want with others means you can get exactly what you want the next time a special occasion rolls around.

Yahoo! Shopping won't make the art of finding the perfect item obsolete, but it can help you make informed choices by showing you what's available, by comparing the product with similar items, and by letting you share the products you've found with others.

HACK #48 Visualize Your Music Collection

Use the Yahoo! Music Engine API to find out which artists appear most often in your collection.

Visualizing an entire music collection has never been easy. Whether the music is in stacks of vinyl records or in racks full of CDs, it's tough to get a picture of all of the artists, albums, and genres that are so unique to each of us. Moving music from the physical world to the digital world of computers has helped, because digital formats can store information about albums and artists that can be extracted and analyzed.

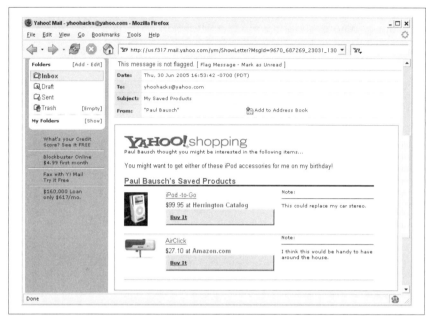

Figure 2-82. Yahoo! Shopping wish list email

This hack helps you visualize your virtual music collection by showing you a list of artists in different font sizes: the larger the font, the more tracks you have by that artist. With this approach, you can see at a glance whether you have more tracks by Kraftwerk or The Propellerheads, and which artists you have the most tracks from.

Using different-sized fonts to represent popularity is sometimes called a *tag map* and was pioneered by the photo-sharing site Flickr **[Hack #67]**.

> You can see the most popular photo tags on Flickr in this
> format at *http://www.flickr.com/photos/tags*.

This hack creates a tag map–like interface for the artists in your music collection by tapping into the Yahoo! Music Engine.

Yahoo! Music Engine

The Yahoo! Music Engine (YME) is a free music player for Windows. It's available for download at *http://music.yahoo.com/musicengine*. If you already use WinAmp or iTunes, you'll find the YME very familiar, and the controls should be intuitive. You can use it alongside your current player or use YME exclusively. If you already have a collection of music files on your computer, you can import them to YME by choosing File → "Add a Folder to My

Music." Once your music has been imported, you can click My Music on the left side and see all of the tracks in your collection.

One feature that separates YME from the pack is its *plug-in* architecture operating behind the scenes. A plug-in is a bit of code that adds a feature to an application that wasn't originally built into the system. Yahoo! has made plug-ins fairly easy to write by making their API available through Java-Script. And because YME contains a web browser, it's possible to write a web page that can control and interact with YME through scripting.

If you're familiar with writing JavaScript for web pages, you'll find writing YME plug-ins fairly painless. In fact, Yahoo! has a page specifically for web developers, explaining how to use HTML and JavaScript to write plug-ins for YME (*http://mep.music.yahoo.com/plugins/docs/webquickstart_page.html*).

The following code is a sample plug-in that you can build and install for YME that helps you visualize the artists in your music collection by popularity.

The Code

The code for this plug-in was written by Dave Brown at Yahoo! and is a standard HTML page with JavaScript. The script queries the YME data-base, gathering a list of the artists in your library. From there, the script counts how many tracks you have from each artist and displays the artist names in the appropriate font size.

To get started, save the following code to a file called *artistCloud.html*:

```
<html>
<head>
<style>
body {
    background-color:#fff;
    font-family:Tahoma, Verdana, Arial;
    color:#354251;
}
.tag {
    margin-bottom: 10px;
    padding: 5px;
}
</style>
</head>

<body>

<script>
// This YME plug-in looks through a music library and prints the names
// of the artists in a font which is proportional to the number of songs
// which are by that artist in the library.
//
// by Dave Brown at Yahoo!
```

```
var minFontSize = 8; // minimum font size in pixels
var maxFontSize = 24; // max font size in pixels
var METADATA_ARTIST = 0; // you should really get this constant from yme.js
                         // available from the Developer SDK.

// Obtain YME's media database which holds the library of tracks:
var mediaDB = window.external.MediaDatabase;

// Get the string name of the artist field, which is used in our database ⏎
queries:
var artistFieldName = mediaDB.Description.GetPredefinedName(METADATA_⏎
ARTIST);

// Get a listing of all unique artist names:
var artistNames = mediaDB.GetUniqueIndexValues(artistFieldName);
var numArtistNames = artistNames.Count;

// For each artist, get a count of how many tracks are by that artist,
// and store it in our array...like a histogram.
// Also store the maximum value we encounter, so we can normalize ⏎
everything.
// (We do normalization because some people may have a large variance of
// tracks per artist, and others a small variance.)

var tracksPerArtist = new Array(numArtistNames);
var maxTracksPerArtist = 0;

for ( i = 0; i < numArtistNames; ++i )
{
    // Get the # of objects in the database for each artist:
    var objectsForArtist = mediaDB.IndexQuery( artistFieldName, ⏎
artistNames(i) );

    // Remember this...
    tracksPerArtist[i] = objectsForArtist.Count;

    // Do we have a new max?
    if ( tracksPerArtist[i] > maxTracksPerArtist )
        maxTracksPerArtist = tracksPerArtist[i];
}

// Print the artists...
for ( i = 0; i < numArtistNames; ++i )
{
    // Set the font size
    var fontSize = minFontSize + Math.floor( maxFontSize * ⏎
(tracksPerArtist[i] / maxTracksPerArtist) );

    // Print the artist:
    document.writeln( "<span class='tag' style='font-size:" + fontSize + ⏎
"px'>" + artistNames(i) + "</span>" );
    }
}
</script>
</body>
</html>
```

Running the Hack

Browse to the directory where you installed YME (usually *C:\Program Files\ Yahoo!\Yahoo! Music Engine*) and save *artistCloud.html* to the *Plugins* directory.

All YME plug-ins are added via the Windows Registry, so you'll need to add a Registry key that defines your plug-in. The following Registry file code will add the necessary information to your Registry. Create a file called *YME_artistCloud.reg* with the following code and be sure to add the correct path to your YME installation:

```
Windows Registry Editor Version 5.00

[HKEY_LOCAL_MACHINE\SOFTWARE\Yahoo\YMP\Plugins\ArtistCloud]
"Enabled"=dword:00000001
"Type"=dword:00000001
"URL"="file://C:\\path to YME\\Plugins\\artistCloud.html"
"Name"="ArtistCloud"
"Description"="Display a list of artists as a tag cloud."
"BitmapFile"="C:\\path to YME\\Plugins\\artistCloud.bmp"
```

Note that there's a setting for `BitmapFile` that points to *artistCloud.bmp*, but the file won't exist unless you create it. `BitmapFile` specifies a 16×16 pixel icon for a plug-in, and you'll need to create your own icon and throw it into the *Plugins* directory if you want a visual ID for your plug-in.

Save the Registry file and double-click the file to add the Registry settings. You'll need to completely restart YME, so click its icon in the system tray and choose Exit. Once it's restarted, you should see the option ArtistCloud in the right column. Click it, and you'll see a list of your artists like the one shown in Figure 2-83.

The ArtistCloud plug-in gives you a new way to visualize your music collection, and you can see at a glance which artists created the most tracks in your collection.

Hacking the Hack

By slightly tweaking the script, you can create a similar tag cloud for the various genres in your collection. Create a copy of *artistCloud.html* called *genreCloud.html*. Edit it to change the value of METADATA_ARTIST to 9, like so:

```
var METADATA_ARTIST = 9;
```

In reality, the number 9 refers to the API variable METADATA_GENRE, and this little tweak is fast, but it doesn't make for readable code. Copy the new file to the YME *Plugins* directory.

> If you want to see a list of all the API variables and their values, take a look at *http://plugins.yme.music.yahoo.com/ plugins/docs/yme.js*.

Figure 2-83. A cloud of artists in Yahoo! Music Engine

Likewise, copy *YME_artistCloud.reg* and edit the file so that every reference to ArtistCloud becomes GenreCloud. Name the file *YME_genreCloud.reg* and run the file. Restart YME, and you should see the GenreCloud plug-in, which you can click to see if Rock beats out Country in your collection, and if Electronic music is more prevalent than Punk.

TraxStats

As you might expect, a number of people are creating plug-ins and sharing them with the world. Yahoo! has an *official unofficial* site for sharing plug-ins at *http://plugins.yme.music.yahoo.com*. One of the plug-ins available at the site, TraxStats by Larry Wang (*http://plugins.yme.music.yahoo.com/archives/2005/03/traxstats.html*), can help you gather statistics about your collection.

Once you download and install the plug-in, you can get some quick reports about your collection. Figure 2-84 shows the number of songs for each artist in a list.

YME is making plug-in development easier for developers and designers, and this might bring about entirely new ways for us to visualize our personal music collections.

Figure 2-84. Viewing the number of songs per artist with TraxStats

HACK #49 Take Yahoo! on the Go

Yahoo! Mobile lets you take much of the power of Yahoo! with you.

Yahoo! Mobile gives you a subset of Yahoo! features for devices with small form factors such as your mobile phone or personal digital assistant (PDA). Yahoo! Mobile is optimized for relatively slow wireless data connections similar to analog modem speeds. Many phones already provide a link to Yahoo! Mobile in the phone's browser, but if you don't spot a link, you can point your phone to *http://mobile.yahoo.com*.

Yahoo! Lite

When you browse to Yahoo! Mobile on your phone, you'll find a simplified home page with many familiar Yahoo! features, such as Search, News, Weather, Sports, and Movies. You'll also see a link that allows you to log in with your Yahoo! ID and password. Once you log in, you'll see personalized options like the ones shown in Figure 2-85.

If you have Yahoo! Mail, Yahoo! Finance portfolios, Yahoo! Movies theater preferences, and other customizations at the Yahoo! web site, you'll find them on Yahoo! Mobile as well.

Some mobile device browsers (such as the Microsoft Internet Explorer for Windows Mobile PCs and Smartphone devices) do not store the Yahoo web

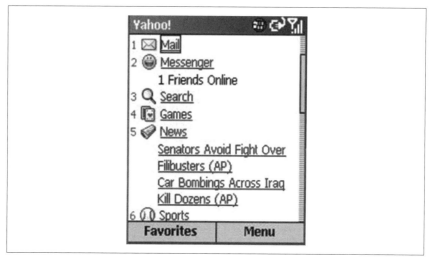

Figure 2-85. Yahoo! Mobile portal page

cookies that allow a login session to persist when you revisit the Yahoo! Mobile page again. If this is the case for your PDA or phone, you might want to consider choosing a password that can be quickly entered using whatever data input options you have (e.g., phone keypad, thumb keyboard, handwriting recognition, etc.). Always keep the security implications for your account [Hack #3] in mind.

Yahoo! Mobile lets you choose the amount of graphics that appears on your mobile device. Figure 2-85 shows a screen from a Microsoft Windows Mobile Smartphone device with the Lite Graphics option turned on. Use this setting if you have a relatively slow wireless data connection such as GPRS, which is about the same speed as some analog 56Kbps modem connections. Scroll to the bottom of the Yahoo! Mobile home page on your phone to change the graphics settings.

Yahoo! Mobile Features

Any of the options on the Yahoo! Mobile home page can be selected by either scrolling through the list or pressing the number on the keypad associated with an option. Here's a closer look at each feature and how it differs from what you'll find on the more familiar Yahoo! web site. Keep in mind that some features listed here aren't available for all mobile devices. You can find out which services are available for your phone or PDA by registering the device via your computer's web browser at the Yahoo! Mobile web site (*http://mobile.yahoo.com*).

Mail

Yahoo! Mail can display up to 200 messages on a single web page when used with a conventional desktop browser. However, Yahoo! Mobile Mail is limited to 10 messages per screen, numbered 1 through 0 (0 is used for the 10th message). The email text body is also truncated and might require several screen updates to display a long email message. You can use the Yahoo! Address Book to retrieve email addresses when composing an email message.

> If the web-based email doesn't fit your work style, subscribing to the Yahoo! Plus premium service allows you to use your mobile device's POP3 email facility to retrieve Yahoo! Mail.

Messenger

The Yahoo! Messenger option works only on mobile devices that directly support it. Choosing it on an unsupported device such as a Microsoft Windows Mobile–based Pocket PC results in a blank screen.

Search

The Yahoo! Mobile Search page gives you a subset of search types, including Local, Images, and Web searches. The Video, Directory, News, and Shopping searches found on the desktop are not provided as search options.

Games

Six low-resolution (mostly text) games are available: Wordaholic, Blackjack, Video Poker, Hangman, 4-In-A-Row, and Dice Slider.

News

The News article selection is as comprehensive as the desktop Yahoo! News option. Thumbnail photographs might be presented along with the text. Selecting the thumbnail photo displays a larger version of the photograph.

Sports

Sports news and scores are provided in extremely brief forms. The scores for a particular game might provide only the score itself and not the more detailed team and individual statistics that many fans crave.

Finance

The portfolios you set up in a desktop browser all show up in Yahoo! Mobile. Drilling down to a specific company results in basic trade information, such as range and volume. You can also get company-specific news and a graphic trading chart for the day.

Weather

A brief version of your local weather is shown and linked at the top level of Yahoo! Mobile. Selecting that link gives you more detailed weather information. The My Weather page shows you eight of your selected cities at a time.

Movies

The Movies option shows you a list of current popular movies. Selecting a movie link leads you to a list of schedules of local theaters showing the movie as well as a summary of the movie itself.

Driving Directions

This feature has a default starting address (your home, for example) and lets you fill in a destination address. The driving directions are provided only in text. Graphic maps are not provided.

Address Book

The Address Book contains all the addresses found in the desktop browser version. One added bonus for phone users is that telephone numbers are presented using the tel: tag. If your phone browser supports it, selecting the web-linked telephone number initiates a voice call to that number.

Calendar

The Calendar shows you tasks and events. The events list can be viewed by day, week, or month.

The Yahoo! Mobile Search screen in Figure 2-86 shows you how Yahoo! reformats the screen for mobile devices. This simplified view lets you work quickly on a small screen.

Figure 2-86. Yahoo! Mobile Search

If you want to browse the Yahoo! Mobile site in a web browser on your desktop before you try it on your phone, visit *http://wap.oa.yahoo.com*. This will give you a chance to try out the features with a quick connection before you need them in the wild. You won't find everything from Yahoo! on your mobile device, but you'll get the basics with Yahoo! Mobile. Many times when you're traveling, that's all you need.

—Todd Ogasawara

Stay Connected with Yahoo! Alerts

#50 Yahoo! Alerts send information that's important to you, when and where you need it.

Alerts are small text messages sent from Yahoo! that can let you know everything from how much snow fell at your favorite ski resort last night, to how a particular stock is faring in the middle of the day, to who was the winner at the end of a ballgame. The key is that alerts keep you up-to-date with information whether you're sitting in front of your computer or out in the world.

To start receiving alerts, all you have to do is let Yahoo! know what you'd like to be alerted about and how you'd like to receive the alert: via email, instant message, or mobile device.

Setting up Alert Devices

The simplest way to start receiving alerts is via any email address, including your Yahoo! Mail address. When you create an alert, specify Email as the delivery method and choose one of the addresses associated with your Yahoo! ID.

Need to add or change an email address associated with your Yahoo! ID? Browse to *http://edit.yahoo.com/config/eval_profile* and log in to add or remove email addresses from your account.

With a bit more work, you can also receive Yahoo! Alerts on a cell phone or pager that supports SMS messages. Before you can set a mobile alert, you'll need to visit *http://mobile.yahoo.com* to associate a mobile device with your Yahoo! ID. From Yahoo! Mobile, you can find out if your device can accept alerts and verify your device so that Yahoo! knows you've authorized it to send alerts. Once set up, you can choose Mobile as the delivery method for an alert. Figure 2-87 shows a weather alert for Corvallis, Oregon, sent to a mobile device.

Figure 2-87. A mobile weather alert for Corvallis, Oregon

You can also receive some alerts via Yahoo! Instant Messenger. Download Yahoo! Instant Messenger at *http://messenger.yahoo.com*, set up an account, and choose Messenger as the delivery method for an alert. Then, any Instant Messenger alerts will pop up on your screen while you're at the computer.

Many alerts also let you choose multiple delivery methods. So, if you have all three device types set up, you could set an alert to give you breaking news from the Associated Press via email, instant messenger, and your pager!

Setting Alerts

As you're browsing around Yahoo! sites such as Yahoo! Travel, Yahoo! Shopping, or Yahoo! Finance, you might see a ringing bell icon and a Set Alert link, as shown in Figure 2-88.

Figure 2-88. Set Alert link at Yahoo! Finance

Clicking this link is the fastest way to set an alert related to the content you're viewing. If you're browsing the San Francisco section of Yahoo! Travel, you can simply click Set Alert to be notified of the best travel fares to the city.

You can also set up alerts by browsing to *http://alerts.yahoo.com* and look-ing through the alerts directory. Here's a sampling of the available alerts:

Auctions
Select an alert based on the category of auction entry, the seller, or a keyword. Searches Yahoo! Auctions and can send updates immediately or summarize once or twice daily.

Avatars
Get updates on new clothes, backgrounds, or any new items for your Yahoo! Instant Messenger avatar.

Best Fares
Select your favorite route and be alerted when the fare drops or increases by $25 or more from the current fare—or if the price goes below a selected amount.

Breaking News
Choose between standard Associated Press alerts with frequent updates or the AP Bulletin, which focuses on the biggest breaking news stories.

Health News
Use these alerts to get health news for words or phrases that you spec-ify. For example, a *diabetes* alert will send summaries of new diabetes-related articles.

Horoscopes
Set your astrological sign and a time to receive your daily horoscope.

Yahoo! Mail
Receive an alert when new mail arrives at your Yahoo! Mail account (available for wireless devices only).

Missing Children
Enter your Zip Code, and you'll be notified of any Missing Children Alerts issued within your area. You might be able to help if you have any information.

News
Subscribe to breaking news alerts, keyword news alerts, and top news within selected categories.

Snowfall
Receive notification when snow levels at your favorite resorts across the world reach a specified minimum. You never know when you might need to take off and ski!

Sports

> Set your favorite teams and get updates during games, or scores when the games end.

Stock Alerts

> Receive daily updates of stock levels for your favorite stocks, or receive notice when they reach a specified numeric or percentage change.

Weather

> Receive daily updates of weather within a specified Zip Code at a specified time.

Yahoo! 360

> Receive an alert when someone sends you a message or adds you as a friend at Yahoo! 360.

Modifying Alerts

Once set, any alert can be modified, temporarily paused, or removed. You can see all of the alerts you've set by browsing to *http://alerts.yahoo.com* and clicking the My Alerts tab. Each alert will show the type, activated status, and delivery method, as shown in Figure 2-89.

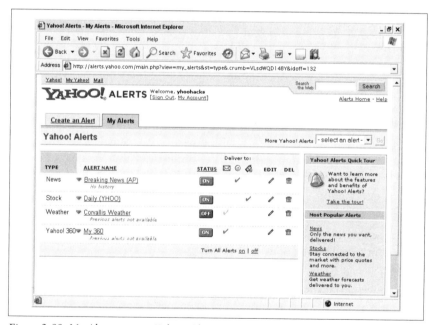

Figure 2-89. My Alerts page at Yahoo! Alerts

To change any of the options you've set for an alert, click the pencil icon. To temporarily stop receiving an alert, click the On or Off status button to change the status. If an alert is listed as Off, you won't receive the alert. Clicking the trash icon and confirming the delete will completely remove an existing alert; you'll stop receiving the alert and you'll need to go through the alert setup process from the beginning if you change your mind and want to receive the deleted alert again in the future.

CHAPTER THREE

Communicating
Hacks 51–67

Over 55 million people around the world have signed up and sent email with Yahoo! Mail. Even if you don't use Yahoo! Mail yourself, the chances are very good that you've received email from a friend, family member, or coworker who uses Yahoo! Mail. By making email accessible through a web browser, Yahoo! has given millions the ability to send and receive email without configuring a client application or knowing what a mail server is. This chapter shows how to manage [Hack #52] and navigate [Hack #51] Yahoo! Mail more effectively and how to use Yahoo! Mail as a universal client [Hack #54] when you need access to other email accounts.

In addition to Yahoo! Mail, Yahoo! provides a number of other tools to connect with friends, meet new people, and collaborate online. Yahoo! Groups [Hack #59] provides a way to discuss topics and plan with others, and Yahoo! 360 [Hack #61] keeps you in touch with friends and family while introducing you to friends of friends. Yahoo! Messenger lets you have real-time conversations with your friends, and adding avatars [Hack #64] adds a new dimension to your discussions. And the photo-sharing service Flickr [Hack #67] allows communities to form around sharing images.

Whether or not you're one of the millions already using Yahoo! tools to connect with others on a daily basis, you're probably already participating in some conversations using Yahoo!, and the hacks in this chapter will show you how to dig a bit deeper into those tools.

 HACK **Navigate Yahoo! Mail**
#51 Find your way around the Yahoo! Mail interface, and speed up common tasks with keyboard shortcuts.

Yahoo! Mail has been a runaway success because it's easy to use. Web-based email gives users an account they can access from any machine with an

Internet connection. You don't have to know how to configure an email client such as Outlook to use Yahoo! Mail; you just need to know how to use a browser. You won't have any trouble using Yahoo! Mail to send messages across the Internet, but by taking a few minutes to learn how Yahoo! Mail is organized, you might find ways to speed up the way you send email.

Yahoo! Mail Layout

You can get to your Yahoo! Mail by browsing to *http://mail.yahoo.com*. You can also type `mail!` into any Yahoo! Search form to go directly to Yahoo! Mail. This even works from external search forms, such as the Firefox Quick Search Box [Hack #13].

> In addition to using the `mail!` shortcut, you can get to most Yahoo! properties by typing the property's name into a Yahoo! search form and adding an exclamation point. Try others, such as `directory!`, `finance!`, `tv!`, and `movies!`.

Yahoo! Mail is really four applications in one, and here's a quick look at how you can use each of them:

Mail
As you'd expect, this is the heart of the application, where you can read and send email via your web browser.

Addresses
This is your personal address book, where you can store not only a contact name and email address, but also phone numbers, home and work addresses, birthdays and anniversaries, and free-form notes about each contact. You can access your address book directly at *http://address.yahoo.com*.

Calendar
This is a space where you can plan your schedule by adding events and tasks to a calendar. You can view the calendar by week, month, or year, and see your tasks as a to-do list. You can also share your calendar with others. Your calendar is available directly at *http://calendar.yahoo.com*.

Notepad
Your notepad is a place for simple text notes to yourself. If you have some class notes, a shopping list, or any sort of simple text, your Yahoo! notepad will make it accessible from any computer with Internet access. You can add notes to your notepad directly at *http://notepad.yahoo.com*.

You can access any of these four applications from the tabs in the Yahoo! Mail navigation bar shown in Figure 3-1.

This navigation bar is available toward the top of every Yahoo! Mail page. In addition to the navigation tabs, it shows you the path to checking and

Figure 3-1. The Yahoo! Mail navigation bar

composing email, searching your email, and editing your preferences with the Mail Options link in the upper-right corner. Be sure to note the location of the Mail Options link, because it's the key to setting your preferences.

Keyboard Shortcuts

If you want to give your mouse muscles a break, you can also navigate with a few built-in keyboard shortcuts. These shortcuts are simply combinations of keys you type to move around within Yahoo! Mail. For example, say you're looking through events in your calendar and you realize you need to fire off an emergency email related to something you've found. You could click the Mail tab and then the Compose button from the navigation bar. Or you could type Ctrl-Shift-P on the keyboard, and you'll find yourself at the new mail form.

It takes a bit of keyboard dexterity to hold both the Ctrl and Shift buttons down while pressing a letter. But once you get the hang of it, you can speed up some of the most common tasks:

Check mail
 Ctrl-Shift-C
Compose new mail
 Ctrl-Shift-P
View folders
 Ctrl-Shift-F
Open the Advanced Search form
 Ctrl-Shift-S
Get help
 Ctrl-Shift-H

These keyboard shortcuts are available anywhere within the Yahoo! Mail application, including your address book, calendar, and notepad.

Custom Keyboard Shortcuts in Firefox

If the built-in keyboard shortcuts aren't enough for you and you use the Firefox browser, there is a way to add your own custom keyboard shortcuts. A Firefox plug-in called Greasemonkey lets users add their own bit of JavaScript to any web site, which means they can add their own features, such as keyboard shortcuts.

To get started you need to install the Greasemonkey plug-in, available at *http://greasemonkey.mozdev.org*. Click the Install Greasemonkey link, and you should receive the plug-in automatically. With that, you're ready to write your code to implement the shortcuts.

Anatomy of a keyboard shortcut. This code builds on top of some JavaScript functions that already exist at Yahoo! Mail. Yahoo! Mail uses a function called addKey( ) to implement its own keyboard shortcuts across the site, and the following Greasemonkey script simply uses that function to add new shortcuts. This also means that the script is entirely dependent on Yahoo!, and if Yahoo! changes the code at any point in the future, this script will become useless.

The primary pieces of the addKey( ) function are the first and third arguments sent. The first argument is the *character code* of the key that is pressed, and the third argument is the location the browser should navigate to when it encounters that code. So, if you'd like to show the address book when you click Ctrl-Shift-A, the first task is to find the character code for the letter A.

Finding the character code for any given keyboard key isn't obvious, but you can accomplish the task with some JavaScript. Add the following code to a blank web page:

```
<script>
document.onkeydown = showKeyCode;
function showKeyCode(e) {
    var code;
    if (!e) var e = window.event;
    if (e.keyCode) code = e.keyCode;
    else if (e.which) code = e.which;
    var character = String.fromCharCode(code);
    alert('Character ' + character + ' code: ' + code);
}
</script>
```

Bring the web page up in a browser, and then press any key. As you press the key, an alert window will let you know the code for the character you just pressed. As you press G, for example, the script will send the alert: Character G code: 71. You'll need the character code for any keyboard shortcut you'd like to create, and once you have them listed, you can move on to the Greasemonkey script.

The code. Save the following code to a file called *yahoo_keys.user.js*. It is important to include the *.user.js* extension because that's how Firefox knows the script is a Greasemonkey script rather than a standard JavaScript file.

```
// ==UserScript==
// @name        Yahoo! Mail Keys
// @namespace   http://hacks.oreilly.com/
// @description Uses existing Yahoo! Mail functions to add a keyboard ⏎
shortcut
// @include     http://*.mail.yahoo.com/*
// ==/UserScript==

(function( ) {

// Trash | CTRL-T
oKey.addKey(84,-1,"location='/ym/ShowFolder?rb=Trash'","shift+ctrl");

// Draft | CTRL-D
oKey.addKey(68,-1,"location='/ym/ShowFolder?rb=Draft'","shift+ctrl");

// General Prefs | CTRL-G
oKey.addKey(71,-1,"location='/ym/Preferences'","shift+ctrl");
```

As you can see, each line of the script is calling the existing addKey( ) function. The first argument is the character code, and the third is the location the browser should visit when that key is pressed. The last line shows that the letter G (character code 71) should bring up the Yahoo! Mail Preferences page.

By studying Yahoo! Mail URLs, you can come up with your own keyboard shortcuts. If you have a custom mail folder called Business that you'd like to access when you press Ctrl-Shift-B, you could add a line to the script like this:

```
// My Business Folder | CTRL-B
oKey.addKey(66,-1,"location='/ym/ShowFolder?rb=Business'","shift+ctrl");
```

Running the hack. To install your keyboard shortcuts, open *yahoo_keys.user.js* in Firefox. From the Tools menu, click Install User Script. Greasemonkey will ask you to confirm that you'd like to install the script for use at Yahoo! Mail. If it all looks good, click OK. From there, you can reload Yahoo! Mail to start using your custom shortcuts.

Although Yahoo! Mail is easy to navigate even without keyboard shortcuts, you might find that you're able to accomplish routine tasks a bit more efficiently without the mouse.

HACK #52 Manage Yahoo! Mail

Take control of your mail by creating folders and filters for incoming messages.

Imagine you've just returned from vacation to find hundreds of messages waiting for you in your Inbox. Wouldn't it be nice to have an administrative assistant to sort that mail into categories and separate the good stuff from the junk? By setting up some folders and filters, you can let Yahoo! play the role of assistant, keeping your incoming mail as organized as possible.

As in any email client, the folders in Yahoo! Mail are simply a way to organize several emails into a group. There are five built-in folders that you can't remove:

Inbox
By default, all incoming mail, except messages marked as spam, arrives in this folder.

Drafts
Any email that you have partially completed and saved for later can be found in this folder. You can also use drafts as a message template for form letters that you send frequently.

Sent
This folder holds a copy of every email you've sent. This folder is enabled by default, but you can disable it by choosing Mail Options → General Preferences, unchecking the box labeled "Save your sent messages in the Sent Items folder," and clicking Save.

Bulk
Email that has been labeled as spam by Yahoo! Mail will arrive in this folder instead of your in Inbox. You can clear the email in this folder at any time by clicking the [Empty] link next to the folder listing, or have Yahoo! automatically delete anything through a setting in Mail Options.

Trash
Deleted mail goes to this folder and is subject to permanent deletion at any time. As with the Bulk folder, you can manually clear this folder at any time by clicking the [Empty] link next to this folder in the folder listing.

You can also create your own folders and give them your own names. Figure 3-2 shows the built-in folders and two custom folders.

Figure 3-2. Yahoo! Mail folders

Sorting with Filters

By using a combination of custom mail folders and *message filters*, you can let Yahoo! Mail do some sorting for you before you ever get to your Inbox. Message filters are simple rules that tell Yahoo! where to place an incoming email if it meets certain criteria that you specify.

For example, many emails from services or mailing lists use a predictable subject line. If you're a member of the photo-sharing site Flickr, all messages from the service include the text [Flickr] in the subject line. Knowing this, you can create a custom folder for Flickr messages and set a custom filter so that the messages won't appear with your regular Inbox mail. Any folder with unread mail will be bold in your list of folders, so even though filtered mail won't show up in your Inbox, you won't miss new mail as it arrives.

To set this up, add a new folder from your list of folders by clicking the Add link and giving it an appropriate title, such as Flickr. You should instantly see a new folder called Flickr in your list of folders. Choose Mail Options → Filters to go to the Filters page. Click the Add button to bring up the Add Message Filter shown in Figure 3-3.

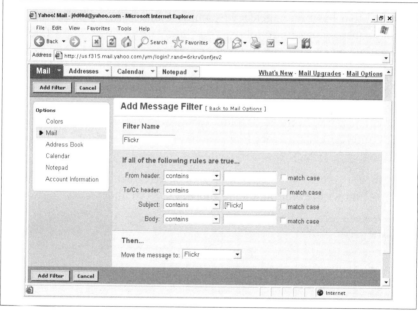

Figure 3-3. Adding a Yahoo! Mail message filter

Give the filter a descriptive title; in this case, Flickr will work. Because the subject line is the predictable part, add the text [Flickr] to the Subject: field in the form. Finally, tell Yahoo! to move the mail to the folder you just created by choosing it from the drop-down list of your folders. Click Add Filter, and Yahoo! Mail will start automatically moving messages that contain [Flickr] in the subject line into the Flickr folder.

> Keep in mind that the more specific you can be when creating a filter, the more accurate it will be. If you set a Flickr filter to look for both [Flickr] in the subject line and flickr.com in the From: header, you'll be sure that forwarded messages from friends with the [Flickr] subject heading won't be filtered into the wrong place.

Adding just a single folder and filter for each mailing list you receive can dramatically streamline your Inbox. As you can see, you can also add filters for specific people or specific text within a message. All of your filters are managed from the Filters page at Mail Options → Filters, where you can put the filters into an order of priority. For example, maybe you want any messages from *bob@example.com* to go into your Bob folder, but you want messages from Bob via a mailing list you're both on to go into the list folder instead. You could simply make the mailing list filter higher in priority than the Bob filter.

Managing Spam

Unsolicited email is a fact of life for anyone with an email account, and no one has yet come up with a way to stop it completely. But there are some steps you can take to help control the number of junk mails you receive.

Use SpamGuard. Yahoo!'s spam-stopping service is called SpamGuard, and it's enabled by default when you create an account. As long as it's enabled, Yahoo! will scan every incoming message for signs that it is spam. If Yahoo! thinks the message is spam, the email will be routed to the built-in Bulk folder instead of your Inbox folder.

You can choose how long messages will stay in the Bulk folder before they're deleted. Just go to Mail Options → Spam Protection and choose a time, from immediate deletion to one month—giving you the option to scan the Bulk folder periodically to make sure you're not missing good email.

Of course if you're a glutton for punishment, you can disable SpamGuard at any time by clicking the Turn SpamGuard OFF link on that same page.

For the spam that slips through the first line of defense, you can report individual messages as spam to Yahoo!. From your Inbox folder—or any of your custom folders—click the box next to any email that is spam. Then, with the unsolicited messages highlighted, click the Spam button. This will report the emails to Yahoo! and move the messages to your Bulk folder.

Block specific addresses or domains. If a specific email sender is getting on your nerves, you can block her manually. First, open the offending message and copy the email address in the From: line at the top of the message. Browse to Mail Options → Block Addresses and paste the address into the Add Block field at the top of the page. Optionally, you can block an entire domain. Simply chop off the @ symbol and everything before it in the email address and put the domain (the part after the @ symbol) into the form instead. Once set, all future mail from the address or domain will automatically be routed to the Bulk folder. You can set up to 100 blocked email addresses or domains.

Use temporary addresses. If you want to do business with a particular online shop, but you're worried that it might sell your email address to spammers, you can sign up with a temporary address. A temporary address is like an alias that you can use to sign up at online services and delete if you start receiving unwanted mail from them at any time.

If your standard Yahoo! Mail address is *example@yahoo.com*, you could create a temporary address, such as *temp21-shop@yahoo.com*, which a third party would never be able to trace to your original address.

Unfortunately, temporary addresses are available only as a feature of Yahoo! Mail Plus, which at the time of this writing is $20 per year.

HACK #53　Create Yahoo! Mail Macros

With a combination of email drafts, direct URL bookmarks, and bookmarklets, you can send complex emails with one click.

In the world of office software, a *macro* is a little bit of code that combines several steps of a process into a single click. Macros take advantage of a computer's ability to automate tasks and can significantly reduce any repetitive task that needs to be done. Taking this thinking to the world of Yahoo! Mail, you can create your own Yahoo! Mail macros to help you send messages.

The normal process of sending a message involves going to Yahoo! Mail, clicking the Compose button, selecting a recipient, typing a subject and message, and clicking the Send button. These steps aren't very laborintensive, but if you find yourself sending the same types of email again and again, there are a few ways you can speed things up.

Drafts

Imagine you send a weekly email with some statistics to a group of coworkers. The introduction, explanation, and ending of the email stay the same from week to week, with only a bit of text in the middle changing each time. The simplest way to automate this type of message is with the built-in Drafts folder at Yahoo! Mail. Draft emails are like templates that can be used and reused as many times as you need.

To create a draft, browse to the standard email form at Yahoo! Mail (*http:// mail.yahoo.com*) by clicking Compose Mail on the navigation menu or pressing Shift-Ctrl-P on the keyboard. Give the email a descriptive subject line, such as "weekly stats message" so you'll remember what the message is for without reading the text of the message. Create the email as if you were sending it out, but when you're finished, click the "Save as a Draft" button instead of clicking Send.

Now, whenever you want to use the email you just composed as a template, click on the Drafts folder from your list of folders and find this message in your list. Click on the message subject to bring the email up for editing. Make any changes you need to the email, add any recipients, and click Send. The message will still be available in your Drafts folder, and you can use the message just like this at any time. If you ever want to remove a draft email from your Drafts folder, manually delete it by checking the box next to the subject and clicking the Delete button.

Yahoo! Mail Bookmarks

Another way to automate common tasks is by creating your own Yahoo! Mail URLs. With some information about how Yahoo! Mail URLs are constructed, you can create a direct link to the Yahoo! Mail form with the fields prefilled for you. For example, if you find yourself sending out the same email over and over again, you could create a direct link to your Yahoo! Mail that includes the full message and subject, saving you some copying and pasting.

To get started, click the Mail tab and then click the Compose button. Note the base URL—everything up to the yahoo.com. It should look something like this:

```
http://us.f317.mail.yahoo.com
```

This base URL will vary based on the localized version of Yahoo! you're using and the way Yahoo! is balancing its servers. With the base URL in hand, add the following to specify the mail form and include your Yahoo! ID:

```
/ym/Compose?insert Yahoo! IDnull
```

So, putting these pieces together will give you blank new mail form, like so:

```
Insert base URL/ym/Compose?insert Yahoo! IDnull
```

To see the form change, add a variable/value pair to the end, using an amper-sand (&), variable, equals sign (=), and value. For example, &to=bob@example.com automatically adds the address *bob@example.com* to the form:

```
Insert base URL/ym/Compose?insert Yahoo! IDnull&to=bob@example.com
```

Here are the variables you can use in the URL:

to
> The email address of the recipient

cc
> An email address of a copied recipient

bcc
> An email address of a blind-copied recipient

subject
> The subject of the email

body
> The text of the message

Using a few of these variables together can give you a fairly complex message that's ready to go without any further action required beyond clicking the Send button. Here's an example:

```
http://us.f315.mail.yahoo.com/ym/Compose?insert Yahoo! IDnull&to=↵
bob@example.com&subject=hello&body=Hi%20Bob%2C%20this%20is%20my%20weekly%20↵
email%20that%20always%20has%20the%20same%20text%2E%20I%20created%20a%20↵
Yahoo%21%20Mail%20URL%20so%20I%20wouldn%27t%20have%20to%20re%2Dtype%20this↵
%20each%20time%2E
```

Note that the message text is *URL-encoded*, which means some characters, such as spaces, are converted to their URL code equivalent (%20 is the URL code equivalent for a space). Look carefully between those %20s and you'll see the text of the message. This encoding is required because some characters (such as spaces) aren't allowed in URLs. Plugging this monster URL into your address bar will bring up a page like the one shown in Figure 3-4, with the fields already filled in.

Bookmark your newly created URL and give it a snappy name, such as "mail to bob!," and you'll have a shortcut to frequently sent mail.

Yahoo! Mail Bookmarklet

Now that you know how to bookmark prefilled mail forms, you can take this a step further to create a Yahoo! Mail *bookmarklet*. A bookmarklet is a bit of JavaScript that lives inside of a browser bookmark that is executed when you click it. Since bookmarklets can interact with the page you're currently viewing in the browser, your Yahoo! Mail bookmarklet can get information like the page title, current URL, and any text you might have highlighted.

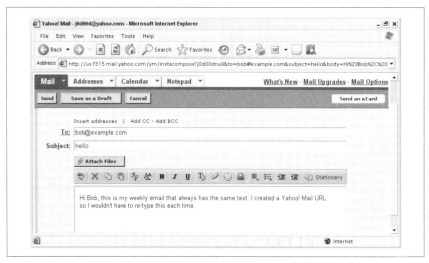

Figure 3-4. A prefilled Yahoo! Mail form

The code. This code creates a Send Link bookmarklet that sends information via Yahoo! Mail about the current web page you're viewing. As with other bookmarklets in this book, first a nicely formatted version of the code is shown, with the usable bookmarklet code to follow:

```
// Dissected JavaScript bookmarklet for Send Link

// Set d to the document object as a shortcut
var d = document;

// Set t to the currently selected text, if available
var t = d.selection?d.selection.createRange().text:d.getSelection();

// Build the body of the email that includes the current
// document title, URL, and any selected text
var b = d.title + '\n\n';
b += d.location.href + '\n\n';
b += '"' + t + '"\n\n';

// Build the URL that will add a bookmark to Yahoo! Bookmarks
var url = 'insert base URL/ym/Compose?insert Yahoo! IDnull&';

// include the tile of the current page as the subject
url += 'subject='+escape(d.title)+'&';

// include the title of the current page
url += 'body='+escape(b)+'&';

// also send a copy of the email to yourself
url += 'cc=insert your email address';

// open a new window to bring up the mail form
```

```
window.open(url,
            '_blank',
            'width=640,height=440,status=yes,resizable=yes,scrollbars=yes');
```

As you can see, this bookmarklet builds the appropriate Yahoo! Mail URL, including a message subject and body in the URL. Both are escaped for URLs with the escape( ) function. The body includes the title of the current site, its URL, and any text that is selected on the page.

And here's the code formatted appropriately for a bookmarklet:

```
javascript:d=document;t=d.selection?d.selection.createRange( ).text:
d.getSelection( );b=d.title+'\n\n'+d.location.href+'\n\n'+'"'+t+'"\n
\n';url='insert base URL/ym/Compose?insert Yahoo! IDnull&subject='+
escape(d.title)+'&body='+escape(b)+'&cc=pb@onfocus.com';void(window
.open(url,'_blank','width=640,height=440,status=yes,resizable=
yes,scrollbars=yes'))
```

It's not nearly as easy to read, but it's much morSe compact. Line breaks and comments have been removed from the code, and the JavaScript has been compacted wherever possible.

Running the hack. Install the bookmarklet by creating a bookmark in your browser. Right-click the bookmark and choose Properties to edit the bookmark. In the Location field, paste the bookmarklet code and rename the bookmark Send Link!.

Imagine you'd like to send a friend a reference to the book pictured in Figure 3-5, along with the highlighted text describing the book.

After you click the Send Link! bookmarklet, a new window opens with title, URL, and the highlighted text prefilled at Yahoo! Mail, as shown in Figure 3-6.

From here, it's just a matter of filling in the To: field and clicking the Send button!

Understanding a bit more about how Yahoo! Mail works can help you streamline any repetitive email tasks or create new features similar to the Send Link! bookmarklet.

HACK #54 Read All Your Email in One Place

With a little setup, you can read email from all of your accounts when you're on the go.

Most of us collect different email addresses like keys on a key ring: we keep adding them for different locations, such as home, work, or post office boxes, and eventually we've got so many keys we can't remember which key unlocks which door. In some situations, it'd be nice to have a single master key to unlock everything, and that's exactly what Yahoo! Mail can accomplish for your email addresses.

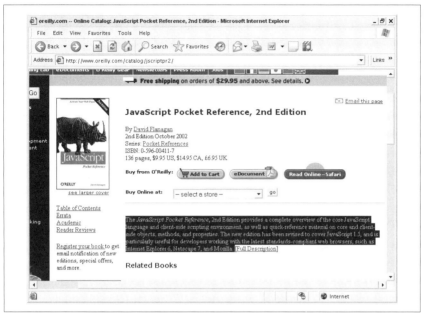

Figure 3-5. Highlighted text to be sent via email

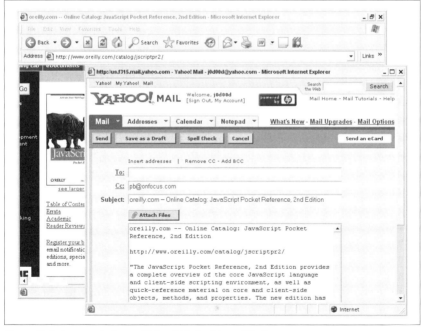

Figure 3-6. A new window at Yahoo! Mail with prefilled text

If you've ever tried to check email while you're traveling, you know how frustrating it can be to check each of your email addresses with a foreign computer or in a place with limited access. While some email can wait until you're back in front of your computer, when you need to stay in touch it's important to have reliable access to your email from any computer with a web browser.

To get started, you'll need a Yahoo! ID [Hack #3] and an activated Yahoo! Mail account. You can get an ID and activate a Yahoo! Mail account at *http:// mail.yahoo.com*. As soon as your account is set up, you can receive email at your Yahoo! address, and you can set up Yahoo! Mail to check your external email accounts as well.

Adding External Mail Accounts

The only requirement for adding an outside account to Yahoo! Mail is that it must be a publicly available Post Office Protocol (POP) account. Chances are very good that all of your email accounts use the POPv3 standard.

If you're using an Internet Message Access Protocol (IMAP) email account, you won't be able to check that account with Yahoo! Mail. Also, Yahoo! Mail does not support encrypted SSL connections for POP accounts, so if your mail server requires an SSL connection, you won't be able to check that account with Yahoo! Mail either.

Yahoo! Mail traffic is not encrypted and can be subject to eavesdropping. If your mail from external accounts is extremely sensitive, you might not want to view it via Yahoo! Mail.

To add an account, log in to Yahoo! Mail and click Mail Options from the upper-right side of the page. Click Mail Accounts to see a summary of your accounts and then click the Add button to start adding an external account.

From here, you just need to choose a name to represent the account, such as *Work* or *School*, and then enter the mail server information that tells Yahoo! Mail how to access that external account. The mail server address will depend on the company that provides your email service, and you'll need to contact them if you don't know the mail server address. You'll also need to include the same username and password you use to check that particular email account. This gives Yahoo! Mail enough information to check the account.

You'll need to choose a color to represent email from each external account. This will help you see at a glance the account each email is from as you view your Yahoo! Mail inbox.

Once your account is set up, you'll see a list of your external mail servers on the left side of the main mail page, as shown in Figure 3-7.

Figure 3-7. A list of external mail servers at Yahoo! Mail

You'll need to click on any external mail server you'd like to check, because Yahoo! Mail will not automatically check them. This means that if you're not ready to deal with a crisis at work while you're on a cruise ship, you can simply avoid clicking the link. After you've clicked the link, Yahoo! will contact your mail server and download any new email. The emails will appear in your inbox, and they'll be highlighted with the color that corresponds to that mail server.

Editing External Mail Accounts

You can access your external mail accounts settings at any time by clicking Mail Accounts from the Mail Options page. To change the settings, highlight an account and click the Edit button. You can modify the settings you entered when you set up the account: mail server, name, password, and account color. And you can also set any of the following additional options:

Deliver To
  You can choose an existing Yahoo! Mail folder from the menu to have all external email sent to a folder other than your Inbox. Use this option if you want to keep external mail from mingling with mail sent to your Yahoo! Mail address.

Override Default POP Port
  If your mail server uses a port other than 110 for POP delivery, you can set the alternate port here.

Leave Mail on POP Server
Check this option to leave a copy of the email on your mail server. With this option checked, Yahoo! will not delete email from your mail server, so you can retrieve it again later with your standard email client. This option is enabled by default.

Retrieve New Messages Only
With this option checked, Yahoo! Mail will download only new messages from your external account, not messages that have already been retrieved. This option is enabled by default.

Use Filters
Enabling this option will apply all of your existing Yahoo! Mail filters [Hack #52] to email from external accounts. You might want to disable this if you'd rather not filter incoming external mail. This option is also enabled by default.

Even though you might be receiving email from an external server, any replies to those messages will be from your Yahoo! Mail address. If you'd rather have your From: address be an external account, you'll need to upgrade to Yahoo! Mail Plus. At the time of this writing, a Plus account is $20 per year. You can read about all of the benefits of Yahoo! Plus at *http://mailplus.yahoo.com*.

Checking Mail on Your Phone

Another benefit of checking your external mail accounts with Yahoo! Mail is that you can read those messages via portable devices. Once the external accounts are set in Yahoo! Mail, you can use any Internet-enabled cell phone to read your mail. Point the phone's browser to *http://mobile.yahoo.com*, sign in, and choose the Mail link. From there, click Check Other Mail, as shown in Figure 3-8.

You'll see a listing of all your external mail servers; click one to view messages from that account. If your current ISP doesn't offer mobile access to your email, the Yahoo! Mail external accounts feature is an easy way to enable it.

While you might not want to read all of your mail through Yahoo! all of the time, it's comforting to know that with a bit of setup, you can receive all of your email from all of your accounts on any computer with a web browser.

Read Yahoo! Mail in Your Preferred Email Client

HACK
#55

Figure 3-8. Checking non-Yahoo! email on a cell phone with Yahoo! Mobile

Read Yahoo! Mail in Your Preferred Email Client

HACK
#55

The standard way to read Yahoo! Mail is with a web browser, but some freely available software called YPOPs! can deliver your Yahoo! Mail to your favorite email client.

Most of us have several email accounts on several systems: one for personal email, two or three for work, and maybe even a Yahoo! Mail account on the side. Most of these accounts are read with Post Office Protocol (POP) email clients such as Outlook Express, Eudora, Thunderbird, or Mac's Mail. But Yahoo! Mail is designed to be read through a web browser. This is handy when you're away from your standard computer, but it can be a hassle when you're on your home machine. To read all of your mail and get completely caught up, you need to open both your email client and a web browser for Yahoo! Mail.

One way to bring all of your email together is to add your standard POP accounts to Yahoo! Mail [Hack #54] so that you can read everything through a web browser. (This is another perk when you're on the road.) But if you're perfectly happy with your email client, there are also ways to route your Yahoo! Mail there.

The most direct route is by upgrading your Yahoo! Mail account to Yahoo! Mail Plus. For an annual fee of $20 (at the time of this writing), Yahoo! Mail Plus adds various features to your account, including direct POP Access. With the upgrade, you'll be able to retrieve your Yahoo! Mail in the same way that you get mail from your other accounts.

Another route is via YPOPs!, open source software that was put together by a handful of developers working in their spare time to solve this very problem. YPOPs! turns your machine into a mini–mail server and at the same time dissects the Yahoo! Mail web interface, translating web text into standard email.

Installing YPOPs!

YPOPs! is available for just about every platform, including Windows, Mac, and Linux. To grab a copy, browse to *http://yahoopops.sourceforge.net*, click the Downloads link toward the top of the page, and find the version for your operating system.

If you're on a Windows machine, you can simply click the download file and install the program. The installation program will ask if you want YPOPs! to start when Windows starts, and you can click No here. (You can easily change this setting once the program is installed.) Once you're finished, the program will start and a new icon will appear in your system tray, as shown in Figure 3-9.

Figure 3-9. The YPOPs! System tray icon

Right-click the new icon and choose Configure from the menu to set up some preferences. Click the Receiving Email preferences shown in Figure 3-10.

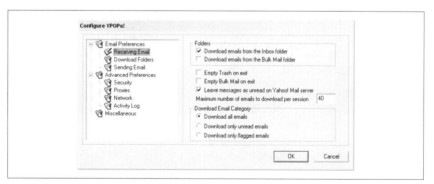

Figure 3-10. The YPOPs! configuration screen

To play it safe, uncheck the "Empty Trash on exit" and "Empty Bulk Mail on exit" options. This will ensure you'll have a backup of every email at Yahoo!. Once you've used YPOPs! for a while, you might want to change these settings, but it's a good idea to proceed cautiously while you're learning how the program works.

Even though YPOPs! has a setting to "Leave messages as unread on Yahoo! Mail server," I've found this doesn't work. No matter what the setting, YPOPs! marks emails as read and moves them to the Trash folder at Yahoo! Mail. If you suddenly have email missing that you expected to be in your inbox, they're probably in Trash!

Once these preferences are set, click OK, and you'll be ready to move on to the final step: configuring your mail client to talk with YPOPs!.

Configuring Your Client

The instructions for configuring your mail client vary a bit between different applications, and the YPOPs! web site has step-by-step instructions for most programs. Browse to the site and choose Configuring Mail Clients in the column on the left, under Documentation. All applications follow a similar pattern, though, that goes something like this:

1. Open your mail client and create a new account. (This is often found under File → New → Account or under Tools → E-Mail Accounts.)
2. Include your full name and your Yahoo! Mail email address.
3. Choose POP or POP3 as the method of delivery.
4. Set the incoming server to 127.0.0.1, which is computer shorthand for "this machine."
5. Set the outgoing server to 127.0.0.1 as well.
6. Set the username to your Yahoo! Mail username (your email address without the @yahoo.com on the end).

And that's it! You should now be able to receive your email from the comfort of your favorite client. Keep in mind that you can access your Yahoo! Mail this way only when the YPOPs! program is running, so it always needs to be on in the background. If you find that you like receiving your mail this way, just click the Configure menu item again and go to the Miscellaneous preferences. You can check the option to automatically start YPOPs! when Windows starts, and you won't have to think about the program again.

HACK #56 Manage and Share Your Schedule

Yahoo! Calendar can help you plan your time, manage an event, remember important events, and share your schedule with friends and family.

When you lead a busy life, time management isn't just an important skill; it's necessary for survival. Without the ability to track important dates and times, you could miss out on key events. While you can accomplish some time management with a pencil-and-paper calendar, once your schedule is digital, you can do much more. Yahoo! Calendar can act as your own personal assistant: reminding you of important dates and times, inviting your friends to a party, and helping your contacts plan a meeting time that's convenient for you.

Yahoo! Calendar (*http://calendar.yahoo.com*) is one piece of Yahoo! Mail, and you can view your calendar at any time by clicking on the Calendar tab at Yahoo! Mail. As you'd expect, you'll find a calendar there that you can view by the Day, Week, Month, or Year. Your Yahoo! Calendar becomes useful when you start adding personal events.

Adding Events

There are a few ways to add events to your calendar, and an overview will help you know when to use each method of adding events.

Event options. To add a detailed event to your calendar, click the Add Event button at the top of any Yahoo! Calendar page. From there, you'll find the Add Event form that contains all of the options available for an event. Here's a look at the available fields:

Title
> You can include a descriptive title for an event, but keep in mind that you're limited to 80 characters. If you like to browse your schedule by the monthly view, you might want to keep event titles fairly short, say under 10 characters.

Event Type
> Choose an event type from around 30 different categories, ranging from Anniversary to Happy Hour to Wedding. The event type you assign will appear on the Event List view of your calendar, and you can sort your events by event type.

Date and Time
> You can give an event a specific date, time, and duration. For birthdays or other events that don't have a specific time, you can set the event as "all day."

Location and Notes
> Use the Location field as a quick description of where the event will be. (You can include more detailed information about the location with the Address and Phone fields.) The Notes field lets you add any

extra information about an event. If set, both of these fields will appear when you hover your mouse over an event title in the Day, Week, or Month view.

Sharing Option
Override your default calendar-sharing option for a specific event by choosing Private, Shows as Busy, or Public. Note that if your calendar is private, setting an event to Public won't change your overall calendar settings.

Repeating Event
If your schedule has some regular patterns, you don't need to add each recurring event by hand. You can set a task that repeats on specific days or at specific times of the month. You can also set an end date or leave the event repeating on your calendar into the future.

Invitations
You can include a list of email addresses separated by commas, and Yahoo! will invite those people to view the event.

Reminders
Have a reminder sent to your Yahoo! Messenger account, email address, or mobile device. Reminders are great for catching birthdays and other events that can slip by.

Address and Phone
You can specify a full address for an event, and Yahoo! will use the information to create a link to a map when you're sending invitations. You can also include a phone number, and Yahoo! will list that as well. If you aren't sending an invitation, you can use this information for you own reference when you view the event details.

When you've filled in the options for an event, click the Save button or Save and Add Another button. One important option on this list is the ability to send invitations to an event.

Invitations. Yahoo! Calendar can also act as an invitation service if you provide a list of emails when you add an event to your calendar. Click Save to add the event, and Yahoo! will give you an extra form to fill out (as shown in Figure 3-11) that will let you customize the message in the email to your guests.

Along with your message, the email will include the event details and a link to a Yahoo! Map of the event location if you include an address. Figure 3-12 shows a Yahoo! Calendar invitation email.

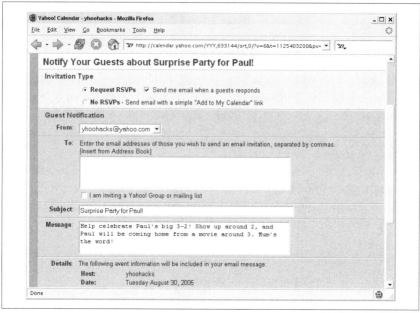

Figure 3-11. The Yahoo! Calendar invitation form

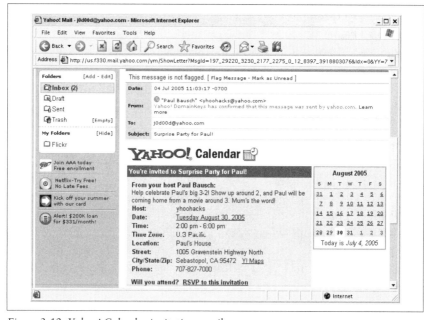

Figure 3-12. Yahoo! Calendar invitation email

In addition to sending out the invitations, Yahoo! Calendar will keep track of your guest list. As guests reply to the invitation, Yahoo! will keep track of who will be attending and will display any notes each guest has added. To see the running list of guests, as shown in Figure 3-13, click on the event in your calendar and click the View Invite list in the upper-right corner of the page.

Figure 3-13. Yahoo! Calendar guest list

From the Invite page, you can add more guests, send an email to all of the guests, invite more people to the event, or add any of the guests to your Yahoo! Address Book.

If you need to cancel your event, you can simply delete the event from your calendar. When you delete an event that has a list of guests associated with it, you'll have the option to notify everyone via email.

Quick Add Event form. If you're overwhelmed by the number of options to fill out when you add an event, you can use the Quick Add Event form, shown in Figure 3-14, that you'll find at the bottom of any calendar view.

Figure 3-14. Yahoo! Calendar Quick Add Event

Type the title for the event, choose the date and time, and click Add. This will instantly add an event to your calendar. You can always fill in the details later by clicking the event title.

Tasks. Similar to events, tasks are listed on the left side of the calendar, and you can use them to build a to-do list. Tasks won't show up on the calendar as events; they're completely independent. You can give each task a due date and a priority, and you can view them all at any time by clicking the Tasks tab.

Time Guides. You can include national holidays, financial events, and sports team schedules on your calendar by adjusting your Time Guides settings. Click Options at the top of any Yahoo! Calendar page, and then click Time Guides under the Events heading. You can choose which types of events you'd like to include or exclude, including your Yahoo! Friends and Groups calendars. Click the Add/Edit link next to any category to make changes. For example, you can click Add/Edit next to Holidays and change the holidays that show up on your calendar. Choose a category from the drop-down menu to see holidays for other continents or religious holidays.

Sharing Your Calendar

Once your calendar is filled with events, you might want to share that calendar with specific Yahoo! users or the world. To start sharing your calendar, you'll need to set your sharing options by going to any Yahoo! Calendar page and choosing Options → Management → Sharing. From the Sharing page, you can set your calendar to be as public or private as you'd like, as shown in Figure 3-15.

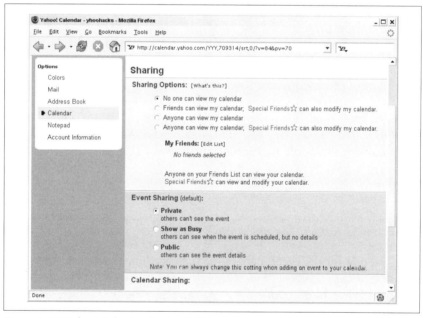

Figure 3-15. Yahoo! Calendar sharing options

The term *Friends* on the sharing options page refers to a specific list of Yahoo! IDs you have approved to view your calendar. Click the Edit List link to add or remove Yahoo! IDs from your list. As you add each Yahoo!

ID, you can also specify whether the member with that ID can modify your calendar. The term *Anyone* literally refers to anyone in the world, whether they have a Yahoo! ID or not. If you choose to make your calendar available to anyone, be sure that the calendar doesn't have personally identifiable information that you wouldn't want some stranger to have. For example, you might not want to let the world know when you'll be away from your house on vacation.

You can also choose a default privacy setting for event details. The "Show as Busy" option will let others know you're busy at a specific time, but it won't let them know where you'll be. The Public setting will let others know the details of your schedule. When you're finished, be sure to click Save at the bottom of the page to modify the sharing options of your calendar.

Once you've made your calendar available to others, you can easily share it by sending the calendar's URL. You'll find the URL at the bottom of the sharing options page, and it's in this predictable format:

```
http://calendar.yahoo.com/insert Yahoo! ID
```

Sharing schedules can help a group plan meetings; it can also keep everyone in your family from missing important dates and times.

HACK #57 Add Contacts to Your Yahoo! Address Book

Add contacts to your Yahoo! Mail Address Book from incoming email or existing desktop address books.

Frequent travelers know the frustration of having data trapped inside desktop applications. Imagine you find yourself in a foreign hotel room—needing to contact your host—only to realize that the email address you need is in your Outlook address book at your office. One solution to this problem is to use a web-based address book, such as the one included with Yahoo! Mail, to keep your contact information available from any computer connected to the Internet. Another reason to keep addresses at Yahoo! is that you'll find it speeds up composing email at Yahoo! Mail. By choosing addresses from your address book, instead of typing in email addresses manually, you'll save some keystrokes and save your brain the work of remembering complex addresses.

One of the biggest hurdles to using a web-based address book, though, is the time involved with building your list of contacts. Luckily, Yahoo! offers a number of ways to enter contact information into your address book—from manually entering each address to importing addresses in batches.

Entering Contacts Manually

The fastest way to enter a single contact into the Yahoo! Address Book is from inside an email. As you're reading an email at Yahoo! Mail, look for the "Add to Address Book" link in the From: line of the mail headers at the top of the email; it will look like Figure 3-16.

Figure 3-16. Add to Address Book link in Yahoo! Mail

Click the link, and you'll see the "Add to Address Book" form with several of the fields prefilled, including first and last name and email address. You can optionally add a phone number and nickname for the contact and click the "Add to Address Book" button to save the contact into your address book.

Though this is simple, it won't work if you're starting a new Yahoo! Mail account or if you haven't received email at your Yahoo! address from the contacts you want to add. To enter a few contacts by hand, browse to *http:// address.yahoo.com* and look for the Quick Add Contact box at the top or bottom of the page. If you're going for speed, the minimum information you need to fill in is a first or last name and an email address; then click the Add button.

To spend a bit more time and build a more complete address book, you can click the Add Contact button found at *http://address.yahoo.com* and you'll have the option to associate much more information with the contact:

Name
> Including first, last, middle, and a nickname. Note that if you use nicknames to address a message when composing email, each nickname should be unique.

Email
> The contact's primary email address and up to two alternates.

Messenger ID
> The contact's Yahoo! ID for receiving instant messages.

Phone Numbers
> Up to seven different numbers, including home, work, mobile, fax, and pager.

Home Information
> The complete address; also space for a URL.

Work Information
> The company name, job title, complete address, and URL.

Important Dates
   Birthday and anniversary information.

Notes
   Any information that doesn't fit in the other categories.

In addition to this information, you can assign your contact to a category that you can set up through the Options link at the top of the page. Categories are handy for grouping contacts by association, such as Friends and Work. If these fields don't meet your needs, you can also add up to four custom fields (also available through the Options link) for extended information.

> If you give a contact a nickname in the address book, you can simply address any future Yahoo! Mail to that nickname.

As you can see, there is a lot of information you can fill out here, and adding more than a handful of contacts this way can become a chore.

Importing Contacts

If you've already entered your contact information in a desktop program such as Outlook, there's no need to go through the hassle again. There are several quicker ways to build up your Yahoo! Address Book.

Using QuickBuilder. If you've been using Yahoo! Mail for any length of time, you probably have a library of emails sitting on Yahoo!'s servers. Clicking through each email, finding the "Add to Address Book" link, and adding each contact could take hours, so Yahoo! built a tool called QuickBuilder. QuickBuilder searches through your existing Yahoo! Mail, looking for contacts to add to your address book.

To get started, browse to your address book and click the QuickBuilder button in the navigation bar. From here, you can select which folders Quick-Builder should look through to find addresses. You can also limit the number of emails QuickBuilder finds by specifying that it should include only addresses that appear more than one to four times in your folders, or addresses from emails received within a specific timeframe. Click Continue to display the list of email addresses QuickBuilder finds. Check the box next to each found address if you'd like to add it to your address book.

You can also add a nickname for each contact before you add it to your address book. Alternately, check the box at the top left of the results to select every email address found. Click Continue to display a list of the addresses that have been added.

Importing from applications. Luckily, all email application designers understand that people migrate between different computers, locations, and email programs on a fairly regular basis, and if you've spent years compiling an address book in another program such as Outlook, you can take advantage of your email application's export features to use your existing data.

The first task in moving your contacts is to find a format that Yahoo! Mail can understand and import. This is called *exporting* your address book, and the exporting process generates a file on your computer that you can send to Yahoo!. First, take a look at the four address book formats that Yahoo! understands:

Microsoft Outlook CSV
> This is a simple text file with comma-separated values (CSV) in a format used by Microsoft Outlook and Outlook Express.

Palm Desktop ABA
> Choose the Address Book Archive (ABA) format if you're importing from a Palm handheld PDA.

Netscape LDIF
> Use the Lightweight Directory Interchange Format (LDIF) option if you're exporting from the Mozilla Thunderbird email client or older Netscape email clients.

Yahoo! CSV
> If you're moving from one Yahoo! ID to another or consolidating multiple Yahoo! Mail accounts into one, you can choose to export into the Yahoo! CSV format and then import the file.

The process for exporting an address book will vary by application, and you can find a list of step-by-step instructions for many email clients in Yahoo! Help at *http://help.yahoo.com/help/us/ab/impexp/index.html*. Generally, you start the export process from the program menu at File → Import and Export. From there, you want to choose to export to a file in one of the formats that Yahoo! understands. You'll also want to give it a memorable name, such as *address_book.csv*, and save it in a memorable location like your desktop.

Now that you have your address book file in a format Yahoo! can understand, browse to your Yahoo! Address Book and click the Import/Export link in the upper-right corner of the page (see Figure 3-17).

As you can see, on this page you choose the format of your file, click Browse... to find the file on your computer, and then click the Import Now button. The next page you'll see is your address book filled with the contact information from your export file.

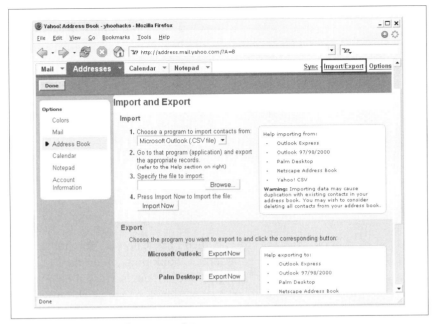

Figure 3-17. Yahoo! Mail Import and Export

Staying in sync. The process of importing contacts from another program works well for moving a large number of contacts between your desktop and Yahoo! Mail. But if you'd like a more incremental approach, Yahoo! offers a program for Windows users called Intellisync for Yahoo!. Intellisync is a program you can download and install that will keep information from certain desktop applications in sync with Yahoo! Mail. Syncing address books is only one service provided by Intellisync, which can move tedious tasks such as importing and exporting contacts to the background. For example, if you add Uncle Joe as a contact in Outlook on your home computer, Intellisync will recognize the addition and add Uncle Joe to your Yahoo! Address Book.

To install Intellisync, click the Sync link in the upper-right corner of your Yahoo! Address Book and make sure your other address book application is listed on the following page. At the time of this writing, Intellisync supports syncing the address book from specific versions of seven applications or platforms: ACT!, Lotus Organizer, MS Outlook, Outlook Express, Palm handhelds, and Pocket PCs. If your current address book isn't supported, Intellisync won't work for you. If you find your version of your application listed, click Install Now to download the program.

Once you've installed Intellisync, you'll need to tell it which address book program you use. Start the program and click the Setup button. Click Application Settings to bring up the configuration window shown in Figure 3-18.

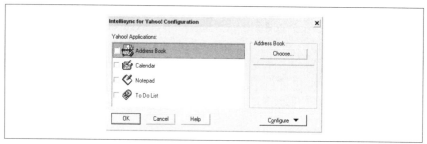

Figure 3-18. Intellisync configuration

Select Address Book from the list and then click Choose... to choose your address book application. Find your address book program on the list, highlight it, and leave "synchronize" checked. From there, save your changes by clicking OK, and you're set up to keep your address books synchronized.

Once you've set up Intellisync, you can run it periodically to sync your address book entries in both places. If Intellisync spots any differences between the two address books, you'll be asked to confirm any edits before they're made, as shown in Figure 3-19.

Figure 3-19. Intellisync address book confirmation

To see the details of any changes, click the Details... button to see exactly which contacts are being sent back and forth.

The process of entering contacts into your Yahoo! address book can be a tedious one, but by taking some time to work with the tools Yahoo! has made available, you can build up your address book in no time and have all of your contacts at your fingertips from any location.

Map Yahoo! Address Book Contacts

#58 Plot the locations of your friends and colleagues on a map of the world with your Yahoo! Address Book and the worldKit mapping application.

The Yahoo! Address Book lets you store more than just names and email addresses. You can store complete contact information for everyone, including street address, city, state, and country. If you have more than a dozen or so contacts stored, you might not realize how geographically dispersed everyone is. This hack plots the locations of all of your Yahoo! Address Book contacts on a map, so you can visualize where your friends, family, and coworkers live.

Plotting each contact's location is possible thanks to Yahoo!'s Address Book export feature, which provides all of your address book data in *comma-separated value* (CSV) format. From there, a freely available web service called Geocoder (*http://geocoder.us*) translates each address into its longitude and latitude. And finally, worldKit (*http://brainoff.com/worldkit*) plots each point on a map.

Preparing Your Address Book

Right now, your address book might be in sloppy condition (mine was), including misspelled addresses, missing states and countries, and abbreviated cities. *Geocoding* requires some degree of accuracy to find good matches, so before getting started, tidy your address book up. It's not necessary to produce a pristine address book, but you need at least a city and country, and a state abbreviation for U.S. locations. Street addresses for U.S. contacts can be used too. You'll likely need to iterate this cleanup a couple of times, with feedback from the geocoding script. Export your contacts by loading *http://address.yahoo.com*, selecting Import/Export, and selecting Export Now! for the Yahoo! CSV format.

The Code

yadr2geo.pl is a Perl script that takes the name of your downloaded address book and outputs a geocoded RSS file to use with worldKit. *Geocoded RSS* refers to any flavor of RSS extended to include item-level latitude and longitude. More details on the format can be found at *http://brainoff.com/worldkit/doc/rss.php#basic*.

This script requires commonly installed modules: URI::Escape for formatting web service requests, LWP::Simple for making those requests, and XML::Simple for parsing the responses.

> This script does not use a module to parse CSV, because
> modules such as Text::CSV assume that a newline indicates a
> new record, while in Yahoo! CSV (and most flavors of this
> unofficial spec) it's legal to include a newline within an entry
> if that entry is quoted. CSV is discussed in more detail at
> *http://www.creativyst.com/Doc/Articles/CSV/CSV01.htm.*

Yahoo! CSV is simple: all entries are guaranteed to be quoted, the first line
gives field names, and there's no extraneous whitespace. So it's straightforward to program a script to parse Yahoo! CSV character by character.
The subroutine getrecord( ) takes an open filehandle as an argument and
returns an array containing the next CSV record.

Save the following code to a file called *yadr2geo.pl*:

```perl
#!/usr/bin/perl -w

use strict;
use XML::Simple qw(XMLin);
use LWP::Simple qw(get);
use URI::Escape qw(uri_escape);

# Map your personal country naming conventions
# to country codes listed at http://brainoff.com/geocoder/countryselect.php
# and change the default country if you wish
my %countrycode = ('USA' => 'US');
my $defaultcountry = 'US';

print <<RSSHEADER;
<?xml version="1.0"?>
<rss version="2.0">
<channel>
    <title>Yahoo! Address Book</title>
    <link>http://address.yahoo.com/</link>
    <description>My geocoded Yahoo! Address Book</description>
RSSHEADER

my (%hash, @vals, $arg, $loc, $lat, $lon, $success, $country);

# First line of Yahoo! CVS is keys
my @keys = @{ getrecord(*STDIN) };

while (! eof(STDIN)) {
    @vals = @{ getrecord(*STDIN) };
    @hash{ @keys } = @vals;

    $success = 0;
    undef($loc);
    $country = $countrycode{ $hash{'Home Country'} } || $defaultcountry;

    # Check for sufficient information to geocode
```

```
if (length($hash{'Home City'}) == 0
    || ($country eq "US" && length($hash{'Home State'}) == 0)) {
    print STDERR "Couldn't geocode: \""
        . join ("\",\"", @vals) . "\"\n";
    next;
}


# Try geocoding US street address
if ($country eq 'US'
    && length($hash{'Home Address'}) > 0) {
    $arg = $hash{'Home Address'} . "," . $hash{'Home City'}
        . "," . $hash{'Home State'};

    eval {
        # Be patient, geocoder.us free service is rate limited
        $loc = XMLin(
            get("http://geocoder.us/service/rest/?address="
            . uri_escape($arg) )
        );
    };

    if (!$@ && defined($loc->{"geo:Point"}->{"geo:long"}) &&
        defined($loc->{"geo:Point"}->{"geo:lat"})) {
        $success = 1;
    }
}

# Try geocoding world city
if ($country ne 'US' || ! $success) {
    if ($country ne "US") {
        $arg = $hash{'Home City'} . "," . $country;
    } else {
        $arg = $hash{'Home City'} . "," . $hash{'Home State'}
            . "," . $country;
    }
    eval {
        $loc = XMLin(
            get("http://brainoff.com/geocoder/rest?city="
            . uri_escape($arg))
        );
    };

    if (!$@ && defined($loc->{"geo:Point"}->{"geo:long"}) &&
        defined($loc->{"geo:Point"}->{"geo:lat"})) {
        $success = 1;
    }
}

if ($success) {
    print <<ITEM;
<item>
    <title>$hash{'First'} $hash{'Last'}</title>
    <geo:lat>$loc->{"geo:Point"}->{"geo:lat"}</geo:lat>
    <geo:long>$loc->{"geo:Point"}->{"geo:long"}</geo:long>
</item>
```

```
ITEM
    } else {
        print STDERR "Couldn't geocode: \""
            . join ("\",\"", @vals) . "\"\n";
    }
}

print "</channel></rss>\n";

#
# "getrecord" returns the next record as an array from an open
#  filehandle. It is a simple state machine, that expects a file
#  formatted in 'Yahoo! CVS'
#
sub getrecord {
    my $fh = shift;
    my $c = "";
    my $st = 0;
    my @record;
    my $entry = "";
    while (defined($c)) {
        $c = getc($fh);
        if ($st == 0) {
            if ($c eq "\n" || ! $c) {
                return \@record;
            } elsif ($c eq "\"") {
                $st = 1;
            } else {
                die "error: parsing state:$st char:$c\n";
            }
        } elsif ($st == 1) {
            if ($c eq "\"") {
                $st = 2;
            } else {
                $entry .= $c;
            }
        } elsif ($st == 2) {
            if ($c eq "\"") {
                $entry .= "\"";
                $st = 1;
            } elsif ($c eq ",") {
                push @record, $entry;
                $entry = "";
                $st = 0;
            } elsif ($c eq "\n") {
                push @record, $entry;
                return \@record;
            } else {
                die "error: parsing state:$st char:$c\n";
            }
        }
    }
    die "error: premature end of file\n";
}
```

The main body of the script builds a hash from the current record, attempts to geocode the address, and outputs an RSS item if it's successful. For U.S. locations with full street address, the REST service from *http://geocoder.us* is employed. It expects an address, city name, and state abbreviation, and it returns a small bit of XML containing a latitude/longitude pair if it's successful. The free service is rate limited, so you'll notice pauses during requests. For non-U.S. locations—and for unsuccessful Geocoder requests—a request is made to the REST interface of the Geocoder at *http://brainoff.com/geocoder*, which expects a city, state abbreviation for U.S. cities, and country code.

The country codes are particular to the GNS (*http://earth-info.nga.mil/gns/html*) database that backs this service. To look up the codes, go to *http://brainoff.com/geocoder/countryselect.php* and select a country; a JavaScript alert will give you the code. You will need to map the country names used in your address book to these codes, by adding entries to %countrycode in the script.

If you use a non-English language on Yahoo!, you might have different field names from the ones expected. The script uses Home Address, Home City, Home State, and Home Country. You might need to examine your CSV export and replace these field names in the code. Similarly, if you wanted to map work addresses, you'd replace Home with Work in each of these field names. Another modification to try is adding a <description> or <link> field to each item, set, for example, to the Personal Website field.

Running the Hack

With the script and the Yahoo! CSV export file (*yahoo.csv*) in place, call the script like this:

```
perl yadr2geo.pl < yahoo.csv > rss.xml
```

The file *rss.xml* will contain each of the entries from your Yahoo! Address Book, along with its geocoded location.

Plotting the Addresses

The final step is to download worldKit from *http://brainoff.com/worldkit* and install it on your server or locally. Loading the included *index.html* in your browser displays the default map. Replace the included *rss.xml* with the output of *yadr2geo.pl* and reload the map. You'll see the locations of your friends spread over the globe, as in the geographically dispersed map in Figure 3-20.

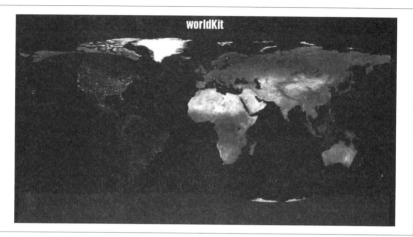

Figure 3-20. Yahoo! Address Book entries plotted on a worldKit map

There are many possible customizations described in the worldKit documentation, from changing the map from global to city scale, to changing the annotation colors according to the category of each contact.

—Mikel Maron

 HACK **Discuss, Share, and Collaborate with Others**

#59 Use Yahoo! Groups to set up a space to share information via email and on the Web.

The Web is redefining how groups of people can work together to achieve a common goal. At one time, forming collaborative relationships meant meeting in the same physical location. By collaborating online, people across the globe can come together to work on a project, exchange information, or simply chat. A family that's distributed across the country can share photos and stories, or a local club can plan meeting times.

Yahoo! Groups is a space that facilitates these kinds of relationships, and at its most basic, Yahoo! Groups provides an easy way to create a *mailing list*. A mailing list is simply a way to send an email to a number of specified email addresses. Some mailing lists are one-way, meaning the list owner sends email to everyone on the list but members don't communicate between each other; these are called *announcement* or *distribution* lists. A two-way list is called a *discussion* list and allows any of its members to send an email to the list; everyone on the list will receive the message. A Yahoo! Group can have either type of mailing list, but Yahoo! Groups are most often thought of as a place for discussion.

Group Features

In addition to its mailing list, every Yahoo! Group has its own group site. Here are the features you'll find at a Yahoo! Groups site:

Messages
> Every message sent to the group via email is archived at the group site, where members can search through past messages or post new messages to the group.

Chat
> A Java™ application that runs in the browser provides real-time chatting for members that are at the group site at the same time.

File, Photo, and Link Sharing
> Members can upload files and photos to share with others. And there's a special section of the group site for sharing links to other sites.

Shared Databases
> The group can work together on a database of information. You can even create your own structure for the data. Prebuilt options include a shared phone book, CD library, recipes, and contact list.

Group Polls
> You can take the pulse of the group by creating a multiple-choice poll question and letting members vote on the choices.

Shared Calendar
> Everyone can keep each other informed of important events by adding event descriptions to the group calendar.

Each Yahoo! Group site offers a number of features that aren't available via email.

Joining a Group

Though you might be tempted to rush into creating your own group, you might find that a group already exists for your favorite topic.

There are millions of public Yahoo! Groups, and you can search for groups or browse by topic at *http://groups.yahoo.com*. Say you're interested in robotics and want to see what people are discussing. You could browse through the categories to Science → Engineering → Mechanical → Robotics and find a listing of around 500 potential groups, as shown in Figure 3-21.

Each Yahoo! Group listing shows the title and description, the number of members, and whether the message archive is open to the public. If the archives are public, you can read through past discussions to see if you're interested in the group. Otherwise, you might have to join the group and try it out.

When you spot a group you might like to join, click the group title and you'll visit the group site, like the one shown in Figure 3-22.

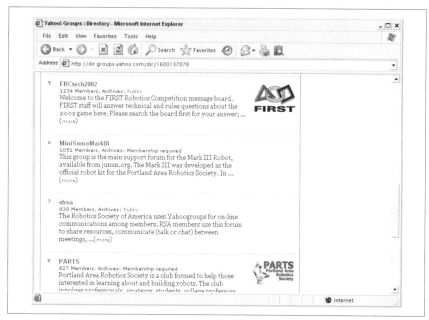

Figure 3-21. A listing of Yahoo! Groups

Figure 3-22. An individual Yahoo! Groups site

Across the top of the group page, you'll notice that it lists the group activity within the past seven days. This includes messages posted to the group and any files, photos, or links shared. This is a good way to get a sense of how active a particular group is. You'll also be able to read the entire group description and read through recent messages if the archives are public. Click Join This Group! to become a member. At this point, you'll need to log in with your Yahoo! ID if you're not logged in already.

After you decide to join a group, you'll need to decide how you'd like to receive messages. You can choose your preferred email address for the group and how you'd like to receive messages at that address:

Individual Emails
> With this setting, you'll receive every individual email sent to the group. This is a good option if you want to be in the thick of daily conversation.

Daily Digest
> A *digest* is a group of all the messages to the group for a day, joined together into one email. This is a good option if you'd like to keep close tabs on the group but don't want to participate heavily in the conversation.

Special Notices
> With this option, you'll receive only messages that the group moderators mark as important. Use this option if you primarily read messages at the group site but want an occasional update.

No Email
> You can read a group exclusively at the group site and avoid any extra messages in your inbox.

You can also choose whether you prefer plain-text or HTML-formatted email.

Once you're a member, you'll be able to post messages to the group, access the archives, and use the extended features of the group site. Keep in mind that some groups require approval from a moderator before allowing you to become a member, and some groups require that all messages sent to the group are approved by a moderator before they're sent on to the entire group.

Creating a Group

To start your own group, browse to *http://groups.yahoo.com* and click the "Start a group now" link. You'll need to log in if you haven't done so already. You can create a group in three steps:

Choose a Category

You need to place your group within a Yahoo! Groups category, even if the group is going to be private. If your group is for a family, you could place it in Family & Home → Families → Individual Families.

Describe the Group

Enter a group name, email address prefix, and description. This description is the group's public face to the world and will appear in the Yahoo! Groups directory if the group is public. The email address prefix will also determine the group site URL, so choose something short and memorable.

Confirm Your Address

Choose your preferred email address to receive messages at the group, and prove you're not a robot by filling out a captcha form, as you may have done when you created a Yahoo! ID [Hack #3].

With the group created, there's nothing more you need to do. You can start inviting people to join your group and start the discussion. You can view your group site by visiting its URL, which is in this format:

```
http://groups.yahoo.com/group/insert email prefix
```

Even though your group is ready to go with the default options, click the Management link on the left side of the home page to see all of your administrative options. The links under the Group Settings headings will let you configure every aspect of your group, from public archives to the look and feel of the group site.

H A C K   Archive Yahoo! Groups Messages with yahoo2mbox
#60

Looking to keep a local archive of your favorite mailing list? With yahoo2mbox, you can import the final results into your favorite mailer.

With the popularity of Yahoo! Groups (*http://groups.yahoo.com*) comes a problem. Sometimes, you want to save the archives of a Yahoo! Group, access the archives outside the Yahoo! Groups site, or move your list somewhere else and take your existing archive with you.

The Code

Vadim Zeitlin had these same concerns, which is why he wrote yahoo2mbox (*http://www.tt-solutions.com/en/products/yahoo2mbox*). This hack retrieves all the messages from a mailing list archive at Yahoo! Groups and saves them to a local file in mbox format. Plenty of options make this handy to have when you're trying to transfer information from Yahoo! Groups. You'll need Perl and several additional modules to run this code, including Getopt::Long, HTML::Entities, HTML::HeadParser, HTML::TokeParser, and LWP::UserAgent.

Running the Hack

Running the code looks like this:

```
perl yahoo2mbox.pl [options] [-o mbox] groupname
```

The options for running the program are as follows:

--help	give the usage message showing the program options
--version	show the program version and exit
--verbose	give verbose informational messages (default)
--quiet	be silent, only error messages are given
--resume	resume an interrupted download
-o mbox	save the message to mbox instead of file named groupname
--start=n	start retrieving messages at index n instead of 1
--end=n	stop retrieving messages at index n instead of the last one
--last=n	get the last specified number of messages from the list
--noresume	don't resume, **overwrites** the existing output file if any
--user=name	login to eGroups using this username (default: guest login)
--pass=pass	the password to use for login (default: none)
--cookies=xxx	file to use to store cookies (default: none, 'netscape' uses netscape cookies file).
--proxy=url	use the given proxy, if 'no' don't use proxy at all (even not the environment variable http_proxy which is used by default), may use http://username:password\@full.host.name/
--country=xx	use the given country code in order to access localized yahoo
--x-yahoo	add X-Yahoo-Message-Num header to identify Yahoo! messages
--delay=n	sleep for the specified number of seconds between requests

So, this command downloads messages from Weird Al Club, starting at message 3258:

```
% perl yahoo2mbox.pl --start=3258 weirdalclub2
Logging in anonymously... ok.
Getting number of messages in group weirdalclub2...
Retrieving messages 3258..3287: ........................... done!
Saved 30 message(s) in weirdalclub2.
```

Here, the messages are saved to a file called *weirdalclub2*. Renaming the file *weirdalclub2.mbx* means that I can immediately open the messages in Eudora, as shown in Figure 3-23. Of course, you can also open the resulting files in any mail program that can import (or natively read) the mbox format.

Figure 3-23. A Yahoo! Groups archive in Eudora

Hacking the Hack

Because this is someone else's program, there's not too much hacking to be done. On the other hand, you might find that you don't want to end this process with the mbox file; you might want to convert to other formats for use in other projects or archives. In that case, check out these other programs to take that mbox format a little further:

hypermail (http://sourceforge.net/projects/hypermail/)
    Converts mbox format to cross-referenced HTML documents.

mb2md (http://www.gerg.ca/hacks/mb2md/)
    Converts mbox format to Maildir. Requires Python and Procmail.

mb2md.pl (http://batleth.sapienti-sat.org/projects/mb2md/)
    Converts mbox format to Maildir. Uses Perl.

—*Kevin Hemenway and Tara Calishain*

H A C K   Explore Your Social Networks
#61   Use Yahoo! 360 to stay in touch with friends, family, and coworkers while viewing their social connections.

You've probably heard the famous theory that says everyone on earth can be connected to anyone else through six degrees of separation. For example, if you really wanted to get in touch with Bill Gates through friends, you could go to someone you know, they could go to someone they know, and you'd eventually reach Bill through no more than six contacts. These relationships make up your social network, and Yahoo! 360 is an attempt to map and expose those connections.

In addition, Yahoo! 360 is a place to keep your friends, family, and coworkers up-to-date with what's happening in your life, as well as a way for you to see what they're up to. It's also a way to meet your friends' friends, and perhaps meet some people you wouldn't have otherwise met. Some of the features you'll find at Yahoo! 360 include:

Your personal profile
Assemble an autobiography and list cities you've lived in, places you've worked, and schools where you've studied. You can also put together lists of favorite movies, music, and television shows.

Weblog
You can keep a personal public journal that will keep your friends up-to-date with your recent thoughts and activities.

Friends list
Assemble a list of your contacts that are on Yahoo! 360 and stay in touch with them.

Yahoo! Network
You can integrate Yahoo! Network data into your personal profile, including Yahoo! Photos you've uploaded, Yahoo! Groups you belong to, and your Yahoo! Local reviews.

Whether you arrive at Yahoo! 360 by invitation or by signing up at *http://360.yahoo.com*, you should take a few steps before you start connecting with others to get the most out of your Yahoo! 360 space.

Create a Profile

Your Yahoo! 360 profile is your public face to others. As people run into your weblog or see your comments on other weblogs, they'll be able to view your profile to learn more about you. When you log into Yahoo! 360, you'll find your profile page full of empty yellow boxes, as shown in Figure 3-24.

This page is a blank canvas that you can begin to fill in with details about yourself. A good place to start is the Edit Basic Info link on the left side of the page. From there, you can enter your name and a nickname, and decide how you want your identity displayed to others.

You can include other bits of information, such as your current location, age, birthday, and primary email address. Most settings allow you to specify a privacy setting, as shown in Figure 3-25, and you'll find similar settings throughout Yahoo! 360.

The default value for information entered into Yahoo! 360 is "just me" (private), and you might want to leave this value alone until you're finished with your Yahoo! 360 space and ready to connect with others. You can always click the Edit Basic Info link later to change your basic info privacy settings.

Once your basic info is set, click Save to return to your profile page. Because photos are used extensively throughout Yahoo! 360, a good next step is uploading a personal photo. The personal photo space is fairly large, so if

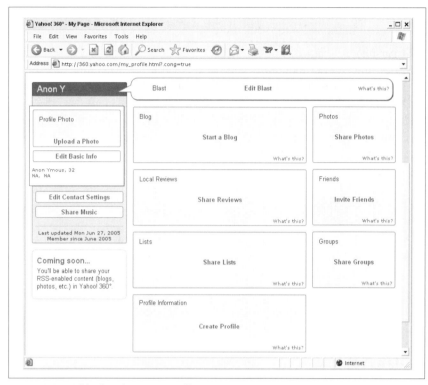

Figure 3-24. A blank Yahoo! 360 profile

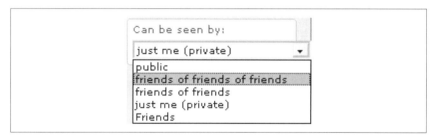

Figure 3-25. Choosing a privacy setting for a piece of information

you'd like to include an image without any distortion, create a personal photo that's 190 pixels wide by 245 pixels high. The photo will need to be in the standard JPEG format. You can upload up to four different photos, and people reading your profile will be able to click on thumbnails to see them at the 190 × 245 size.

With your personal photos in place, click the Create Profile link at the bottom of your profile page. This is where your autobiography begins, and you can tell people as little or as much about yourself as you'd like. Yahoo! 360 provides a space for describing yourself, forms for listing places you've lived, worked, or gone to school, a space to list your home page, a way to list languages you speak, and a spot for your favorite quote. Click Save when you're finished, and you should start to see your profile page taking shape.

Click Share Lists to add lists of things you're interested in. These lists help you connect with other Yahoo! 360 members by interest. You can list general interests, favorite books, movies, music, and television shows.

Finally, click Edit Contact Settings on the left side of your profile page and decide how you'd like to receive messages from other Yahoo! 360 members. You can allow anyone to contact you, just people you've designated as friends, or friends of friends within your network. You can also adjust the settings for Yahoo! 360 friend invitations and Yahoo! Messenger settings. Now that you have a home base set and you've decided how you'd like to be contacted, you can start connecting with others.

Start Blogging

A *blog* (short for *weblog*), is a public journal that can be a way to share opinions, a place to describe recent activities, or simply a space to chronicle interesting things you find on the Web. To set up your blog, go to your profile page and click the "Start a Blog" link and give your new weblog a title and description. You can also choose to activate a Simple URL for your blog. The default URLs for Yahoo! 360 weblogs aren't easy to pass around. Here's what a standard Yahoo! 360 blog URL looks like:

```
http://blog.360.yahoo.com/blog-W.nEFiYoc6l2SMTF4MyXaOE-
```

But you can enable a Simple URL that contains your Yahoo! ID and is much more manageable, something like this:

```
http://blog.360.yahoo.com/yhoohacks
```

Yahoo! 360 uses the first, more complex URL as the default, so that your Yahoo! ID isn't immediately available to others. If you don't mind sharing your Yahoo! ID with others, though, you can have a much simpler URL to share with friends and family.

Next, choose who can see your blog: anyone (public), friends in your network, or just you (completely private). If you choose the public option, you can also publish a *site feed*. With a site feed, others can subscribe to your weblog through My Yahoo! or other RSS newsreaders. Finally, choose who can comment on your posts and click the Begin Blog button.

You'll find yourself at your weblog, without any posts. Click the Compose New Entry link on the left to write your first message to the world. Just as with email, each post has a title and a body (entry content). In most browsers you can format the text of your post with the controls just above the Entry Content area. Figure 3-26 shows some of the formatting options available, including bold, italics, links, smileys, and lists.

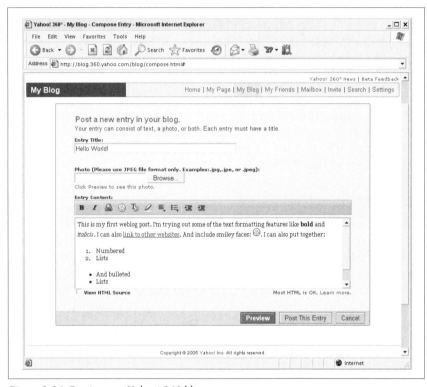

Figure 3-26. Posting to a Yahoo! 360 blog

If you're familiar with HTML, you can skip the formatting buttons and write the HTML yourself by selecting the View HTML Source option. Be aware that your HTML options are limited; you'll need to brush up on what's allowed at Yahoo! 360 by clicking the "Learn more" link under the Entry Content area.

If you include a photo with your post, the photo will appear at the top of the post when it's published. The photo will be scaled to 284 pixels wide once it's uploaded to Yahoo! 360. The photo will appear directly under the title and above the main body of the post once the post is published.

Once you're happy with your entry, click Post This Entry to make the post available on your blog. Who can read your words will depend on your privacy settings. An occasional blog entry is an unobtrusive way to keep friends, coworkers, and family up to speed on what's happening in your life. Plus, your friends and family can add their own comments to your posts, which keeps a public dialogue going.

Another option available on your Yahoo! 360 blog is a tool for building a *blogroll*. A blogroll is simply a list of links to other blogs and sites you enjoy. To add sites to your blogroll, click the My Blog link at the top of any Yahoo! 360 page and click the Edit Blogroll link. From there, you can add sites by typing in a site's name and URL. If you're moving from another weblog service and already have a blogroll, you might want to automate this process [Hack #62].

Connect with Friends

The strength of Yahoo! 360 lies in your connections with other members. As you add people to your friends list, you'll see their recent activity and they'll see yours. Figure 3-27 shows a Yahoo! 360 home page listing the latest information from friends.

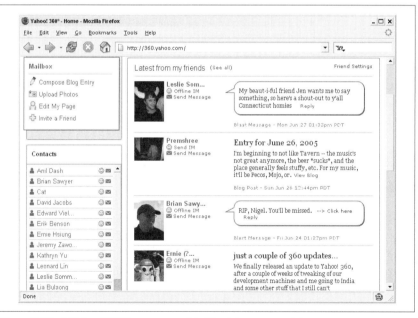

Figure 3-27. A Yahoo! 360 home page with friends' current activity

There are a few different ways to build your own friends list. You can click the Home link at the top of any Yahoo! 360 page and then click the "Invite a Friend" link from the left side of the home page. From there, you can send an invitation email and personal message to someone you know. If she accepts your invitation, joins Yahoo! 360, builds a profile, and starts posting to a weblog, she'll be listed as a contact, and you'll see her latest activity on your home page.

Another way to spot friends is by browsing your existing friends' lists. If we're all connected by six degrees, you shouldn't have to surf other friends' lists long before you find people you know. You can also click the Search link at the top of any Yahoo! 360 page to search for people you know, or you can enter specific criteria such as location, age, or schools attended to find people you don't know (yet).

You can also click My Page at the top of any Yahoo! 360 page to get to your profile. If you've assembled lists of books, music, and movies you enjoy, you can click those titles to see other Yahoo! 360 members who share that interest. For example, if you've listed Kraftwerk as a musical favorite, simply click the Kraftwerk link to see others who like the German electronic group. If you see someone you'd like to add to your friends list, click the Invite link next to his name. If he accepts your invitation, he'll be added to your friends list, and you'll see his latest activity on your home page.

In addition to weblog posts and comments, you can communicate privately with other Yahoo! 360 members through your Mailbox. As you'd expect, you can reach your Yahoo! 360 Mailbox by clicking the Mailbox link at the top of any Yahoo! 360 page. Whenever you see someone you'd like to talk with, click the Send Message link next to her name. The messages are similar to email, but your email address isn't exposed in the process. This way, you can contact people with as little or as much anonymity as you'd like.

HACK #62 Import an Existing Blogroll to Yahoo! 360

Moving your blog to Yahoo! 360 and already have a blogroll? Automate adding blogroll links with OPML and Perl.

A prominent feature of most weblogs is a list of links to other weblogs running down the side of the page. This list is called a *blogroll*, and they're so popular that a service called Blogrolling (*http://www.blogrolling.com*) is there to help people maintain large lists of links and easily include them on their own weblog.

Yahoo! 360 [Hack #61] also features a blogroll and a blogroll manager (*http://blog.360.yahoo.com/blog/blogroll.html*). To add a link to your blogroll, add the site name and URL into the form. If you'd like to add more links, click the Add Another button at the top of the page to reveal more fields. Adding a handful of links this way is fine, but if you already have a list of 10 or more sites you'd like to include, this can get tedious quickly. Luckily, there's a standard way of exchanging links that can make the job faster.

As more and more services offer the ability to create blogrolls or lists of links, the way to exchange these lists is an XML format called Outline Processor Markup Language (OPML). OPML can be used to syndicate lists of just about anything. Sites such as Blogrolling and the newsreader Bloglines (*http://www.bloglines.com*) use OPML to import and export long lists of web sites. For example, at Bloglines, you can subscribe to your favorite web sites to read their posts. Using Bloglines on a regular basis, you can accumulate a list of hundreds of sites. If you'd like to use this same list of accumulated sites with another service, you can use Bloglines's export function to get an OPML list of the site names and URLs.

Each individual entry in an OPML file exported from Bloglines looks like this:

```
<outline title="O'Reilly Radar" htmlUrl="http://radar.oreilly.com/"
type="rss" xmlUrl="http://radar.oreilly.com/index.rdf"/>
```

As you can see, the OPML file contains the title and URL of the site, and the location of the site's RSS feed. Having your list of favorite sites in this structured way can help you automate adding the sites to your Yahoo! 360 blogroll. Figure 3-28 shows a Yahoo! 360 blogroll that's been imported with the code in this hack.

Instead of typing in each entry by hand into the Yahoo! 360 form, you can let Perl do the heavy lifting for you.

The Code

This code relies on a nonstandard component called WWW::Mechanize to handle the automation. Among other things, WWW::Mechanize can log in to web sites and fill out forms—perfect for adding a batch of entries to the Yahoo! 360 blogroll editor. You'll also need to install the Yahoo!-specific component WWW::Yahoo::Login, which works with WWW::Mechanize to log in to your Yahoo! account.

Once the components are installed, save the following code to a file called *import_blogroll_360.pl* and be sure to add your Yahoo! ID and password to the script. Also, take a look at your current blogroll form (available at *http://blog.360.yahoo.com/blog/blogroll.html*) and count the number of rows you see. If you're starting with a blank blogroll, the number should be 3. Add this number to the code at the line my $i = *n*. This will tell the script where to begin adding links and will ensure that any current links you have at your Yahoo! 360 blogroll won't be overwritten.

Import an Existing Blogroll to Yahoo! 360

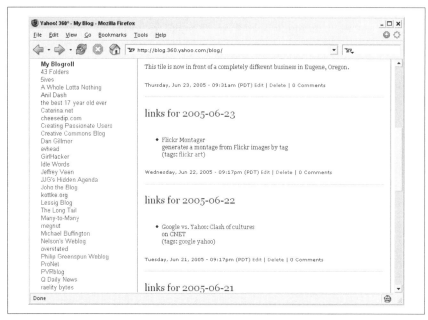

Figure 3-28. A Yahoo! 360 imported blogroll

```perl
#!/usr/bin/perl
# import_blogroll_360.pl
# Imports links from an OPML file into Yahoo! 360 Bookmarks
# Usage: import_blogroll_360.pl <OPML FILE>

use strict;
use WWW::Yahoo::Login qw( login logout );
use WWW::Mechanize;

# Open the incoming file
open(OPML, "@ARGV") || die "usage: import_blogroll_360.pl <OPML >";
my @opml = reverse <OPML>;

my $mech = WWW::Mechanize->new( );

# Log into Yahoo! 360
my $resp = login(
    mech    => $mech,
    uri     => 'http://blog.360.yahoo.com/blog/blogroll.html',
    user    => 'insert Yahoo! ID',
    pass    => 'insert Yahoo! Password',
);

# Set the beginning field value
my $i = n;
my $form = $mech->current_form( );

# If login succeeded, loop through the OPML
```

```
    if ($resp) {
        # Parse the OPML
        foreach my $link (@opml) {
            # Depending on the flavor of OPML you're parsing
            # you may need to edit this regex
            while ($link =~ /<outline title="(.*?)" htmlUrl="(.*?)"[^>].*/gi) {
                $i++;
                my $title = $1;
                my $url = $2;
                # Set title field
                my (%titleattr);
                $titleattr{name} = "title_$i";
                $titleattr{value} = $title;
                $form->push_input("text", \%titleattr);
                $mech->field("title_$i", $title);
                # Set URL field
                my (%urlattr);
                $urlattr{name} = "url_$i";
                $urlattr{value} = $url;
                $form->push_input("text", \%urlattr);
                $mech->field("url_$i", $url);
                print "$title - $url\n";
            }
        }
        $mech->field("amt",$i);

        # Submit the form
        $mech->click("save");
    } else {
        warn $WWW::Yahoo::Login::ERROR;
    }
```

This script is set to parse the output from Bloglines, and other services might have slightly different flavors of OPML that will require some changes. Even though OPML is emerging as a standard, the format is flexible and different services implement it in different ways. For example, Bloglines uses a `title` attribute to indicate the title of a site, while some others use a `text` attribute. If the flavor of OPML that you're working with is different, change the line that contains the format of the <outline> tag (bold in the code).

Running the Hack

To run the code, call it from the command line and pass in the name of your OPML file. So if your Bloglines export file is named *bloglines_export.xml*, you'd invoke the script like this:

```
perl import_blogroll_360.pl bloglines_export.xml
```

Once executed, the script logs in to Yahoo! 360 with your Yahoo! ID and password and analyzes the blogroll form. From there, it loops through the OPML file, adding the proper fields and values to the Yahoo! 360 form. Once it's through the file, `$mech->click("save")` does the work of clicking the Save button, and you'll have your old blogroll in a new location!

H A C K **Add an API to Your Yahoo! 360 Blog**
#63 Start using third-party services with your Yahoo! 360 blog by adding your
own API.

Yahoo! 360 is a site designed to help you keep in touch with friends, family,
and coworkers. In addition to sharing reviews, photos, and lists of your
favorite music and movies, Yahoo! 360 lets you post messages in a blog. Of
course, Yahoo! isn't the only place you can keep a blog. Services such as
Blogger (*http://www.blogger.com*) and TypePad (*http://www.typepad.com*) will
also host a blog for you. But if your friends are all chatting away on Yahoo!
360, you might want to keep a journal there, where you and your friends can
all connect.

At the time of this writing, Yahoo! 360 is in beta testing, and its developers
are working on the features they intend to offer for a wider release. Unfortunately, this means the blog portion of Yahoo! 360 isn't as robust as some of
the other weblog services, and Yahoo! 360 doesn't yet offer a way to post to
your weblog from third-party services. For example, if I keep a weblog on
Blogger, I can post photos to that weblog from Flickr (*http://www.flickr.com*),
a photo-sharing application recently acquired by Yahoo!. That's because
Blogger offers an application programming interface (API) that lets other services access data programmatically.

Even though Yahoo! 360 doesn't offer an API, with a bit of scripting you can
mimic a weblog API and start posting through third-party tools.

What You Need

To implement this hack, you'll need access to a publicly available web server
that can run Perl scripts, and several external modules. Here's a look at the
modules you need, what they provide, and where you can find them:

XMLRPC::Transport::HTTP
    This module handles all of the formatting of XML-RPC requests and
    responses required for the metaWeblog API interface. The module is part
    of a larger package called SOAP::Lite. To read the documentation, go to
    *http://search.cpan.org/~byrne/SOAP-Lite-0.60a/lib/XMLRPC/Transport/
    HTTP.pm*.

LWP::Simple
    This module allows you to download the contents of pages from the
    Web. It is available at *http://search.cpan.org/~gaas/libwww-perl-5.803/
    lib/LWP/Simple.pm*.

WWW::Mechanize
> Also known as Mech, this module can automate interactions with a web site. This hack uses Mech to log in to Yahoo! and post items to a Yahoo! 360 weblog. To download the module and read its documentation, go to *http://search.cpan.org/~petdance/WWW-Mechanize-1.12/lib/WWW/Mechanize.pm*.

WWW::Yahoo::Login
> This module is an extension of Mech that handles logging in to Yahoo! sites. Find it ar *http://search.cpan.org/~struan/WWW-Yahoo-Login-0.10/lib/WWW/Yahoo/Login.pm*.

Image::Size
> This module can find the dimensions in pixels of any image. It's used in this hack to find the dimension of images posted from Flickr. You can read more at *http://search.cpan.org/~rjray/Image-Size-2.992/Size.pm*.

If you're missing any of these modules, you can install each of them with CPAN, like this:

```
perl -MCPAN -e shell
cpan> install insert package name
```

With the modules in place, you're ready to move on to the script.

The Code

This code doesn't fully implement all of the functions you'll find in the metaWeblog API. Instead, it implements two methods: getUsersBlogs and newPost. These two methods are the bare minimum needed to interface with other systems and add new weblog posts.

As you'd expect, getUsersBlogs returns a list of weblogs that a particular user can post to at a weblog service. Because Yahoo! 360 users are limited to one blog per Yahoo! ID, this function simply logs in to Yahoo! and fetches the name of the user's Yahoo! 360 blog. The newPost function also logs in to Yahoo!, changes the incoming text of a post if necessary, and adds the text as a new post to the Yahoo! 360 weblog.

Save the following code to a file called *Y360_api.pl*:

```
#!/usr/bin/perl
# Y360_api.pl
# Implements a minimalist metaWeblog API for Yahoo! 360 blogs.
# You can read more about the metaWeblog API here:
# http://www.xmlrpc.com/metaWeblogApi
#
# Usage: send metaWeblog API requests for methods:
#
#       getUsersBlogs
#           Returns the name and URL of a Yahoo! 360
```

```
#               blog for the given user.
#          newPost
#               Adds a post with the incoming text to
#               a Yahoo! 360 blog for the given user.

use strict;
use XMLRPC::Transport::HTTP;

XMLRPC::Transport::HTTP::CGI
  -> dispatch_to('metaWeblog')
  -> handle
;

package metaWeblog;
use WWW::Yahoo::Login qw( login logout );
use WWW::Mechanize;
use Image::Size 'html_imgsize';
use LWP::Simple;

my $mech = WWW::Mechanize->new(autocheck => 1);

sub getUsersBlogs {
    my($app, $msg, $user, $pass) = @_;

    # Set some defaults
    my $blog_url = "http://blog.360.yahoo.com/blog/";
    my $blog_name = "My Yahoo! 360 Blog";

    # Log into Yahoo! 360
    my $mech = WWW::Mechanize->new( );
    my $login = login(
        mech    => $mech,
        uri     => 'http://blog.360.yahoo.com/blog/',
        user    => $user,
        pass    => $pass,
    );

    # Get weblog URL and title
    if ($login) {
        my $html = $mech->response( )->content( );
        if ($html =~ m!<h2>(.*?)</h2>!mgis) {
            $blog_name = $1;
        }
        if ($html =~ m!<li><a href="(.*?)">View Blog</a></li>!mgis) {
            $blog_url = $1;
        }
    }

    # Send the response
    my @res;
    push @res, { url => SOAP::Data->type(string => $blog_url),
        blogid => SOAP::Data->type(string => "1"),
        blogName => SOAP::Data->type(string => $blog_name) };
    \@res;
}
```

```
sub newPost {
    shift if UNIVERSAL::isa($_[0] => __PACKAGE__);
    my($blog_id, $user, $pass, $item, $publish) = @_;

    # Log into Yahoo! 360
    my $mech = WWW::Mechanize->new( );
    my $login = login(
        mech    => $mech,
        uri     => 'http://blog.360.yahoo.com/blog/compose.html',
        user    => $user,
        pass    => $pass,
    );

    # Add width/height to image tags (for Flickr posts)
    if ($item->{description} =~ m!(.*?<img src="(.*?)" .*?)( )(/>.*)!mgis) {
        my $file = get($2);
        my $size = html_imgsize(\$file);
        $item->{description} = "$1 $size $4";
    }

    # Write post description to a file
    open(FILE, ">> post.txt") or die("Couldn't open post.txt\n");
    print FILE $item->{description} . "\n\n";

    # Remove initial div tag from del.icio.us posts
    $item->{description} =~ s!<div class="delicious-link">(.*?)</div>⏎
!$1!gis;

    # Strip line breaks
    $item->{description} =~ s!\n!!gis;

    # If login succeeded, add post and send a successful
    # response with the generic 1000 as the post ID
    if ($login && $item->{title}) {
        my $form = $mech->form_name("blog_compose");
        $mech->field("title", $item->{title});
        $mech->field("contents", $item->{description});
        $mech->click("post");
        SOAP::Data->type(string => "1000");
    } else {
        return error $WWW::Yahoo::Login::ERROR;
    }
}
```

This script is built specifically to work with the API-related services at Flickr [Hack #67] and del.icio.us—a bookmark manager available at *http://del.icio.us*. The newPost subroutine reformats incoming text based on the text that these services provide. For example, Flickr doesn't provide height and width attributes for image tags in the HTML it produces, and Yahoo! 360 requires those attributes in weblog posts. So this script uses the Image::Size module to add those attributes to the text.

Running the Hack

To run the hack, upload *Y360_api.pl* to a publicly available web server and note the URL. It should look something like this:

```
http://example.com/Y360_api.pl
```

Be aware that this URL is sometimes referred to as an *API Endpoint*, so don't let the jargon throw you off. Whenever a service asks for a URL, this is the one you should use.

The final step is to test out your new API at a third-party service. Since the script was built specifically for Flickr, that's a good place to start. Follow the steps to set up a weblog at Flickr [Hack #98] and choose MetaWeblogAPI Enabled Blog as your weblog type, enter your script's URL as the Endpoint, and include your Yahoo! ID and password.

Flickr will contact your script behind the scenes with a getUsersBlogs request, and your script will send back the title and URL of your Yahoo! 360 weblog. Once your weblog is set up in Flickr, you can click the Blog This button above any photo and choose your Yahoo! 360 weblog (see Figure 3-29).

Figure 3-29. The Blog This button at Flickr

From there you can compose your post at Flickr and see the finished product as a post on your Yahoo! 360 blog like that shown in Figure 3-30.

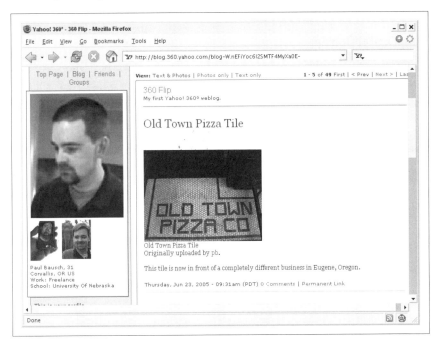

Figure 3-30. A Flickr image posted to a Yahoo! 360 blog

The code takes a bit of time to set up, but once you wire this shortcut for yourself, you may find that you use both Yahoo! 360 and Flickr more often.

HACK #64 Create a Yahoo! Avatar

Make a custom caricature of yourself and watch it smile or cry along with you as you chat through Yahoo! Instant Messenger.

Having an instant messaging conversation on the computer is a bit like having a conversation with a blindfold on. You can "hear" what the other person is saying clearly by reading what he types, but other cues, such as facial expressions, are completely absent. Without seeing and hearing the person you're chatting with, it's hard to pick up on emotional overtones such as humor, sadness, or sarcasm. This is exactly why we've developed text shortcuts to convey emotions over the Internet—for example, using an *emoticon* to indicate smiling, or using an abbreviation such as LOL to indicate that you're laughing out loud.

Yahoo! has taken this idea of conveying emotion a step beyond such text shortcuts by creating cartoon-like characters called *avatars* to stand in for some of these emotional cues during Yahoo! Instant Messenger conversations. With a little work, you can create your own avatar that's unique to your personality and let it stand in for you as you chat with people online.

Your Digital Double

To create the Internet representation of *you*, browse to the Yahoo! Avatars site (*http://avatars.yahoo.com*). (You'll need to be at a Windows computer and have the Flash plug-in installed for your browser.) Once you're there, log in and choose the gender of your avatar (male or female); all other options will flow from this choice. You can then go on a virtual shopping spree to change the look of your avatar in a number of ways:

Appearance
Match your skin color, face shape, eye color, or hairstyle.

Apparel
Dress your avatar up in different tops and bottoms.

Extras
Give your avatar bags, jewelry, scarves, sports items, pets, hats, or holiday-specific items.

Backgrounds
Put your avatar in a specific location, such as a school or vacation spot.

Branded
Give your avatar the latest brand-name apparel.

As you go from section to section changing your avatar, you can keep track of your changes on the Previewing Changes panel on the left side of the page, as shown in Figure 3-31.

As you click different apparel items or extras, you'll find them listed under the "What I'm trying on" box below the preview panel. When you find a combination you like, click Save to move the list of items to the "What I'm wearing" box. If you ever find that you've accidentally added a ski outfit and your avatar is in a beach scene, click the Clear button to revert to your last saved avatar.

There are quite a few customizations to click through, and if you ever spot something you'd like to come back to, you can add an outfit or scene to your Favorites section to keep them just a click away. (You can see your favorites at any time by clicking the My Favorites link from the Yahoo! Avatars toolbar.) You can also save entire avatars to your Favorites list, giving you quick access to fairly complex combinations quickly. But keep in mind that if you ever decide to change genders, you'll lose all of your previously saved avatars!

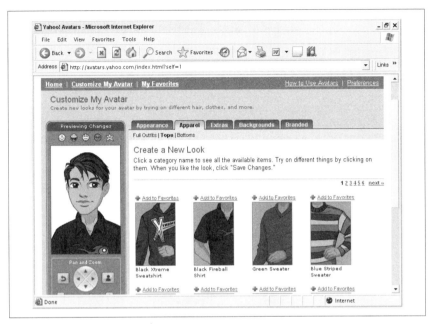

Figure 3-31. Dressing up a Yahoo! avatar

Getting Moody

Just as your avatar can reflect your physical appearance to some degree, your avatar can also reflect your mood. At the top of the preview panel in Figure 3-31, you can see five face icons that represent different moods. Clicking on each face changes your avatar to display a different emotion, such as happy, excited, sad, or angry. Figure 3-32 shows the whole range of available emotions.

Figure 3-32. A Yahoo! avatar showing its emotions

There's also a *special* mood that changes based on the selections you've made for your avatar's facial appearance. If you don't set a specific mood for your avatar when you're in the designing process, you avatar will still emote while you're chatting.

Once your avatar is set, start Yahoo! Instant Messenger and log in. Double-click an ID in your friends list to bring up a chat window, and click the small head icon next to the Send button. This will make your avatar visible to you while you're chatting with others. If your friend on the other end is also using the Windows version of Yahoo! Instant Messenger, she'll see your avatar as well.

As you're chatting, you might notice that your avatar changes expression from time to time. For example, if you type LOL in a conversation, your avatar will have a big smile for a moment and return to its normal expression. There is a whole series of words and emoticons that will change the expression of your avatar. Here are a few of the most common expressions that avatars can display, along with different strings you can type to trigger each one:

Neutral
> happy, nice, or :) (the standard smiling emoticon)

Excited
> hehe, haha, rotf (for "rolling on the floor"), lol, or excited

Sad
> boo, hoo, or :((the frowning face emoticon)

Angry
> hmmph, grr, or angry

To trigger the special mood for a specific avatar, you can type (*). A complete list of avatar-altering words is available at *http://help.yahoo.com/help/us/avatar/avatar-14.html*.

You can also change the mood of your avatar by clicking the avatar within Yahoo! Instant Messenger and choosing Set Avatar Mood To. This option allows you change between the five basic moods shown in Figure 3-32.

While using an avatar can never replace face-to-face communication, Yahoo! Instant Messenger avatars communicate some extra information about identity and emotions as you're communicating in an environment that's largely limited to text.

Add a Content Tab to Yahoo! Messenger

HACK #65 With a bit of Registry hacking, you can add a custom content tab to Yahoo! Instant Messenger.

Yahoo! Messenger (*http://messenger.yahoo.com*) is more than just a way to have conversations with your friends. It's is also a way to keep up with your favorite Yahoo! content. Across the bottom of the Yahoo! Messenger window, you'll find a series of *content tabs*. Each tab gives you instant access to some information you'd normally find on the Yahoo! web site, such as weather, stock quotes, news headlines, or your Yahoo! calendar. Figure 3-33 shows a series of content tabs in Yahoo! Messenger, with the Yahoo! Buzz tab selected.

Figure 3-33. The Yahoo! Buzz content tab in Yahoo! Messenger

The Yahoo! Buzz tab gives you a quick summary of what you'll find at the Yahoo! Buzz site (*http://buzz.yahoo.com*), tracking trends in Yahoo! searching. You can customize which tabs appear in Yahoo! Messenger by choosing Messenger → Preferences from the top menu and selecting the Content Tabs category from the left pane. From there, you can choose from around a dozen different tabs to show or hide from your Yahoo! Messenger interface.

> This hack describes the latest version of Yahoo! Messenger for Windows. At the time of this writing, the Mac version of Yahoo! Messenger has four content tabs, and there's no way to add custom tabs to the interface.

The choices you'll find in your Yahoo! Messenger settings are static, and you can't add or remove tabs you find from within the preferences interface. But this hack shows how to add your own content tab to Yahoo! Messenger by tweaking some settings behind the scenes.

> Thanks to Marcus Foster at Yahoo! for sharing this method of adding a tab!

Inside Your Registry

All of the content tabs within Yahoo! Messenger are defined within the Windows Registry, a database that stores system settings. You can take a look at the settings for each of the tabs by viewing the settings in the Registry Editor. Start the Registry Editor by clicking Start → Run and typing regedit.

> Be very careful when editing your Registry settings. If you change the wrong setting, you could do irreparable harm to your system. Just be aware that the Registry settings are vital to your system, and if you're not comfortable tooling around in sensitive areas, you might want to skip this hack!

With the registry editor open, browse to the following key: HKEY_CURRENT_USER\Software\Yahoo\Pager\View\. Beneath the View key, you'll find a series of registry keys with the prefix YMSGR_. These are the available content tabs, and you can highlight each to see the system settings. Figure 3-34 shows the Registry key for the Yahoo! Buzz tab, with its system settings in the right pane.

Figure 3-34. Yahoo! Messenger content tab settings in the Registry

The important settings to note are Display Name, Display Bmp, and content url. The first two set the tab name and icon. And because each tab display is simply a web page, the content url value is where you'll find the page for a particular tab. In fact, you can visit any tab page in Internet Explorer including the Yahoo! Buzz content tab at *http://tools.search.yahoo.com/ym/buzz*.

The key to adding your own tab to Yahoo! Messenger is creating a new Registry key with content url set to a URL of your choosing. And the easiest way to create a new key with all of the proper settings is to copy an existing key. Inside the Registry Editor, highlight the YMSGR_buzz key, right-click, and click Export. Save the key as *YMSGR_buzz.reg*, and you'll be set to create your own tab.

So, what type of web page makes a good content tab? The best content tab page will be compact, with its contents viewable in a small space. Most pages probably won't fit very well into a content tab, and you'll have to design a page specifically for use within Yahoo! Messenger. If you've already added a Yahoo! Bookmarks sidebar [Hack #30] to your browser, you'll know there's already a page available to display your Yahoo! Bookmarks in a small space. There isn't a Bookmarks content tab currently available in Yahoo! Messenger, but the following Registry changes will add one.

The Code

Copy the *YMSGR_buzz.reg* file and to a new file and name the new file *YMSGR_bookmarks.reg*. Open the file in Notepad and make the following changes to the Registry settings within. Note that the changes are in bold.

```
Windows Registry Editor Version 5.00

[HKEY_CURRENT_USER\Software\Yahoo\Pager\View\YMSGR_bookmarks]
"Display Name"="Bookmarks"
"Display Bmp"="YView\\ybang.bmp"
"default"=dword:00000001
"insert"=dword:00000001
"enable browsing"=dword:00000001
"Stat Letter"="B"
"click count"=dword:00000000
"persistent"=dword:00000001
"content url"="http://my.yahoo.com/tearoff/sites.html"
"MinHeight"=dword:0000001e
"PreferHeight"=dword:000000d1
"Resizable"=dword:00000001
"Refreshable"=dword:00000000
```

The key name has been changed to YMSGR_bookmarks and the display name is set to Bookmarks. There isn't a custom icon for the Bookmarks tab (because it doesn't exist yet), so the icon has been changed to *ybang.bmp*, a generic Yahoo! icon included when you install Yahoo! Messenger.

> If you want to go the extra mile for your custom content tab, you could create your own icon to display it. Use the icons in the *YView* directory of your Yahoo! Messenger installation as a guide.

Finally, the content url setting points to your Yahoo! Bookmarks minimalist display URL.

Running the Hack

Click Save in Notepad to save your modified Registry file, and then double-click *YMSGR_bookmarks.reg*. Confirm that you'd like to add the settings to the Registry, and you should receive a message that the contents were added. Restart Yahoo! Messenger and keep in mind that even if you close the Yahoo! Messenger window it can still be running in the taskbar. You'll need to completely restart the program and then bring up the Content Tabs category in your Preferences. You should see the new option to add a Bookmarks tab, as shown in Figure 3-35.

Figure 3-35. Adding a new content tab in Yahoo! Messenger

HACK

Add a Content Tab to Yahoo! Messenger   #65

Highlight the Bookmarks tab, click the Show button, and click OK to close your Preferences. You should see the new tab along the bottom of Yahoo! Messenger. Click the Bookmarks tab with the generic Yahoo! icon, and you should see your Yahoo! Bookmarks appear in the content pane, as shown in Figure 3-36.

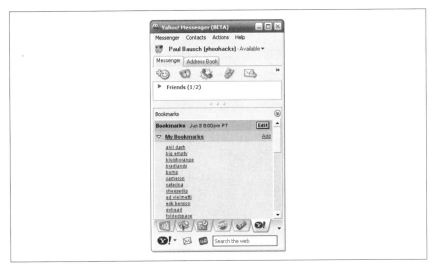

Figure 3-36. The Bookmarks content tab in Yahoo! Messenger

Of course, a custom content tab doesn't have to be Yahoo! content as in this example. Because content tabs are simply standard URLs, you could easily create your own pages and have instant access to your own custom information while you're chatting with friends.

Hacking the Hack

Sites specifically designed for mobile devices like cell phones and PDAs work extremely well as Yahoo! Messenger content tabs. If you can track down a URL for a mobile site, you can create your own tab. For example, Yahoo!'s photo-sharing service Flickr [Hack #67] has a mobile site available at *http://flickr.com/mob*. Change the key and display names in the Registry file, and set content url to the Flickr mobile URL. Once you run the file, restart Yahoo! Messenger and add the new tab. You'll end up with the content shown in Figure 3-37.

With the Flickr tab in place, you can easily keep tabs on the photos your friends are posting without opening up a web browser.

Figure 3-37. Flickr mobile in a Yahoo! Messenger content tab

Yahoo! also has a mobile site (*http://wap.oa.yahoo.com*); you could easily set up a Yahoo! tab and have access to all your personalized Yahoo! content in a single Yahoo! Messenger tab.

H A C K   Send Instant Messages Beyond Yahoo!
#66   In a world where your friends are using different instant messaging systems, speak with all of them using Trillian.

If Yahoo! Instant Messenger is your favorite way to chat with friends, ideally everyone you know would also use Yahoo! Instant Messenger. But the world isn't a perfect place, and there are many competing instant messaging applications, including AOL Instant Messenger (AIM), ICQ, Microsoft's MSN Messenger, and Apple's iChat. Unfortunately, a friend using AIM can't talk with another friend using ICQ. And neither of these friends would be able to chat with you on Yahoo! Instant Messenger. Instead of trying to convince everyone you know to switch to your favorite application—or installing four different programs—you could switch to a universal instant messaging program: Trillian.

Cerulean Studios, the company behind Trillian, recognized this communication breakdown between instant messengers and decided to make a program that could speak with all of them. Trillian lets you chat with anyone on Yahoo!, AIM, ICQ, or MSN. It works by connecting directly with servers for each service and mimicking the messages sent from the standard messaging program. The basic version is free, and Trillian Pro offers a few more features for $25.

Trillian runs only on Windows 98 or above, so Linux and Mac users are out of luck. You'll also need an account with each service you'd like to communicate with. But to get started, you'll just need your Yahoo! ID and password.

> Mac OS X users might want to try the freely available Fire application, which is similar to Trillian. You can download Fire from *http://fire.sourceforge.net*.

Installation and Setup

From the Cerulean Studios homepage (*http://www.ceruleanstudios.com*), click Downloads and then click the Download button on the next page. Because Cerulean Studios distributes the program through its partner CNet, the download link takes you to Download.com (*http://www.download.com*). From there, choose Download Now to get the program. Double-click the installation file to install Trillian.

When you launch Trillian for the first time, you'll see the Trillian First Time Wizard, which will step you through setting up the program. On the Choose Features page, make sure that Yahoo! Messenger is selected and click Next. When you see the "Connect to Yahoo! Messenger" page as shown in Figure 3-38, enter your Yahoo! username and password.

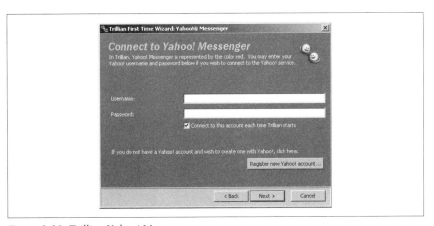

Figure 3-38. Trillian Yahoo! Messenger setup

If you already have a contact list in Yahoo! Instant Messenger, Trillian will get the list of contacts when it connects with Yahoo!. (Trillian will do the same for accounts on other systems as well.) If the connection works as planned, you should see a list of your contacts across instant messaging systems, as shown in Figure 3-39.

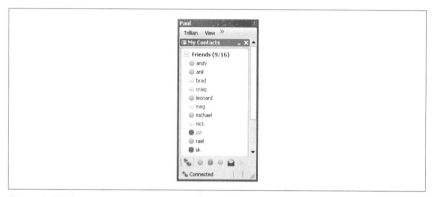

Figure 3-39. Instant messaging contacts from different platforms

The contacts are color-coded, with Yahoo! users in red. To add a Yahoo! contact at any time, choose Trillian from the top menu and then choose Add Contact or Group. From there, select Yahoo as the medium, and fill out the form you see in Figure 3-40 with your friend's Yahoo! ID and a brief message.

Figure 3-40. Adding a Yahoo! contact in Trillian

You can also set up multiple Yahoo! IDs with Trillian and connect to any or all of them at once. This is handy if you have a separate account for personal and work contacts, or multiple Yahoo! IDs for different situations. To add a new Yahoo! ID at any time, choose Trillian from the top menu, then Connections → Manage My Connections. Click "Add a New Connection" at the bottom of the page and then choose Yahoo. Then add a Yahoo! username and password, and Trillian will connect with that ID as well.

What You'll Miss

The Windows versions of both Yahoo! Instant Messenger and Trillian work well for sending text messages back and forth, but there are some differences between the programs you should be aware of. Unlike Yahoo! Instant Messenger, Trillian doesn't offer instant access to other Yahoo! features, such as LaunchCast, Games, Stock Quotes, Weather, and your Yahoo! Calendar and Address Book. The one notable exception is Yahoo! Mail, which Trillian will check periodically. If new mail arrives while you're using Trillian, it will display a new mail alert (like the one shown in Figure 3-41) .

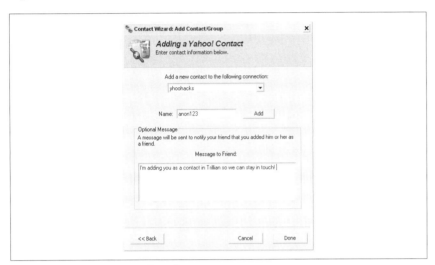

Figure 3-41. Trillian new mail notification

Trillian users will also miss out on some Yahoo! Instant Messenger features, such as Audibles, which feature animated characters saying humorous phrases, and Trillian users won't see the animated avatars that show a cartoon-like representation of the chat participants.

Beyond these differences, Trillian is a great way to stay in touch with people if their favorite instant messenger isn't the same as yours.

Store, Sort, and Share Your Photos

H A C K
#67

Flickr makes it easy to share your photos with the world.

At its most basic, Flickr is a web application that helps you create a public journal of photos. You can upload your photos to Flickr and see them appear on a web page with the most recently added photo on top. But once you start playing with Flickr, you'll quickly find that it's much more sophisticated. In fact, Flickr is an open platform for storing, arranging, sharing, discussing, and discovering photos with people across the globe.

What began as an independent project by a small company called Ludicorp was recently purchased by Yahoo! and is in the process of being integrated more closely with Yahoo!. At the time of this writing, Flickr is still very much an independent application, and you'll need your own Flickr account to upload photos (a Yahoo! ID will not work). You can create a free Flickr account by browsing to *http://www.flickr.com* and clicking the pink "Sign up now!" button.

> A basic Flickr account is free, lets you upload up to 20 MB in photos per month, show up to 200 of your photos, and create three individual galleries (which Flickr calls *sets*). You can also upgrade to a paid Flickr Pro account, which gives you much more storage and unlimited sets. At the time of this writing, a Flickr Pro account is $24.95 per year.

Once you've created an account, you can add some information about yourself to your profile that will tell others a bit about you. Flickr is a social application, and unlike some sites where uploading photos feels like a lonely process, adding photos to Flickr feels like a group activity.

Store

The first step in getting to know Flickr is to upload some of your photos. The steps required to move photos from your camera to your computer vary widely, so that will have to be left as an exercise for the reader. But once photos are on your computer, there are several ways to move them to Flickr.

From your browser. The simplest way to upload photos is via your web browser and the "Upload Photos to Flickr" page (*http://www.flickr.com/photos/upload*). Click Browse… next to one of the blank fields on the page, and a new window will let you choose an image file on your local computer. Figure 3-42 shows what choosing a file looks like on Windows XP.

When you highlight a photo and click Open, the previously blank field will be filled in with the local path to the image file. You can upload up to six photos at a time and set tags and privacy settings for each photo in the group. Clicking Upload sends your photos to Flickr, which might take some time, depending on the size of your photos and your connection

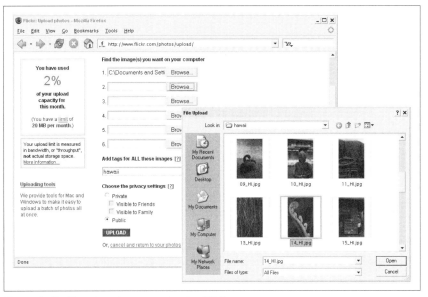

Figure 3-42. Choosing photos to upload to Flickr

speed. Once your photos have been uploaded, you'll have the option to add titles and descriptions to each of them. It's easy to add titles and descriptions later as well.

You can set default privacy options for every photo you upload, by clicking Your Account from the top of any Flickr page and choosing Default Photo Privacy from the menu. Or you can browse directly to *http://www.flickr.com/ profile_photoconf.gne* to set options such as who can see your photos, who can comment, and who can add notes and tags.

From your desktop. Once you're completely hooked on Flickr, you might want to upload entire sets of photographs at a time. You can find a number of ways to upload photos on the Tools page (*http://www.flickr.com/tools*). The tools are programs you can download and install on Windows or Macintosh computers that allow you to upload a number of photos at once. Figure 3-43 shows the Windows Flickr Uploadr in action; you can simply drag images from the Windows File Explorer and drop them onto the Flickr Uploadr window.

Once you've added all of the photos you want to send to Flickr into the Flickr Uploadr, click the Upload... button. You'll also have the option to add tags to the photos or change the default privacy settings for those photos.

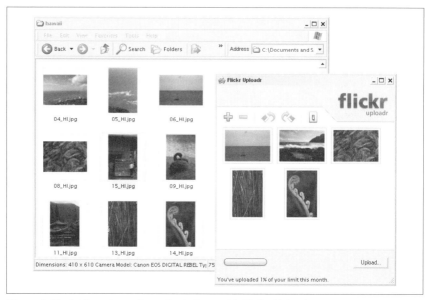

Figure 3-43. Adding photos from the desktop with Flickr Uploadr

From an email address. In addition to uploading photos via the Web or a desktop application, you can send photos to Flickr by email. Click the Your Account link from the top of any Flickr page and choose "Uploading photos by email" under the Photo Settings heading. You can also browse directly to *http://www.flickr.com/profile_mailconf.gne*.

Once there, you'll find a randomly generated email address that's unique to your Flickr account. You can use the address to send photos to Flickr as email attachments. This option is particularly handy for cell phone cameras, because you can snap your photo on the go and post it directly to Flickr without making a trip to your home computer.

Sort

You'll find every photo you upload in your Flickr *photostream*. A photostream is simply a list of every photo you've uploaded in reverse-chronological order (i.e., the photo you uploaded most recently is listed first). And once your photos are in your photostream, there are a number of ways you can organize them beyond the chronological listing.

Tagging. Tagging is a simple form of organization that lets you associate keywords with each of your photos. Unlike traditional categorization schemes, tags are free-form: you can use any words, numbers, or phrases you like. Figure 3-44 shows a photo at Flickr with its tags listed just to the right of the photo.

Figure 3-44. A photo with tags at Flickr

The photo was taken in the town of Kaneohe, Hawaii, at a Buddhist temple, and the photographer has tagged the photo with the words *temple*, *Kaneohe*, and *Hawaii*. By clicking any tag, you'll see all of your photos tagged with that particular word. And by clicking the globe icon next to any tag, you'll see photos by everyone at Flickr tagged with that word.

Organizing. The key to more complex organization is the Flickr tool called Organizr. Organizr runs in your browser and you'll need the free Macromedia Flash Player (*http://www.macromedia.com/go/getflashplayer*) installed to use it. You can fire up Organizr by clicking the Organize link at the top of any Flickr page.

Inside Organizr, you'll find your photos in the main window. You can view all photos, limit your photos by date, or search your titles, descriptions, and tags. The sliders below the main window adjust the dates you'd like to view (see Figure 3-45).

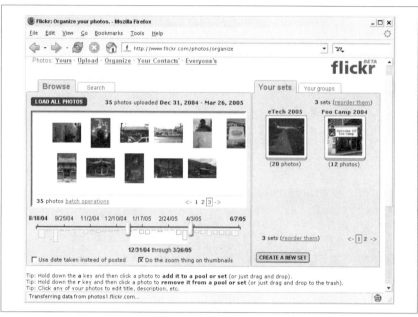

Figure 3-45. Sorting photos with Flickr Organizr

Inside Organizr, you can create and edit photo *sets*. A set is group of photos that you assemble into an individual gallery. Once you've created a set and given it a title, you can drag a photo from the main window and drop it into a set on the right to add the photo to the set. From there, you can arrange the photos in a set into a specific order. Figure 3-46 shows what the cover page of a set looks like to someone browsing a set for the first time.

Free Flickr accounts are limited to three sets, but you can create an unlimited number of sets with a Flickr Pro account.

The "View as slideshow" link on the front page of a set will let someone see the group of photos as Flash presentation. Viewers don't even have to type on the keyboard or click their mouse; they can sit back and watch the photos dissolve in and out as the presentation automatically moves from one picture to the next.

Share

One of the primary benefits of using Flickr is that once your photos are uploaded, they are accessible to anyone with a web browser.

Figure 3-46. A Flickr photoset

Free to the public. The easiest way to share all of your photos is to create a simple URL, called a *Flickr address*, that you can share with others. Browse to *http://www.flickr.com/profile_url.gne* and choose a simple word as your address. The format of the URL will look like this:

```
http://www.flickr.com/photos/insert your word
```

It's important to choose your Flickr address carefully, because your choice is permanent; you can't edit your Flickr address once you've created it. The newly created URL will point directly to your photostream, and you can give the URL to your friends and family or link to your photostream from another web site using the URL.

Once your photos are on Flickr, you can also share them by automatically posting them to a weblog **[Hack #98]** or by displaying your latest photos with a Flickr badge **[Hack #99]**. Flickr also provides RSS feeds for photostreams, groups, and tags, so once your photos are in the system, there are myriad ways for others to view them.

One benefit of these methods of sharing is that others viewing your photos don't need to be members of Flickr to see them. They don't have to go through an account creation process simply to look at your photos. But if someone does go the extra mile to become a Flickr member, there are several more ways to connect and share photographs.

Flickr community. Flickr works best when your friends and family are also participating at the site. Once someone has an account, you can add him as a friend, family member, or contact.

> Keep in mind that whichever category another Flickr member is in will determine which photos of yours she can see if you alter the default privacy settings for a particular photo.

As you build a group of contacts at Flickr, you'll be able to easily browse their photos just as they can browse yours. Clicking the Your Contacts' link in the Photos: bar at the top of any Flickr page will show the latest photos added by all of your contacts, and it's a great way to keep up with your friends. You can also browse a full list of your contacts by clicking the People link at the top of any page and then clicking someone's name to see his photostream. Figure 3-47 shows a contact list at Flickr.

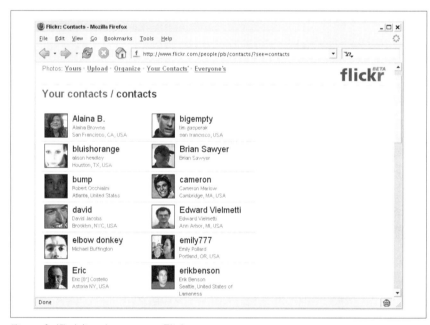

Figure 3-47. A list of contacts at Flickr

The Groups feature lets anyone form a public discussion and photo-sharing space at Flickr. In addition to sending photos to a *group photo pool*, you can post messages to the group and carry on a conversation. For example, there's a group called The Bookshelf Project (*http://www.flickr.com/groups/bookshelf*). The members there share photos of their home bookshelves and discuss the topic of storing books.

If you're interested in a specific topic, chances are good that someone has created a specific Flickr Group devoted to it. You can browse a full list of groups, organized by topic, at *http://www.flickr.com/groups_browse.gne*. Figure 3-48 shows the Flickr Group for this book, which you'll find online at *http://www.flickr.com/groups/yahoohacks*.

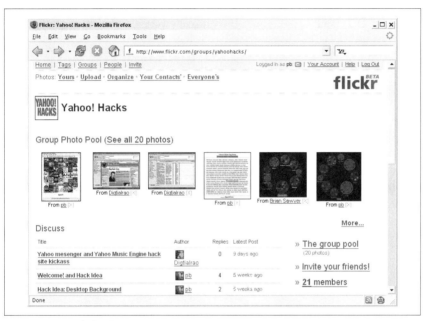

Figure 3-48. A Flickr Group page

Flickr members can also comment on each other's photos, help out with tagging, and even add notes to specific areas of a photo. And, as always, these features are contingent on the permissions you set for your photos.

CHAPTER FOUR

Web Services
Hacks 68–76

As you've already seen, Yahoo! provides an impressive amount of information on its sites. And through the years, private hackers have found ways to use Yahoo! data in their scripts and programs. A search for Yahoo! in the Perl module repository CPAN (*http://search.cpan.org*) will turn up hundreds of modules written by independent programmers who wanted to automate some piece of Yahoo! for their own purposes. Most of these Perl modules—and any code in other languages—rely on *screen scraping* to fetch the data. That is, the program downloads a Yahoo! web page and picks through the HTML to find the interesting data. Screen scraping isn't a reliable way to fetch data, because a single change to the HTML means a change to the code is necessary to keep it working.

In February 2005, Yahoo! opened up a much more reliable and developer-friendly path to its data, giving outside developers, tinkerers, and Yahoo! customers programmatic access to some of the data available on Yahoo! sites. This means that if you want to integrate information you find on Yahoo! into your own applications or web sites, Yahoo! Web Services has opened the door for you.

What Are Web Services?

The term *web service* refers to a set of standards for exchanging data between two systems. Though the systems may be built with completely different platforms, the web service protocols allow the systems to exchange information. For example, a service built with Perl scripts on a Linux machine could exchange information with a Visual Basic application on a Microsoft computer because both platforms can speak the common web service language.

Sometimes a web service is referred to as an *application programming interface* (API), a similar pre-Web concept. The terms are used interchangeably throughout this book.

The phrase *web service* has also come to describe a specific method of exchanging data using XML files sent over the familiar HTTP protocol. XML is a textual, structured representation of data that both computers and humans can read, and HTTP is the standard protocol for delivering content across the Web. Yahoo! has implemented a straightforward XML over HTTP architecture for its web services.

Yahoo! Web Services

Yahoo! has chosen a web services standard called REST for delivering most of its data. If you've used the Web, you'll be familiar with how REST works. A specially constructed URL will return the data you're after—just as the URL for a document on the Web returns that document. Instead of a web page (HTML document), REST requests return an XML document. The key to using Yahoo! Web Services is learning how to construct the proper request URLs.

Before creating your own request URLs though, it'd be good to know exactly what you can get your hands on through the API.

What's Available

Not every piece of data available at Yahoo! is available via web services. For example, movie showtimes [Hack #42] and television schedules [Hack #44] are still limited to the Web. But you can get access to Yahoo! Search results and a few services that aren't available via the Web.

The list of web services that Yahoo! provides is continually evolving, and you should browse to the Yahoo! Developer Network (*http://developer.yahoo.net*) to keep up with additions and changes. At the time of this writing, the services available include:

Search
> As you'd expect, you can access search results across the Web, Image, Local, News, Video, Audio, Shopping, and Contextual [Hack #97] Searches.

Text Analysis
> In addition to the search results, you can access some features of the Yahoo! Search pages including Related Queries and Spelling Suggestions. You can also access the Content Analysis feature that extracts keywords from text.

My Web

You can access information from Yahoo!'s My Web [Hack #7], giving you the ability to integrate your saved pages into other applications.

Maps

By specifying the URL of a geo-encoded RSS file, you can plot your own points [Hack #91] on an interactive Yahoo! Map.

Flickr

Purchased by Yahoo! in 2005, Flickr [Hack #67] joined the Yahoo! family with a fully realized web services offering of its own. You can use the Flickr API to programmatically access every facet of the photo-sharing service from adding photos to browsing information about Flickr members.

RSS

While RSS is not technically a web service, it's important to keep in mind that Yahoo! offers RSS feeds across their sites, and the feeds provide a simple way to integrate data with your web site.

Along with offering web services, Yahoo! has started a conversation with developers at the Yahoo! Developer Network. Browse to the Community Resources page (*http://developer.yahoo.net/community*) to see how other developers are using Yahoo! data in their applications.

Yahoo!'s Terms

Yahoo! has made this data available for free, but there are a few rules you have to play by to keep your access to the data. The key rule to keep in mind is that Yahoo! data can't be used in commercial applications. That means you can't use the API in an application you plan to sell or on a web site you charge people to access. Yahoo! also asks that you add attribution somewhere in your application. Adding the phrase "Powered by Yahoo! Search" to a site that uses Yahoo! data will fulfill the requirement.

 If you're a lawyer (or think like one) you can read the complete Yahoo! APIs Terms of Use at *http://developer.yahoo.net/terms*.

If the API is free, what's in it for Yahoo!? Yahoo! Search Evangelist Jeremy Zawadony said, "By exposing interesting pieces of Yahoo! to the larger developer community, we think they'll build applications that benefit both us and our users." In addition to showing you some basic code to access Yahoo! in various programming languages, this chapter will show you some of the applications that outside developers are building with Yahoo! data.

Request limits. Yahoo! imposes some limits on the number of requests that can be made per day. The request limit can vary by service, but at the time of this writing, you're limited to 5,000 queries per day for most services. Yahoo! tracks usage by *IP address* (a numeric address for every machine connected to the Internet), so a single machine can't make more than 5,000 requests in a single day.

If you ever reach the limit, you'll receive an HTTP 403 "Forbidden" error that indicates you're over your limit for the day.

Application IDs. Yahoo! also requires that for every application you build, you include an ID unique to the application with every request the application makes. You can request a unique ID at any time by browsing to *http:// api.search.yahoo.com/webservices/register_application*. You'll need to be logged in with your Yahoo! ID to request an application ID.

Keep in mind that Yahoo! doesn't use application IDs to monitor request limits; the ID is simply used to track your application usage. In turn, Yahoo! provides the usage data for your application IDs at *http://api.search.yahoo.com/ webservices/register_application*. Figure 4-1 shows the Application ID report available at the Yahoo! Developer Network.

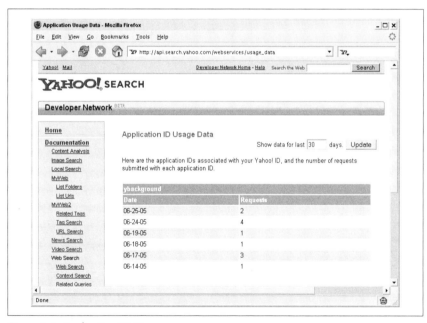

Figure 4-1. Application ID Usage page

Making Requests

Now that you know the rules, you can start making Yahoo! Web Service requests by assembling URLs for the different services.

Search and Text. The Search, Text, and My Web services all use the same structure for request URLs. The URL starts with the base service URL, *http://api.search.yahoo.com*. From there, you add a service name, version number, and specific function to the URL. Calling the Web Search (webSearch) function of the Web Search service (WebSearchService) looks like this:

```
http://api.search.yahoo.com/WebSearchService/V1/webSearch
```

At the time of this writing, all Yahoo! Search services are in Version 1, so the V1 parameter will be consistent throughout. As Yahoo! upgrades the service in the future, this parameter might change.

The final step to assembling the proper URL is adding parameters to the query. The only parameters required for a web search are appid and query, so a Web Search request could be as simple as:

```
http://api.search.yahoo.com/WebSearchService/V1/webSearch?appid=insert app ⌐
ID&query=insert query
```

Once you have the query built, you can even plug the URL in your browser's address bar to bring up the response XML and see exactly which information you'll receive. Figure 4-2 shows a Yahoo! Search response for the term hacks in a browser.

Every Yahoo! service contains a different set of potential request parameters you can use to modify your requests. For example, the Yahoo! Web Search service allows you to filter searches by language (language), country (country), adult content (adult_ok), document type (type), or Creative Commons license (license). Each service also has parameters for controlling the page of the response. Just as the Web Search lists responses across a number of pages, Yahoo! Search Web Services also breaks the responses into pages. You can adjust the response by specifying the number of results (results) up to 50 per page and specifying the result position (start) the current page should start with.

You can read the full documentation and find all of the parameters available for each of the services at the developer site (*http://developer.yahoo.net*).

Maps. To create your own map with custom points, you'll need an application ID and the URL of a specially prepared RSS file on your own server. You can assemble these pieces into a URL like this:

```
http://api.maps.yahoo.com/Maps/V1/AnnotatedMaps?appid=insert app ⌐
ID&xmlsrc=insert RSS url
```

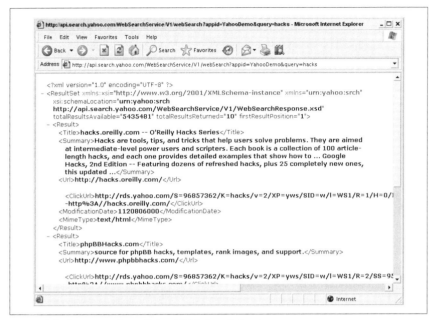

Figure 4-2. A response from Yahoo! Web Search Services

The Maps API is a bit different because you're receiving not XML, but a fully realized HTML document. You'll find a custom map example [Hack #91] in Chapter 5.

Flickr. At the time of this writing, the Flickr API operates under different rules from other Yahoo! Search APIs. You'll need to request a Flickr API Key at *http://www.flickr.com/services/api/key.gne* to make requests, and you have the option of using a REST, XML-RPC, or SOAP interface for the requests. You can find a complete list of API methods available for Flickr at *http://www.flickr.com/services/api*.

RSS. You'll find Yahoo! RSS documents throughout Yahoo! sites, and you don't need anything extra to use them. Simply copy the RSS URL and paste it into your favorite RSS newsreader, or integrate the files with your own web sites. Yahoo! doesn't limit access or require an application ID to use RSS, and the feeds aren't covered by the Yahoo! Web Services terms of service.

Working with Responses

The way to parse XML responses will be unique to your development environment, and this chapter provides basic examples in nine different languages. Typically, you'll need two pieces of software that aren't always built into your environment of choice: code to handle HTTP requests and code to parse XML responses.

Yahoo! responses are in a proprietary XML format that's unique to the Yahoo! APIs. The top-level tag in Yahoo! Search API responses is `<ResultSet>`, with a number of `<Result>` tags holding information about each individual result.

Each result detail will vary by service, but typically you'll receive all of the data necessary to duplicate what you find on the corresponding Yahoo! site. For example, each Web Search result includes the following XML tags: `<Title>`, `<Summary>`, `<Url>`, `<ClickUrl>`, `<MimeType>`, `<ModificationDate>`, and `<Cache>`. As you can tell from the tag names, the data you'll receive is almost identical to the data on a Yahoo! Web Search results page outlined in the introduction to Chapter 1.

The key to understanding what's available and how you can use it is simply playing with data and building some sample applications. The hacks in this chapter should give you a head start on integrating Yahoo! data into your own programs.

HACK #68 Program Yahoo! with Perl

Grabbing data from Yahoo! Search Web Services can be quite easy with just a little bit of Perl.

Perl is great for getting things done quickly, and fetching search results from Yahoo! is no exception. This hack shows a simple way to access Yahoo! with Perl, using minimal code. Think of it as a doorway to Yahoo! that you can drop into your own Perl scripts, or that you can use as a starting point for more complex applications. This script will accept a keyword or phrase, contact Yahoo! Search, and print out the first 10 results.

What You Need

In the spirit of keeping things easy, this hack uses two *simple* modules that may already be installed on your system: `LWP::Simple` (*http://search.cpan.org/~gaas/libwww-perl-5.803/lib/LWP/Simple.pm*) makes the HTTP request; `XML::Simple` (*http://search.cpan.org/~grantm/XML-Simple-2.14/lib/XML/Simple.pm*) parses the XML response. If you need to install these modules, you can use CPAN for each module:

```
perl -MCPAN -e shell
cpan> install XML::Simple
```

On a Windows system with ActivePerl, you can install these modules from the command line with the Perl package manager, like this:

```
ppm install LWP-Simple
```

The only other piece you'll need is a unique application ID from Yahoo!, which you can pick up at *http://api.search.yahoo.com/webservices/register_application*.

The Code

This code builds a Yahoo! Search Web Services request URL using the keyword passed to it when the script is run. Then it parses the response and prints it out in a readable format. Save the following code to a file named *yahoo_search.pl*:

```perl
#!/usr/bin/perl
# yahoo_search.pl
# Accepts a search term and shows the top results.
# Usage: yahoo_search.pl <Query>
#
# You can create an AppID, and read the full documentation
# for Yahoo! Web Services at http://developer.yahoo.net/

use strict;
use LWP::Simple;
use XML::Simple;

# Set your unique Yahoo! Application ID
my $appID = "insert your app ID";

# Grab the incoming search query
my $query = join(' ', @ARGV) or die "Usage: yahoo_search.pl <query>\n";

# Construct a Yahoo! Search Query with only required options
my $language = "en";
my $req_url = "http://api.search.yahoo.com/";
    $req_url .= "WebSearchService/V1/webSearch?";
    $req_url .= "appid=$appID";
    $req_url .= "&query=$query";
    $req_url .= "&language=$language";

# Make the request
my $yahoo_response = get($req_url);

# Parse the XML
my $xmlsimple = XML::Simple->new( );
my $yahoo_xml = $xmlsimple->XMLin($yahoo_response);

# Initialize results counter
my $i;

# Loop through the items returned, printing them out
foreach my $result (@{$yahoo_xml->{Result}}) {
    $i++;
    my $title = $result->{Title};
    my $summary = $result->{Summary};
    my $url = $result->{Url};
    print "$i. $title\n$summary\n$url\n\n";
}
```

The final print command sends the information from Yahoo! to STDOUT. You can change what this script shows by rearranging the variables and making this last line more or less complex.

Running the Hack

Simply call the script from the command line:

```
perl yahoo_search.pl insert word
```

And be sure to enclose phrases or multiple keywords in quotes:

```
perl yahoo_search.pl "insert multiword phrase"
```

Figure 4-3 shows the Yahoo! Search results for the phrase "minimalist Perl".

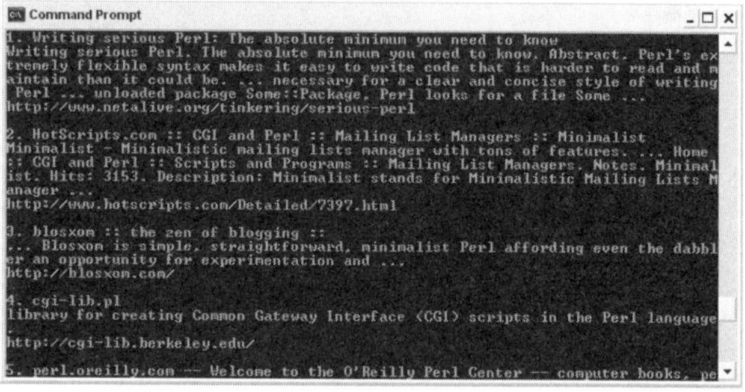

Figure 4-3. Yahoo! Search results for "minimalist Perl"

This hack uses minimalist Perl to demonstrate how quickly Yahoo! data can be included in Perl scripts, and this technique can be used as a building block for more advanced scripts. In fact, most of the Perl scripts in this book use this basic method of accessing Yahoo! Search Web Services.

HACK #69 Program Yahoo! with PHP 5

Take advantage of some of the latest features in PHP to quickly add Yahoo! data to PHP-powered pages.

The recursively named PHP Hypertext Processor language is a popular choice for building dynamic web applications. In fact, Yahoo! itself has made PHP its development platform of choice across the company. The PHP platform is continually evolving, and the latest version (Version 5) includes a handy XML parser called *SimpleXML*. As the name implies, it's easy to work with. And as long as the XML that SimpleXML is parsing is fairly simple, it's the perfect tool for getting XML data into objects PHP can easily manipulate.

Yahoo! Search Web Services responses definitely qualify as simple XML, and this hack shows how easy it is to request and parse this data with PHP. You'll need PHP 5 for this hack, but you won't need any external modules.

The Code

Save the following code to your web server in a file called *yahoo_search.php*.

Don't forget to grab a unique application ID for this script at *http://developer.yahoo.net*.

```php
<?php
// yahoo_search.php
// Accepts a search term and shows the top results.
// Usage: yahoo_search.php?p=<Query>
//
// You can create an AppID, and read the full documentation
// for Yahoo! Web Services at http://developer.yahoo.net/

// Set your unique Yahoo! Application ID
$appID = "insert your app ID";

// Grab the incoming search query, and encode for a URL
$query = $_GET['p'];
$query = urlencode($query);

if ($query == "") {
    print "usage: yahoo_search.php?p=&lt;Query&gt;";
    die;
}

// Construct a Yahoo! Search Query with only required options
$language = "en";
$req_url = "http://api.search.yahoo.com/";
$req_url .= "WebSearchService/V1/webSearch?";
$req_url .= "appid=$appID";
$req_url .= "&query=$query";
$req_url .= "&language=$language";

// Make the request
$yahoo_response = file_get_contents($req_url);

// Parse the XML
$xml = simplexml_load_string($yahoo_response);

// Initialize results counter
$i = 0;
?>
<html>
```

```
<body>
<h2>Yahoo! Search Results</h2>
<ol>
<?php
// Loop through the items returned, printing them out
foreach ($xml->Result as $result) {
    $i++;
    $title = $result->Title;
    $summary = $result->Summary;
    $summary = preg_replace("/</i","&lt;",$summary);
    $clickurl = $result->ClickUrl;
    $url = $result->Url;
    print "<li><div style=\"margin-bottom:15px;\">";
    print "<a href=\"$clickurl\">$title</a><br />";
    print "$summary<br />";
    print "<cite>$url</cite></div></li>\n";
}
?>
</ol>
-- Results Powered by Yahoo!
</body>
</html>
```

This script uses the value of the querystring variable p to build a Yahoo! Web Search request URL and fetches the XML with the file_get_contents() function. Once the script has the XML in the $yahoo_response string, it calls the SimpleXML function simplexml_load_string( ), which parses the XML and makes the data available to PHP as an object. Finally, the script loops through the objects, using print to send the data to the browser.

Running the Hack

To run the script, point your web browser to the location of the script on your server and add the querystring variable p:

```
http://example.com/yahoo_search.php?p=insert word
```

You can add multiple words by encoding spaces for URLs. For example, here's the search string for "PHP encoding":

```
http://example.com/yahoo_search.php?p=PHP%20encoding
```

Figure 1-1 shows the results of a search for simpleXML.

As the results indicate, you can read the official documentation for PHP's SimpleXML function at *http://www.php.net/simplexml*. With this function, working with Yahoo! Search Web Services data is much more intuitive than with earlier versions of PHP.

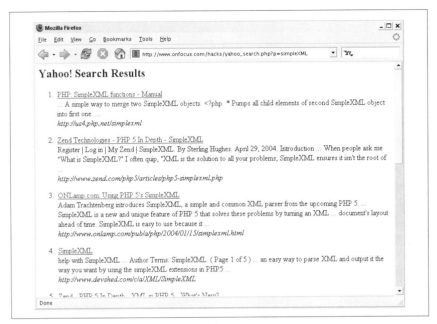

Figure 4-4. Yahoo! Search results for "simpleXML."

HACK #70 Program Yahoo! with Python

Use the existing Yahoo! library for Python to build applications quickly.

The Yahoo! Developer Network web site (*http://developer.yahoo.net*) provides a number of tools to help developers build applications with Yahoo! data. Their Yahoo! Search Web Services software development kit (SDK) includes a handy Python library called pYsearch that does most of the heavy lifting (making requests and parsing responses) for you. This means you have a simple set of commands to learn and interact with, rather than having to take the time to learn how Yahoo! request URLs should be formatted. In exchange for this ease of use, you'll need to spend a few minutes installing the library.

Download the SDK (at *http://developeryahoo.net/download*) and unzip its contents to install the pYsearch library. From a command prompt, change directories to the newly unzipped SDK files and then change into the */python/pYsearch* directory. In this directory, you'll find *setup.py*, which you'll need Python 2.2.3 to run. If you can't install a newer version, or if you'd rather not, there's a quick

way to make the library compatible with older versions of Python. Just add the
following code to *setup.py*, toward the top of the script:

```
# add for Python versions that don't understand "classifiers"
import sys
if sys.version < '2.2.3':
    from distutils.dist import DistributionMetadata
    DistributionMetadata.classifiers = None
    DistributionMetadata.download_url = None
```

Once *setup.py* is ready to go for your system, install it from the command
prompt with these two commands:

```
python setup.py build
python setup.py install
```

If everything works as it should, the pYsearch library will now be available
to your Python scripts.

The Code

This simple Python script uses the pYsearch library to return Yahoo! Web
Search responses. Save this code to a file called *yahoo_search.py* and be sure
to add your own unique application ID:

```
#!/usr/bin/python
# yahoo_search.py
# A quick Yahoo! Web Search script using Yahoo!'s
# pYsearch library availble in the Y!WS SDK
# [http://developer.yahoo.net/download/]
# Usage: python yahoo_search.py <Query>

import sys, string, codecs

# Use the pYsearch functions
from yahoo.search import webservices

# Grab the query from the command line
if sys.argv[1:]:
    query = sys.argv[1]
else:
    sys.exit('Usage: python yahoo_search.py <query>')

# Include your unique application ID
appID = 'insert your app ID'

# Query Yahoo!
search = webservices.create_search('web', appID)
```

```
search.language = "en"
search.results = 10
search.start = 1
search.query = query

# Parse the results
try:
    results = search.parse_results()
except Exception, err:
    print "Got an error: ", err
    sys.exit(1)

# Tell standard output to handle utf-8 encoding
sys.stdout = codecs.lookup('utf-8')[-1](sys.stdout)

# Start counter
count = search.start

# Print out the results
for result in results:
    print "%s. %s\n%s\n\n%s\n\n" % (count, result.Title, result.Summary, ⏎
result.Url)
    count += 1
```

The key to using the pYsearch library is importing the webservices module at the top of the script. From there, the script calls the create_search function, sets some parameters, and uses parse_results to get the entire Yahoo! response. And the last print command formats the response and displays it for the user.

The web search type is specified in the create_search function, but keep in mind that you could use any of Yahoo!'s search services here.

Running the Hack

Run the script on the command line:

python yahoo_search.py *insert word*

And, as usual, enclose multiple words in quotation marks:

python yahoo_search.py *"insert multiword phrase"*

Figure 4-5 shows the results for "learning Python".

Python is known as a language that can assemble complex applications quickly; if you're planning to integrate Yahoo! data with a Python application, it's that much faster because most of the hard work is done for you already in the pYsearch library.

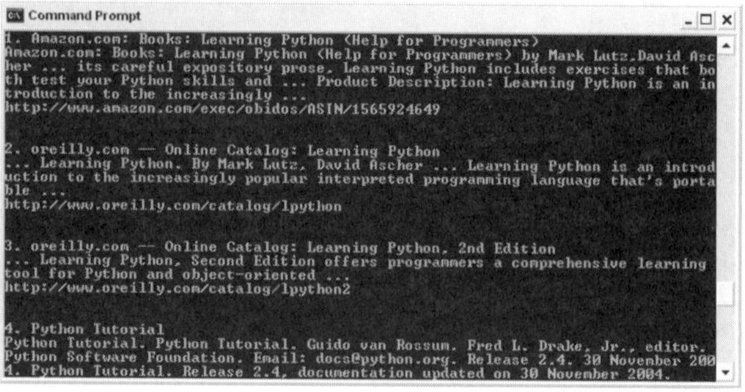

Figure 4-5. Yahoo! Search results for "learning Python"

Program Yahoo! with VBScript

HACK #71   Build Yahoo! searches into Windows programs or ASP pages with VBScript.

VBScript is a general-purpose scripting language for Windows, and it gets its name from Visual Basic, its big brother of a programming language. With a few tweaks here and there, the code in this hack could add Yahoo! searching to Office applications or an ASP-powered web page. This hack is written to run as a Microsoft Windows Script and it provides just the basics for building a Yahoo! Search query and presenting the results.

Microsoft Windows Script is built into the fabric of the Windows operating system and is used primarily by system administrators to automate some tasks involved with—you guessed it—system administration. But Microsoft Windows Scripts can also be used to automate applications and send data back and forth between programs.

What You Need

If your Windows installation is up-to-date, you shouldn't need to install anything extra to run this hack. But if it's been a while since you've run Windows Update, you might want to grab the latest version of Microsoft Windows Script at *http://www.microsoft.com/scripting*. From that page, click Downloads and choose Microsoft Windows Script 5.6 or later for your version of Windows.

This hack also relies on the Microsoft XML Parser to sort the results from Yahoo!. Your system should already have a version of the parser installed, but if you run into trouble, you can always download the latest version at *http://msdn.microsoft.com/xml*. Once you're there, click XML Downloads and choose the latest XML Core Services package you can find.

As always, be sure to grab a unique Yahoo! application ID for this script at *http://api.search.yahoo.com/webservices/ register_application*.

The Code

Like any other script, the code is simply plain text in a standard text file. You could even use Notepad to save the following code to a file called *yahoo_search.vbs*:

```vbscript
' yahoo_search.vbs
' Accepts a search term and shows the top results.
' Usage: cscript yahoo_search.vbs <Query> //I
'
' You can create an AppID, and read the full documentation
' for Yahoo! Web Services at http://developer.yahoo.net/

'Set your unique Yahoo! Application ID
Const APP_ID = "insert your app ID"

'Grab the incoming search query or ask for one
If WScript.Arguments.Length = 0 Then
    strQuery = InputBox("Enter a search Term")
Else
    strQuery = WScript.Arguments(0)
End If

'Construct a Yahoo! Search Query
strLanguage = "en"
strReqURL = "http://api.search.yahoo.com/" & _
            "WebSearchService/V1/webSearch?" & _
            "appid=" & APP_ID & _
            "&query=" & strQuery & _
            "&language=" & strLanguage

'Start the XML Parser
Set MSXML = CreateObject("MSXML.DOMDocument")

'Set the XML Parser options
MSXML.Async = False

'Make the Request
strResponse = MSXML.Load(strReqURL)

'Make sure the request loaded
If (strResponse) Then

    'Load the results
    Set Results = MSXML.SelectNodes("//Result")

    'Loop through the results
```

```
For x = 0 to Results.length - 1
    strTitle = Results(x).SelectSingleNode("Title").text
    strSummary = Results(x).SelectSingleNode("Summary").text
    strURL = Results(x).SelectSingleNode("Url").text
    strOut = (x + 1) & ". " & _
             strTitle & vbCrLf & _
             strSummary & vbCrLf & _
             strURL & vbCrLf & vbCrLf
    WScript.Echo strOut
Next

'Unload the results
Set Results = Nothing

End If

'Unload the XML Parser
Set MSXML = Nothing
```

This code accepts a query on the command line when the script runs, or it asks the user for a query with the InputBox( ) function. From there, the script uses the query to build the proper Yahoo! Web Search request. The results from the request are passed through the Microsoft XML Parser and formatted for display. WScript.Echo sends the results to the user.

Running the Hack

There are a couple of different ways to run the code. The most useful way to see the results is to run the script from a command prompt in interactive mode. Open a command prompt and type the following command:

```
cscript yahoo_search.vbs insert word //I
```

Be sure to include multiword searches in quotes:

```
cscript yahoo_search.vbs "insert multiword phrase" //I
```

The //I switch tells Microsoft Windows Script to output any results to the command line. Figure 4-6 shows this in action for the search term vbscript.

If you want to, though, you can just double-click the *yahoo_search.vbs* file as you would any other program. You'll be prompted for a search word, and the results will be shown one at a time—all 10 of them—in window prompts like the one shown in Figure 4-7.

While this isn't the handiest way to view search results, it shows that adding Yahoo! data to VBScript applications can be accomplished fairly quickly.

Figure 4-6. Yahoo! Search results for "vbscript"

Figure shows a Windows Script Host dialog:

Windows Script Host

1. VBScript Tutorial
HTML,CSS,JavaScript,DHTML,XML,XHTML,ASP,ADO and VBScript tutorial from W3Schools. ... HOME. VBScript Tutorial. VB HOME ... In our VBScript tutorial you will learn how to write VBScript, and how to insert these scripts into your HTML documents ...
http://www.w3schools.com/vbscript

OK

Figure 4-7. The top Yahoo! Search result for "vbscript" in a window prompt

HACK #72 Program Yahoo! with ColdFusion

ColdFusion MX includes all of the tools necessary to work with the Yahoo! API.

ColdFusion is a development platform for creating web applications. Its tag-based template structure is a popular choice for HTML developers who want to move to more dynamic content and are already familiar with using tags. In fact, if you were to glance at a ColdFusion script, you might think the code was standard HTML. Putting together a ColdFusion template is a lot like putting together an HTML page, but you can draw on resources such as databases and web services to bring in dynamic content.

You'll need to be running a version of ColdFusion MX or later to use this hack, because it relies on the XmlParse function that was added with the MX release. This function can take an XML document, such as the responses from Yahoo! Search Web Services, and turn it into an object that Cold-Fusion scripts can work with.

The Code

This hack shows how you can quickly use the ColdFusion Markup Language (CFML) to bring in content from Yahoo! Search Web Services. This script assembles the proper request URL based on a querystring variable and gets a response from Yahoo! with the <cfhttp> tag. Then the XmlParse function makes the data available to the script, and the <cfloop> tag goes through each bit of data, adding it to the page.

Save the following code to a file called *yahoo_search.cfm* and upload it to your server:

```
<!---
yahoo_search.cfm
Accepts a search term and shows the top results.
Usage: yahoo_search.cfm?p=<Query>

You can create an AppID, and read the full documentation
for Yahoo! Web Services at http://developer.yahoo.net/
--->
<html>
<body>
<h2>Yahoo! Search Results</h2>
<ol>
<!--- Set your unique Yahoo! Application ID --->
<cfset appID = "YahooTest">

<!--- Grab the incoming search query --->
<cfset query = "#URL.p#">

<!--- Construct a Yahoo! Search Query with only required options --->
<cfset req_url = "http://api.search.yahoo.com/">
<cfset req_url = req_url & "WebSearchService/V1/webSearch?">
<cfset req_url = req_url & "appid=#appID#">
<cfset req_url = req_url & "&query=#query#">
<cfset req_url = req_url & "&language=en">

<!--- Make Request --->
<cfhttp url="#req_url#" method="GET" charset="utf-8">
    <cfhttpparam type="Header" name="charset" value="utf-8" />
</cfhttp>

<!--- Parse Response --->
<cfset response = #XMLParse(cfhttp.fileContent)#>
<cfset results = #response.ResultSet.Result#>

<!--- Loop Through Response --->
<cfoutput>
<cfloop from="1" to="#ArrayLen(results)#" index="i">
    <li><div style="margin-bottom:15px;">
    <a href=\"#results[i].ClickUrl.xmlText#\">#results[i].Title.xmlText#</a>
    #results[i].Summary.xmlText#<br />
    <cite>#results[i].Url.xmlText#</cite></div></li>
</cfloop>
</cfoutput>
</ol>
-- Results Powered by Yahoo!
</body>
</html>
```

Take a look at the <cfhttp> tag in the script. Note that the charset attribute is utf-8 and that a <cfhttpparam> tag was used to set a charset header for the request with the utf-8 value. This is a bit of extra work, but it's necessary to make sure ColdFusion and Yahoo! Search Web Services are speaking the same language.

Running the Hack

Bring up the page in a browser to see it in action:

```
http://example.com/yahoo_search.cfm?p=insert word
```

Separate multiple words with URL-encoded spaces, as in this search for "ColdFusion MX":

```
http://example.com/yahoo_search.cfm?p=ColdFusion%20MX
```

You should see the top Yahoo! Search results for ColdFusion MX, as shown in Figure 4-8.

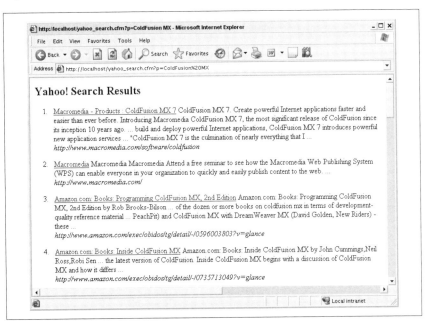

Figure 4-8. Yahoo! Search results for "ColdFusion MX"

As you can see, ColdFusion MX includes all of the tools you need to make Yahoo! Search Web Services requests and work with the responses. Integrating Yahoo! data with existing ColdFusion applications can be accomplished with just a few lines of code.

Program Yahoo! with XSLT

#73   Transform Yahoo! Search Web Services responses into HTML with an XSLT stylesheet.

The Extensible Stylesheet Language (XSL) is a tag-based template system that can transform any XML document into any other text format, including other flavors of XML or, more commonly, HTML. Like a scripting language, XSL defines what data should go where on a page. You'll still need to use a scripting language to perform the transformation from XML into HTML, and the entire process is encapsulated in the term *XSL transformations* or *XSLT*.

At first glance, an XSL stylesheet looks a lot like an HTML page, and it often contains HTML tags. But unlike HTML, each stylesheet must be valid XML and must contain a number of tags that describe how the XML should be processed. While an HTML document can have a few unclosed tags here and there and still display a web page, XSL is very strict and will fail if it's not properly formed.

Responses from the Yahoo! Search Web Services are in XML and can be transformed directly into an HTML page with a bit of XSL.

The Code

Each stylesheet is organized into one or more templates that define how data from the source XML document should be arranged. The templates within a stylesheet contain a mix of XSL processing tags and HTML.

To try a transformation out, first create the stylesheet. Save the following XSL to a text file called *yahoo_search.xsl*:

```
<?xml version="1.0" encoding="UTF-8" ?>
<xsl:stylesheet version="1.0" xmlns:xsl="http://www.w3.org/1999/XSL/↵
Transform">
<xsl:template match="/">
<html xmlns="http://www.w3.org/1999/xhtml">
<head>
<meta http-equiv="Content-Type" content="text/html; charset=utf-8" />
<title>Search Results</title>
</head>
<body>
    <h1>Search Results</h1>
        <!-- Begin Search Results -->
    <ol>
    <xsl:apply-templates select="//ResultSet/Result"/>
    </ol>
        <!-- End Search Results -->
    <p>Powered by Yahoo!</p>
```

```
</body>
</html>
</xsl:template>

<xsl:template match="ResultSet/Result">
    <li style="margin-bottom:10px;">
        <a>
        <xsl:attribute name="href">
            <xsl:value-of select="ClickUrl"/>
        </xsl:attribute>
        <xsl:value-of select="Title"/>
        </a><br />
        <xsl:value-of select="Summary"/><br />
        <xsl:value-of select="Url"/>
    </li>
</xsl:template>

</xsl:stylesheet>
```

In addition to the stylesheet, you'll need a scripting language to make the request and perform the transformation. Every development environment has XSLT tools you can use; this example uses Perl. As with most of the Perl examples in this book, you'll need the component LWP::Simple to make Yahoo! API requests. And to work with XSL, you'll need the XML::XSLT module.

This script accepts a search query term, assembles the Yahoo! API request URL, and fetches the response. Then it uses the XML::XSLT module to apply the stylesheet to the XML response and it prints the results. To create the script, save the following code to a file called *yahoo_xslt.cgi*:

```
#!/usr/bin/perl
# yahoo_xslt.cgi
# Accepts a search term and shows the top results.
# Usage: yahoo_xslt.cgi?<query>
#
# You can create an AppID, and read the full documentation
# for Yahoo! Web Services at http://developer.yahoo.net/

use strict;
use XML::XSLT;
use LWP::Simple;

# Set the XSL stylesheet
my $xslfile = "yahoo_search.xsl";

# Set your unique Yahoo! Application ID
my $appID = "insert Application ID";

# Grab the incoming search query
my $query = join(' ', @ARGV);
unless ($query) {
    print "Content-type: text/plain\n\n";
    print "Usage: yahoo_xslt.cgi?query";
```

```
    exit;
}

# Construct a Yahoo! Search Query with only required options
my $language = "en";
my $req_url = "http://api.search.yahoo.com/";
    $req_url .= "WebSearchService/V1/webSearch?";
    $req_url .= "appid=$appID";
    $req_url .= "&query=$query";
    $req_url .= "&language=$language";

# Make the request
my $yahoo_response = get($req_url);

# Transform the response
my $xslt = XML::XSLT->new ($xslfile, warnings => 1);
$xslt->transform ($yahoo_response);

# Print the transformation
print "Content-Type: text/xml\n\n";
print '<!DOCTYPE html PUBLIC "-//W3C//DTD XHTML 1.0 Strict//EN" ',
    '"http://www.w3.org/TR/xhtml1/DTD/xhtml1-strict.dtd">';
print $xslt->toString;

# Clean up
$xslt->dispose( );
```

Running the Hack

To run the code, upload both files to a web server and bring up the script in a browser, adding a search term like this:

```
http://example.com/yahoo_xslt.cgi?insert query
```

So searching for the phrase "Elements of Style" looks like this:

```
http://example.com/yahoo_xslt.cgi?Elements%20of%20Style
```

Figure 4-9 shows the results of the script in a browser, with the XML formatted as HTML with the stylesheet.

Hacking the Hack

This example was written with Perl, but you could make Yahoo! API requests with your favorite development environment. If you were to re-create this example in PHP, Python, or Visual Basic, the XSL stylesheet would stay the same and only the script that makes requests and processes the transformation would change.

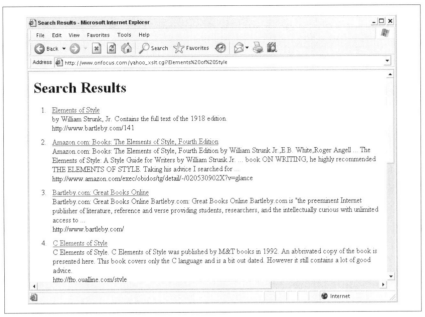

Figure 4-9. Yahoo! Search API response transformed with XSLT

Program Yahoo! with Java

HACK #74

Java's native support for working with XML makes parsing Yahoo! Search
Web Services responses a snap.

Simple REST, XML-over-HTTP interfaces like the one Yahoo! provides are
most often associated with scripting languages such as Perl or PHP, while
Java—a compiled language—is viewed as a better tool for working with
more complex web services protocols. If Java is your preferred language,
some new tools in the latest version have made it even easier to work with
services like the Yahoo! API.

Java 1.5 added native support for working with XML documents using
XPath. This means that if you know the XML format ahead of time, you can
retrieve a specific piece of the document with a simple query. For example,
every Yahoo! response includes an attribute called `totalResultsAvailable` in
the `<ResultSet>` tag, which holds the value of the total number of results
Yahoo! has for that particular query. If you'd like to grab this value with
XPath, you can use this simple query:

```
/ResultSet/@totalResultsAvailable
```

This hack presents a quick example using Java's built-in XML and XPath tools to work with Yahoo! Search Web Services. This native support means you won't need to download any external XML parsers; you simply need the latest version of Java.

What You Need

If you don't have Java 1.5 or higher, you'll need the latest Java Developer Kit (JDK™), available at *http://java.sun.com*. On the right side of the page, you'll find a section called Popular Downloads. Click the link for Java 2 Standard Edition (J2SE™) 5.0 and download the JDK. Don't confuse this with the Java Runtime Environment (JRE), because you'll need the complier included with the JDK.

Once you've downloaded the file for your system, install the JDK and you'll be set to compile and run the hack.

The Code

This simple Java program accepts a query term, builds the appropriate Yahoo! Search Web Services URL with that term, and parses the response. Then the program lists the top 10 URLs for that search term. The code uses XPath queries to pick out the total results available and each URL in the response.

Save the following code to a file called *WebSearch.java* and be sure to include a unique application ID:

```java
import org.w3c.dom.Document;
import org.w3c.dom.Node;
import org.w3c.dom.NodeList;
import org.xml.sax.SAXException;

import javax.xml.parsers.DocumentBuilder;
import javax.xml.parsers.DocumentBuilderFactory;
import javax.xml.parsers.ParserConfigurationException;
import javax.xml.xpath.XPath;
import javax.xml.xpath.XPathConstants;
import javax.xml.xpath.XPathExpressionException;
import javax.xml.xpath.XPathFactory;
import java.io.IOException;
import java.io.UnsupportedEncodingException;
import java.net.MalformedURLException;
import java.net.URL;
import java.net.URLEncoder;
import java.text.MessageFormat;

/**
 * Simple demonstration of the Yahoo! Web Search Service using Java 1.5's
 * XML support.
 */
public class WebSearch {
```

```
// Need to have an application ID to call the Yahoo! services.
private static final String APPLICATION_ID = "insert app ID";

// URL format for the request. The simplest request includes the
// application ID and the query. See the service documentation for
// a list of additional parameters.
private static final String WEB_SEARCH_URL_FORMAT =
        "http://api.search.yahoo.com/WebSearchService/V1/↵
webSearch?appid={0}&query={1}";

/**
 * Main program that takes a query and executes it as a web search
 * using the Yahoo! Web Search Service.
 *
 * @param args Command line arguments. There should be at least 1.
 */
public static void main(String[] args) throws ↵
UnsupportedEncodingException,
        MalformedURLException, XPathExpressionException,
        ParserConfigurationException {
    // Make sure a query was given.
    String query = null;
    if(args.length == 0) {
        System.out.println("Usage: java WebSearch <query>");
        System.exit(1);
    }
    else {
        // Construct the query from the command line arguments.
        query = prepareQuery(args);
    }

    // Construct the URL. Inject the URL encoded application ID and
    // the search query.
    URL url = new URL(MessageFormat.format(WEB_SEARCH_URL_FORMAT,
        new Object[]{URLEncoder.encode(APPLICATION_ID, "utf-8"),
        URLEncoder.encode(query, "utf-8")}));
    System.out.println("Request URL = " + url.toString());

    // Create an XPath engine.
    XPath xpath = XPathFactory.newInstance().newXPath();

    // Execute the query.
    Document responseDocument = null;
    try {
        // We need a Document to use XPath.
        DocumentBuilder builder = DocumentBuilderFactory.newInstance()↵
.newDocumentBuilder();
        responseDocument = builder.parse(url.openStream());
    }
    catch (IOException e) {
        // Error calling the service.
        System.err.println("Error calling the service: " + e.toString(↵));
        e.printStackTrace(System.err);
        System.exit(1);
    }
    catch (SAXException e) {
```

```
        // Error parsing the XML.
        System.err.println("Error parsing the XML: " + e.toString());
        e.printStackTrace(System.err);
        System.exit(1);
    }

    // Query the XML for the total results available.
    String totalResultsAvailable = (String) xpath.evaluate(
        "/ResultSet/@totalResultsAvailable",
        responseDocument,
        XPathConstants.STRING);
    System.out.println("Total results available for '" + query + "' is "
        + totalResultsAvailable);

    // Query the XML for the URLs.
    NodeList urls = (NodeList) xpath.evaluate("/ResultSet/Result/Url",
        responseDocument, XPathConstants.NODESET);
    for(int i = 0; i < urls.getLength(); i++) {
        Node urlNode = urls.item(i);
        System.out.println("URL " + (i + 1) + ": "
            + urlNode.getTextContent());
    }
}
/**
 * Simple method that stitches together an array of strings into
 * a single string. Used to take multiple command line arguments
 * and turn it into a single query string.
 *
 * @param args The individual strings to stitch together.
 * @return A new string containing each of the strings passed in, all
 * seperated by spaces.
 */
private static String prepareQuery(String[] args) {
    String query;
    StringBuffer queryBuffer = new StringBuffer();
    for (int i = 0; i < args.length; i++) {
        queryBuffer.append(args[i]);
        if((i + 1) < args.length) {
            queryBuffer.append(" ");
        }
    }
    query = queryBuffer.toString();
    return query;
}
}
```

To compile this code, open up a command prompt and type the following:

```
javac WebSearch.java
```

This should create the compiled *WebSearch.class*, which you can now run.

Running the Hack

From the same command prompt, you can run the code like so:

```
java WebSearch insert term
```

In response, the program shows the request URL it used, total results for that query, and the top 10 URLs. Figure 4-10 shows results for the term "Java XML".

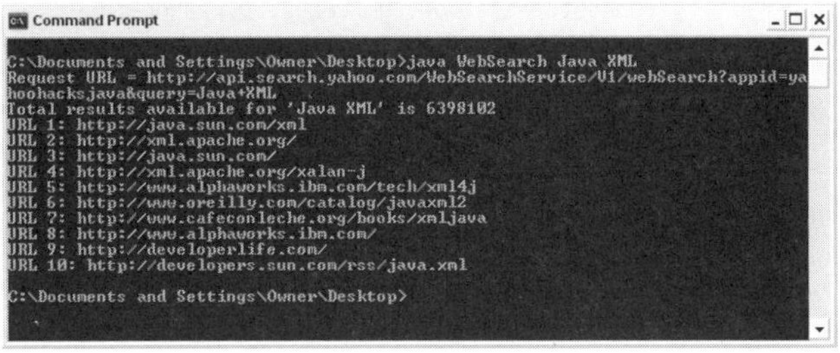

Figure 4-10. Yahoo! Search results for "Java XML"

As you can see, handling REST queries and responses with Java is fairly quick work!

—Ryan Kennedy

HACK #75 Program Yahoo! with Ruby

Use a Yahoo! Ruby library to include Yahoo! data in your Ruby scripts.

The Yahoo! Developer Network web site (*http://developer.yahoo.net*) provides a number of tools to help developers build applications with Yahoo! data. Their Yahoo! Search Web Services software development kit (SDK) includes libraries for various programming languages; Ruby, unfortunately, is not one of them. However, I have developed a Ruby library, which is available at *http://premshree.seacrow.com/code/ruby/yahoo-ruby*.

The library is easy to use; there's no "installation" as such. Just copy the contents and place it in any suitable directory. The library is just one file, *yahoo-ruby.rb*, which you need to place in the *lib/ruby/site_ruby* directory of your Ruby installation. Once it is in place, whenever you want to use the Ruby API for Yahoo! Search Web Services, simply include require yahoo-ruby in the script. Using this Ruby library means you'll never have to know how to construct Yahoo! Search Web Services URLs, or even know what the XML looks like. The library handles all of the work of communicating with Yahoo!'s server.

The Code

This simple Ruby script uses the Ruby library to return Yahoo! Web Search responses. Save this code to a file called *yahoo_search.rb* and be sure to add your own unique application ID:

```ruby
#!/usr/bin/ruby
# yahoo_search.rb
# A simple Yahoo! search script using the
# Ruby API (http://premshree.seacrow.com/code/ruby/yahoo-ruby)
# Usage ruby yahoo_search.rb <query>

# include the yahoo-ruby API
require 'yahoo-ruby'

# get the query parameter
query = ARGV[0]? ARGV[0] : exit

##
# create a web search object:
# Arguments:
# 1. App ID (You can get one at http://developer.yahoo.net)
# 2. The query
# 3. type can be one of: 'all', 'any' or 'phrase'
# 4. The no. of results
##
obj = WebSearch.new('insert app ID', query, 'all', 3)

# store the results -- returns an array of hashes
results = obj.parse_results

# now loop over each item in results, and display the title, summary and URL
results.each { |result|
    print "Title:\t#{result['Title']}\n"
    print "Summary:\t#{result['Summary']}\n"
    print "URL:\t#{result['Url']}\n"
    print "=====================================\n\n"
}
```

The first thing this script looks for is the yahoo-ruby API. Then the script looks for the query argument; if an argument is not present, the script exits. After fetching the query from the command line, the script creates a WebSearch object and then calls the parse_results function to get the results as an array of hashes.

To use a different Yahoo! Search service—Image search, for example—you need to create a different object.

Running the Hack

Run the script on the command line:

```
ruby yahoo_search.rb insert query
```

So a search for the term ruby would look like this:

```
ruby yahoo_search.rb ruby
```

Figure 4-11 shows the results of the search.

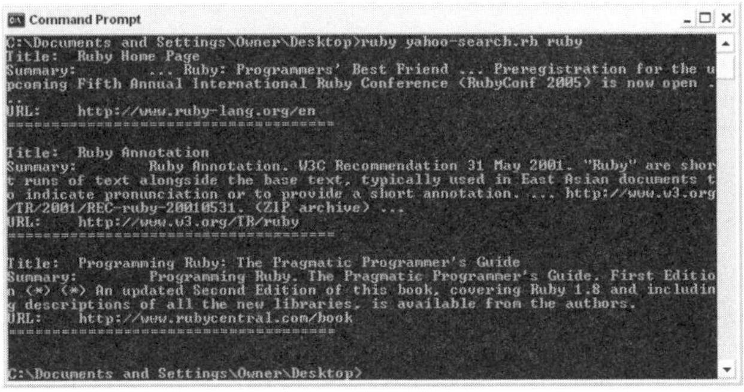

Figure 4-11. Yahoo! Search results for "ruby"

As you can see, using the yahoo-ruby library means you can integrate Yahoo! data within your Ruby applications with a few lines of code.

—*Premshree Pillai*

HACK #76 Program Yahoo! with REBOL

With REBOL, you can build a graphical interface to Yahoo! with minimal code.

Relative Expression-based Object Language (REBOL) is a technology that provides a lightweight method of distributed computing and communication. REBOL is a *messaging language*, which means it was built specifically to send messages across Internet protocols. REBOL is available for free, and there are two variations available for download:

REBOL/Core
    This is the kernel, the heart of REBOL, with a command-line interface.

REBOL/View
    This is a graphical client version, an extension of REBOL/Core for developers who want to work visually.

This hack creates a simple Yahoo! Image search widget with the REBOL/View variation. The widget allows you to enter a keyword, display the first image in the results, and navigate between other results with Previous and Next buttons. This type of graphical user interface (GUI), which uses buttons in a familiar desktop-style application, is quite a bit different from the scripting, command-line applications in this book.

To begin, download REBOL/View for your platform at *http://www.rebol.com/ view-platforms.html*. Next, you'll need to download a modified version of Gavin F. McKenzie's SAX XML parser at *http://premshree.seacrow.com/code/ rebol/xml-parse.r/view*. Place *xml-parse.r* in the working directory where you'll create the widget.

The Code

Unlike with most GUI frameworks, creating GUIs is a breeze in REBOL.

 In the following commented code, note that comments in REBOL begin with a semicolon.

Save the following code to a file called *yahoo.r* and be sure to include your own Yahoo! application ID:

```
REBOL [
    Title:  "Yahoo Search Web Services"
    File:  %yahoo.r
    Date:  22-May-2005
    Author: "Premshree Pillai"

    Purpose: {
        Yahoo! Search Web services demo
    }
]
;;
; load the SAX XML Parser
;;
do %xml-parse.r


;;
; set the Application ID
;;
APP_ID: 'insert App ID'


;;
; This function takes two parameters
; 1. query
; 2. Application ID
; It returns the results as an array of maps
; The parsing bit is done by the parse handlers within the parser.
;;
ImageSearch: func [query app_id] [
    return parse-xml+ read rejoin
[http://api.search.yahoo.com/ImageSearchService/V1/imageSearch '?query=' ⏎
query '&appid=' app_id]
]


;;
```

```
; Define a layout
;;
out: layout [
    ;;
    ; This will appear as the heading in the widget
    ;;
    H3 400 {
        Yahoo Search Web Services
        demo using REBOL
    }

    ;;
    ; tells REBOL to place following elements across
    ;;
    across
    query: field
    button "Search" [
        ImageSearchResults: ImageSearch query/text 'rebol-yahoo' APP_ID
        curr_count: 1 ; current result no.
        img: load to-url ImageSearchResults/:curr_count/3/2
        backface/image: img
        show backface
    ]

    ;;
    ; tells REBOL to place the following elements below
    ;;
    return

    ;;
    ; A text box
    ;;
    backface: text 400x300 center

    return

    ;;
    ; Navigate to previous search result
    ;;
    button "Previous" [
        curr_count: curr_count - 1
        img: load to-url ImageSearchResults/:curr_count/3/2
        backface/image: img
        show backface
    ]

    ;;
    ; Navigate to next search result
    ;;
    button "Next" [
        curr_count: curr_count + 1
        img: load to-url ImageSearchResults/:curr_count/3/2
        backface/image: img
        show backface
    ]
```

```
        pad 0x5
    ]

    ;;
    ; Display the widget!
    ;;
    view out
```

This minimal widget has no error handling. However, this code should give you a sense of how to use Yahoo!'s Search Web Services with REBOL. Note that the work of parsing the XML response is handled by the handlers in the SAX XML Parser. Modifications to the parse handler functions are commented with my name (Premshree Pillai). If you need to use any of the other Yahoo! Search Web Services, you might need to modify the SAX handlers.

Running the Hack

If you're on Windows, simply double-click the filename and a widget should pop up. If you're running Unix, run the hack from the command line, like so:

```
rebol yahoo.r
```

Figure 4-12 shows the result for a search for Pink Floyd.

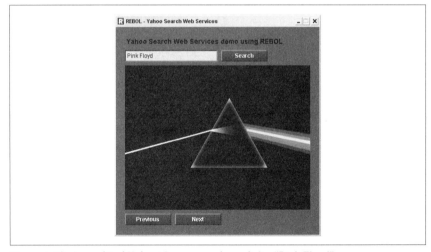

Figure 4-12. A graphical Yahoo! Image search result for "Pink Floyd"

You can click the Next and Previous buttons to browse other Yahoo! Image search results.

—Premshree Pillai

CHAPTER FIVE

Applications
Hacks 77–91

Basic sample code can get you started with Yahoo! Web Services, but to get to know what's available and how you might use the features of the API, this chapter shows you some more fully realized applications. They range from seriously useful applications (such as Grokker [Hack #77] and TagCloud [Hack #88]) that extend Yahoo! features into new directions, to the seriously silly (such as Web of Letters [Hack #82] or yReplacer [Hack #86]). This chapter intends to give you a taste of what's possible when a company like Yahoo! opens its database to outside developers, tinkerers, and hackers.

The hacks in this chapter merely scratch the surface of what's possible, and you'll find many more examples of Yahoo! Web Services applications in the wild. The best place to spot new applications is at the Yahoo! Developer Network application list (*http://developer.yahoo.net/wiki/index.cgi?ApplicationList*). The list is open to the public; if you build your own Yahoo! application, be sure to add it so others can see what you've built—whether it increases productivity or is a fun distraction.

 Visualize Yahoo! Web Search Results

#77 A service called Grokker groups Yahoo! Web Search results into a categorized, animated display.

When you type a query at Yahoo! Web Search (*http://search.yahoo.com*), Yahoo! will return a list of sites in an order that Yahoo! thinks is best. This is a great way to view results when you're looking for a specific bit of information, but it's not as helpful if you want to quickly get a broad overview of a general topic. A free web service called Grokker (*http://www.grokker.com*) takes the top 158 Yahoo! Web Search results for a query, categorizes the documents in the results, and displays them as groups in a visual map.

Imagine you're looking for information about DNA; type in the term DNA and you'll get the familiar sequential list of sites, as shown in Figure 5-1.

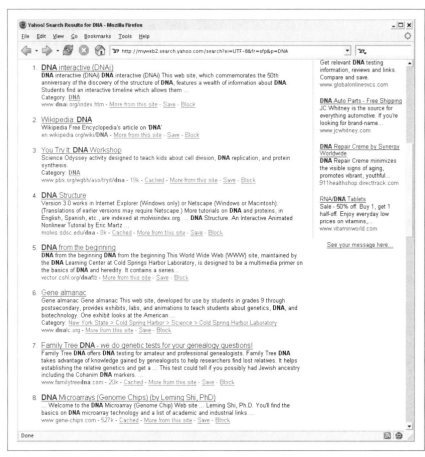

Figure 5-1. Yahoo! Search results for DNA

You'll find some sites with information about DNA, but it's difficult to find patterns within the results. You could mentally categorize sites as you browse through the pages of results, but Grokker can do the categorization for you, quickly giving you a sense of the type of information related to the query DNA. Perform the same query at Grokker, and you'll see the radically different display of results shown in Figure 5-2.

It takes a few minutes to orient yourself to a Grokker map, but once you know how to read the results, you can scan a large amount of information fairly quickly.

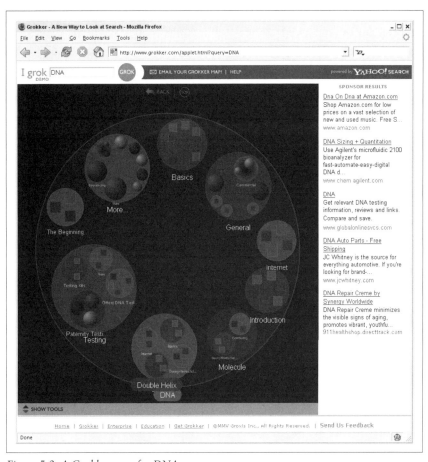

Figure 5-2. A Grokker map for DNA

Each circle on a Grokker map represents a category, and each square represents a specific document in the search results. You can click within a circle to zoom in on a category and see the documents within. As you can see, Grokker grouped results for the query DNA into categories such as Basic, Testing, and Molecule. The highlighted Double Helix category is within a top-level Structure category. And within the Double Helix category are four squares that represent documents that discuss the Double Helix structure of a DNA molecule. At a glance, you can see some patterns emerging from the search results that you couldn't get from a simple list of documents.

A circle shaded like a sphere on a Grokker map represents a category with several results. To see more details within the category, you can click the sphere to zoom in. As you zoom in to different parts of the search results, you can find more details about the documents in the results. Figure 5-3 shows a document detail within the Double Helix category.

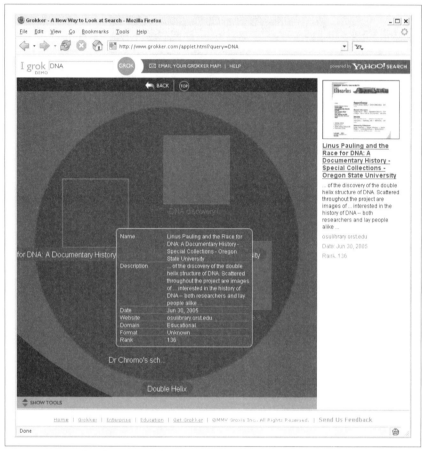

Figure 5-3. Site details on a Grokker map

As you click to view document details, you'll see a thumbnail preview and summary of the document in the right frame. To zoom back to your original view of the map, click the Top link at the top of map.

In addition to the automatic categorization on a Grokker map, you can create your own categories within search results. From the main map, right-click any empty space and choose Create from the menu. This will create a blank circle. Click just below the circle to give your new category a title and then start clicking and dragging documents or categories into your new category, as shown in Figure 5-4.

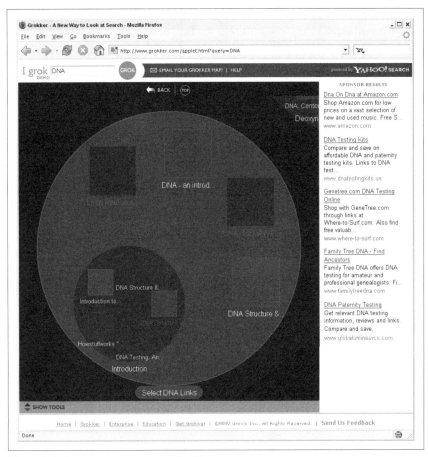

Figure 5-4. A custom category on a Grokker map

A custom category is a handy way to assemble a handful of documents to explore from the hundreds of documents on the original Grokker map. Similarly, you can delete any categories from the results by right-clicking a circle and choosing Delete from the menu.

Once you put the time into customizing a Grokker map, you can share it with others and save it for yourself by clicking the Email Your Grokker Map link at the top of the page. Fill out the form, and Grokker will send a link to your custom map to any addresses you specify.

In the lower-left corner of the map, you'll see a Show Tools link. These tools let you search within the map, filter sites by date and Yahoo! rank, and adjust the look and feel. You can change from a circular map to a square map, or change the colors to dark text on a light background.

Another benefit of using Grokker maps is that you'll find sites deep within search results that otherwise you might never have seen. You'd need to read through eight pages of Yahoo! Web Search results to see all of the documents that make up a single Grokker map. If nothing else, playing with this Yahoo! visualization should bring some results to your attention that you wouldn't have seen otherwise.

Find Links to Any Web Site

#78 Yahoo! can tell you which sites link to any other site, and yLinkbacks uses Yahoo! Search Web Services to find links to the current page you're browsing.

When you browse to a web site you've never seen before, you don't have very much advance knowledge about the site. You might know that you've followed a link from a particular site that you read frequently, or you might have found the site in some search results for a certain search term. Of course, the site itself can tell you quite a bit, but that still doesn't give you any clues about where the site fits into the larger Web. With some searching at Yahoo!, you can get extra info about a site by using the special link: syntax.

If you want to find what sites are linking to any other particular site, you can browse to *http://search.yahoo.com* and enter this query: link:*insert URL*. Instead of standard search results, Yahoo! will display a list of the sites that link to the URL you've specified in the query. For example, if you'd like to find out where the O'Reilly Hacks site fits into the Web, you could search for link:http://hacks.oreilly.com.

In the results, you immediately get a sense of how many pages link to the site and what kinds of sites are linking there. If you're browsing the Web, leaving a site to do a quick Yahoo! link: search can be annoying if you'd just like to get this sense about the current site you're visiting. To find the sites, you need to copy the current URL from your browser address bar, open a new window or tab, browse to Yahoo!, and then assemble the proper query. It's a quick process, but you can speed it up considerably with a bit of classic ASP and a JavaScript bookmarklet.

This hack uses JavaScript to get the URL of the current page you're viewing in your browser. From there, it passes the URL to a server-side script that assembles the proper Yahoo! query and fetches the top 10 results with Yahoo! Search Web Services. A new pop-up window will give a quick look at which sites are linking to the current page, without leaving your place.

The Code

The first part of this hack is a server-side script that retrieves the search results and formats them for display. The HTML result will end up being inserted into a separate pop-up browser window above the current page.

The script accepts a URL with the querystring variable q. From there, it creates a Yahoo! Search Web Services URL using the special link: syntax.

To create the script, save the following code to a file called *yl.asp* and be sure to include your own unique application ID in the code:

```
<html>
<head>
    <style type="text/css">
        body {
            background-color:#fff;
            color:#000;
            font-family:verdana,sans-serif;
            font-size:11px;
            margin:0px;
            padding:0px;
            border:0px;
        }
        li{padding:1px;padding-bottom:2px;}
    </style>
    <title>Yahoo Linkbacks</title>
    <base target="_new"/>
</head>

<body>
<script language="JavaScript" type="text/javascript">
    //bring window to top, necessary for Mozilla/Firefox
    window.focus( );
</script>
<%

On Error Resume Next
Response.Buffer = True
'' Expecting a URL string to be in the querystring "q"
szQ = Request("q")
If (szQ <> "") Then %>

<div style='text-align:center;width:98%;'>
    <a style='font-weight:bold;'
      href="http://search.yahoo.com/search?p=link:<% =szQ %>">Yahoo ⏎
Linkbacks</a>
    <br/>
    for <a href="<% =szQ %>" title="<% =szQ %>">this url</a>
</div>

<!-- Display a temporary "Loading" message while looking up images -->
<div id="ldDiv"
 style='font-weight:bold;text-align:center;width:98%;padding-top:20px;'>
Loading...</div>
<% Response.Flush %>

<ul style="margin:4px;padding:4px;">

<%    Dim objXML, xml
    szStr = ""
    szUrl = ""
    szTitle = ""
```

```
        szSummary = ""
        set xml = Server.CreateObject ("MSXML2.ServerXMLHTTP.3.0")

        szGetString = ("http://api.search.yahoo.com/" &_
                       "WebSearchService/V1/webSearch?" &_
                       "appid=[YOUR_APPLICATION_ID]&results=10&query=link:" & szQ)

        xml.Open "GET", szGetString, False
        xml.Send
        set objXML = xml.responseXML

        If (objXML.getElementsByTagName("Result").length>0) Then
            If (objXML.getElementsByTagName("Result").length>10) Then
                nLen = 10
            Else
                nLen = objXML.getElementsByTagName("Result").length-1
            End if
            For z = 0 to nLen

                '' Get each "Result" Node and loop through
                '' its childNodes to get Url, Title and Summaries
                Set nGb = objXML.getElementsByTagName("Result")(z)
                set o18 = nGb.childNodes
                For k = 0 to o18.length-1
                    Select Case (o18.item(k).nodeName)
                        Case "Title"
                            szTitle = o18.item(k).text
                        Case "Summary"
                            szSummary = o18.item(k).text
                        Case "Url"
                            szUrl = o18.item(k).text
                    End Select
                Next

                If (szSummary <> "") Then szSummary = ": " & szSummary

                szStr = szStr & ("<li><a href='" & szUrl & "'>" & szTitle & ↵
"</a>")
                szStr = szStr & (szSummary & "</li>")

                szUrl = ""
                szTitle = ""
                szSummary = ""
            Next
        End if
        If (szStr <> "") Then
            Response.write(szStr)
        Else
            Response.write("<li>No Results Found</li>")
        End if

        set xml = Nothing
        set objXML = Nothing
    End if %></ul>

    <script language="JavaScript" type="text/javascript">
```

```
// Hide the "Loading" message when page is fully loaded
document.getElementById("ldDiv").style.display="none";
</script>
</body>
</html>
```

Upload *yl.asp* to a public web server to make it available to the bookmarklet. The bookmarklet is a bit of JavaScript that resides in a bookmark and calls the ASP page in-context by sending the URL of the page currently in the browser.

Running the Hack

Add the following code to an existing bookmarklet by adding it to the location field. Be sure to include the URL of the server-side page, *yl.asp*:

```
javascript:function p(){window.open(('http://example.com/yl. asp?q='+⏎
document.location. href),'nsm','width=250,height=350,directories=no,⏎
location=no,menubar=no, scrollbars=yes,status=no,toolbar=no,⏎
resizable=no,left=0,top=0,screenx=0,screeny=0')}p( )
```

Name the bookmarklet *yLinkback*, and you should be set for easy access to linking information. For example, if you browse to the photo-sharing web site Flickr (*http://www.flickr.com*) and click the yLinkback bookmark, you'll see a pop-up window like the one shown in Figure 5-5.

Figure 5-5. The yLinkbacks pop-up window at Flickr

A quick survey of the sites there shows that Flickr is linked by many personal weblogs, and this can let you know that the site is probably a favorite with the weblog community. Once you have the yLinkbacks bookmarklet installed, you can gather some quick information like this for any web site you visit. If you'd rather not build your own version of the hack, you can install the bookmarklet at *http://www.kokogiak.com/yahoo_linkbacks.html*.

—*Alan Taylor*

Import Yahoo! Local Listings into Your Address #79 Book

A freely available program called gvcard can help you import a Yahoo! Local listing into your email address book, cell phone, or any application that understands vCard.

Have you ever wondered why it is so darn hard to import search results from Yellow Pages sites like Yahoo! Local (*http://local.yahoo.com*) into other programs? Whether you are at your desk or using your fancy Treo 650, wouldn't it be nice if you could import these addresses, phone numbers, and URLs directly into your address book? Now you can.

gvcard (*http://gvcard.sf.net*) is a free program that wraps common Yellow Pages services from Yahoo! and Google and makes their results available in the vCard format. gvcard is written in Python and the source code is available via CVS.

gvcard comes in four flavors (all four versions are available at the gvcard web site):

- A standalone CGI script that you can run from any web site
- A command-line client you can run locally just about anywhere
- A *weblet* version of the CGI script that you can also run locally
- A plug in for IMSmarter.com (*http://imsmarter.com/developer.php*) that allows you to access gvcard over IM

At the heart of gvcard is the vCard standard: a simple text-based format that almost all phone book, address book, and calendaring applications understand. vCard allows these programs to share contact information across a wide variety of platforms. By wiring vCard up to Yahoo! Local, gvcard helps you avoid searching for the same information twice. Best of all, it makes local business information easy to take with you on all kinds of portable devices, from PDAs to cell phones—even those without Internet access.

HACK
#79

Import Yahoo! Local Listings into Your Address Book

You can view the complete vCard standard at *http://www.imc.org/pdi*, but it's easy to see how it works in an example:

```
BEGIN:VCARD
FN:Coupa Cafe
ORG:Coupa Cafe
ADR;DOM;POSTAL;WORK:538 Ramona St;;;Palo Alto;CA;;
TEL;Work;VOICE;PREF:(650) 322-6872
URL:http://www.coupacafe.com/
UID:http://www.coupacafe.com/
NOTE:***Directions: http://xrl.us/fbu5 ***Search: http://xrl.us/fbu4
VERSION:2.1
END:VCARD
```

Every line in the vCard has a tag and value, such as ORG:Coupa Cafe, which identifies this vCard as being for the organization Coupa Cafe. It also has additional bits of metadata that work similarly to XML's attributes, such as PREF, which indicates that the work phone number listed is the preferred mode of contact. Unfortunately, the vCard standard predates the widespread adoption of XML as the Web's "one true metadata format," so some of its features are a bit archaic. Thankfully, we don't have much need for its advanced features.

 If you're interested in playing around with vCards, the following handy site has a simple CGI that will generate them from an HTML form: *http://www.vcardprocessor.com/try.htm*.

Accessing Yahoo! Local is a snap, thanks to Yahoo!'s excellent web services support. Like all Yahoo! APIs, Yahoo! Local works via REST, a simple technique whereby a client makes a standard HTTP request using GET parameters and receives an XML response. The client application—in this case, gvcard—needs to be able to correctly format the request based on user input and then parse and present the response. Here's a sample Yahoo! Local query:

```
http://api.local.yahoo.com/LocalSearchService/V1/localSearch?appid=insert ↵
App ID&query=pizza&zip=94306&results=2
```

And here's an excerpt of the response it generates:

```
<ResultSet xsi:schemaLocation="urn:yahoo:lcl http://api.search.yahoo.com/↵
LocalSearchService/V1/LocalSearchResponse.xsd" totalResultsAvailable="93" ↵
totalResultsReturned="2" firstResultPosition="1">
<ResultSetMapUrl>↵
http://local.yahoo.com/mapview?stx=pizza&csz=Palo+Alto%2C+CA&city=↵
Palo+Alto&state=CA&radius=5&ed=BVD56a131DxIV6V7_5O_wO8KQY1.bxtOAd8qew-- ↵
</ResultSetMapUrl>
<Result>
```

```
<Title>Round Table Pizza Palo Alto</Title>
<Address>3407 Alma St</Address>
<City>Palo Alto</City>
<State>CA</State>
<Phone>(650) 494-2928</Phone>
<Rating/>

<Distance>0.28</Distance>
<Url>⏎
http://local.yahoo.com/details?id=21395990&state=CA&stx=pizza&csz=Palo+Alto⏎
+CA&ed=o9pJ_q160Sy74qzFN72IOcSInA8HkgnO3mChobdW6IFvjLcw9NpqoONCOIKIFIrT⏎
</Url>
<ClickUrl>⏎
http://local.yahoo.com/details?id=21395990&state=CA&stx=pizza&csz=Palo+⏎
Alto+CA&ed=o9pJ_q160Sy74qzFN72IOcSInA8HkgnO3mChobdW6IFvjLcw9NpqoONCOIKIFIrT⏎
</ClickUrl>

<MapUrl>⏎
http://maps.yahoo.com/maps_result?name=Round+Table+Pizza+Palo+Alto&desc=⏎
6504942928&csz=Palo+Alto+CA&qty=9&cs=9&ed=o9pJ_q160Sy74qzFN72IOcSInA8H⏎
kgnO3mChobdW6IFvjLcw9NpqoONCOIKIFIrT⏎
</MapUrl>
<BusinessUrl>http://www.roundtablepizza.com/</BusinessUrl>

<BusinessClickUrl>http://www.roundtablepizza.com/</BusinessClickUrl>
</Result>
</ResultSet>
```

Most of the elements in this XML are straightforward and map pretty closely to the corresponding fields in the vCard. Because some of the URLs are lengthy, gvcard often uses a URL rewriting service from *http://www.metamark.net* to keep the URL lengths manageable. Other than that, the data is copied directly from Yahoo! Local XML responses to the vCard.

The Code

Although gvcard comes in several varieties, each with its own user interface, they all work according to the following basic four-step procedure:

1. Get input, consisting of a search term (such as pizza in our previous example) and a location (such as 94301 or "Palo Alto, CA").

2. Pass the request to Yahoo! Local and parse the response.

3. Create a vCard using the appropriate fields.

4. Present the result for easy import into an address book application.

gvcard is written in Python, and even if you're not familiar with Python, the following code example should be straightforward.

At the heart of all gvcard versions is the *lookup.py* module. Its job is to formulate the request and parse the response. This is accomplished with two simple classes, YahooLocalRequest and YahooParser:

```
class YahooLocalRequest:
    def __init__(self, searchTerm, location):
        self.baseUrl_ = "http://api.local.yahoo.com/LocalSearchService/V1/⏎
localSearch"
        self.params_ = {"appid":"gvcard-python",
                        "query": searchTerm,
                        "location": location
                        }
        self.url_ = "%s?%s" % (self.baseUrl_, urllib.urlencode(self.params_))
        self.request_ = urllib2.Request(url=self.url_)

    def fetchRaw(self):
        f = urllib2.urlopen(self.request_)
        self.contents_ = f.read( )
        return self.contents_
```

gvcard also works with Google Local, which is a nearly equivalent service. However, Google does not provide a web services API for its Local search, and the code to interface with it is much more complicated. Feel free to compare the two if you ever need to make the case for web services to somebody.

If you're familiar with python's urllib2 module, this code will look completely familiar. Take the search term and location (along with an appid, which is assigned by Yahoo!), URL-encode them, and retrieve the raw XML as text via HTTP. The YahooParser does the rest (no pun intended):

```
class YahooParser:
    def __init__(self):
        self.results_ = {}

    def get(self, xml, tag, default=""):
        rs = xml.getElementsByTagName(tag)
        if not rs:
            return default
        element = rs[0]
        textNode = element.firstChild
        if textNode:
            return textNode.data
        else:
            return default

    def feed(self, data):
        dom = xml.dom.minidom.parseString(data)
        rs = dom.getElementsByTagName("ResultSet")[0]
```

```
            for i, result in enumerate(rs.getElementsByTagName("Result")):
                self.results_[i] = { "phone" : self.get(result, "Phone"),
                                     "directionsUrl" : self.get(result, ⤶
   "MapUrl"),
                                     "homepageUrl" : self.get(result, ⤶
   "BusinessUrl"),
                                     "city" : self.get(result, "City"),
                                     "state" : self.get(result, "State"),
                                     "zip" : "",
                                     "street" : self.get(result, "Address"),
                                     "name" : self.get(result, "Title"),
                                     "searchUrl" : self.get(result, "ClickUrl")
   }
            return self.results_
```

The feed( ) method constructs a Python dictionary that holds the relevant data for each result. Use the get( ) method as a simple wrapper for python's xml.minidom module, whose API is not entirely well suited to the kind of parsing we're doing here.

Finally, the results of the search are passed to the makevcard module, which looks like this:

```
def generateVCard(name, street, city, state, zip, phone, url=None,
location=None, note=None, searchUrl=None):
    text = ""
    text += "BEGIN:VCARD\n"
    text += "FN:%s\n" % name
    text += "ORG:%s\n" % name
    text += "ADR"
    text += ";DOM;POSTAL;WORK:"
    text += "%s;" % street
    text += ";;%s;%s;%s;\n" % (city, state, zip)
    text += "TEL;Work"
    text += ";VOICE"
    text += ";PREF"
    text += ":%s\n" % phone
    if url:
      text += "URL:%s\n" % url
      text += "UID:%s\n" % url

    if not note:
        note = ""
    if searchUrl:
        note += " ***Search: %s" % searchUrl
    if note:
        text += "NOTE:***Directions: %s\n" % note
    text += "VERSION:2.1\n"
    text += "END:VCARD\n"
    return text
```

Import Yahoo! Local Listings into Your Address Book

HACK
#79

The vCard is then presented to the user in a form that is easy to import. Because the CGI version of gvcard is the most widely used, let's take a look at its inner workings:

```
form = cgi.FieldStorage( )
try:
    location = form["location"].value
except KeyError:
    if recentLocations:
        location = recentLocations[0]
    else:
        location = ""
try:
    search = form["search"].value
except KeyError:
    search = ""
```

As you can see, this code handles the input from the web form and verifies that the user has entered information.

Running the Hack

To pull it all together into a script, start by using Python's built-in cgi module to get the query parameters. Next, the program emits the actual HTML that the user will see:

```
cprint( "<html><head>" )
cprint( "<TITLE>Local Google -> vCard: %s</TITLE></head><body>" % mode )

cprint( "<form>Business name: <input name='search' value='%s'><br>" % ⏎
search )
    cprint( "Location: <input name='location' value='%s'> (e.g. Palo Alto, ⏎
CA or 94301)<br>" % location )
    cprint( "Choose a local search provier: <SELECT name=searchType>" )
    options = ("Google", "Yahoo")
    for option in options:
        if option == searchType:
            sel = " SELECTED"
        else:
            sel = ""
        cprint("<OPTION %s>%s</OPTION>" % (sel,option))
    cprint( "</SELECT><br>")
    cprint( "<input type=submit value=Search> Show at most" )
    cprint( "<SELECT name=maxResults><OPTION>1</OPTION><option>2</option>
<OPTION>5</OPTION><OPTION>10</OPTION><OPTION SELECTED>25</OPTION></SELECT>
results<br></form>" )
```

If you've been provided with search terms, go ahead and run the search, using the lookup module:

```
if search and location:
        if location in recentLocations:
            recentLocations.remove(location)
```

```
recentLocations.insert(0, location)
tpl = (search, location)
if tpl in recentSearches:
    recentSearches.remove(tpl)
recentSearches.insert(0, tpl)

results, url = lookup.resultsForQuery(searchTerm=search, ⏎
location=location, searchType=searchType)
    cprint( "<b>Results</b> (from <a href='%s'>these raw search ⏎
results</a>):<p>" % url)
```

Next, present a list of all the results, in a simple, stripped-down HTML for-mat. This HTML page renders equally well on most cell phone and PDA web browsers, allowing access to gvcard from a wide variety of devices:

```
for valueDict, vc in results[:maxResults]:
    for entry in ResultTemplate.split("\n"):
        oe = entry
        for k, v in valueDict.items():
            entry = entry.replace("$%s" % k, v)
            if oe != entry:
                cprint( entry )
    qs = urllib.urlencode(valueDict)
    cprint( "vCard: <a href='vcardcgi.cgi/card.vcf?%s'>download here</a><br>⏎
"% qs )
    cprint( "<hr>" )
```

One technique to note here is the use of a simple template to present each result. The template (called `ResultTemplate` in the preceding code fragment) looks like this:

```
ResultTemplate = """
$name<br>
$street<br>
$city, $state $zip<br>
$phone<br>
<a href='$homepageUrl'>$homepageUrl</a><br>
<a href='$searchUrl'>$searchType Link</a> - <a href='$directionsUrl'>
Directions</a><br>
"""
```

This template could easily be changed to something more graphically rich, perhaps incorporating some additional elements of Yahoo! Local (such as its mapping features) that are not currently supported by gvcard.

The last aspect of gvcard for which the CGI script is responsible is to pro-vide the user a way to easily import the vCard into her address book pro-gram of choice. Since gvcard is designed to work with the widest possible array of programs and platforms, this is a bit tricky. Notice the line from the previous fragment that looked like this:

```
cprint( "vCard: <a href='vcardcgi.cgi/card.vcf?%s'>download here</a><br>" ⏎
% qs )
```

This constructs a link to another part of gvcard, the *vcardcgi.cgi* script. It's responsible for emitting the vCard data itself, using the correct MIME type: text/x-vcard. Keep in mind that not all browsers recognize the vCard MIME type, but most know about the vCard file extension *.vcf*, which is why the link is written with the trailing /card.vcf. Many browsers will assume this is the filename of the file being downloaded and invoke the right program to handle it.

A freely accessible running instance of the gvcard CGI script is available at *http://www.speakeasy.org/~ericries/gvcard/lookupcgi.cgi,* so feel free to try it out. Bookmark this URL in your phone, PDA, or handheld's web browser and surprise yourself with how many times it comes in handy. At the very least, you'll save yourself a few bucks in calls to 411.

—*Eric Ries*

HACK Create a Yahoo! Local MIDlet
#80 Use Java for mobile devices to access the Yahoo! Local API on a mobile device.

The Yahoo! Local Search service allows you to search the Internet for businesses near a specified location. With the availability of a REST web service interface to Yahoo! Local Search, it is quite simple to implement an application that enables mobile devices to access Yahoo! Local Search. It might save you the cost of expensive 411 calls to find out the phone number or the address of a business when you are traveling.

Before you build the hack, it might help to familiarize yourself with a couple of important terms you'll encounter:

MIDlet
    A *MIDlet* is a Java application for small devices like cell phones. More specifically, it's a Java 2, Micro Edition (J2ME™) application that is conformant with the Mobile Information Device Profile (MIDP) specification.

J2ME
    J2ME is a group of Java APIs for creating applications on small devices like cell phones, pagers, PDAs, and set-top boxes.

This hack shows you how to build a MIDlet that allows users to perform local search, implemented over Yahoo! Local Search API, from a mobile device.

What You Need

To use this hack, you'll need a Handspring Treo 600 running the Web-Sphere Everyplace Micro Environment (WEME), which you'll find at *http://www.palmone.com/us/support/jvm.*

You'll also need the Sun Java Wireless Toolkit Version 2.2, which you can find at *http://java.sun.com/products/j2mewtoolkit*, and the Eclipse development environment with the EclipseME plug-in for building MIDlets, available at *http://eclipseme.org.*

The Code

The code for this hack is organized into three files:

LocalSearch.java
    MIDlet described in more detail below

LocalSearchResponseHandler.java
    SAX event handler class used to parse the response from Yahoo! Local Search

URLUTF8Encoder.java
    Utility class used to encode special characters in the URL

> You can download the complete code for this hack at *http://mobile-j2me.blogspot.com.*

The code in *LocalSearch.java* handles most of the work. This file implements the MIDlet interface requirements, describes the application interface, and handles any user interaction. Here's a look at the key methods in *LocalSearch.java*:

```
// package/import statements
public class LocalSearch extends MIDlet implements CommandListener
{
    // Data members

    public LocalSearch( )
    {
        // Create the UI forms and the buttons/commands
    }
    protected void startApp( ) throws MIDletStateChangeException
    {
        // Set the display to the main form
    }
    protected void pauseApp( )
    {
```

```
    // Not used
}
protected void destroyApp(boolean unconditional)
{
    // Not used
}
public void commandAction(Command c, Displayable s)
{
    // Handle commands from the UI
    // Retrieve data entered by the user
    // Invoke Yahoo! Local Search (see doYahooLocalSearch())
    // Parse the response
    // Display the results or error to the user
}
// Invoke Yahoo Local Search and get response
private String doYahooLocalSearch() throws IOException
{
    // Invoke Yahoo Local Search
    String url =
    "http://api.local.yahoo.com/LocalSearchService/V1/localSearch?"
    + "appid="
    + appID
    + "&query="
    + URLUTF8Encoder.encode(query)
    + "&results="
    + results
    + "&start="
    + start
        + "&zip=" + zip;

    return(postViaHttpConnection(url).toFormattedString());
}
private LocalSearchResponseHandler postViaHttpConnection(String url) ⏎
throws IOException
{
    // POST a HTTP request with the URL
    // Retrieve the response (XML document)
    // Invoke parseXML()
}
// Parse the response XML document using SAX and retrieve
// the needed information
private LocalSearchResponseHandler parseXML(InputStream is) throws ⏎
SAXException, IOException
{
}
}
```

The following code is a SAX handler that retrieves the title, phone number, and address from each of the businesses that Yahoo! returns. Here are the key methods in *LocalSearchResponseHandler.java*:

```
// package/import statements
class LocalSearchResponseHandler extends DefaultHandler
```

```
{
    // Data members

    public void startElement(String uri, String localName, String qName, ⏎
    Attributes attributes) throws SAXException
    {
        // Keep track of QNames
        qNameStack.push(qName);

        // Get the # of results available and the # of results
        // returned in the response
        if (qName.equals(ELEM_RS))
        {
            totalResultsAvailable=attributes.getValue(ATTR_TRA);
            totalResultsReturned = attributes.getValue(ATTR_TRR);
        }

        currentElementContent = "";
    }

    public void characters(char[] ch, int start, int length)
            throws SAXException
    {
    currentElementContent = currentElementContent + new String(ch, start, ⏎
    length);
    }

    public void endElement(String uri, String localName, String qName)
            throws SAXException
    {
        // Get current QName
        qName = (String) qNameStack.peek();

        // Get the title, phone, address of the listing
        if (ELEM_TITLE.equals(qName))
        {
            titles.addElement(currentElementContent);
        }
        else if (ELEM_PHONE.equals(qName))
        {
            phones.addElement(currentElementContent);
        }
        else if (ELEM_ADDRESS.equals(qName))
        {
            addresses.addElement(currentElementContent);
        }

        // Pop QName, since we are done with it
        qNameStack.pop( );
    }

}
```

Running the Hack

Once you have the source files in place, you can build the application from within Eclipse by right-clicking the project and selecting Build Project. Or to package the application, right-click the project and select J2ME → Create Package.

Upload the resulting *YahooWebServices.jar* file to a publicly accessible web server. Then use the IBM MIDlet manager on the Treo to download the MIDlet at the appropriate URL.

Once the code is installed, launch the IBM MIDlet manager from the handheld. You should see a screen similar to that shown in Figure 5-6.

Figure 5-6. MIDlet manager

> You can also use the MIDlet manager to install a different MIDlet or get a new version of the Yahoo! Web Services MIDlet.

From the manager, select the Yahoo Web Services MIDlet and click Launch. The main screen of the MIDlet will appear, as shown in Figure 5-7.

Figure 5-7. MIDlet entry form

There are five fields you can fill in on the form. AppID identifies the user of Yahoo! Local Web Services. By default, its value is set to YahooDemo, but you can get your own app ID at *http://api.search.yahoo.com/webservices/register_application*. The Query field is for the business you're looking for; Results is for the number of results that you want to see on the results screen; and Start identifies the point from where you would like to see the results from the complete list. Finally, ZIP is for the Zip Code that identifies the location where you want to do the search.

Enter the name of a local business or type of business along with your Zip Code and click Search. You should see results like those shown in Figure 5-8.

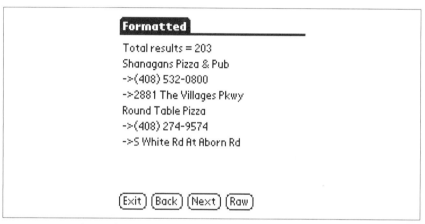

Figure 5-8. MIDlet results

If the top results aren't quite what you're looking for, you can click Next to see more.

Assembling this hack takes a bit of work, but it's an excellent example of seamlessly integrating Yahoo! data into unusual places, such as applications for mobile devices.

—Deepak Nadig

HACK Import Yahoo! Local Listings into Excel
#81 Bringing Yahoo! Local Search results into a spreadsheet can help you sort, view, and visualize local businesses.

Having access to the Yahoo! Local API is like being able to effortlessly move entries from the physical Yellow Pages to your computer. And dumping the entries into a structured environment like Excel can give you a new way to look at Yahoo! Local Search results.

Imagine that you find yourself in Corvallis, Oregon, and you'd like to find a spot to sit down, grab a bite to eat, and surf the Internet wirelessly. A Yahoo! Local Search for wifi near the Corvallis Zip Code (97333) will turn up several results for businesses that have wireless Internet access, as shown in Figure 5-9.

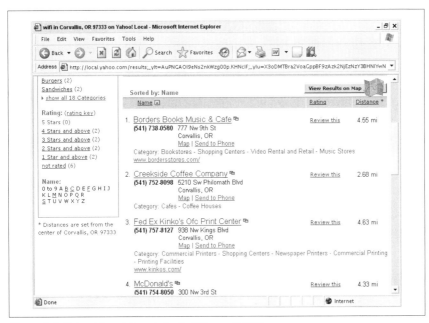

Figure 5-9. Yahoo! Local Search for "wifi" near 97333

Unfortunately, Yahoo! Local won't tell you which places have *free* wireless access, so you'd have to call each of the businesses to ask them. You could scroll and click through the web page and jot down each phone number, or you could take advantage of the Yahoo! Local API to import the list into a spreadsheet for quick reference to the phone numbers.

Exporting Yahoo! Local Search to a Spreadsheet

Programmer Rikul Patel has already done much of the work involved with importing results into a spreadsheet. His program, called Yahoo! Local Search To Excel, is available for free at *http://rikulpatel.com/ylocalsearch.php*. It's available on Windows only, and you'll need a spreadsheet program such as Excel to view the results.

Once you download the program, there's nothing to install. Double-click *YLocalSearch.exe* and you'll see a form like the one shown in Figure 5-10.

Figure 5-10. The Yahoo! Local Search To Excel form

Type in a query, Zip Code, and radius, and then click Local Search. Behind the scenes, the program asks Yahoo! for the data and formats the response as a *comma-separated value* (CSV) file. The program will ask you to name the file, so call it something appropriate, like *corvallis_wifi.csv* in this example. If Excel is installed on your system, *corvallis_wifi.csv* should open in Excel when you double-click it, and you'll see a spreadsheet like the one shown in Figure 5-11.

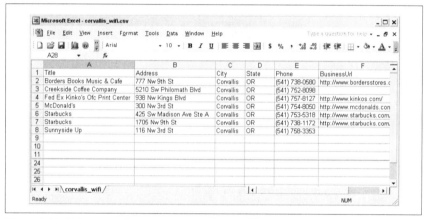

Figure 5-11. Yahoo! Local results in an Excel spreadsheet

The spreadsheet includes the name, address, city, state, and phone number of the business. If Yahoo! has a web site listed for the business, that's included as well. With the data in the spreadsheet, you can then add your own columns, mix it with existing data, or even create charts based on the data. And this definitely makes for a quick list of phone numbers you can call to see who has free wireless in the area.

Using Perl

Yahoo! Local Search To Excel is easy to use, but the output isn't very flexible. To access some of the other data available through the Yahoo! API—such as distance and user ratings—you'll need to write your own code. Luckily, this is fairly quick work with a scripting language like Perl.

The code. Much like the previous program, this Perl script accepts a query and a Zip Code and assembles a CSV file with results from a Yahoo! Local Search. As with most of the other Perl examples in this book, you'll need to have LWP::Simple and XML::Simple installed on your system for requesting and parsing Yahoo! data. You'll also need the Getopt::Simple module for handling the command-line parameters. Save the following code to a file called *yahoo_excel.pl*:

```perl
#!/usr/bin/perl
# yahoo_excel.pl
# Accepts a query and zip code and returns a CSV
# list of results you can open in Excel.
# Usage: yahoo_excel.pl -q <query> -z <zip code>
#
# You can create an AppID, and read the full documentation
# for Yahoo! Web Services at http://developer.yahoo.net/

use strict;
use Getopt::Simple qw($switch);
use LWP::Simple;
use XML::Simple;

# Set your unique Yahoo! Application ID
my $appID = "insert app ID";

# Get/Set the command line options
my $options =
{
  q =>
    {
    type    => '=s',
    env     => '-',
    default => '',
    verbose => 'Specify a query',
    order   => 1,
    },
  zip =>
    {
    type    => '=f',
    env     => '-',
    default => '',
    verbose => 'Specify a zip code',
    order   => 2,
    },
};
my $option = Getopt::Simple->new();
if (!$option->getOptions($options,
    "Usage: yahoo_excel.pl -q [query] -z [zip code]")) {
  exit(-1);
}

# Make sure the command line options have values
```

```
my $query = $$switch{'q'};
my $zip = $$switch{'zip'};
if ((!$query) || (!$zip)) {
    print "Usage: yahoo_excel.pl -q <query> -z <zip code>";
    exit;
};

# Construct a Yahoo! Local Query with only required options
my $language = "en";

my $req_url = "http://api.local.yahoo.com/";
    $req_url .= "LocalSearchService/V1/localSearch?";
    $req_url .= "appid=$appID";
    $req_url .= "&query=$query";
    $req_url .= "&zip=$zip";

# Make the request
my $yahoo_response = get($req_url);

# Parse the XML
my $xmlsimple = XML::Simple->new( );
my $yahoo_xml = $xmlsimple->XMLin($yahoo_response);

# Loop through the items returned, printing as CSV
print "\"Title\",\"Address\",\"Distance\",\"Rating\"\n";
foreach my $result (@{$yahoo_xml->{Result}}) {
    my $title = $result->{Title};
    my $address = $result->{Address};
    my $distance = $result->{Distance};
    my $rating = $result->{Rating};
    if (!eval($rating)) {
        $rating = "";
    }
    print "\"$title\",\"$address\",\"$distance\",\"$rating\"\n";
}
```

With a bit more control over the file, you can decide which columns you'd like to include in your spreadsheet. As you can see in the last line of this code, the script prints the title of the business, the address, the distance from the center of the Zip Code, and the rating as an average of Yahoo! user ratings for that business.

Running the hack. Run the code from the command line by passing in the two parameters: -q followed by a query, and -z followed by a Zip Code. If you're still looking for wireless hotspots in Corvallis, you might call the script like this:

```
perl yahoo_excel.pl -q wifi -z 97333
```

If all goes well, you should see a block of text scroll past with all of the options. Because you'd rather read the results in a spreadsheet, you should pipe the results to a CSV file, like so:

```
perl yahoo_excel.pl -q wifi -z 97333 > wifi.csv
```

Double-click the newly created *wifi.csv* to see the results of the query, and you should have something like what's shown in Figure 5-12.

	A	B	C	D	E	F	G	H
1	Title	Address	Distance	Rating				
2	Creekside Coffee Company	5210 Sw Philomath Blvd	2.68					
3	Starbucks	425 Sw Madison Ave Ste A	4.11	4.5				
4	Sunnyside Up	116 Nw 3rd St	4.2					
5	McDonald's	300 Nw 3rd St	4.33					
6	Borders Books Music & Cafe	777 Nw 9th St	4.55					
7	Fed Ex Kinko's Ofc Print Center	938 Nw Kings Blvd	4.63					
8	Starbucks	1705 Nw 9th St	5.51	4				
9	McDonald's	2250 Nw 9th St	5.96					
10								
11								
26								

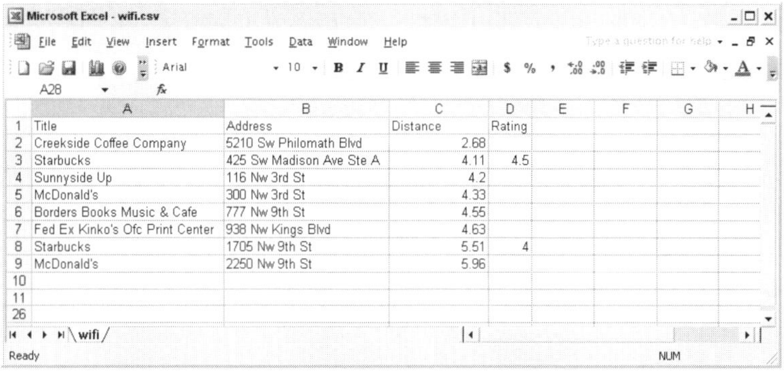

Figure 5-12. Custom Yahoo! Local results in an Excel spreadsheet

With a custom script, you can now quickly see not only which businesses offer wireless Internet access, but also how close they are and how Yahoo! users have rated each business. The key to the hack is that, thanks to Yahoo!'s open API, you can add the search results to other programs such as Excel and structure the data in ways that are useful to you.

HACK #82 Spell Words with Yahoo! Images

Web of Letters combines Yahoo! Image Search results to spell a single word.

The Web of Letters is a PHP script that uses the Yahoo! Image Search API to grab images of letters from all over the Web to spell words. The results—a combination of photos and illustrations—are always surprising and can even look like modern art. You simply type a word into a web form, and the script assembles the images.

The key to the hack is transforming the user's word into the proper Yahoo! query. When the user enters `hello`, the code queries Yahoo! Image Search for each letter in the word—`"letter h"`, `"letter e"`, `"letter l"`, and so on—eventually spelling the complete word, as shown in Figure 5-13.

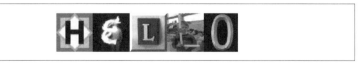

Figure 5-13. The word "hello" assembled from Yahoo! Images

When the character is a number, the query syntax is "number 1", "number 2", etc. When the character is a symbol, the code queries Yahoo! for its full name; the symbol & becomes ampersand.

You can try a working Web of Letters is at *http://blog.outer-court.com/yahoo/letters.php5*.

The Code

Web of Letters uses PHP5, and you can start by creating a file called *letters.php5*. In addition to a standard HTML head, add the following code to accept a query parameter q:

```
$q = ( isset($_POST['q']) ) ? $_POST['q'] : '';
```

Then add the following XHTML snippet, which will ask the user for input:

```
<form action="letters.php5" method="post"><div>
Enter anything:
<input type="text" size="40" maxlength="40" name="q"
       value="<?= toAttribute($q) ?>" />
<input type="submit" value="Display" />
</div></form>
```

Print the query in the input box if something has been posted already, but make sure to convert it to an HTML attribute value using the toAttribute function:

```
function toAttribute($s)
{
    $s = toXml($s);
    $s = str_replace('"', '&quot;', $s);
    return $s;
}

function toXml($s)
{
    $s = str_replace('&', '&amp;', $s);
    $s = str_replace('<', '&lt;', $s);
    $s = str_replace('>', '&gt;', $s);
    return $s;
}
```

The heart of the code shows the images retrieved from Yahoo!.

> The script accepts only words of up to 40 letters. It's also wise to implement a cache when you query Yahoo!; "letter b" will be used for every b, but we do not need to query Yahoo every time for this.

```
if ($q != '')
{
    ?><p style="margin-top: 50px">Spelling
        <em><?= toXml($q) ?></em>
            (reload for variations):</p><?

    if ( strlen($q) <= 40 )
    {
        for ($i = 0; $i < strlen($q); $i++)
        {
            $letter = substr($q, $i, 1);
            switch ( strtolower($letter) )
            {
                case '.':
                    showImage('dot');
                    break;

                case '_':
                    showImage('underscore');
                    break;

                case '-':
                    showImage('minus');
                    break;

                case '/':
                    showImage('slash');
                    break;

                case ':':
                    showImage('colon sign');
                    break;

                case '$':
                    showImage('dollar');
                    break;

                case '0':
                case '1':
                case '2':
                case '3':
                case '4':
                case '5':
                case '6':
                case '7':
                case '8':
                case '9':
                    showImage('"number ' . $letter . '"');
                    break;

                case '!':
                    showImage('"exclamation mark"');
                    break;
```

```
                    case '?':
                        showImage('"question mark"');
                        break;

                    case 'a':
                    case 'b':
                    case 'c':
                    case 'd':
                    case 'e':
                    case 'f':
                    case 'g':
                    case 'h':
                    case 'i':
                    case 'j':
                    case 'k':
                    case 'l':
                    case 'm':
                    case 'n':
                    case 'o':
                    case 'p':
                    case 'q':
                    case 'r':
                    case 's':
                    case 't':
                    case 'u':
                    case 'v':
                    case 'w':
                    case 'x':
                    case 'y':
                    case 'z':
                        showImage('"letter ' . $letter . '"');
                        break;

                    default:
                        echo '<br />';
                        break;
                }
            }
        }
        else
        {
            echo '<p>Up to 40 letters only.</p>';
        }
    }
```

The switch-case clause calls the `showImage` function that grabs 20 images from Yahoo! for every query and then displays one at random:

```
function showImage($q)
{
    $max = 20;
    $s = '';
```

```
$url = 'http://api.search.yahoo.com/ImageSearchService/' .
       'V1/imageSearch?appid=insert app ID&' .
       'query=' . urlencode($q) .
       '&results=' . $max;

$dom = new domdocument;
$dom->load($url);

$xpath = new domxpath($dom);
$i = rand(0, $max - 1);
$source = $xpath->query('//Result/Thumbnail/Url')->
          item($i)->firstChild->data;
echo '<img src="' . $source . '" ' .
     'style="width:80px; height:80px" alt="" />';
}
```

Running the Hack

Upload *letters.php5* to your server and view it with your browser. Type a word in the form and click Display. You should see a group of letters spelling your word, like the results for Yahoo! Hacks shown in Figure 5-14.

Figure 5-14. "Yahoo! Hacks" spelled by the Web of Letters

As you can see in Figure 5-14, all images are scaled to 80 pixels by 80 pixels, so they have the same size. The script uses inline styles, but you might want to move the style definitions into a separate CSS stylesheet to keep the HTML lean.

With Web of Letters, you can use the power of images across the Web for some fun. Happy writing—and no ransom notes, please!

—Philipp Lenssen

HACK #83   Randomize Your Windows Desktop Background

Use the Yahoo! Image Search web service to spin a virtual roulette wheel and let fate choose your desktop background image.

People love to change their desktop backgrounds. It's one of the first skills that new computer users learn, and even old computer pros fiddle with their desktop background image on a fairly regular basis. Browsing through the aisles of your local computer shop, you'll find CDs full of scenic imagery that you can use as your desktop background pictures. But why shell out money for custom backgrounds, when you can use the entire Web as your source for background images?

The Yahoo! Image Search is a good place to start your search for a new desktop background. Point your browser to *http://search.yahoo.com/images* and type in a query, such as landscape. You should find many thumbnails of images, such as the ones in Figure 5-15, which would make suitable desktop backgrounds.

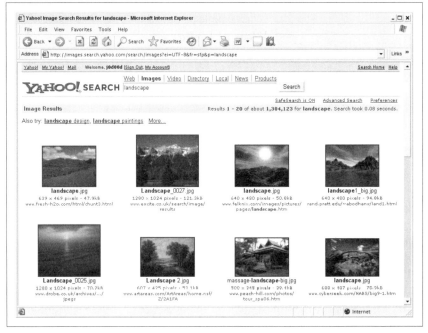

Figure 5-15. Yahoo! Image Search results for "landscape"

Underneath each photo is the name of the image file, its size in pixels, and the URL where the image was found. The closer the image is to the size of your current desktop, the better it will look as a background. To find out your desktop's current resolution, right-click anywhere on your desktop, choose Properties from the menu, and click the Settings tab. The current size of your desktop is listed under Screen Resolution and is typically 800 pixels wide by 600 pixels tall, or a bit larger at 1024×768. As monitors have been getting bigger, desktop sizes have been increasing as well.

To find the best images to use as backgrounds, perform an advanced image search (*http://search.yahoo.com/images/advanced*) and set the Size option to "large" or "wallpaper." This will exclude any images that wouldn't make good desktop backgrounds, such as buttons or icons. You can also include some search meta keywords with your query to find images with a specific size. For example, if your desktop is 1024×768, you could use the query landscape width:1024 height:768 to find only images that match your desktop resolution. The width and height keywords tell Yahoo! Image Search to return only images with the specified size.

From the search results, click on an image that's close to your desktop size to see the page on which Yahoo! found the original image. From the top frame, click the View Image link to display the original image by itself in your browser window. Right-click anywhere on the image and choose "Set as Wallpaper" in Firefox or "Set as Background" in Internet Explorer. Then you can close your browser and see your new background image!

This process is easy to follow anytime you're ready for a new background, but with a little scripting, you can speed things up and let chance decide which picture you should use.

The Code

This hack contacts Yahoo! via its Web Services API, performs an image search, chooses one of the responses at random, downloads the image, and sets it as your desktop background. Because Windows expects desktop backgrounds to be the bitmap image type and most web images are JPEGs, the script will also have to convert any image from a JPEG to a bitmap.

This conversion process is out of the scope of the Windows scripting environment, and this hack uses a third-party ActiveX component that converts JPEG files to bitmaps. An ActiveX component is a piece of software that is meant to be used by other programs, and it usually performs a specific task. Alex K. Angelopoulos wrote this particular component, called Convert to Bitmap, and published it on his web site. You can download a copy at *http://dev.remotenetworktechnology.com/wsh/comwsh.htm*. Once you've downloaded the file and unzipped the contents, you'll need to install the component so it's available to scripts. From a command line, browse to the directory where you unzipped the package and type the following command:

```
Regsvr32 GfxConverter.ocx
```

With the component installed, you'll be set to run the script. Save the following code to a file called *Y!background.vbs*:

```
'----------------------------------------------------
' Y!Background.vbs
'
' Finds a random image via the Yahoo! Image API and
' sets it as the desktop background image.
'
' This script depends on GfxConverter.ocx that you
' download here:
'
' http://dev.remotenetworktechnology.com/wsh/comwsh.htm
'
' Click/Save "Convert to Bitmap", unzip, and install
' from the command line, like this:
'
' Regsvr32 GfxConverter.ocx
'
' Edit the following line to change the "theme" of
' your background. Double-click this file to run it.
'----------------------------------------------------
strQuery = "landscape"


'----------------------------------------------------
' the Yahoo! App ID -- Please don't change this
'----------------------------------------------------
Const APP_ID = "ybackground"


'----------------------------------------------------
' Using the query, find a random image via Yahoo!
'----------------------------------------------------
'Construct a Yahoo! Search Query
strReqURL = "http://api.search.yahoo.com/" & _
            "ImageSearchService/V1/imageSearch?" & _
            "appid=" & APP_ID & _
            "&query=" & strQuery & _
            "&results=50" & _
            "&adult_ok=0"


'Start the XML Parser
Set MSXML = CreateObject("MSXML.DOMDocument")

'Set the XML Parser options
MSXML.Async = False

'Make the Request
strResponse = MSXML.Load(strReqURL)
If MSXML.parseError.errorCode <> 0 Then
    WScript.Echo("Error! " + MSXML.parseError.reason)
End If

'Make sure the request loaded
```

```
If (strResponse) Then

    'Find the total available
    Set ResultSet = MSXML.SelectSingleNode("//ResultSet")
    intTotalReturned = ResultSet.getAttribute("totalResultsReturned")

    'Pick a random number
    Randomize
    RandomNumber = Int(intTotalReturned * Rnd + 1)

    'Load the results
    Set Results = MSXML.SelectNodes("//Result")

    'Loop through the results
    For x = 0 to Results.length - 1
    If x = RandomNumber Then
            strImageURL = Results(x).SelectSingleNode("Url").text
    End If
    Next

    'Unload the results
    Set Results = Nothing
    Set ResultSet = Nothing

End If


'If no image URL is found, send a message
If strImageURL = "" Then
    WScript.Echo "No image found! Try again."
    WScript.Quit
End If


'------------------------------------------------------
' Save the image locally to the root c:\ folder
'------------------------------------------------------
Set fs = CreateObject("Scripting.FileSystemObject")
Set xmlhttp = CreateObject("Msxml2.SERVERXMLHTTP")
xmlhttp.Open "GET", strImageURL, false
xmlhttp.Send(Now)

fs.CreateTextFile "c:\" & strImageFile & ".jpg"

'Create a Stream instance
Dim objStream
Set objStream = CreateObject("ADODB.Stream")

'Open the stream
objStream.Open
objStream.Type = 1 'adTypeBinary
objStream.Write xmlhttp.responseBody
objStream.SaveToFile "c:\" & strQuery & ".jpg", 2 'adSaveCreateOverwrite
objStream.Close
Set objStream = Nothing
```

```
Set xmlhttp = Nothing
Set fs = Nothing

'----------------------------------------------------
' Convert the jpeg to a bitmap
'----------------------------------------------------
Set Converter = CreateObject("Gfx.Converter")
Converter.ToBitmap "c:\" & strQuery & ".jpg", "c:\" & strQuery & ".bmp"
Set Converter = Nothing

'----------------------------------------------------
' Set the newly created bitmap to background
' and refresh
'----------------------------------------------------
strRegRoot = "HKEY_CURRENT_USER\Software\Microsoft\" & _
             "Internet Explorer\Desktop\General\"
strRegRoot2 = "HKEY_CURRENT_USER\Control Panel\Desktop\"

Set Shell = WScript.CreateObject("Wscript.Shell")
Shell.RegWrite strRegRoot & "BackUpWallpaper", "c:\" & strQuery & ".bmp"
Shell.RegWrite strRegRoot & "Wallpaper", "c:\" & strQuery & ".bmp"
Shell.RegWrite strRegRoot2 & "Wallpaper", "c:\" & strQuery & ".bmp"
Shell.Run "%windir%\System32\RUNDLL32.EXE " & _
          "user32.dll,UpdatePerUserSystemParameters", 1, False
Set Shell = Nothing
```

Note that the first line of the script sets the theme of your desktop background. If you'd like something different from landscape images, simply edit this line to whatever you'd like to see.

Also keep in mind that you can tweak the request URL variable strReqURL to get different results. The URL is currently set to exclude adult images: adult_ok is set to 0. If you change this value to 1, you might find adult images in your results. Of course, changing the strReqURL value to something more adult-oriented will have an effect on the content of the search as well. Even with the filter set to keep adult images out, understand that Yahoo!'s filter isn't perfect and some adult images might find their way into the mix.

Running the Hack

Before you run the script, make sure you understand the risks. This will replace your current desktop background with a random image from the Web, so be sure you have a backup of your current desktop background image before you proceed; otherwise, you might lose it forever. Also, remember that you're grabbing images from any web site; while the risk is minimal, some malicious code can find its way into image files. Make sure your antivirus program is up-to-date before playing around with this code.

When you're ready to run the script, double-click the script file or run it from the command line:

```
Y!Background.vbs
```

You should see your desktop background change. If you're not happy with the image, run the script again. You can keep running the script until you settle on something you like—for example, the nice landscape in Figure 5-16.

Figure 5-16. A random Windows desktop background via Yahoo!

If you want the random fun to continue, you can place this script in your Startup folder and you'll find a new background every time you log in to your machine. The Startup folder is located at *C:\Documents and Settings\ <Your Name>\Start Menu\Programs*.

Hacking the Hack

For even more random desktop background fun, add the script as a scheduled task by selecting Start → Settings → Control Panel → Scheduled Tasks and choosing Add Scheduled Task. You can set it to run as frequently as you'd like, from once a week to once an hour.

Leaving your desktop background to chance is definitely a risky game, but you might find some great images from across the Web in the process.

Randomize Your Mac Desktop Background

#84 Leave your Mac desktop picture to chance with Yahoo!, Perl, and AppleScript.

Windows users aren't the only ones who can experience the fun that is random desktop backgrounds [Hack #83]. By using Yahoo! as your own image database, you can automatically change your Mac desktop background picture when the mood strikes.

If you use Mac OS X just to browse the Web and send email, you might not be aware that there's a powerful Unix-based operating system under the hood. In fact, in addition to AppleScript (the Mac scripting language), Mac OS X ships with Perl installed. This hack takes advantage of both Perl and AppleScript to bring some randomness to your desktop.

The Code

Perl is a great language for making HTTP requests and working with the responses. But it's not as good as AppleScript at performing Mac system tasks, such as setting a desktop image. Luckily, a Perl module called Mac::AppleScript lets you execute AppleScript code from within your Perl scripts. To install this module, open a Terminal window and type the following command:

```
sudo perl -MCPAN -e 'install Mac::AppleScript'
```

Before you begin, you'll need to install a couple of other Perl modules. As with most of the Perl examples in this book, you'll need LWP::Simple and XML::Simple to make Yahoo! requests and parse responses.

Once these prerequisites are installed, save the following code to a file named *ybackground.pl*:

```
#!/usr/bin/perl
# ybackground.pl
# Accepts a query term and sets a Mac desktop background
# with that theme.
# Usage: ybackground.pl <query>
#
# You can read the full documentation
# for Yahoo! Web Services at http://developer.yahoo.net/

use strict;
use LWP::Simple;
use XML::Simple;
use Mac::AppleScript qw(RunAppleScript);

# Please leave this Yahoo! Application ID
```

```
my $appID = "ybackground-mac";

# Grab the incoming search query
my $query = join(' ', @ARGV) or die "Usage: ybackground.pl <query>\n";

# Construct a Yahoo! Search Query with only required options
my $language = "en";
my $req_url = "http://api.search.yahoo.com/";
    $req_url .= "ImageSearchService/V1/imageSearch?";
    $req_url .= "appid=$appID";
    $req_url .= "&query=$query";
    $req_url .= "&results=50";
    $req_url .= "&adult_ok=0";

# Make the request
my $yahoo_response = get($req_url);

# Parse the XML
my $xmlsimple = XML::Simple->new( );
my $yahoo_xml = $xmlsimple->XMLin($yahoo_response);

# Grab a random image URL from the results
my $rnd = int(rand(@{$yahoo_xml->{Result}}));
my $url = $yahoo_xml->{Result}->[$rnd]->{Url};

# Save the image locally
my $time = time;
my $image = get($url);
open IMAGE,">$query-$time.jpg";
print IMAGE $image;
close IMAGE;

# Set the image as the current
# desktop background

RunAppleScript(qq(
tell application "Finder"
    set desktop picture to document file "$query-$time.jpg"
end tell));
```

This code creates a unique image file each time the script is run, using the time the file was downloaded as part of the title. The last four lines of the script are where the AppleScript runs, via the RunAppleScript function, setting the desktop background to the newly downloaded file.

If you know the specific size of an image you'd like to download, you can modify the script to look for that size. For example, if your desktop size is set to 1024×768, a smaller image that's stretched might not look as good as an image that is 1024×768 without resizing.

To find only images that are a certain size you can use the `height:` and `width:` meta keywords when you construct the Yahoo! URL. If you only want images that are 1024 pixels wide, change the line in the script where you set the query, like so:

```
$req_url .= "&query=$query width:1024";
```

With the width set appropriately, you'll be sure to get only images that fit the width of your desktop.

Running the Hack

You can run the script from the command line, adding a desktop theme, like this:

```
perl ybackground.pl insert theme
```

Running the script with the `lightning` search term sets your background to something that looks like Figure 5-17.

Figure 5-17. A random Mac desktop background via Yahoo!

While the idea of leaving your desktop background to chance might seem frightening, you might be surprised at the quality of some of the images Yahoo! has found across the Web.

Mash Up Images from Around the Web

The Yahoo! Image API provides access to thousands of images across the Web, and developers are recombining these images into new applications that let you play along.

In the music world, a *mash-up* combines two or more existing songs into something entirely new. A mash-up might have a song from the Beatles in the background and vocals from Snoop Dogg in the foreground, while blending in a *Sesame Street* song at the same time. The Yahoo! Image Search web service offers programmatic access to thousands of images, and some developers are using this service to create their own visual mash-ups—combining disparate images into games, interesting visualizations, or random works of art. Here are a few interactive examples that will give you a taste of what's being mashed together with the Yahoo! Image Search API.

Yahoo! Buzz Demo

The Yahoo! Buzz Demo is an alternative way to read the news. When you browse to *http://buzz.progphp.com*, you'll find an oval-shaped collage made up of over 100 different images, each representing a current top news story. As you move your pointer over each image in the collage, the image pops to the foreground so that you can see it clearly, and a summary of the news story the image represents is displayed in the middle of the page, as shown in Figure 5-18.

Clicking an image takes you directly to that image's original location on the Web, and clicking the center news story takes you to the full story at Yahoo! News. In addition to top stories, you can browse images based on other news categories, or use your own term.

Rasmus Lerdorf, a Yahoo! employee, built the Yahoo! Buzz Demo to show what's possible with the Yahoo! Image Search web service. The demo uses PHP to pull in news stories from Yahoo! News RSS and the Yahoo! News API, images from around the Web via the Yahoo! Image API, and some crafty CSS to pull everything together. While it won't replace the front page of the paper anytime soon, the Buzz Demo is a fun way to find stories. If you'd like to take a look behind the scenes, you can view the complete source code at *http://buzz.progphp.com/buzz.phps*.

Search Collage Generator

Siddharth Uppal put together around 100 lines of Perl that grabs up to 50 images for any given query and assembles them into a single collage. He used the existing Yahoo::Search module (available at *http://search.cpan.org/ ~jfriedl/Yahoo-Search-1.4.7/lib/Yahoo/Search.pm*) to assemble Yahoo! Image

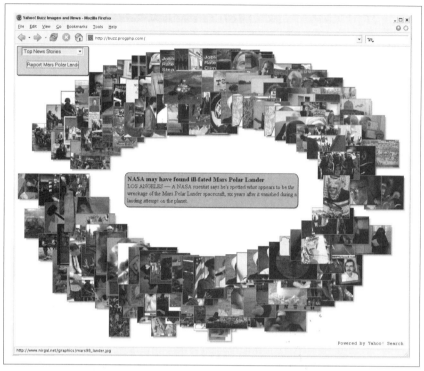

Figure 5-18. A visual look at top news stories

API requests and return the results as Perl-friendly objects. The script then puts each image into a collage on a web page, resizing each image to the same size within HTML <img> tags.

You can download a copy of the script at *http://upster.blogspot.com/2005/03/ yahoo-image-search-collage-generator.html* and run it from the command line like this:

```
perl yahoo_collage.pl --query insert query
```

The output is HTML, so you'll want to send this output to a new file. For example, you can create a collage of portraits from around the Web by calling the script like this:

```
perl yahoo_collage.pl --query portrait > portrait.html
```

After you run this script, *portrait.html* will show you a collage similar to the one in Figure 5-19.

The script also provides the HTML necessary to share your collage with the world. You can simply cut and paste the HTML in the <textarea> at the bottom of the page and paste it into your weblog or web publishing tool to show off your creation.

Figure 5-19. A collage generated with the query "portrait"

Yahoo! Memory Game

Remember those memory games you played as a kid, where you had to turn over cards of matching pictures? Swedish developer Nisse Bryngfors re-created the game with the Yahoo! Image API and Flash. When you browse to *http://bryngfors.com/index.php?page_id=10*, you'll find a blank game form titled "Dynamiskt memory spel," and a "Search images" field in which you can type a search term. Enter a term, click Go!, and the game will be populated with 28 silver tiles.

Clicking a silver tile reveals an image that has been gathered via the Yahoo! Images API. Somewhere under another tile is the same image, and it's your mission to find all of the matches as quickly as possible. Figure 5-20 shows a game in progress using the term fire.

If you'd like a shorter game, you can decrease the number of tiles. Sometimes, seeing what images the Yahoo! Image API returns is as entertaining as the game itself!

HACK

#86 Illustrate Any Web Site

The yReplacer Yahoo! game replaces words on any web page with an image.

Some books are better with pictures, and some web pages would be better with illustrations. You can't edit every text-heavy page on the Web yourself, but you can have some fun swapping words with images thanks to a clever script called *yReplacer*.

With yReplacer, you can highlight any word on a web site and click a bookmarklet to swap that word with a matching image from Yahoo! Image

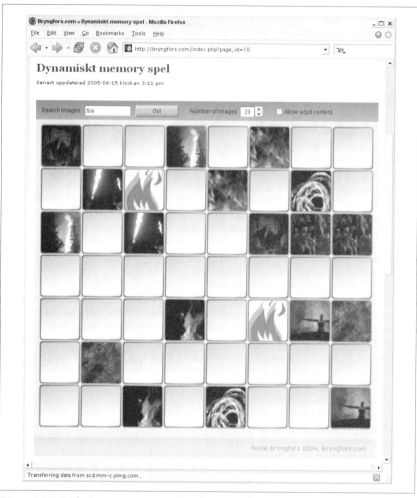

Figure 5-20. A Flash memory game using the query "fire"

Search. So the word *Martians* on a page could become a picture of the cartoon character Marvin the Martian, or the word *planet* could become a picture of Saturn.

This hack is composed of two parts: a server-side script that retrieves the search image from Yahoo! and displays it, and a bookmarklet that initiates the swap. You can install the bookmarklet from yReplacer's permanent home on the Web at *http://www.kokogiak.com/yreplacer.html*, or you can build this hack yourself with the following code.

The Code

The first part of this hack is server-side retrieval of a random image, written here in VBScript for classic ASP. This script accepts an incoming word with the querystring variable q, sends a request to the Yahoo! Image API, and selects a random result from the response. The script then uses the random image to write some HTML to display the image, which will end up in an HTML <iframe> element inside the page the script is called from.

Save the following code to a file called *yr.asp* and be sure to create and use a unique application ID for the script:

```
<html>
<head>
<style type="text/css">
    body{background-color:#fff;color:#000;margin:0px;padding:0px;border:
0px;}
</style>
</head>

<body scroll="no">
<%
On Error Resume Next
Response.Buffer = True

'' Expecting a search term to be in the querystring "q"
szQ = Request("q")
If (szQ <> "") Then
    Dim objXML, xml
    set xml = Server.CreateObject("MSXML2.ServerXMLHTTP.3.0")

    szGetString = ("http://api.search.yahoo.com/" &_
                   "ImageSearchService/V1/imageSearch" &_
                   "?appid=[YOUR_APPLICATION_ID]&results=10&query=" & szQ)

    xml.Open "GET", szGetString, False
    xml.Send
    set objXML = xml.responseXML

    If (objXML.getElementsByTagName("Result").length>0) Then

        '' Fetch a random image within the set returned
        Randomize
        ano = Int(((objXML.getElementsByTagName("Result").length-1) * Rnd))

        Set oGb = objXML.getElementsByTagName("Result")(ano)
        Set oTn = oGb.getElementsByTagName("Thumbnail")(0)

        Response.write("<a target='_top' href='")
        Response.write(oGb.getElementsByTagName("RefererUrl")(0).text)
        Response.write("'><img title='" & szQ & "' alt='" & szQ & "' ")
        Response.write("src='" & oTn.getElementsByTagName("Url")(0).text & ⏎
"'")
        Response.write(" style='border:0px;'/></a>")
    End if
```

```
Set oGb = Nothing
Set oTn = Nothing
set xml = Nothing
set objXML = Nothing

End if %>
</body>
</html>
```

Upload *yr.asp* to a publicly available web server and you're halfway there!

Now we need to call the ASP page in-context so that it will swap an image for selected text. To do this, we'll use JavaScript embedded in a book-mark—also known as a *bookmarklet* or *favelet*. This JavaScript is designed to function in either IE4+ or Mozilla/Firefox.

Here's the yReplacer JavaScript bookmarklet code, expanded for easy reading. Note that you'll need to include the location of *yr.asp* in the code:

```
function p( ){
    u='http://example.com/yr.asp?q=';
    if(document.all){
        //IE version
        r=document.selection.createRange( );
        r.pasteHTML('<iframe scrolling=no style=\'width:75;height:75;border↵
:0;\' src=\''+u+r.text+'\'/>')
    }else{
        //Mozilla/Firefox version
        var g=window.getSelection( );
        r=g.getRangeAt(0);
        f=document.createElement('IFRAME');
        f.setAttribute('scrolling','no');
        f.setAttribute('style','width:75;height:75;border:0');
        f.setAttribute('src',u+g);
        r.deleteContents( );
        r.insertNode(f)
    }
}
p( );
```

This JavaScript inserts an HTML <iframe> in place of the currently selected word and uses *yr.asp* with that word as the source for the frame.

Running the Hack

With *yr.asp* on a publicly available server and the JavaScript code ready to go, the last step is formatting the JavaScript for a bookmarklet. Here's the same yReplacer bookmarklet JavaScript code in the single-line format neces-sary for bookmarklets:

```
JavaScript:function p( ){u='http://example.com/yr.asp?q=';if(document.↵
all){r=document.selection.createRange( );r.pasteHTML('<iframe scrolling=no↵
style=\'width:75;height:75;border:0;\' src=\''+r.text+'\'/>')}else{var↵
g=window.getSelection( );r=g.getRangeAt(0);f=document.↵
```

```
createElement('IFRAME');f.setAttribute('scrolling','no');f.↵
setAttribute('style','width:75;height:75;border:0');f.↵
setAttribute('src',u+g);r.deleteContents( );r.insertNode(f)}}p( )
```

Add the code to an existing bookmark or favorite by pasting the code into the location property of the bookmark. Give the bookmarklet a name, such as yReplacer, and you'll be ready to illustrate the Web. For example, H. G. Wells's *War of the Worlds* is filled with wonderful imagery, but not wonderful images. Figure 5-21 shows the text of the book, which is freely available online.

Figure 5-21. A text-heavy web page with the yReplacer bookmarklet ready for use

As you read, you can highlight a word, click the yReplacer bookmarklet, and have a new, illustrated *War of the Worlds*, as shown in Figure 5-22.

Replacing words with random Yahoo! Image Search results won't yield a new masterpiece, but the results can be surprisingly accurate and humorous.

—Alan Taylor

Add Links to a Block of Text Automatically

Auto-Linker uses the Yahoo! API to add relevant links to keywords in any text.

Isn't the task of inserting links into web pages mundane? The Yahoo! Auto-Linker solves this problem by automatically substituting keywords in any text with hyperlinks to top Yahoo! searches for that keyword. The result of

Add Links to a Block of Text Automatically

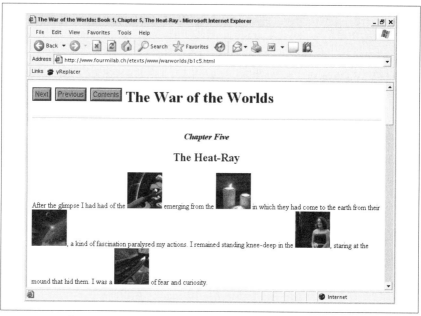

Figure 5-22. The same web page, now illustrated with yReplacer

this hack can be useful and inspiring, bizarre, or just plain amusing. The Auto-Linker accepts a bit of text via a web page form like the one shown in Figure 5-23 and returns the same block of text with hyperlinks inserted.

Figure 5-23. The Auto-Linker text-entry form

At *http://blog.outer-court.com/yahoo/autolinker.php5*, you can play with a working version of Auto-Linker and see how it works in detail. Once you're comfortable with it, you can build your own version with the code in this hack.

The Auto-Linker makes use of two Yahoo API services when it auto-links a given text. First, it finds the significant phrases within the text using Yahoo's Term Extraction (*http://developer.yahoo.net/content/V1/termExtraction.html*).

Second, it uses the Yahoo! Web Search (*http://developer.yahoo.net/web/V1/ webSearch.html*) to find the top web page for this phrase. All that's left to do is add the corresponding HTML link to each occurrence of the phrase within the text.

The Code

The code for Auto-Links is PHP5, so save the following code to a file called *autolinker.php5*:

```
<html>
<body>
<?php
$text = ( isset($_POST['text']) ) ? $_POST['text'] : '';
$rel = ( isset($_POST['rel']) ) ? $_POST['rel'] : '';
$engine = ( isset($_POST['engine']) ) ? $_POST['engine'] : '';
$text = stripslashes($text);

$maxLength = 2000;
if ( strlen($text) >= $maxLength ) {
    $text = substr($text, 0, $maxLength - 1) . '...';
}

echo '<h1>Auto-Linker</h1>';

if ($text == '')
{
?>
<p>This tool uses the Yahoo API to link significant words and phrases from a
text you provide.</p>

<form action="autolinker.php5" method="post"><div>
<textarea style="font-size: 90%" name="text"
        cols="58" rows="8"></textarea><br />

Relation:
<select name="rel">
    <option value="">[Default]</option>
    <option value="nofollow">Nofollow</option>
</select>

  Search Engine:
<select name="engine">
    <option value="yahoo">Yahoo</option>
    <option value="google">Google</option>
</select>

<input type="submit" value="Submit" />
</div></form>
<?
}
```

This code makes sure that if the text parameter has not been submitted, the script presents a <textarea> to be filled out. The user can also choose between links returned from Yahoo! or a Google web search.

Once the text is submitted to the script, the actual auto-linking takes place. Here is the else clause that triggers auto-linking:

```
else
{
    $sLinked = autoLink($text, $rel, $engine);
    echo '<p style="font-size: 105%;">' .
        $sLinked . '</p>';
    showCopyable($sLinked);
    echo '<p><a href="autolinker.php5">[Auto-Linker Home]</a></p>';
}
```

The showCopyable function just inserts a <textarea> where the user can copy the HTML source of the auto-linked result. The auto-linking core is in the autoLink function:

```
function autoLink($s, $rel, $engine)
{
    $s = strip_tags($s);
    $sRel = ($rel != '') ? ' rel="' . $rel . '"' : '';

    $url = 'http://api.search.yahoo.com/ContentAnalysisService/' .
        'V1/termExtraction.xsd?appid=insert App ID&' .
        'context=' . urlencode($s); //*See footnote

    $dom = new domdocument;
    $dom->load($url);
    $xpath = new domxpath($dom);
    $xNodes = $xpath->query('//Result');

    $counter = 0;
    $maxLinks = 10;
    foreach ($xNodes as $xNode)
    {
        if (++$counter > $maxLinks) { break; }
        $phrase = $xNode->firstChild->data;

        $phraseUrl = '';

        if ($engine == 'google') {
            $phraseUrl = getTopLinkGoogle($phrase);
        }
        else {
            $phraseUrl = getTopLinkYahoo($phrase);
        }

        if ($phraseUrl != '')
```

```
{
    $s = preg_replace('@( ' . $phrase . ')@ei',
        '\' <a href="' . $phraseUrl .
        '">\' . trim(\'$1\') . \'</a>\'',
        $s, 4);
    }
}
$s = str_replace("\r\n", '<br />', $s);

return $s;
}
```

The autoLink function takes the parameters s (the whole text), rel (the link relation, either default or nofollow), and engine (the search engine, either yahoo or google). Then the function requests the list of significant phrases from the Yahoo! API. Yahoo! recommends using a POST request for longer text, but a GET request, as used here, also works. Yahoo!'s returned XML looks like this, with all lowercase values:

```
<?xml version="1.0" encoding="UTF-8"?>
<ResultSet ...>
    <Result>superman</Result>
    <Result>clark kent</Result>
    <Result>super powers</Result>
</ResultSet>
```

The script applies an XPath expression to this XML to iterate through all Result elements to get their values. The preg_replace function searches for the phrase (in this example, blank before the phrase is to catch words only, and we make sure the replace is case-insensitive).

The link will be taken from either Yahoo! or Google, using these two functions:

```
// We grab results from Yahoo's "REST" API again
// using PHP5's nice native XML functionality.

function getTopLinkYahoo($q)
{
    $url = 'http://api.search.yahoo.com/WebSearchService/' .
        'V1/webSearch?appid=insert app ID&max=1&q=' .
        urlencode($q); //*See footnote
    $dom = new domdocument;
    $dom->load($url);
    $xpath = new domxpath($dom);
    $topUrl = $xpath->query('//Url')->item(0)->firstChild->data;

    return $topUrl;
}

// A tiny screen-scraping function avoids the overhead
// of Google's SOAP API; this code will need
```

```
// adjustments whenever Google drastically changes their
// result-page HTML.

function getTopLinkGoogle($q)
{
    error_reporting(E_ERROR | E_PARSE);
    $dom = new domdocument;
    $dom->loadHTMLFile('http://www.google.com/search?' .
                'hl=en&q=' . urlencode($q) . '&num=1');
    $xpath = new domxpath($dom);
    $s = $xpath->query(
            "//p[@class='g']/a[@href]")->item(0)->getAttribute('href');
    if ( ! ( strpos($s, 'spell=1') === false ) &&
            ! ( strpos($s, '/search?') === false ) )
    {
        $s = $xpath->query(
                "//p/a[@href]")->item(1)->getAttribute('href');
    }

    return $s;
}
```

Running the Hack

To run the code, upload *autolinker.php5* to a web server and point your browser there. Add some text to the form and you should get a response similar to the one shown in Figure 5-24.

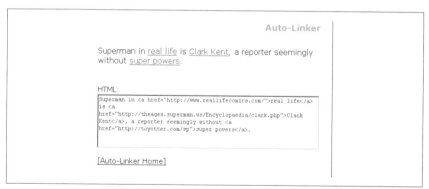

Figure 5-24. Some auto-linked text

Now that all pieces of the hack are in place, nothing stops you from quickly spicing up any text with relevant hyperlinks!

—*Philipp Lenssen*

Visualize News Topics as Tags

#88 Two services, Yahoo! News Tag Soup and TagCloud, use the Yahoo! Contextual Web Search API to help you visualize which topics are mentioned the most across Yahoo! News and your favorite sites.

As you consume the news each day, you get a general sense of what the big stories are. If CNN is leading the hour with news about the Supreme Court, you open the newspaper to find a story about the Supreme Court on the front page, and then you spot a Supreme Court story at the top of Yahoo! News, you can bet the Supreme Court is the hot topic. But this general way of identifying a hot topic isn't as precise as actually analyzing the content itself to quantify which keywords are mentioned most often throughout a day.

With digital information, it's possible to track exactly which words are used more frequently than others. And there are a number of ways you can categorize information to make that tracking easier. One system of categorization is called *tagging*, in which people add keywords to an article, photo, or web site in order to organize that bit of information. Each keyword is referred to as a *tag*, and lots of fun can be had analyzing the tags.

A popular way to visualize tag usage is in the form of a *tag map* that displays more popular tags in a larger font. So popular tags appear large, and less-popular tags appear small. With one glance at a tag map, you can see which topics are hot.

Now, imagine you have a source of information, but no people to tag it for you. That's where the Yahoo! Contextual Web Service can help. This service lets you send an arbitrary amount of text, and it will automatically extract keywords from that text. The service ignores common words such as *a*, *and*, or *the* and returns the more unique words from a text. For example, the Yahoo! Contextual Web Service analysis of the text of this hack returned phrases such as *supreme court*, *hot topic*, and *search api*.

By automatically extracting keywords from text, you can create computer-generated tags and perform similar sorts of analysis on those tags.

Yahoo! News Tag Soup

Seeing a more precise picture of news keywords was the motivation behind a service by John Herren called Yahoo! News Tag Soup (*http://yahoo.theherrens.com*). By sending stories from Yahoo! News through the Yahoo! Contextual Web Service and storing the resulting keywords, you can visualize trends in the day's news as a tag map.

Figure 5-25 shows the Yahoo! News Tag Soup for June 28, 2005.

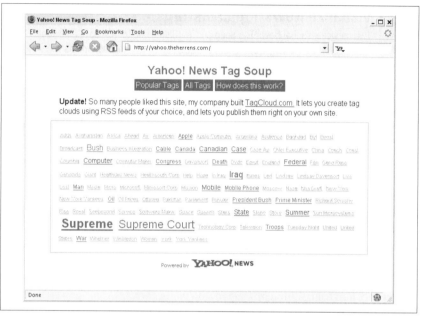

Figure 5-25. A tag map with topics culled from Yahoo! News stories

As you can see, the Supreme Court was in the news that day. When you click on the tags at Yahoo! News Tag Soup, the service provides a list of stories that contain that particular keyword, as shown in Figure 5-26.

Yahoo! News organizes stories by importance, or into broad categories such as politics, business, or technology. Yahoo! News Tag Soup is a completely new way to browse news stories, made possible thanks to Yahoo!'s open technology.

Not content to focus solely on Yahoo! News, the creator of Tag Soup helped build a way for you to assemble your own personal news visualizations from any source.

Your Personal Tag Cloud

John Herren's company IonZoft, Inc., took the idea behind Yahoo! News Tag Soup and made it accessible to others. The application is called TagCloud (*http://www.tagcloud.com*) and it's a free service. To get started, browse to the TagCloud web site and create an account.

Once you're logged in, you can create a personalized cloud. The Cloud Name must be unique across the system, so you might need to choose something unusual. For instance, the cloud name *oregon* is probably taken by someone

Figure 5-26. A list of Yahoo! News stories by tag

else already, but *oregon2112* is probably available. Use the Description to identify what types of news sources you're going to analyze with your cloud. Click Create Cloud and you'll have an empty space you can start filling up with personal news and information.

TagCloud relies on RSS feeds as input, and you can add individual feeds one at a time by clicking the Feeds tab and entering the URL. If you already have a list of feeds you read at a service such as Bloglines (*http://www.bloglines.com*), you can import several at once by clicking the Import OPML tab and specifying an OPML file that contains a list of your feeds.

Once you have a few feeds included in your cloud, click the View tab at the top of the page. You should see a list of tags that have been extracted from your feeds, with each tag a different size based on its frequency, as shown in Figure 5-27.

Click on any tag to see a list of matching stories and posts across your feeds. This is a useful way to visualize what topics are hot on a specific group of sites. You can also publish your TagCloud to your web site, so you can share your slice of the news with others.

Click Implementation Guide at the top of any TagCloud page and you'll see how easy it is to add a TagCloud to a remote site. You simply need to copy

Figure 5-27. A personal TagCloud

two lines of JavaScript and paste them into your site. The TagCloud service does the rest. Figure 5-28 shows a personal TagCloud included as a sidebar on a weblog.

As readers click on a tag, they'll find a list of posts and stories from your selected feeds that have that keyword.

Listing your personal TagCloud on your weblog, or reviewing it privately for fun, is a great way to keep a visual handle on the day's news.

  HACK
#89 # Get Related Terms Instantly with Ajax

Pull Yahoo! related search suggestions into a web page without clicking a link, a form button, or the Refresh button.

Though widely used, JavaScript has never been considered an indispensable development language. That perception is changing, though, thanks to improvements in web browsers. Now that most widely used web browsers support a standard form of JavaScript, developers can spend their time writing code rather than tweaking the code they've already written. Since a single block of code can work across different browsers, JavaScript is back in the spotlight.

JavaScript's most impressive use is in combination with XML-based services, such as Yahoo! Web Services. Because JavaScript can make requests from the

Figure 5-28. A personal TagCloud on a weblog

user's machine and doesn't require a page refresh, information can be updated almost instantly without the user clicking a link, clicking a form button, or reloading the page. This makes very interactive, dynamic pages possible. The name for this type of JavaScript is Asynchronous JavaScript + XML, or Ajax for short.

This hack is a simple Ajax application that uses Yahoo! Web Services as a data source. As you type in standard HTML text input, JavaScript is in constant communication with the Yahoo! API. With every letter added, the script checks to see if Yahoo! has *related search suggestions* for the current search term. Related search suggestions are simply phrases that are related to any query, and they're displayed below the text input as you type. This way, if you're typing `activeX control` into the form, you can see suggested alternate terms like `active volcanoes` and `free activeX` along the way.

The Code

This script relies on the XML HTTP object to send and receive responses from a server, and to parse those responses into objects that JavaScript can manipulate. When the page loads, an XML HTTP object is created. The user-input text field has an onkeyup event, so that when the user's input has a keystroke, the getAlts( ) function contacts the Yahoo! Search Web Services, looking for related search terms. If there are no related terms, nothing happens. If related terms are found, the printResponse( ) function formats the related search terms as HTML and prints them to the page with the innerHTML property of a <div> tag below the form.

This code is a standard HTML file, and it doesn't need to reside on a web server. Simply open a text editor, such as Notepad, add the following code, and name the file *relatedterms.html*:

```
<!DOCTYPE HTML PUBLIC "-//W3C//DTD HTML 4.01 Transitional//EN">

<html>
<head>
    <title>Related Terms</title>
    <script language="javascript" type="text/javascript">
    // netscape.security.PrivilegeManager.⌐
enablePrivilege("UniversalBrowserAccess");
    var xmlhttp=false;
    /*@cc_on @*/
    /*@if (@_jscript_version >= 5)
    // Verify that the browser can load the xmlHttp object.
    try {
      xmlhttp = new ActiveXObject("Msxml2.XMLHTTP");
    } catch (e) {
      try {
       xmlhttp = new ActiveXObject("Microsoft.XMLHTTP");
      } catch (E) {
       xmlhttp = false;
      }
    }
    @end @*/
    if (!xmlhttp && typeof XMLHttpRequest!='undefined') {
      xmlhttp = new XMLHttpRequest( );
    }

    // Accepts a related term, and makes it a Yahoo! link
    function getLink(r) {
        var o = "<a href=\"http://search.yahoo.com/search?p="
        o = o + escape(r) + "\">" + r + "</a>";
        return o;
    }

    // Accepts the Yahoo! Search Web Services response, and
    // prints to the page as HTML
    function printResponse(xml) {
        // netscape.security.PrivilegeManager.⌐
enablePrivilege("UniversalXPConnect");
        var results = xml.getElementsByTagName("Result");
        var numOfResults = results.length;
        if (numOfResults > 0) {
```

```
        var out = "";
        for (var i=0;i<numOfResults;i++) {
            out = out + "<li>" + getLink(results[i].firstChild.nodeValue) + ⏎
"</li>";
        }
        var s = document.getElementById('suggest');
        s.innerHTML = "You might also try:<ul>" + out + "</ul>";
        }
    }


    // Accepts a full or partial search term, and looks for
    // related terms with a Yahoo! Search Web Services request
    function getAlts(t) {
        var yurl = "http://api.search.yahoo.com/WebSearchService/V1/"
        yurl = yurl + "relatedSuggestion?appid=YahooDemo&query=" + ⏎
escape(t);
        // netscape.security.PrivilegeManager.⏎
enablePrivilege("UniversalXPConnect");
        try {
            xmlhttp.open("GET", yurl, true);
        }
        catch (E) {
            alert(E);
        }
        xmlhttp.onreadystatechange = function( ) {
            if (xmlhttp.readyState==4) {
                printResponse(xmlhttp.responseXML);
            }
        }
        xmlhttp.send(null)
    }
    </script>
</head>

<body>
<h2>Yahoo! Related Terms</h2>
<form>
    <input name="txt" type="text" value="" onkeyup="getAlts(this.value)" />
</form>
<div name="suggest" id="suggest"></div>
</body>
</html>
```

As you can see, the HTML for this page is straightforward, and the work is done in the JavaScript section in the <head> of the page. Be sure to request a unique application ID for the script and use it in the code.

Running the Hack

To avoid potential problems with *cross-site scripting* exploits, by default browsers do not allow JavaScript to call pages from other domains. And because Yahoo! Search Web Services are at another domain, this script will require some browser tweaks to run. If you were to implement this script on a web site, you'd need to set this up in a different way. But this example is intended to show what's possible with Ajax, rather than the perfect way to deploy an Ajax application to other users.

When you open this page in Internet Explorer, you'll probably see a yellow security warning like the one shown below the Address bar in Figure 5-29.

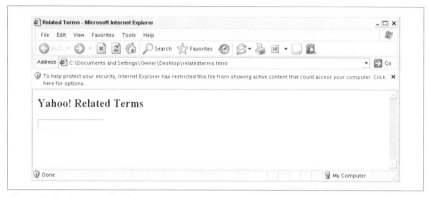

Figure 5-29. Internet Explorer security warning

Click the yellow banner, and choose Allow Blocked Content... to let the script contact Yahoo!.

For Firefox, you'll need to uncomment the following text by removing the double slashes at the beginning of its line in *relatedterms.html*:

```
netscape.security.PrivilegeManager.enablePrivilege("UniversalXPConnect");
```

This will allow the browser to contact a remote domain, and the first time it tries to run, you'll see a request to allow the privilege change, as shown in Figure 5-30.

Figure 5-30. Firefox security request

Check the "Remember this decision" box and then click the Allow button. If you ever spot this dialog while browsing a file that you didn't write, you'll want to click Deny instead. But because you're in control of the information being passed around, you can be sure you're not doing anything malicious.

With the security settings behind you, you can start playing with the script. As you type, the JavaScript contacts Yahoo! for suggestions. Try searching for the tech term activeX Component, and you'll see different suggestions appear along the way. After you type the first six letters (active), several suggestions appear below the form, as shown in Figure 5-31.

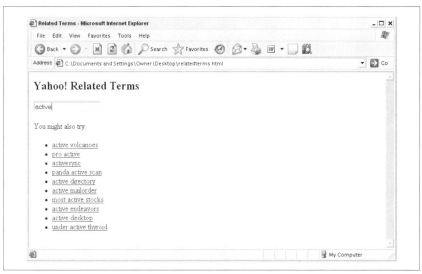

Figure 5-31. Yahoo! related terms for "active"

Keep typing, and new suggestions appear as you type the X, as shown in Figure 5-32.

Click any of the suggestions to view the search results for that phrase at Yahoo!. The complete phrase activeX Control will yield even more suggestions.

HACK
#90 Compare the Popularity of Related Search Terms

By gluing together two different kinds of Yahoo! Web Services requests, you can find the most widely used alternate search requests for any given topic.

Though the Yahoo! Search engine is something each of us use in isolation, from Yahoo!'s perspective searching is a group activity. They have the ability to analyze each individual query and group it together with other, similar queries. When you do a web search on Yahoo!, you can get a glimpse of these similar phrases. Figure 5-33 highlights the list of "Also try:" phrases for a search on the term robot.

Yahoo! has also exposed some of this group data in the Related Suggestions feature of Yahoo! Search Web Services.

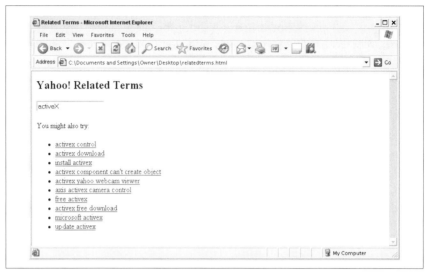

Figure 5-32. Yahoo! related terms for "activeX"

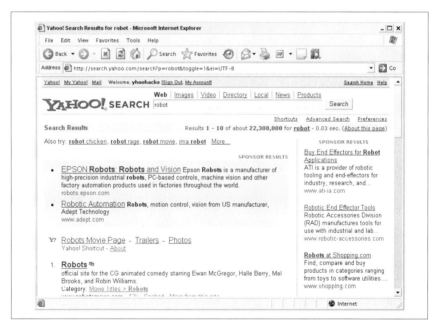

Figure 5-33. "Also try:" related suggestion on Yahoo! Search results

Related Suggestions returns a list of alternate phrases for any given search
term or phrase. For example, if I ask Yahoo! for related suggestions for the
term robot, Yahoo! will return a long list of alternates, including industrial
robots, toy robots, humanoid robots, building robots, and so on. This not

only gives you a window to what other robot-minded Yahoo! users are searching for, but it can also help you refine your own query to find just the information you're looking for.

Yahoo!'s API returns up to 50 related search terms, but some terms have just a few related examples. The robot example returns 50 related terms, but android returns only 14. Though the API returns the related terms, it doesn't tell you which of those terms is the most popular across the Web. However, a standard web search includes the totalResultsAvailable tag, which lets you know how many pages Yahoo! has indexed with the term. Gluing these two pieces together is a perfect job for Perl, and with a few dozen Yahoo! Search Web Services queries, you can put together a report about the popularity of related search terms.

The Code

This hack relies on several nonstandard Perl modules that you might need to install before you can run the script. As with most examples in this book, LWP::Simple makes API requests and XML::Simple parses the response. In addition, URI::Escape is used to encode queries so they can be used in a URL, and Number::Format is used as a quick way to add commas to large numbers.

Because this script makes trips to the Yahoo! server in different ways, the code for accessing Yahoo! has been encapsulated into the query_yahoo( ) function, which returns a parsed XML response based on the parameters sent to it.

> The function accepts a results value that tells Yahoo! how many search results to return. By changing this value, you can find more or fewer related search terms.

Save the following code to a file called *pop_related.pl*:

```perl
#!/usr/bin/perl
# pop_related.pl
# Accepts a search term, finds related search terms, queries
# Yahoo! to find the total results available for each, and
# prints a report with the popularity of each related term.
# Usage: pop_related.pl <query>
#
# You can create an AppID, and read the full documentation
# for Yahoo! Web Services at http://developer.yahoo.net/

use strict;
use LWP::Simple;
use XML::Simple;
```

Compare the Popularity of Related Search Terms

```perl
use URI::Escape;
use Number::Format;

# Set your unique Yahoo! Application ID
my $appID = "insert your app ID";

# Grab the incoming search query
my $query = join(' ', @ARGV) or die "Usage: pop_related.pl <query>\n";

# Initialize some variables
my ($final_related, $final_total);

# Define the file header
format STDOUT_TOP=
            Related Search Terms

query: @<<<<<<<<<<<<<<<<<<<<<<<<<<<<<<<<<<<<<<<<
       $query
--------------------------------------------------
Related Search                          Total
--------------------------------------------------
.

# Define the line-item details
format STDOUT=
@<<<<<<<<<<<<<<<<<<<<<<<<<<<<<<<<<<<<<< @>>>>>>>>
$final_related, $final_total
.

# Make the API call with query_yahoo() function
my $yahoo_xml = &query_yahoo($appID,"relatedSuggestion",25,$query);

# Initialize results array
my @popresults;

# Loop through the items returned, printing them out
foreach my $related (@{$yahoo_xml->{Result}}) {
    my $query = uri_escape($related);
    my $query = "\"$query\"";

    # Make the API call with query_yahoo() function
    my $yahoo_xml = &query_yahoo($appID,"webSearch",1,$query);

    # Grab Total Available Results for related term
    my $total =  $yahoo_xml->{totalResultsAvailable};

    # Store in a hash, add to results array
    my $thisRelated = {
                        related => $related,
                        total => $total,
    };
    push @popresults, $thisRelated;
}
```

```
# Sort the array,
@popresults = sort({ $$b{total} <=> $$a{total} } @popresults);

# And print the results
for my $pop(@popresults) {
    $final_related = $$pop{related};
    $final_total = $$pop{total};
    my $x = new Number::Format();
    $final_total = $x->format_number($final_total,2);

    write;
}

# This function assembles a Y!WS URL and retuns a parsed response
sub query_yahoo () {
    my ($appID,$type,$results,$query) = @_;

    # Construct a Yahoo! Search Query with only required options
    my $req_url = "http://api.search.yahoo.com/";
        $req_url .= "WebSearchService/V1/$type?";
        $req_url .= "appid=$appID";
        $req_url .= "&query=$query";
        $req_url .= "&results=$results";

    # Make the request
    my $yahoo_response = get($req_url);

    # Parse the XML
    my $xmlsimple = XML::Simple->new();
    return $xmlsimple->XMLin($yahoo_response);
}
```

The response is formatted with the built-in format method and its write command. The format is set for standard output on the command line, or STDOUT, but could easily be switched to a Perl filehandle if you'd rather print the results to a text file automatically.

Running the Hack

To run the code, simply call it from a command line, adding the term you'd like to search for:

```
perl pop_related.pl insert word
```

And if you want to pipe the results to a text file, you could call it like so:

```
perl pop_related.pl insert word > insert text file
```

Figure 5-34 shows the results of the robot search, with the output sent to a file called *pop_robot.txt*, like this:

```
perl pop_related.pl robot > pop_robot.txt
```

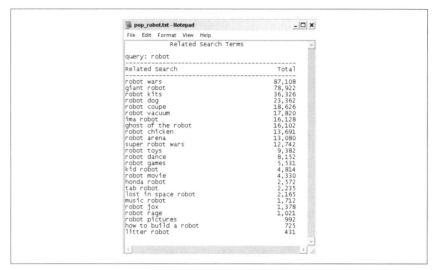

Figure 5-34. Popular related searches for the term "robot"

Now that you know the popularity of giant robot trumps that of robot chicken, you can be sure to give the next robot you build an appropriate name!

H A C K   **Plot Multiple Points on Your Own Map**
#91   Use the Yahoo! Maps Web Service to plot several locations on a map at once.

An online mapping service such as Yahoo! Maps (*http://maps.yahoo.com*) is a vast improvement over the multifold paper maps that are stashed in your glove compartment. Enter your starting address and an end address at Yahoo! Maps, and you'll get a detailed map, along with directions that include every turn you need to make to reach your destination. Finding a single address on a map is easy, but plotting several unique points on an interactive map used to be a task that only map service providers could accomplish.

Yahoo! has opened this ability to anyone with a bit of scripting knowledge, and you can plot dozens of points on a map instantly with the Yahoo! Maps Web Service (*http://developer.yahoo.net/maps*). The key to plotting several points is building a Yahoo! Maps Annotation file: an XML file with information about the points you want to plot on your map. If you're familiar with the syndication format RSS, you're most of the way there. The Yahoo! Maps Annotation file uses the RSS 2.0 format with some proprietary extensions that describe locations. This hack shows how to put together an RSS file that Yahoo! Maps will understand, and it explains how that file plots points on a Yahoo! Map.

Assembling Your Locations

Imagine it's Saturday morning, and you've decided to spend the day going to garage sales in your area. You open the paper, find a list of garage sales in the classified ads, and want to choose the most efficient route for visiting the sales. Unless the paper provides a list of sales on a map, it's difficult to visualize where each address is located. This is where the Yahoo! Maps Web Service can help.

To start building your map, you need to have your location data in a digital format. A spreadsheet works well for data entry, so open Excel and add the addresses you want to plot on a map. This hack expects the data in five columns, in this order: address, city, state, Zip Code, and notes about the address. Now you can copy the garage sale addresses from the paper and include notes about what you're most interested in at that particular sale. Figure 5-35 shows a sample spreadsheet in Excel.

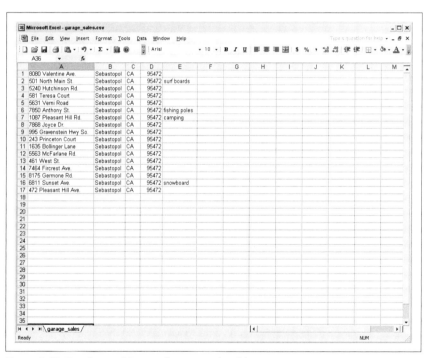

Figure 5-35. Excel spreadsheet with garage sale addresses

Once you've added all the addresses you want to plot, save the file in the plain text comma-separated value (CSV) format and call the file *garage_sales.csv*. Now that your location data is in a digital format, you can easily convert the CSV file into the Yahoo! Maps Annotation format with some Perl.

The Code

This script accepts a filename for a CSV file and uses the data in the file to
create a geo-aware RSS 2.0 file. You won't need any extra modules, so you
can simply save the following code to a file called *csv_to_geoRSS.pl*:

```perl
#!/usr/bin/perl
# csv_to_geoRSS.pl
# Converts a CSV file with addresses to geo-aware RSS
# Usage: csv_to_geoRSS.pl <CSV File>

use strict;

# Open the incoming file
open(CSV, "<@ARGV" ) or die "Can't open @ARGV : $!";

# Change the .csv extension to .xml for RSS file
my $RSSfile = $ARGV[0];
$RSSfile =~ s!csv$!xml!;

# Open the RSS file for writing
open(RSS, ">$RSSfile") or die "Can't open file: $!";

print RSS<<"HEADER_END";
<?xml version="1.0"?>
<rss version="2.0" xmlns:geo="http://www.w3.org/2003/01/geo/wgs84_pos#"
    xmlns:ymaps="http://api.maps.yahoo.com/Maps/V1/AnnotatedMaps.xsd">
<channel>
HEADER_END

# Loop through the CSV file, adding items
while(<CSV>) {
   chomp;
   my($address, $city, $state, $zip, $notes) = split(/,/, $_);

   print RSS<<"ITEM_END";
    <item>
        <title>$address</title>
        <link />
        <description>$notes</description>
        <ymaps:Address>$address</ymaps:Address>
        <ymaps:CityState>$city, $state</ymaps:CityState>
        <ymaps:Zip>$zip</ymaps:Zip>
        <ymaps:Country>us</ymaps:Country>
    </item>
ITEM_END
}
```

```
# Finish the RSS
print RSS "</channel>\n";
print RSS "</rss>";

# Close the files
close CSV;
close RSS;
```

As you look through the script, you can see that the RSS format contains the standard <title>, <link>, and <description> tags. It also has some Yahoo!-specific extension tags including <ymaps:Address>, <ymaps:CityState>, <ymaps:Zip>, and <ymaps:Country>. Because the garage sales in this example don't have titles or links, the address is used as a title and the link tags are blank in the final RSS file. You could easily add more columns to the spreadsheet to hold titles or links.

Also keep in mind that if your source spreadsheet file data contains commas (in the address or note columns, for example), you may need to adjust the script to accommodate. Try saving the spreadsheet as a tab-delimited file and changing the line in the code that separates data by commas so that it instead separates data by tabs:

```
my($address, $city, $state, $zip, $notes) = split(/\t/, $_);
```

This measure should help ensure your data lines up properly in the RSS file.

Running the Hack

To create the RSS file, pass the name of your CSV file to the script, like so:

```
perl csv_to_geoRSS.pl garage_sales.csv
```

The script will create a file called *garage_sales.xml* that contains the properly formatted RSS for plotting points on a Yahoo! Map. Upload the RSS file to a publicly available web server and note the URL. The RSS file needs to be available online so Yahoo! Maps can use the data.

Building the Map

Once your RSS file is in place, building your map is simply a matter of constructing the proper Yahoo! Maps URL. You'll need a Yahoo! Application ID, which you can pick up at *http://api.search.yahoo.com/webservices/register_application*. With your Application ID and RSS URL, link to your custom map like this:

```
http://api.maps.yahoo.com/Maps/V1/AnnotatedMaps?appid=insert App ⏎
ID&xmlsrc=insert RSS URL
```

For this example, the URL would be:

```
http://api.maps.yahoo.com/Maps/V1/AnnotatedMaps?appid=insert App ⏎
ID&xmlsrc=http://example.com/garage_sales.xml
```

When you browse to the URL, Yahoo! fetches the RSS file and plots the addresses on a map, like the one shown in Figure 5-36.

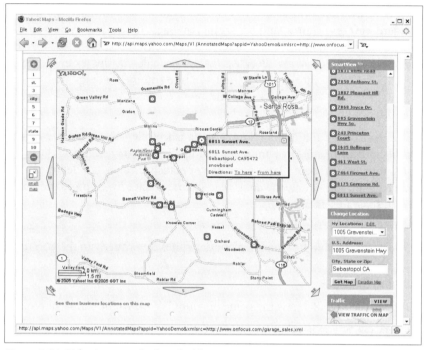

Figure 5-36. Yahoo! map with plotted addresses

Hover over the points on the map to see details, including notes about each address. You can also click the Printable Version link at the top of the page to see a numbered map of the points and a list of the addresses below the map—perfect for taking with you to those garage sales. Beyond personal use, you now have a unique map you can share with others via email or on the Web.

Hacking the Hack

This hack gives the most basic example of plotting several points on a map, and there are more ways to use the Yahoo! Maps service. If you have longitude and latitude data instead of addresses, you can use geoRSS 2.0

(*http://brainoff.com/worldkit/doc/rss.php*) to plot points. geoRSS is a standard RSS file with extra `<geo:lat>` and `<geo:long>` tags or specially formatted text in the `<description>` tag to describe coordinates.

If you want to change the look and feel of your map, you can add special tags that provide alternate icons for plotted points. You can also design your own pop up to describe items and give the pop-up URL in a `<ymaps:ItemUrl>` tag. You can read the complete Yahoo! Maps API documentation at *http://developer.yahoo.net/maps*.

## CHAPTER SIX

Webmastering
Hacks 92–100

According to Nielsen/Netratings (a company that tracks Internet usage), Yahoo! served results for 908 million searches in the month of May 2005. With millions of people relying on Yahoo! to point them to information across the Web, it makes sense that if you publish online you'll want to make sure your content is listed [Hack #92] at any appropriate Yahoo! site. And if you're publishing sensitive material, you might want the opposite [Hack #93].

In addition to sending traffic to your site, Yahoo! has a number of tools you can use to augment your site. Letting your readers know when you're online [Hack #95], giving your readers contextual search [Hack #97], and publishing your photos [Hack #99] can add unique features to an existing web site. And, of course, the presence of RSS throughout Yahoo!'s sites means you can write your own code to syndicate data such as messages from a Yahoo! Group [Hack #100] to your own web site.

Yahoo! offers more than just a bit of extra traffic to webmasters, and this chapter shows you how to take advantage of some of the services available.

Get Your Site Listed at Yahoo!

#92 Put your site in front of Yahoo! searchers by suggesting it for inclusion.

Millions of people use Yahoo! to find information, and having your site in Yahoo! Search or the Yahoo! Directory can mean more sales, more conversations with people you wouldn't have met otherwise, and more hits for your web site. However, letting Yahoo! know that your site exists can be a bit confusing. There's a distinction between Yahoo! Search (*http://search.yahoo.com*) and the Yahoo! Directory (*http://dir.yahoo.com*), and the process for submitting your site to each is a bit different.

Yahoo! Search

If other sites on the Web link to your site, chances are good that Yahoo! has already added your site to its *index*. An index is simply another name for the total list of sites that Yahoo! is watching. Yahoo! Search relies on a *crawler* to find new sites and keep current sites up-to-date. If a site that's currently in Yahoo!'s index has linked to your site, the crawler has probably already visited your site and automatically added it to Yahoo!'s index.

You can see if Yahoo! is already indexing your site by searching for it with the url: meta keyword [Hack #1]. Browse to *http://search.yahoo.com* and enter a query like this:

    url:http://insert your site

So a query to find the O'Reilly Hacks site looks like this:

    url:http://hacks.oreilly.com

It's important to include the full URL with the http:// prefix. Click Search; if a result is returned, it means that Yahoo! is already visiting your site periodically and you don't need to submit your URL. If you don't see a result, you can tell Yahoo! about your site for free.

Browse to *http://submit.search.yahoo.com/free/request* and enter your site's primary page URL into the form. You'll need to have a Yahoo! ID [Hack #3] to submit your site, and you'll have to log in before submitting a site. Once Yahoo! has your URL on file, the Yahoo! crawler will visit your site within a few weeks and make your site available to searchers.

If you operate a site for mobile devices, there's a separate form you can use to submit your site URL at *http://search.yahoo.com/free/mobile/request*. And if you run a site for kids, you can submit a site to Yahooligans! (*http://yahooligans.yahoo.com*) at *http://add.yahoo.com/fast/add?+Kids*.

Yahoo! Directory

While Yahoo! Search tries to include as many sites as possible in its index, the Yahoo! Directory is more like an exclusive club, where sites have to be approved by Yahoo! Editors. Because Yahoo! wants to maintain a highly useful directory, the steps for inclusion are a bit more involved.

To see if your site is already listed in the Yahoo! Directory, browse to *http://dir.yahoo.com* and search for the title of your site. If you don't see your site among the results, you can suggest your site to the Yahoo! Directory.

The first thing you need to determine about your site is whether it's commercial or noncommercial, because you'll need to pay $299 to submit a commercial site. According to Yahoo!, "If your site sells something, promote[s] goods and services, or represents a company that sells products and/or services," your site is commercial and should be listed somewhere in the Business and Economy category within the directory. If your site is purely personal, informational, or not-for-profit, your site is noncommercial. A banner ad or text ad on your site doesn't necessarily make your site commercial; if you have such an ad, it'll be up to the Yahoo! Editors to decide whether your site is commercial.

Adding a noncommercial site. The first step to adding a noncommercial site is to find the appropriate category for your site. If you know of some sites that are similar to yours, you might try searching for the titles of those sites within the directory to see how they're categorized. Otherwise, start browsing through the directory at *http://dir.yahoo.com* for the most appropriate place for your site. If your site is a personal home page, browse to "Society and Culture" → People → Personal Home Pages. If your site is a weblog, you'll want to browse to "Computers and Internet" → Internet → World Wide Web → Weblogs.

Once you've found the appropriate category, click the "Suggest a Site" link at the top of the page. Choose Standard Consideration and follow the instructions for adding a site. You'll have the option to include a site title, URL, geographic location, and description. If you have suggestions about other categories that your site might be appropriate for, you can include those suggestions in notes to Yahoo! Editors.

Once you've made your submission, the waiting game begins. Yahoo! doesn't guarantee that all sites submitted will be reviewed, and many sites are not included in the directory. If your site doesn't show up in the directory within two or three weeks, you can resubmit your site using the same process. Multiple submissions in a short period of time could exclude your site from consideration altogether. To be guaranteed a response about your site's placement within the directory, you can submit your site as if it were a commercial site, paying the commercial fee.

Adding a commercial site. To add a site to the commercial side of the Yahoo! Directory, you'll need to use a service called Yahoo! Directory Submit. The service requires a nonrefundable fee of $299 to review a site, with an annual fee of $299 to maintain the listing. Adult sites must pay $600 for review and as an annual fee due to extra work involved with reviewing them. Keep in mind that the initial $299 fee will guarantee that a Yahoo! Editor will review your site, but paying the fee does not guarantee that your site will be included in the Yahoo! Directory.

The Yahoo! Directory Submit terms of service state that
"Yahoo! Directory does not accept listings for online gam-
bling sites and prescription drug sites." If your site is related
to either of these businesses, you might want to take a closer
look at the submission terms, which are available at *https://
ecom.yahoo.com/dir/reference/submit*.

Once you agree to the fees and terms, you'll need to include your site information, including title, URL, geographic location, description, and any additional information that might help Yahoo! Editors categorize your site. You
can also provide a username and password for your site if your site requires
membership.

Once you have submitted your site, Yahoo! will respond within seven business days, letting you know whether your site will be listed in the directory.
If your site is denied a listing, you can appeal the decision once within 30
days.

Updating your listing. As your site changes, chances are good that you'll need
to update your Yahoo! Directory listing once in a while. You can suggest
changes to your listing at *http://add.yahoo.com/fast/change*.

Yahoo! RSS

Many sites offer RSS feeds of their content, and Yahoo! has some tools specifically for RSS publishers. A good place to start is the Yahoo! Publisher's
Guide to RSS, available at *http://publisher.yahoo.com/whatis.php* and shown
in Figure 6-1.

The Publisher's Guide contains a wealth of information about RSS, tools for
generating "Add to My Yahoo!" buttons, and a form for submitting your
RSS feed for indexing by Yahoo!.

As you update your RSS feed, you can notify My Yahoo! that you've done so
by pinging the service at this URL:

```
http://api.my.yahoo.com/rss/ping?u=insert your feed's URL
```

Doing this will ensure that your readers there will have your latest content as
soon as that content is added.

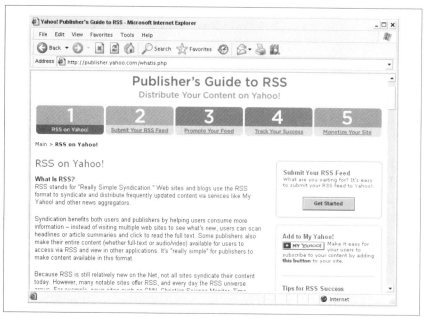

Figure 6-1. Yahoo! Publisher's Guide to RSS

Hide Part of Your Web Site from Yahoo!

#93   Though many sites do whatever they can to be found and ranked highly in Yahoo! Search results, there might be parts of your site that you want to keep private.

The Web is considered a public place, used to share pages of information with anyone in the world who wants to view them. But, to a lesser degree, the Web is also used to share information with small groups, or even a single individual. Because Yahoo! indexes as much of the Web as it can, these semipublic spaces can also be included in Yahoo! Search results. With just a bit of work, you can tell Yahoo! exactly which pages are meant for public consumption and which pages shouldn't be included in Yahoo! Search results. In addition, some sections of sites might not be a good introduction to the site, and you might want to control where people enter.

Yahoo! scans the Web with a program called Slurp. Slurp is a *bot* (short for *robot*) that visits and indexes web pages, makes a copy of the page for Yahoo!, and follows any links in the page looking for more pages to index. In addition to standard web pages, Slurp copies other files it finds along the way, such as PowerPoint presentations, PDF files, Word documents, Excel spreadsheets, and XML data files. Because of Slurp's link-following nature, many people think that if a page or document isn't linked from a page on their site that Yahoo! won't find it and it'll be out of view. But Slurp doesn't follow links exclusively; Slurp also looks for common filenames. And if a particular file is linked from another site, Slurp might find it that way.

Server Authentication

The best way to keep pages and files out of view of the general public is to place them behind *server authentication*. Server authentication is the web server's attempt to verify the identity of a particular user by requesting a username and password. The authentication is set at the server level.

Slurp can't enter a username and password if it encounters a server authenticated page, so you can be sure that anything behind this wall will not be indexed. You can set authentication permissions on a directory or file, and it's fairly easy to set up with both Apache and Microsoft's Internet Information Server (IIS).

Imagine you have a directory on your server called */private* and you'd like to keep any pages or files out of Yahoo! Search results. Apache includes many ways to set authentication, but a straightforward method involves setting a *.htaccess* file. The *.htaccess* file tells Apache how to configure a particular directory, and you can add a *.htaccess* file to the */private* directory with the following information:

```
AuthName "Please enter you login info."
AuthType Basic
AuthUserFile /your/path/to/.htpasswd
AuthGroupFile /dev/null
require user insert user name
```

Note that AuthUserFile points to a file that contains the username and password of the authenticated user, and you'll need to change */your/path/to/* to a real directory on your server that's not accessible via the Web. The next step is to create that password file with the *htpasswd* tool. Enter the following command from a command prompt:

```
htpasswd -c /your/path/to/.htpasswd insert user name
```

This creates the proper *.htpasswd* file for that user and puts in place all of the pieces for basic HTTP authentication.

To get the same results on a Windows server running IIS, open the IIS manager and find the directory you'd like to protect. Right-click the directory and choose Properties → Directory Security. Click Edit under "Anonymous Access and Authentication Control," and you'll see the window shown in Figure 6-2.

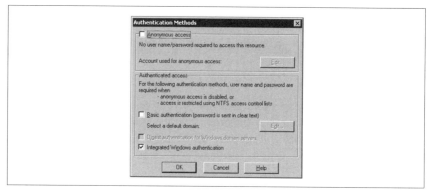

Figure 6-2. Authentication Methods prompt in IIS

Uncheck the "Anonymous access" box to require authentication. Check "Integrated Windows authentication" for a bit more security or "Basic authentication" for the most basic HTTP authentication. Once you set one of these, only authenticated users will be able to view the files or subdirectories of */private*, and Slurp won't be allowed in.

robots.txt Exclusions

If server authentication seems like overkill and you'd rather make your directory or files available to everyone except Slurp, you can do so with a *robots.txt* file, which indicates how you'd like robots to behave at your site. Well-behaved bots (such as Slurp) check for *robots.txt* before indexing anything, to make sure they're acting as the site owner wants them to.

With *robots.txt*, you can tell Slurp that you'd like it to exclude certain directories or files from its crawl. For example, if you'd like Slurp to skip a directory called */private*, save the following line to a file called *robots.txt*:

```
User-agent: Slurp
Disallow: /private/
```

You can also tell Slurp to skip specific files:

```
User-agent: Slurp
Disallow: /Private.doc
Disallow: /Private.html
```

Once you've listed all of the files and directories you'd like to hide, add *robots.txt* to the root directory of your web site, so it has a URL like this:

```
http://example.com/robots.txt
```

If a human reads your *robots.txt* file, they'll see a list of the files and directories you've asked Yahoo! not to index. While *robots.txt* will keep some bots away, it won't keep people from viewing the files. Private files should always be placed behind server authentication where a password is required to access them.

If you'd like to deny entry to all robots across all areas of you site, you can use a wildcard, like this:

```
User-agent: *
Disallow: /
```

Keep in mind that only bots that adhere to the *robots.txt* standard will play by the rules. People are free to build bots any way they want, and some ignore *robots.txt* altogether. Luckily, Slurp will always play by the rules.

robots Meta Tags

Another way to guide the Slurp bot on a page-by-page basis as it crawls your web site is through special HTML *meta* tags. Meta tags add extra information to a web page and are located toward the top of the page, between the <head></head> tags. To keep Slurp from indexing a particular page, add the following tag:

```
<META NAME="robots" CONTENT="noindex">
```

This will insure that the page will not show up in Yahoo! Search results. Many web crawlers look for this tag, and adding this robots tag will affect more than Yahoo! Other search engines, such as Google, will also skip the page.

If you'd like search engines to index the page, but not keep a copy in their cache, you can use the following tag:

```
<META NAME="robots" CONTENT="noarchive">
```

Using this tag will mean your page will show up in search results, but the search engine will not store a copy of the page that their users can view. Again, this will affect more than just Yahoo!, because many search engines also obey this tag.

Now that you know how to speak Slurp's language, you can make sure that your private or semiprivate information doesn't turn up in Yahoo! Search results, and you can control what Yahoo! sees in the first place.

Search Your Web Site with Yahoo!

#94 Offer your readers a way to search your site—without hiring a team of developers to build it.

As a serious web addict, I'm frequently frustrated by sites that don't offer a way to search their content. Navigating through a maze of different sections, trying to find that one piece of information I'm after feels like a waste of time. Often I'm forced to leave the site, bring up Yahoo! Web Search, and use its `site:` meta keyword. The `site:` shortcut lets you specify that the search results should be limited to a single domain.

For example, if you browse to *mountaindew.com*, you're immediately blasted with metal music and an extreme Flash animation showing various extreme sports. But all I'm after is the number of calories in a can of soda, and there's not a search form in sight. I could try clicking on a few of the menu items, but I'd probably find more images of skateboarding than useful information. So I surf over to Yahoo! and type:

```
site:mountaindew.com calories
```

In a few seconds, I have a specific link deep within the *mountaindew.com* site that has the information I'm after, as shown in Figure 6-3.

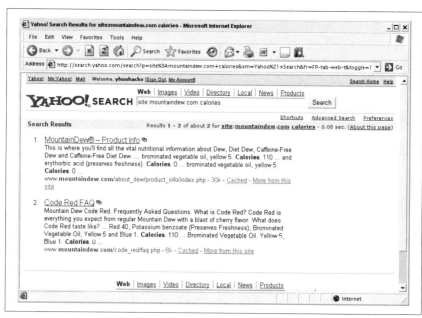

Figure 6-3. Search results for "calories" limited to mountaindew.com

PepsiCo, Inc. (the owners and operators of *http://www.mountaindew.com*) probably has the budget and team of developers to build its own search engine for the site if it wanted to. But many individuals and small businesses don't have that luxury. Since Yahoo! is probably already indexing any pages you have on the Web, you could easily give your readers a shortcut to searching your site with a custom Yahoo! search form.

The Code

In addition to the site: meta keyword, some tweaks to a standard Yahoo! Web Search URL will also limit results to a single domain. Here's a search URL that will return the same results as the previous example:

```
http://search.yahoo.com/search?p=calories&vs=mountaindew.com
```

As you can see, the p querystring variable holds the search query and the vs variable indicates the domain to limit the search results to. Armed with this information, here's a bit of HTML that will build the proper URL:

```html
<form action="http://search.yahoo.com/search">
<input type="text" name="p" size="34" />
<input type="submit" value="Search" />
<div>
<input type="radio" name="vs" value="" id="websearch" />
   <label for="websearch">Search the web</label>
<input type="radio" name="vs" id="sitesearch"
   value="insert your domain" checked="checked" />
   <label for="sitesearch">Search this site</label>
</div>
</form>
```

Running the Hack

All you need to do to customize the code is insert your domain name in the second radio input tag. You can add this HTML to any existing web page to provide your readers with a way to search your site. In a browser, the result looks like Figure 6-4.

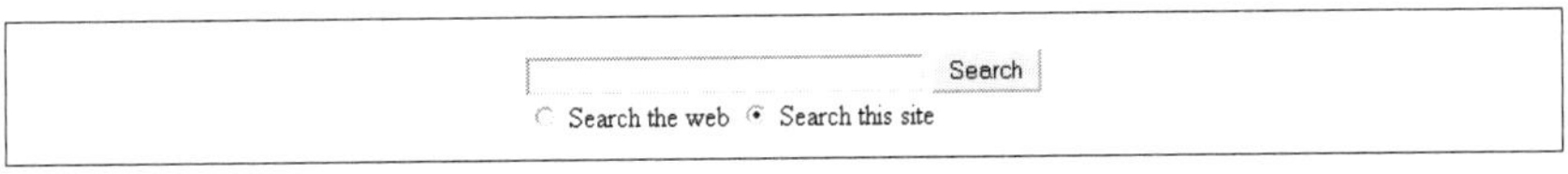

Figure 6-4. Custom Yahoo! search form

The "Search this site" option will be selected by default, but users could also search the entire Web from the form. While this won't make your site as extreme as *http://www.mountaindew.com*, at least your visitors will be able to find exactly what they're after.

HACK Add Presence to Your Web Site
#95

Let your visitors know when you're online by connecting your site to Yahoo! Messenger.

The Web is great for *asynchronous* communication. That is, I can post something to my web site at 4:00 a.m., and you can read what I've written at any point after that. We don't need to be sitting at our computers at the same time to share information. However, if both of us want to have a real-time text conversation—similar to a telephone coversation, but typed rather than spoken—the Web doesn't work nearly as well, and that's where instant messaging can help.

Yahoo! Instant Messenger is a program that lets you communicate with other people in real time. If you and a friend both have Yahoo! Instant Messenger and you're both at your respective computers at the same time, you can send messages back and forth instantly. The program lets you set a status that lets others know whether you're currently available. This status, or *presence*, is available only to people who have you on their Yahoo! Instant Messenger friends list and who have the program open. But with some simple HTML, you can make your presence known to anyone browsing your web site.

Yahoo! has opened a back door to the current online status of Yahoo! members, called the Online Presence Indicator. Thanks to a predictable image URL, you can display a graphic on your web site that tells people whether you're available to chat. If one of your readers also has Yahoo! Instant Messenger, he'll be able to click the graphic to send you an instant message.

The only thing you'll need to run this hack is a copy of Yahoo! Instant Messenger (*http://messenger.yahoo.com*). You'll also need to be sure that your Yahoo! Profile allows others to view your online status. To verify that others can view your online status, go to *http://edit.profiles.yahoo.com/config/edit_identity* and make sure that the box to "hide my online status" is unchecked, as shown in Figure 6-5.

The Code

If you want the lightning-fast way to add presence to your web site, Yahoo! offers some cut-and-paste HTML at *http://messenger.yahoo.com/messenger/help/online.html*. But by taking some time to understand how to put together your own presence HTML, you can customize the look of the presence indicator and get it to behave the way you want it to.

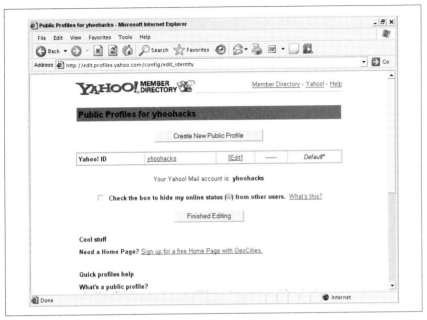

Figure 6-5. Yahoo! Profile setting to hide online status

The key to writing the presence HTML lies in knowing how to build a custom URL that indicates any member's online status. The following URL shows the basic format:

```
http://opi.yahoo.com/online?u=insert your Yahoo! ID&m=g&t=2
```

There are three required variables in the URL that you can play with to get different results:

u   A Yahoo! member ID.

m   The method Yahoo! will use to deliver the status. g returns a graphic and t returns text.

t   The type of text or graphic to send. The value should be a number between 1 and 3: use 2 for the largest graphic, 1 for a medium-sized graphic, and 3 for the smallest.

To test a URL, simply type it into your browser. Using the example URL with m set to g (for a graphic) and t set to 2 will return an online or offline image like the ones in Figure 6-6.

Figure 6-6. Online and offline images with type set to 2

By changing the value of t, you can change the images. For example, the following URL will display an online or offline image like the ones in Figure 6-7:

```
http://opi.yahoo.com/online?u=insert your Yahoo! ID&m=g&t=1
```

Figure 6-7. Online and offline images with type set to 1

The final option, with t set to a value of 3, is simply an image of a face, as shown in Figure 6-8.

Figure 6-8. Online and offline images with type set to 3

The image will automatically change based on your Yahoo! Instant Messenger status. You can confirm this change by bringing up the image URL in your browser, going on- or offline in Yahoo! Instant Messenger, and then reloading the image.

Running the Hack

To add the image to your site, add it as the src of an image tag, like so:

```
<img src="http://opi.yahoo.com/online?u=insert your Yahoo! ID&m=g&t=2" />
```

This tag will add the presence indicator to your web site, and with one more step you can let people send you an instant message by clicking the image. Yahoo! provides a page that lets someone send you an instant message regardless of whether she has Yahoo! Instant Messenger installed. Use this URL:

```
http://messenger.yahoo.com/edit/send/?.target=insert your Yahoo! ID
```

If your visitor has Yahoo! Instant Messenger installed, a chat dialog will pop-up and she can start chatting with you. If she doesn't have the program, Yahoo! will provide a web pop-up window to let her send a message.

Putting it all together, you should end up with something like the following HTML:

```
<a href="http://messenger.yahoo.com/edit/send/?.target=insert your Yahoo! ID">
<img src="http://opi.yahoo.com/online?u=insert your Yahoo! ID&m=g&t=2"
border="0" /></a>
```

This will display your online status to viewers of your web site and let people click to send you a message when you're available. Figure 6-9 shows the image in action on a remote site.

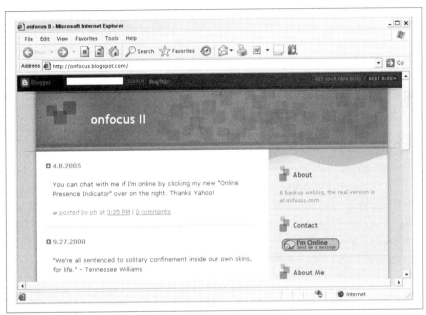

Figure 6-9. The Online Presence Indicator at a remote site

With some presence on your site, you'll be able to let people know when you're online, and you'll give them the opportunity to communicate with you instantly.

Syndicate Rich Media
HACK #96

Media RSS can tell Yahoo! and the world about your audio and video.

Web publishers have been using the syndication format RSS to move text around the Internet since 1999. Typically, an RSS feed contains summaries of news stories or weblog posts and URLs that point to the permanent location of those pieces of text. The type of content that could be delivered via RSS expanded when the format added support for *enclosures*. Enclosures are like email attachments and can be used to include any type of binary file, including audio and video.

This support for enclosures led to a new form of audio distribution called *podcasting*, which lets people subscribe to audio shows via an RSS file and automatically download new episodes to an iPod or other portable media player. This new distribution method has generated an explosion of independent audio content and a new audience for that content.

Looking forward, it's not hard to imagine a similar scenario with video content. Anyone with a computer and a digital video camera can produce their own content, and the Internet is a perfect distribution system for those digital bits. Video syndication poses some additional challenges, but Yahoo! has already started building the tools necessary for video syndication.

Introducing Media RSS

Yahoo! wanted something more flexible for publishers of audio and video than a single "attachment" for items in their RSS feed. And they wanted publishers to be able to describe those media files in a structured way. Unfortunately, the enclosure capabilities of RSS don't quite fit the bill. While you can definitely include a video file as an enclosure, you can't include multiple files or describe the files in a structured way.

One of the strengths of the RSS syndication format is the fact that anyone can extend the format with modules. And Yahoo! has taken the enclosure features of RSS a step further with its Media RSS module.

> You can read the specification for Media RSS at *http://search.yahoo.com/mrss* or read through the frequently asked questions at *http://search.yahoo.com/mrss/mrss*.

Beyond giving publishers a bit more control, this more fine-grained approach to describing media within RSS helps Yahoo! discover video to index for Yahoo! Video Search [Hack #11]. Because many audio and video publishers include their media files in special player pop-up windows, finding and indexing the video is not as simple as finding and indexing web pages. Yahoo! is encouraging people who provide audio and video to use Media RSS as a way to tell Yahoo! what to include in their video search engine.

Here's a look at some of the ways Media RSS expands the enclosure capabilities of RSS:

Multiple files
 The `<media:group>` tag allows for multiple media files within a single `<item>`. This way, a single news story that contains several video clips could include each of the clips within a single RSS item.

Metadata
 The `<media:content>` tag includes nine attributes that describe the video file, including `url`, `type`, `bitrate`, `duration`, `height`, and `width`.

Thumbnails
Publishers who want to supply a thumbnail for a video file can use the <media:thumbnail> tag and include a thumbnail url, height, and width.

Credits
The <media:credit> tag can be used to indicate who put together the content. A role attribute indicates a title, and the tag itself holds someone's name.

Text
The <media:text> tag could be used to include lyrics, a transcript, or some related text. The type attribute specifies whether the text is plain or HTML.

Player
Publishers who want to control the way a video or audio clip is played can provide a URL to a web-based player with the <media:player> tag.

Categorization
Each media file included in a Media RSS file can be categorized with the <media:category> tag, giving more information about the content of the file.

To use the extended capabilities of the Media RSS Module, you simply need to declare the Media RSS namespace in the opening RSS tag, like this:

```
<rss version="2.0" xmlns:media="http://search.yahoo.com/mrss">
```

This declaration gives computers parsing the file some indication of how the file should be used, and it gives curious people viewing the file a way to look up the precise way the <media:> tags should be used, so they can understand what they're looking at.

Automating Media RSS

Most RSS feeds today are generated with content management software. After you write a news story or weblog post, you don't even have to think about the RSS that describes it. The RSS is generated automatically for you. As Media RSS evolves, it will likely be generated by software as well, and this hack illustrates how a simple script can generate Media RSS for you.

Imagine you have a directory full of video on your server. The video might be linked from various web pages on your site, but you'd like to be sure that all of your video files are indexed by Yahoo! Video so they'll appear in Yahoo! Search results. This script solves the problem by creating a Media RSS file based on a directory full of media files that's suitable for submitting to Yahoo!.

The Code

This code is an ASP file written with VBScript that can be used on Windows servers. Save the following code to a file called *mRSS.asp* and be sure to alter the three values at the top to match your setup:

```
<%
'-----------------------------------------------------------------
' mRSS.asp
'
' Finds video files in a directory and generates a Media RSS file
' describing those video files.
'-----------------------------------------------------------------
' Change these values to fit your setup.
'
' BASE_URL is the publicly available address for the directory
' MEDIA_ADULT indicates whether or not the files are for adults only
' MEDIA_EXTS is a list of recognized media extensions that you want
'            to include in the Media RSS file
'
Const BASE_URL = "http://insert/path/to/videos/"
Const MEDIA_ADULT = "false"
Const MEDIA_EXTS = "avi,mov,mp3,mpg,mpeg,wmv"

' Set content type for the page
Response.ContentType = "text/xml"

%><?xml version="1.0"?>
<rss version="2.0" xmlns:media="http://search.yahoo.com/mrss">
<channel>
<title>My Site Videos</title>
<link>http://www.example.com/</link>
<description>Various videos I've produced</description>
<%
' Start the FileSystem Object
Set fs = Server.CreateObject("Scripting.FileSystemObject")

' Find the current directory
thisPath = Request.ServerVariables("path_info")
lastS = InStrRev(thisPath,"/")
thisPath = Mid(thisPath,1,lastS)
thisFullPath = Server.MapPath(thisPath)

' Load the current directory
Set fsFolder = fs.GetFolder(thisFullPath)
Set fsFiles = fsFolder.Files

    ' Loop through each file in the directory and
    ' check the extension. If it's a recognized
    ' type, build the RSS item
    For Each Item in fsFiles
        strName = Item.Name
```

```
        intDot = InStrRev(strName,".") + 1
        strShortName = Left(strName,intDot - 2)
        strExtension = LCase(Mid(strName,intDot,Len(strName)))
        If InStr(MEDIA_EXTS,strExtension) Then
            strSize = Item.Size
            dtmDate = Item.DateCreated
            dtmMod = Item.DateLastModified
            strType = Item.Type
            response.write "<item>" & Chr(13)
            response.write "  <title>" & strShortName & "</title>" & Chr(13)
            response.write "  <link>" & BASE_URL & strName & "</link>" & ↵
Chr(13)
            response.write "  <media:content url=""" & BASE_URL & strName ↵
& """"
            response.write "  fileSize=""" & strSize & """"
            response.write "  type=""" & getType(strExtension) & """ />" ↵
& Chr(13)
            response.write "    <media:adult>" & MEDIA_ADULT & "</media:↵
adult>"
            response.write Chr(13) & "</item>" & Chr(13)
        End If
    Next

' Clean up the objects
Set fsFiles = Nothing
Set fsFolder = Nothing
Set fs = Nothing
%>
</channel>
</rss>
<%
' This function translates a file extension
' into its content type
Function getType(ext)
    Select Case ext
        Case "avi"
            getType = "video/avi"
        Case "mov"
            getType = "video/quicktime"
        Case "mp3"
            getType = "audio/mpeg"
        Case "mpeg","mpg"
            getType = "video/mpeg"
        Case "wmv"
            getType = "video/x-ms-wmv"
    End Select
End Function
%>
```

This code loops through the files in a directory and checks the file extension
against the list of extensions set as MEDIA_EXTS. If the extension is one of the

set types, the script creates an RSS item using the filename as the `<title>`, and the value set in `BASE_URL` plus the filename as the `<link>`.

The script then adds a minimal `<media:content>` tag to describe the file and the `<media:adult>` tag to indicate whether the file has adult content. This value is hardcoded into the script, so you'll need to keep your adult files separate from your kid-friendly files. You can change how the script treats the file by setting the `MEDIA_ADULT` variable to `true` or `false` at the top of the script.

Running the Hack

To run the code, place *mRSS.asp* in a directory that is available on the Web and contains media files, and bring its URL up in a browser. For example:

```
http://example.com/videos/mRSS.asp
```

You should see an RSS feed with a list of all the media files in the directory. Each `<item>` in the feed will correspond to a file and should look something like this:

```
<item>
  <title>My_Home_Video</title>
  <link>http://example.com/videos/My_Home_Video.wmv</link>
  <media:content url="http://example.com/videos/My_Home_Video.wmv"
    fileSize="5676202"
    type="video/x-ms-wmv"/>
  <media:adult>false</media:adult>
</item>
```

This simple feed doesn't take advantage of all the features of Media RSS, but it's enough to build a feed suitable for submitting to Yahoo! Video.

> You can validate any RSS feed—including Media RSS—with the Feed Validator (*http://www.feedvalidator.org*). Simply plug in your RSS feed URL into the form, and the validator will fetch the feed and point out any problems.

Submitting Video to Yahoo!

Once you have an RSS feed filled with pointers to rich media, you can submit the feed to Yahoo! to be sure your video is available to Yahoo! searchers. Browse to *http://search.yahoo.com/mrss/submit* and add your RSS feed URL to the form. You can also include your email address, web site URL, and company name, but these are optional. Once Yahoo! has your Media RSS URL in its database, a Yahoo! crawler will begin visiting your feed and indexing your video.

If you put time and energy into publishing independent content, describing it with Media RSS can help you reach a wider audience by making the content available through Yahoo! Video Search.

Add Contextual Search to Your Blog

#97 Y!Q gives your readers the ability to search for content directly related to your posts.

Say you're reading a weblog about astronomy and you run across a post about *refraction*, a stellar optical illusion caused by the atmosphere. If you want to learn more about refraction, you'll need to leave the weblog, browse to your favorite search engine, type in refraction, and start browsing through the results. Unfortunately, the search is lacking any context, and though you will get results related to astronomical refraction, you'll also find many results about lenses, the human eye, and physics. Most likely, you were interested in the term *refraction* as it relates to astronomy.

Yahoo! is addressing this problem by bringing search capabilities to remote sites such as weblogs with a feature called Y!Q. Y!Q is a *contextual search*, which means a Y!Q search uses additional information to refine the search results. If the astronomy weblog had a Y!Q search link embedded with every post, you could have clicked the link to see the top related results without leaving the weblog—and within an astronomical context.

Weblogs are particularly suited for contextual search, because each post is a unique burst of text with its own topic. A related search link can give readers a path to explore more about a particular topic. And adding the feature to your weblog is just a matter of knowing some HTML.

Most weblog systems provide a template system for defining how posts should be displayed within a page. Adding a Y!Q search form is just a matter of editing your template. Every page that will host a Y!Q search must include the JavaScript Y!Q library. Open your template and add the following code somewhere between the <head> and </head> tags in the page:

```
<script language="javascript" type="text/javascript"
    src="http://yq.search.yahoo.com/javascript/yq.js"></script>
```

Next, you'll need to add some HTML to the section of the template that describes how posts should be displayed. Here's a simple bit of HTML from a Blogger (*http://www.blogger.com*) template that describes how to display the text of a post:

```
<div class="post-body">
    <p><$BlogItemBody$></p>
</div>
```

And here's the same code, with the addition of a Y!Q Search Related Info link:

```
<div class="post-body">
    <div class="yqcontext">
    <p><$BlogItemBody$></p>
    <form action="http://yq.search.yahoo.com/search" method="post">
        <input type="hidden" name="context" value="<$BlogItemBody$>" />
        <div class="yqact">
            <input class="yqbt" type="submit" value="Search Related Info"
                onclick="return activateYQ(this)" />
        </div>
    </form>
    </div>
</div>
```

The <div> tag with the class yqcontext tells Y!Q what to highlight when someone clicks the Search Related Info link. And the <form> creates the Search Related Info link. Within the form, the hidden element named context tells Yahoo! what information is related to the search. In this case, the Blogger-specific <$BlogItemBody$> tag sets the value of context to the full text of the post when the weblog is published.

You could also narrow this value to the title of the post by using the <$BlogItemTitle$> tag instead. Other weblog systems have special tags for categories related to the post or a post excerpt. You might need to experiment with the context to see which information gives the best related results.

Once you save your template changes and republish your weblog, you should see the Search Related Info link after every post, as shown in Figure 6-10.

When a reader clicks the link, a new window appears within the page, highlights the context, and shows the top few related search results, as shown in Figure 6-11.

At this point, the reader can review the top results, click one to visit another site, close the Related Search Results box, or type his own query in the search field. Even though he types his own search query, Y!Q still retains the context of the post. Figure 6-12 shows the Y!Q Search Results page, along with the keywords extracted from the context text.

The reader can review the keywords and rerun the search with a different context, or he can completely turn off the related search feature to find more general results.

This example has shown the bare minimum needed to implement Y!Q. But there are quite a few options you can customize, most with hidden

Figure 6-10. Y!Q Search Related Info links on a weblog

form elements you can add to the Y!Q HTML. Here are some of the possible customizations:

Search Specific Sites
> You can use a hidden input tag named `siteRestriction` to limit Y!Q results to a single web site, including your own site. Set the `value` attribute of the tag to a list of sites separated by spaces.

Number of Results
> By default, you'll see the top three results in a Y!Q box, but you can change this with a hidden input tag named `YSTResultsMax`.

Add Contextual Search to Your Blog

Figure 6-11. Y!Q Related Search Results box

More Context

    If there's some context you'd like to provide beyond what your readers see, you can use a hidden tag named `siteContext` for a brief paragraph of text, or a hidden tag named `p` to add specific keywords to the context.

Custom Logo or Text

    You can add your own logo or text to the Y!Q box with hidden input tags named `c1`, `c2`, and `c3`. The value of the tags can be plain text or HTML, so you could include the HTML necessary to have your own logo in the Y!Q box, for example.

Look and Feel

    You can play with the entire look and feel of the box by creating your own stylesheet. The default stylesheet for Y!Q (*http://yq.search.yahoo.com/javascript/defaultTheme.css*) is a good basis for building your own.

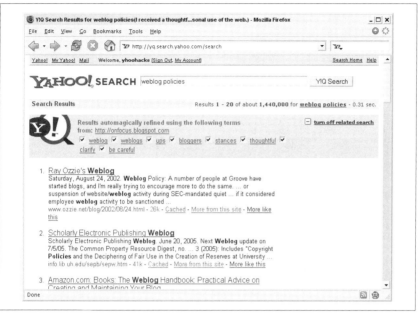

Figure 6-12. Y!Q Search Results page

You can find a full list of Y!Q customization options for publishers at *http://yq.search.yahoo.com/publisher/embed.html*.

By adding a Y!Q search to your weblog, you'll be giving your readers a smarter search tool that lets you set the context for their research.

Post Photos to Your Blog

#98

If you take a few minutes to enter some information about your weblog at Flickr, you can post photos directly to your weblog with a single click.

Even though many weblog systems offer tools to help you upload and include images with your posts, you might find that Flickr is a nice alternative to the standard photo tools. Once you upload a photo to Flickr [Hack #67], you have several options for including that photo in your weblog posts.

Blog This

The most direct way to send a photo from Flickr to your weblog is through the Blog This button above each of your photos, as shown in Figure 6-13.

To enable the Blog This button, you need to give Flickr some information about your weblog.

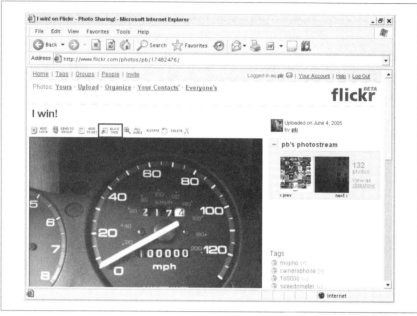

Figure 6-13. The Blog This button above a photo at Flickr

Configuring a weblog. Setting up Flickr to post to a weblog is a simple process. Click Your Account at the top of any page at Flickr and then click Your Blogs under the section labeled Blogging. You'll find a list of any weblogs you've already set up, or you can click "Set up a new blog" to add a new weblog to your account.

The first step to setting up a new weblog is telling Flickr which weblog tool you use. Flickr supports the following weblog systems:

Blogger
    http://blogger.com

TypePad
    http://sixapart.com/typepad

Movable Type
    http://sixapart.com/movabletype

LiveJournal
    http://sixapart.com/livejournal

WordPress
    http://wordpress.org

Manila
    http://www.manilasites.com

If you use a weblog tool that's not listed, check your tool's documentation to see if your tool uses one of the supported weblog application programming interfaces (APIs). An API allows a third-party tool such as Flickr to add posts to your weblog. Flickr supports the following APIs:

ATOM
> This API is an emerging independent standard for programmatic weblog access and is supported by many tools, including Blogger and the latest versions of Movable Type. You can see the details of the API at *http://atomenabled.org*.

BloggerAPI
> This is the first weblog API implemented by Blogger. It is no longer actively developed but might be supported in some tools.

MetaWeblogAPI
> This is also an older API that some tools, including WordPress, support. You can read more about the API at *http://www.xmlrpc.com/metaWeblogApi*.

If your weblog tool supports one of the above APIs, you just need to know the *API Endpoint*: a URL to which Flickr should send API requests. The documentation should give you the API Endpoint URL, and with that in hand, you can move on to the second step.

Once you've chosen your tool or supported API, you'll need to enter the username and password you use at your weblog tool. Flickr will use this information to contact the weblog tool and fetch information about your weblog or the multiple weblogs you maintain there. Choose your weblog from the list, click Next, and verify the information on the following page. If you don't feel comfortable storing your weblog tool's password with Flickr, you can uncheck the box labeled "Store your password?" Click All Done and you'll be ready to start posting pictures!

Posting to your weblog. With your weblog set to go at Flickr, browse to one of your photos that you'd like to post to a weblog. Click the Blog This button above the photo and choose one of your weblogs from the list, as shown in Figure 6-14.

Figure 6-14. Choosing a blog with the Blog This button

Once you choose your weblog, you'll have the option to compose your post at Flickr (see Figure 6-15).

Figure 6-15. Composing a weblog post at Flickr

Click Post Entry, and Flickr will automatically send the text and photo to your weblog. Figure 6-16 shows the example post at a Blogger-powered weblog.

The nice part about using the Blog This feature of Flickr is that you don't have to write the HTML necessary to link to a photo. You can simply point and click to add a post with a photo to your weblog. Flickr assembles the necessary HTML behind the scenes.

If you want to change the HTML that Flickr uses, you can alter the way Flickr lays out the photo and text for your weblog posts. To customize a post layout for one of your weblogs, browse to the Your Blogs page at Flickr and click Layout. You'll see several options, as shown in Figure 6-17.

You can even create a custom post layout template, if you want to go beyond the existing options.

Roll Your Own Post

While the Blog This feature at Flickr works well for posting a single photo along with some text, it doesn't work as well for posting multiple photos

Figure 6-16. A weblog post via Flickr

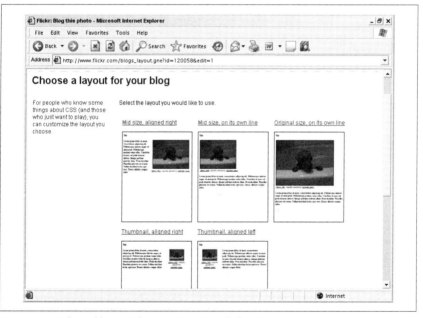

Figure 6-17. The weblog post layout options at Flickr

within a single post. And you might find that your post layouts are so unique that a single template won't work. In each of these cases, you'll need to write your own HTML to display images in your weblog posts. Even though you'll be doing some of the work on your own, Flickr can still make your life easier by hosting and processing your images.

The key to writing your own HTML to display images is finding a direct URL for the images you upload. But there's more than just one URL per image. For every image you upload to Flickr, there are five image sizes available, each with its own URL. This lets you choose the appropriate image size for the post or use a thumbnail instead of a full image.

> Keep in mind that the larger your photo, the longer it takes your readers to download the photo. And large photos won't always fit within the design constraints of a standard weblog. If your weblog text fits within a 400 pixel-wide column, posting an 800 pixel-wide photo will break the design.

To find URLs for each of the image sizes available, click the appropriately titled All Sizes button above any photo you've uploaded to Flickr. You'll find the All Sizes page (see Figure 6-18), which includes the size options listed across the top of the page, along with the dimensions of the photo in that particular size.

As you click each image size in the menu, you'll find a unique URL listed underneath the photo. Each URL has a similar format that looks something like this:

    http://photos11.flickr.com/17422514_fff01711bb_o.jpg

Notice that the URL starts with a Flickr domain, followed by a filename made up of two alphanumeric IDs and a final letter (separated by underscores) before the extension .jpg. That final letter is a *URL code* that represents the size of a Flickr photo, and understanding the codes can help you create or change links to different photo sizes on the fly. Here's a quick look at the different photo sizes available at Flickr:

Large

This size is the original size of the photo before it was uploaded to Flickr. If you uploaded a photo that was 800 pixels wide by 600 pixels high, you can access the original by clicking the Large size. The URL code for this size is o, which probably stands for "original." If the original image you uploaded was extremely large, you may also have the URL code b available for the large image size.

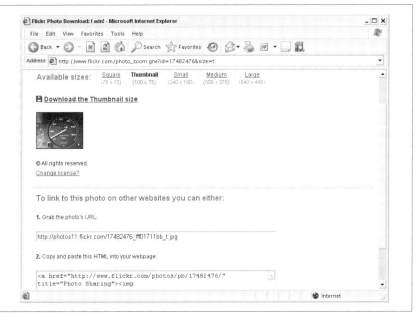

Figure 6-18. The All Sizes page for an image at Flickr

Medium

    The Medium size is what you see on a Flickr photo detail page. This size will be 500 pixels at its longest dimension, depending on the orientation of the photo. There is no URL code for Medium photos, because this is the default size.

Small

    Small photos are 240 pixels at the longest dimension and are used on photostream pages as thumbnails. The URL code for Small photos is m, possibly because at one time this size was considered medium.

Thumbnail

    This size is 100 pixels at its longest dimension and can be used to link to a larger version of the photo. The URL code for Thumbnail-sized photos is t.

Square

    The Square photos are versions of the original cropped to a square of 75×75 pixels. You'll find this size of photo in use on your Flickr home page when you're logged in. This is a handy size to use if you need to know the exact width and height of a photo. The URL code for square photos is s.

Once you know the size of the photo you'd like to display in your post, copy the URL. Then you can use the URL in an HTML image tag to display the photo, like this:

```
<img src="http://photos11.flickr.com/17422514_fff01711bb_m.jpg" width="240"
height="180" alt="speedometer" />
```

Once you're writing your own HTML, you can combine multiple images, link images to unique web pages, or create more complex layouts than are possible with Flickr's Blog This feature. Figure 6-19 shows a single post at LiveJournal with several photos hosted at Flickr.

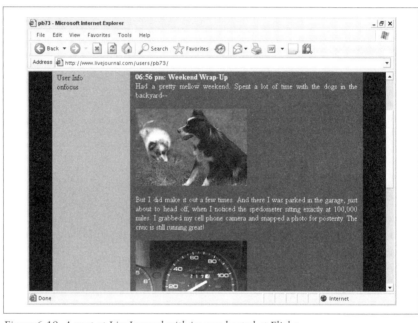

Figure 6-19. A post at LiveJournal with images hosted at Flickr

While you might not need this level of control for every post you make, knowing what's available to you can give you the freedom to get creative with your weblog posts.

 HACK #99 Feed Your Latest Photos to Your Web Site

Flickr provides a number of ways to syndicate your photos to another web site.

Adding photos to an existing web site can be a complex chore. You have to upload each photo to your site, write some HTML to display each photo on a page, and create duplicate, resized images if you want to show thumbnails of the photos. If you already use Flickr [Hack #67] to share your photos, there are several tools at your disposal that simplify the process of sharing your photos on a remote web site.

Even though you upload your photographs to Flickr—and they're stored on Flickr's servers—your photos aren't locked in at the site. Flickr is an open system that allows you to access your photos in a number of ways and display them anywhere you'd like. One of the easiest ways to show your photos on another site is with a Flickr badge.

Flickr Badges

Though it sounds like something you might wear on your uniform, a Flickr *badge* is simply a bit of code that displays photos on a remote web site. Figure 6-20 shows a simple Flickr badge with three photos on a remote web site.

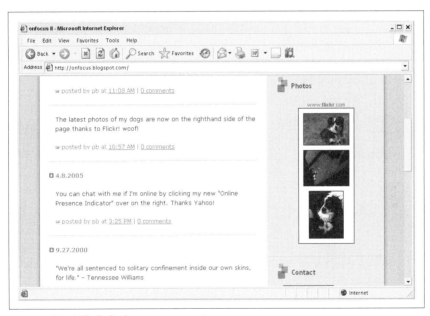

Figure 6-20. A Flickr badge on a remote site

You can create your own Flickr badge in a simple five-step process. Browse to the "Create your own Flickr badge" page at *http://www.flickr.com/badge_new.gne*, and log in if you aren't already.

Keep in mind that you'll need a unique Flickr ID and password to use the tools. You can create a free account at *http://
www.flickr.com/register.gne*. Although Yahoo! has purchased Flickr, at the time of this writing a Yahoo! ID will not
work on Flickr.

Creating a Flickr badge is the process of making a number of decisions
about the badge. Here's a look at the steps:

1. Choose the type.

   You can decide between basic static HTML or an animated, Flash-based
   badge. The animated badge shows a bit of movement and fades thumbnails in and out. Choosing Flash will mean your visitors will need the
   Macromedia Flash plug-in installed for their browser in order to see
   your photos.

2. Choose the photos.

   You can choose to display your latest photos or those of your photos
   that are tagged with a specific term. In addition, you can display photos
   from a group you're a member of, all photos with a certain tag, or, if
   you're feeling generous, all public photos.

3. Set the layout (HTML only).

   When you're building an HTML badge, you have a number of options
   for the layout. You can choose to show your personal buddy icon,
   which links to your Flickr profile page. You can choose the number of
   photos you'd like to show, the size of the thumbnails, and the orienta-
   tion of the badge: horizontal or vertical. Finally, you can choose to show
   the latest photos or a random sampling.

4. Choose colors.

   If you want the badge to fit in seamlessly with your remote site's design,
   you can adjust the background, border, and link colors. The preview at
   the bottom of the page will show your changes in progress.

5. Copy and paste code.

   On the last page, you can preview your badge and then copy the code
   for it by highlighting the badge and clicking Ctrl-C.

The code for a static HTML badge is a combination of CSS, HTML, and
JavaScript and should look something like this:

```
<!-- Start of Flickr Badge -->
<style type="text/css">
#flickr_badge_source_txt {padding:0; font: 11px Arial, Helvetica, Sans serif;
   color:#666666;}
```

```
#flickr_badge_icon {display:block !important; margin:0 !important;
    border: 1px solid rgb(0, 0, 0) !important;}
#flickr_icon_td {padding:0 5px 0 0 !important;}
.flickr_badge_image {text-align:center !important;}
.flickr_badge_image img {border: 1px solid black !important;}
#flickr_www {display:block; padding:0 10px 0 10px !important;
    font: 11px Arial, Helvetica, Sans serif !important; color:#3993ff
!important;}
#flickr_badge_uber_wrapper a:hover,
#flickr_badge_uber_wrapper a:link,
#flickr_badge_uber_wrapper a:active,
#flickr_badge_uber_wrapper a:visited {text-decoration:none !important;
    background:inherit !important;color:#3993ff;}
#flickr_badge_wrapper {background-color:#ffffff;border: solid 1px #000000}
#flickr_badge_source {padding:0 !important;
    font: 11px Arial, Helvetica, Sans serif !important; color:#666666
!important;}
</style>
<table id="flickr_badge_uber_wrapper" cellpadding="0" cellspacing="10"
border="0">
 <tr>
    <td>
    <a href="http://www.flickr.com" id="flickr_www">
    www.<strong style="color:#3993ff">flick
    <span style="color:#ff1c92">r</span></strong>
    .com</a>
    <table cellpadding="0" cellspacing="10" border="0" id="flickr_badge_↵
wrapper">
        <script type="text/javascript"
src="http://www.flickr.com/badge_code_v2.gne?count=3&display=latest&size=t↵
&layout=v&source=user&user=33853652177%40N01">
        </script>
        </table>
        </td>
 </tr>
</table>
<!-- End of Flickr Badge -->
```

The CSS style definitions at the top of the code format how the badge looks. You can modify this CSS at any point to change how the badge looks on your site. Immediately after the <style> tags, the standard HTML <table> holds the photos.

The <script> tag does the work of displaying the photos. As you can see in the src attribute, the JavaScript file resides at *http://www.flickr.com* and displays photos based on the parameters passed in the URL. Many of the decisions you made while running through the badge creation process are encapsulated in this URL. For example, the count variable will be set to the number of photos you told the badge to display, and the layout variable will be set to v or h, depending on your choice of vertical or horizontal layout.

If you need to change your badge, try studying the fairly self-explanatory variables in the URL and changing values. That way, you can make changes quickly without running through the badge-creation process again.

Flickr Feeds

Another way that Flickr makes photos available for use on other sites is through standard XML syndication formats. Browse to your photos, scroll to the bottom of the page, and you'll see the feed options shown in Figure 6-21.

> Feeds for pb's photostream Available as RSS 2.0 and Atom   ☐ MY Y!

Figure 6-21. Flickr feed options at the bottom of a Flickr page

You'll find feeds in the popular RSS and Atom formats. Click the link to view the feed or copy the URL. You can also click the "Add to My Yahoo!" button with the plus sign to watch that particular group of photos on your My Yahoo! page. You'll find the same feed listing at the bottom of group pages and pages showing photos with a particular tag.

Each feed contains the 10 most recently added photos for a particular user, group, or tag. The item nodes in the feed contain all of the details you need to display the photo on a remote site: the title, a link to the photo on Flickr, and a bit of HTML for displaying a photo thumbnail and caption. Here's a look at an item in a Flickr RSS feed. Note that this example has been formatted for readability; the actual feed includes escaped HTML with tags like <p> rendered as the escaped <p>.

```
<item>
    <title>Ultimate Championships</title>
    <link>http://www.flickr.com/photos/pb/16469233/</link>
    <description>
        <p><a href="http://www.flickr.com/people/pb/">pb</a> posted a photo:⏎
</p>
        <p><a href="http://www.flickr.com/photos/pb/16469233/"
            title="Ultimate Championships">
            <img src="http://photos10.flickr.com/16422514_40ac8021f5_m.jpg"
            width="240" height="161" alt="Ultimate Championships"
            style="border: 1px solid #000000;" /></a></p>
        <p>the women's championship game was washington vs. stanford</p>
    </description>
    <pubDate>Mon, 30 May 2005 11:01:15 -0700</pubDate>
    <author>nobody@flickr.com (pb)</author>
    <guid isPermaLink="false">tag:flickr.com,2004:/photo/16469233</guid>
</item>
```

The <title> and <link> elements hold the title of the photo and a link to the photo, as you'd expect. The <description> element holds the block of HTML you can use on a remote site.

The most common use of RSS is for viewing new items in a newsreader, but there's no reason you can't use this same feed to create a custom Flickr badge. Parsing XML is the perfect job for Perl, and with a few lines of code you can build your own badge.

The code. This Perl script uses the LWP::Simple module to fetch a Flickr feed and the XML::RSS module to parse the feed and display its contents. Make sure you have these modules on your server, and then save this code to a file called *flickr_feed.pl*. Be sure to include a valid Flickr feed URL that contains the photos you want to syndicate.

```
#!/usr/bin/perl
# flickr_feed.pl
# Transforms a Flickr Feed into HTML
# Usage: flickr_feed.pl

use strict;
use XML::RSS;
use LWP::Simple;

# Grab the feed.
my $flickr_feed = 'insert Flickr feed URL';
my $feed = get($flickr_feed);

# Start RSS Parser
my $rss = new XML::RSS;

# parse the feed
$rss->parse($feed);

# initialize item counter
my $i;

# print the title, link, and description of each RSS item
foreach my $item (@{$rss->{'items'}}) {
    $i++;
    my $desc = "$item->{'description'}\n";

    # remove the "posted by" text
    $desc =~ s!<p>.*?posted a photo:</p>!!;

    # use thumbnails instead of medium images
    $desc =~ s!_m!_t!;

    # remove the width and height attributes from image tags
    $desc =~ s!width=".*?" height=".*?"!!;
```

```
    # remove the paragraph tags
    $desc =~ s!</?p>!!g;

    # print the item
    print "$desc<br />";
    print "<a href=\"$item->{'link'}\">";
    print "$item->{'title'}</a><br /><br />";

    # set the number of photos
    last if ($i == 3);
}
```

This code downloads the Flickr feed and massages the HTML in the
<description> tag, removing some text. Then it prints each item in the feed,
until it hits the number specified in the last line of the script.

Running the hack. You can run this code from the command line by calling
the script like this:

```
perl flickr_feed.pl
```

And you'll probably want to set the script to run on a regular schedule with
the Windows Task Scheduler or cron on Unix-based systems.

Using an XML feed instead of a preprogrammed Flickr badge is a bit more
work, but it gives you some more control over the presentation. You can
create your own CSS styles and classes to make the photos appear as you
want them to. Figure 6-22 shows a custom Flickr badge created with this
script and displayed on a remote site.

Figure 6-22. A custom Flickr badge

Hacking the Hack

Even though the Flickr feeds contain most of the information associated with each photo, you can still do more with the Flickr API. The API provides programmatic access to anything at Flickr, not just photos. You can read the full documentation at *http://www.flickr.com/services/api*.

In addition to titles and captions, you can get access to everything else, from the number of comments people have left about a photo, to notes left by others, to technical data (EXIF tags) from the camera that took the photo! Building a custom badge with the API will be more technically complex than parsing an RSS feed, but if you really want access to all of your data stored at Flickr, it's available!

Display Messages from a Yahoo! Group on Your Web Site

Use RSS to display the latest messages from a Yahoo! Group on a remote web site.

Really Simple Syndication (RSS) is a standard XML format designed for syndicating content across web sites. The fact that there are so many tools available that can work with RSS means it really is simple to work with.

Yahoo! has embraced RSS and offers RSS feeds for many of their features, including search results, news headlines, and Yahoo! Groups. Many people use Yahoo! Groups alongside another web site, or in cooperation with several web sites, so the following hack offers an excellent example of how this simple XML format can add a lot of value to an existing site.

The first step is to find the feed URL for the Yahoo! Group you're interested in. If the Yahoo! Group allows anyone to view the message archive, you should find a bright orange XML icon on the front page, like the one shown in Figure 6-23.

If you don't see the XML icon, you can ask the group moderator to change the settings to allow anyone to view the group archives, which will enable the feed. The steps for the moderator are:

1. From the group's front page, click Management at the bottom of the menu on the left side of the page.

2. Click Messages on the right side of the page, under Group Settings.

3. Click Edit next to Posting and Archives.

4. Change the Archive Options at the bottom of the page to Anyone and click Save Changes.

HACK
#100

Display Messages from a Yahoo! Group on Your Web Site

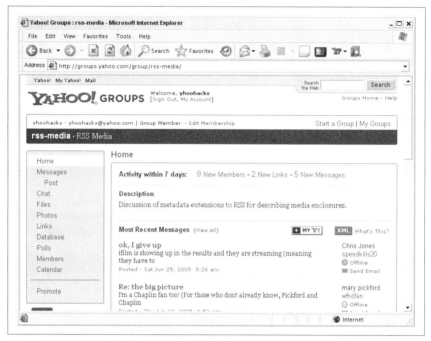

Figure 6-23. XML feed indicator on a Yahoo! Group

After the moderator completes these steps, the orange XML icon should appear. Right-click the icon and choose Copy Link Location or Copy Short-cut. The feed URL will now be on your virtual clipboard, ready for pasting where you need it.

If you click the icon instead of copying the URL (in a browser that displays XML), you'll get a sense of what the RSS format looks like. Figure 6-24 shows what the Yahoo! Groups RSS feed looks like.

Looking at the feed, you can see that the basic tags of each RSS <item> that represent a post to the group are <title>, <link>, <description>, and <pubDate>. The first two tags hold what you'd expect them to: the title of the message and a link to the message on the web archive, respectively. The <description> tag holds the first few lines from the message, and <pubDate> holds the date the message was originally sent. With this format, it's easy for a script to grab the information and display it on another site.

The Code

Instead of parsing the XML by hand with XML::Simple (as in most of the Perl hacks in this book), this script uses a module tailor-made for working with RSS called, appropriately enough, XML::RSS. This module features some

Display Messages from a Yahoo! Group on Your Web Site

HACK
#100

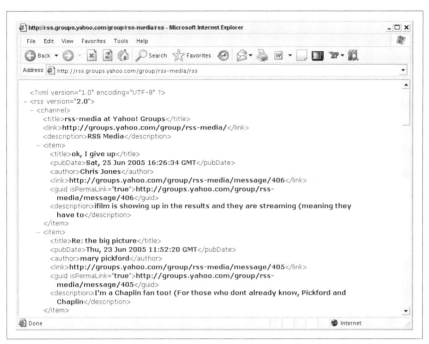

Figure 6-24. A Yahoo Groups! RSS feed

handy shortcuts when parsing RSS, and it makes working with the format even easier. To install XML::RSS on your system, you can use CPAN from the command line like this:

```
perl -MCPAN -e shell
cpan> install XML::RSS
```

The other module you'll need is LWP::Simple, which will fetch the RSS from Yahoo!.

Save the following code to a file called *write_feed.pl*:

```perl
#!/usr/bin/perl
# write_feed.pl
# Accepts an RSS feed URL and prints as HTML.
# Usage: write_feed.pl <RSS Feed URL>

use LWP::Simple;
use XML::RSS;

# Grab the incoming feed URL
my $url = join(' ', @ARGV) or die "Usage: write_feed.pl <RSS Feed URL>\n";

# Make the request
my $rss = get($url);
```

```
# Parse the RSS
my $xmlrss = new XML::RSS();
$xmlrss->parse($rss);

# Print the feed Header with title
print "<h3>" . $xmlrss->channel('title') . "</h3>";
print "<ul>";

# Loop through the items returned, printing them out
foreach my $item (@{$xmlrss->{'items'}}) {
        my $title = $item->{'title'};
        my $url = $item->{'link'};
        my $description = $item->{'description'};
        print "<li><a href=\"$url\">$title</a></li>\n";
}

# Print the feed Footer
print "</ul>";
```

The XML::RSS parse() function turns the RSS from Yahoo! into an object that Perl can work with. From there, the final foreach loops over each item in the feed and prints the results with a bit of HTML formatting.

Running the Hack

To run the script, call it from the command line, supplying a feed URL:

```
perl write_feed.pl insert feed URL
```

This will print the HTML to the command line, which probably isn't the effect you're after. To pipe the output to a text file, add one to the end like this:

```
perl write_feed.pl insert feed URL > insert text file
```

And here's a look at writing a Yahoo! Groups feed directly:

```
perl write_feed.pl http://rss.groups.yahoo.com/group/rss-media/rss > mrss.html
```

Once run, the newly created *mrss.html* file will contain the script's output, which will look something like Figure 6-25.

The final step to including this file in an existing web site is to drop it in as a *server-side include*. This can be as simple as adding a line to an existing dynamically generated web page, like so:

```
<!--#include virtual="/mrss.html" -->
```

Of course, be sure to replace the name of the file with the name of your HTML.

You could run this script manually once in a while, but it's much handier to let the server handle it. You can add your script as a cron job to run every

Display Messages from a Yahoo! Group on Your Web Site

HACK
#100

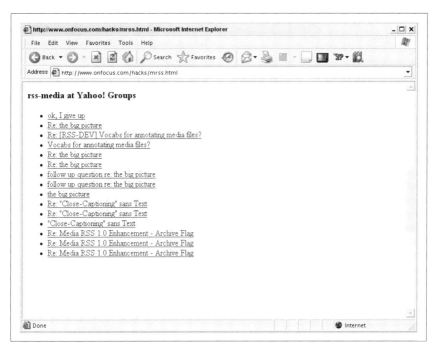

Figure 6-25. A converted Yahoo! Groups RSS feed at another domain

few hours, and you won't ever have to touch it again. Any new messages sent to the Yahoo! Group will also show up on your remote web site. It's a quick way to keep visitors to your site up-to-date with activities happening somewhere else.

Index

Symbols

& (ampersand)
  search queries and, 18
  spelling words with images, 354
  Yahoo! Mail URLs, 226
' (apostrophe), 120
* (asterisk), 276
@ (at sign), 224
\ (backslash), 150
: (colon), 44
= (equals sign), 108
! (exclamation point), 9, 217
> (greater-than sign), 44
< (less-than sign), 44
– (minus sign), 5, 7
( ) (parentheses), 6, 112
+ (plus sign), 49
" " (quotation marks) (see quotation
        marks)
; (semicolon), 324
_ (underscore), 426

A

about:cache file, 33
about:config file, 32
ACT!, 245
ActiveX Control, 122, 359
Acxiom, 159
"Add to My Yahoo!" icon, 148
Add/Edit Buttons (Yahoo! Toolbar), 47
addKey( ) function, 219, 220

address book
  adding to, 159, 241–246
  exporting, 244
  importing listings, 336–343
  mapping contacts, 247–252
  one-click access, 46, 48
  property shortcut, 10
  syncing, 245–246
  Yahoo! Mail and, 217
  Yahoo! Mobile and, 209, 210
Address field (Yahoo! Calendar), 237
address! property shortcut, 10
addresses
  blocking specific, 224
  Flickr address, 291
  groups and, 256
  importing, 241
  mail server, 230
  mapping to, 157–158
  plotting, 251, 252, 396
  temporary, 224
  Yahoo! Maps and, 392
adult content
  desktop images, 362
  filtering, 15, 16
  Yahoo! services and, 298
adult_ok parameter, 298, 362
advanced searches (see Yahoo!
        Advanced Search)
advertising
  cookies and, 65–68
  Sponsor Results, 2

We'd like to hear your suggestions for improving our indexes. Send email to *index@oreilly.com*.

AIM (AOL Instant Messenger), 282
airport shortcut, 9
Ajax, 382–387
alerts
    email, 48
    functionality, 91
    overview, 211–215
Also Try, 2
American Heritage Dictionary, 164
American Heritage Spanish
        Dictionary, 164
ampersand (&)
    search queries and, 18
    spelling words with images, 354
    Yahoo! Mail URLs, 226
Angelopoulos, Alex K., 359
announcement lists, 252
AOL Instant Messenger (AIM), 282
API Endpoint, 272, 423
API variables, 205
APIs (application programming
        interfaces)
    accessing data, 350
    adding to blogs, 268–273
    Buzz Game, 60, 61
    comparing search terms, 389
    mash-up images, 367–369
    memory games, 369
    spelling words with images, 353
    weblogs and, 423
    (see also web services)
apostrophe ('), 120
appid parameter, 298
Apple
    Dashboard feature, 161
    iChat, 282
    Quicktime plug-in, 164
AppleScript, 364–366
application IDs
    gvcard and, 339
    Perl and, 300
    plotting map points, 395
    unique, 297
    VBScript and, 308
application programming interfaces (see
        APIs)
applications
    adding links automatically, 373–378
    Ajax, 382–387
    automating, 308

comparing search terms, 387–392
creating MIDlets, 343–348
finding links, 332–336
grouping search results, 327–332
illustrating web sites, 369–373
importing from, 244
importing listings into address
        book, 336–343
importing listings into
        Excel, 348–353
mash-up images, 367–369
OPML, 123, 124
overview, 327
plotting maps, 392–397
Python and, 307
random Mac desktop, 364–366
random Windows desktop, 358–363
spelling words with images, 353–357
visualizing news topics, 379–382
archives
    group email, 253, 255
    Yahoo! Buzz Log, 57
    Yahoo! Group and, 435
    yahoo2mbox, 256–258
area codes, 9
Artymiak, Jacek, 74–81
Ask Yahoo!, 91
aspect keyword, 45
aspect ratio, 45
ASPs, VBScript and, 308, 372
asterisk (*), 276
asynchronous communication, 408
at sign (@), 224
ATOM API, 423
Atom feed, 49, 432
authentication, 403
AuthUserFile setting, 403
Auto-Linker, 373–378
automobile loan calculations, 116
autos property, 91
avatars
    creating, 273–276
    Trillian program and, 285
    Yahoo! Instant Messenger and, 213

B

background images, random
    Macintosh, 364–366
    Windows, 358–363

backslash (\), 150
Bakken, Stig Saether, 43
banking property, 91
banking-related calculators, 114
Bartlett's Familiar Quotations, 164
Battelle, John, 71
Bausch, Paul, 25–31
bcc variable, 226
Beattie, Russell, 72
Biafore, Bonnie, 102–108
Block link
    My Web and, 25, 26, 27
    purpose, 4
Blog This button, 421–424
Blogger service, 268, 422
BloggerAPI, 423
<$BlogItemBody$> tag, 418
<$BlogItemTitle$> tag, 418
Bloglines RSS reader
    importing blogrolls, 265
    importing bookmarks, 122
    OPML applications, 124, 267
Blogrolling web service, 122, 128, 264,
        265
blogrolls
    defined, 263
    importing, 264–267
blogs (see weblogs)
body variable, 226
bonds
    calculators related to, 115
    tracking, 92–97
bookmarklets
    defined, 110, 118
    finding links, 335
    installing, 120
    shortening URLs, 63
    translation, 22–24
    Yahoo! Mail, 226–228
    Yahoo! Travel and, 193
    yReplacer and, 369, 372
bookmarks
    accessing, 91
    bookmarklets and, 110, 118
    Currency Converter and, 110
    del.icio.us, 73
    importing, 25, 122–124
    managing, 49, 271
    movie showtimes, 169
    one-click adding, 118–122

opening in sidebars, 124–127
publishing, 128–130
Yahoo! Mail URLs, 225–226
bot (see robots)
box office charts, 168
Brown, Dave, 203
browsers
    about:config file, 32
    context menus and, 149
    cookies and, 65–68
    cross-site scripting, 385
    JavaScript and, 382
    opting out of cookies, 66
    SafeSearch Lock and, 16
    SmartSort tool, 199
    transferring bookmarks, 128
    uploading photos, 286
    Yahoo! Mail and, 233
    Yahoo! Toolbar, 46–52
browsing
    international stock exchanges, 94
    Yahoo! Directory and, 81–83
    Yahoo! Shopping, 197
Bryngfors, Nisse, 369
Bulk folder, 221, 223
Bureau of Labor Statistics, 182
Burke, Sean, 175
businesses, finding, 156–159
buzz score, 56, 58

C

<Cache> tag, 300
Cached link, 4
caches
    prefetch results and, 32
    spelling words with images, 354
Cadenhead, Roger, 123, 124
calculators, 112–117
calendar! property shortcut, 10
calendars
    finding dates, 57
    managing and sharing, 235–241
    one-click access, 46
    property shortcut, 10
    shared, 253
    vCard standard, 336
    Yahoo! Mobile and, 210
    Yahoo! TV and, 188–191
Calishain, Tara, 83–86, 86–90, 256–258

Cantoni, Brian, 63
captcha image, 12, 256
cars property, 91
categories
    calculating links, 86
    contacts and, 243
    Flickr members and, 292
    grouping results into, 327–332
    groups and, 256
    managing email, 220
    search results and, 4
    tracking additions, 84
    Yahoo!, 74
CC (Creative Commons), 37–41
cc variable, 226
cell phones
    checking mail via, 232
    content tabs, 281
    importing listings into address
        book, 336–343
    MIDlets and, 343
    monitoring traffic conditions, 163
    movie showtimes, 169
    sending information to, 158
    sending photos to Flickr, 288
    tracking portfolios, 96
    viewing movie lists, 178–182
    web cookies and, 207
    Yahoo! Alerts, 91, 211
    Yahoo! Mobile and, 207
Cerulean Studios, 282
<cfhttp> tag, 311, 313
<cfhttpparam> tag, 313
<cfloop> tag, 311
CFML (ColdFusion Markup
        Language), 311–313
CGI
    overview, xviii
    vCard, 337, 341, 342
cgi module (Python), 341
channel lineup, 139, 183
character codes, 219
charset attribute, 313
charts, spotting trends with, 61–62
chats
    avatars and, 276
    groups and, 253
    instant messenger, 410
    Yahoo! 360, 268
    (see also instant messenger)

Choose Buttons option (Yahoo!
        Toolbar), 47
circles (Grokker), 329
classifieds property, 91
<ClickUrl> tag, 300
CNET News.blog: Yahoo weblog, 70
ColdFusion Markup Language
        (CFML), 311–313
collages, 367
colon (:), 44
colors
    email accounts, 230
    Flickr badges, 430
    Grokker maps, 331
    instant messenger contacts and, 284
    My Yahoo! pages, 142–143
    My Yahoo! Ticker and, 154
Columbia Encyclopedia, 164
comic strips, 140
command-line scripts, xvi–xvii
comma-separated values format (see
        CSV format)
.comment variable, 119
communicating
    adding APIs to blogs, 268–273
    adding contacts to address
        book, 241–246
    archiving group messages, 256–258
    creating avatars, 273–276
    exploring social networks, 258–264
    group collaboration, 252–256
    importing blogrolls, 264–267
    managing Yahoo! Mail, 220–224
    mapping contacts, 247–252
    navigating Yahoo! Mail, 216–220
    overview, 216
    reading email in one place, 228–232
    reading email in preferred
        client, 233–235
    sharing calendars, 235–241
    storing and sharing photos, 285–293
    Trillian, 282–285
    Yahoo! Mail macros, 224–228
    Yahoo! Messenger content
        tab, 276–282
commute, monitoring, 160–163
configuration
    email clients, 235
    weblogs, 422, 423

contacts
    adding to address book, 241–246
    Flickr community, 292
    mapping, 247–252
    Yahoo! 360 profile and, 261
content management software, 413
content, reusing legally, 37–41
content tabs (Yahoo!
        Messenger), 276–282
content url setting (Yahoo!
        Messenger), 279, 280, 281
context menus, 149–151
contextual searches
    adding to weblogs, 417–421
    visualizing news topics, 379–382
    web services and, 295
conversion
    currencies, 108–112
    JPEG to bitmap, 359
Conversion Calculator, 164
convert shortcut, 112
Convert to Bitmap (ActiveX
        component), 359
cookies
    opting out of advertiser, 65–68
    SafeSearch settings, 16
    Yahoo! ID, 13
    Yahoo! Mobile and, 207
copyrights, 37, 42
country parameter, 298
CPAN module repository
    displaying messages on sites, 436
    overview, 294
    Perl and, 300
    Yahoo! 360 and, 269
crawlers, 151–155, 399, 405
Creative Commons (CC), 37–41
CSS stylesheets, 357
CSV (comma-separated values) format
    gvcard and, 336
    Microsoft Outlook, 244
    parsing, 248
    Perl and, 350
    plotting contact location, 247
    plotting map points, 393–395
    Yahoo! Local Search To Excel
        program, 350
csz variable, 162
Ctrl-Shift-C (check mail) shortcut, 218
Ctrl-Shift-F (view folders) shortcut, 218

Ctrl-Shift-H (help) shortcut, 218
Ctrl-Shift-P (compose new mail)
        shortcut, 218, 225
Ctrl-Shift-S (open Advanced Search
        form) shortcut, 218
currencies, converting, 108–112
Currency Converter (Yahoo!
        Finance), 108–112

D
Dashboard (Macintosh), 161
databases
    shared, 253
    TV show, 183
Date field (Yahoo! Calendar), 236
date keyword, 44
Date::Manip module, 132
Daypop weblog search, 74
debugging, FAQs for, xix
Decliners link (Yahoo! Buzz), 57
define shortcut, 8
del.icio.us bookmark manager, 73, 271
<description> tag
    HTML and, 433, 434
    RSS format, 395, 436
desktop
    random Mac background, 364–366
    random Windows desktop, 358–363
digests, 255
directions, location, 157–158
directories, 82
directory search (see Yahoo! Directory)
discussion lists, 252
Display Bmp setting (Yahoo!
        Messenger), 279
Display Name setting (Yahoo!
        Messenger), 279
distribution lists, 252
<div> tag, 130, 383, 418
documents
    fromtitle keyword, 45
    search results and, 3, 4
domains, blocking, 224
Donamraju, Ravi, 72
.done variable, 119
Drafts folder, 221, 225
driving directions, 210
duration keyword, 44

E

eavesdropping, 230
Eclipse environment, 344, 347
EclipseME plug-in, 344
Edit Web Query dialog box, 105
editorial cartoons, 140
education! property shortcut, 10
email
    adding contacts manually, 242–243
    alerts, 48, 211–212
    archiving group, 256–258
    creating macros, 224–228
    creating TV watch lists, 191
    displaying on web sites, 435–439
    enclosures and, 411
    exporting address books, 244
    favorite TV listings, 184
    group collaboration, 252–256
    importing listings into address
        book, 336–343
    invitation service, 237
    long URLs and, 63
    managing, 220–224
    movie showtimes, 169
    one-click access, 46
    reading in one place, 228–232
    reading in preferred client, 233–235
    Save and Share link, 201
    sending photos to Flickr, 288
    shortcuts for, 218
    stock updates, 97–101
    Yahoo! Alerts, 91
    Yahoo! Mobile and, 209
    (see also Yahoo! Mail)
Email field (Yahoo! Address Book), 242
emoticons, 273, 276
emotions, avatars and, 275–276
enclosures, 411
encryption, 97, 230
entertainment news, 168
equals sign (=), 108
error code 500, xix
escape( ) function, 120, 228
Event Type field (Yahoo!
        Calendar), 236
events
    adding, 236–240
    canceling, 239
    privacy setting, 241
    (see also calendars)

Everything Yahoo!, 70
Excel (Microsoft)
    Buzz Game, 58–62
    downloading financial
        data, 102–108
    importing listings into, 348–353
    Slurp program and, 402
exclamation point (!), 9, 217
EXIF tags, 435
exporting
    address book, 244
    contacts, 247
    searches to spreadsheets, 349–350
    web site lists, 265
Extensible Stylesheet Language
        (XSL), 314
external mail accounts
    adding, 230, 231
    editing, 231, 232

F

fact-checking, 163–167
facts shortcut, 8
fair use, 37
Fandango, 169
fare trackers, 139, 213
feed( ) method, 340
feed URLs
    adding, 146, 148
    context menus and, 149
    defined, 137
    finding, 144–145
    messages on web sites, 435, 438
Feed Validator, 416
files, sharing, 253
filesize keyword, 44
Filo, David, xiii, 81
filters
    adult content, 15, 16
    external accounts and, 232
    managing email, 220–224
    spiders and, 81
finance! property shortcut, 10
financial markets, tracking, 91, 92–97
FIND function, 108
Fire application, 283
Firefox browser
    adding Yahoo! Search types, 53–55
    Clear Recent Searches option, 52
    cookie settings, 67

Firefox browser (*continued*)
    desktop pictures, 359
    getting related terms instantly, 386
    Greasemonkey plug-in, 31–34,
        218–220
    importing bookmarks from, 123
    keyboard shortcuts, 218–220
    pop-up windows and, 50
    property shortcuts, 10
    search box, 51
    searchplugins directory, 54
    View Source feature, 145
    Yahoo! ID and, 12
    Yahoo! Toolbar, 47
first party, 67
FishHoo! fishing search engine, 89
Flash plug-in
    avatars, 274
    Flickr badges, 430
    memory games, 369
    photo slideshow, 290
Flickr address, 291
Flickr badges, 291, 429–432
Flickr photo-sharing service
    adding APIs to blogs, 271, 272
    email subject lines, 222
    feeding photos to web sites, 428–435
    mobile site, 281
    overview, 73
    posting photos to blogs, 421–428
    storing/sharing photos, 285–293
    tag maps, 202
    web services and, 296, 299
    weblogs and, 268
    yLinkback bookmark, 335
folder class (CSS), 130
.folder variable, 119
folders
    external mail accounts, 231
    managing email, 220–224
    QuickBuilder tool and, 243
    shared, 25, 27, 29
    Startup, 363
    viewing, 218
follow_link function, 190
fonts
    My Yahoo! page, 143
    tag maps, 379
    Yahoo! Music Engine, 202, 203
<form> tag, 418

format method, 391
formats
    address books, 244
    date, 185
    Yahoo! Advanced Search, 18
    Yahoo! Video Search, 43
Foster, Marcus, 277
fromsite keyword, 45
fromtitle keyword, 45
fromtld keyword, 44
Furl, 74
FUSE vision, xiii

G

games
    memory, 369
    property shortcut, 10
    Trillian program, 284
    Yahoo! Mobile and, 209
    yReplacer, 369–373
games! property shortcut, 10
garbage characters, 63
Geocoder web service, 247, 251
geocoding, 247–252
geoRSS, 396
get( ) method, 340
GET request, 337, 377
Getopt::Long module, 257
Getopt::Simple module, 351
getUsersBlogs method, 269, 272
Gift Finder (Yahoo! Shopping), 198
GNS database, 251
Google News, 71
Google search engine
    Firefox and, 51, 53
    gvcard and, 336, 339
    link counts, 86–90
    Open Directory Project, 81, 88, 89
    Yahoo! Finance and, 93
    Yahoo! Search and, 34–37
gossip, TV-related, 183
graphical user interface (GUI), 323, 324
graphs, spotting trends with, 61–62
Gray's Anatomy of the Human
    Body, 164
Greasemonkey plug-in (Firefox), 31–34,
    218–220
greater-than sign (>), 44
Grokker service, 327–332

groups
    archiving messages, 256–258
    collaborating in, 252–256
    creating, 255–256
    displaying email, 435–439
    Flickr community, 292
    joining, 253–255
    one-click access, 46
    RSS feeds, 291
    sharing information, 252–253
GUI (graphical user interface), 323, 324
gvcard, 336–343

H

hackers, xv, 11
hacks, xv, xvi–xvii
Hall, David, 43
<head> tag, 145, 385, 405
health news, 213
health property, 92
height keyword
    Flickr, 271
    random desktop pictures, 359, 366
    video searches, 44
help shortcut, 218
Hemenway, Kevin, 83–86, 86–90,
        256–258
Herren, John, 379
Hitchcock, Alfred, 174
Home Information field (Yahoo!
        Address Book), 242
horoscopes, 92, 213
hostname: keyword, 6
hotels shortcut, 9
Hsiung, Ernie, 72
HTML
    adding web site presence, 408
    ColdFusion and, 311
    email format, 255
    feed URLs and, 145
    Flickr and, 424, 430, 430–432
    hiding portions of web sites, 407
    mash-up images, 368
    screen scraping and, 184, 294
    spelling words with images, 354
    vCards, 337, 341
    XSLT stylesheets and, 314–316
    YME and, 203
    Y!Q and, 417
HTML::Entities module, 257

HTML::HeadParser module, 257
HTML::LinkExtor module, 87
HTML::TableExtract module, 179
HTML::TokeParser module, 257
htmlUrl attribute, 124
htpasswd tool, 403
http:// prefix, 399
HTTP protocol
    basic authentication, 403
    403 "forbidden" error, 297
    getting related terms instantly, 383
    Perl and, 364
    REST service and, 337
    web services and, 295
hyperlinks, 373
hypermail program, 258

I

IBM MIDlet manager, 347
iChat (Apple), 282
icons
    "Add to My Yahoo!", 148
    desktop backgrounds and, 359
    generic Yahoo!, 279, 281
    Google, 51
    monitoring traffic conditions, 161
    NEW!, 83
    new window link, 3
    newspaper, 154
    padlock, 12
    pencil, 120
    personal buddy, 430
    PICK!, 82, 83
    ringing bell, 212
    sunglasses, 83
    XML, 144, 149, 435
    Y!, 154
    yellow folder, 27
ICQ, 282
<iframe> element, 371, 372
IIS (Internet Information Server), 403
images (see Yahoo! Image)
Image::Size module, 269, 271
IMAP (Internet Message Access
        Protocol), 230
<img> tag, 367
Import Data dialog box, 103
Important Dates field (Yahoo! Address
        Book), 243

importing
    addresses, 241
    from applications, 244
    blogrolls, 264–267
    bookmarks, 122–124
    contacts, 243–246
    listings into Excel, 348–353
    web site lists, 265
    Yahoo! Local listings into address
        book, 336–343
IMSmarter.com, 336
Inbox folder, 221, 223
indexes, 86, 399, 402
innerHTML property, 383
installation
    bookmarklets, 120
    Intellisync for Yahoo!, 245
    pYsearch library, 305, 306
    Trillian program, 283–284
    Yahoo! Local Traffic widget, 162
    Yahoo! Toolbar, 47–48
    YPOPs!, 234–235
instant messenger
    avatars, 213, 273–276
    functionality, 408–411
    gvcard and, 336
    Trillian, 282–285
    Yahoo! Alerts, 91, 212, 213
insurance property, 92
Intellisync for Yahoo!, 245–246
Internal Server Error, xix
Internet
    emoticons, 273
    group collaboration, 252–256
Internet Explorer browser
    adding RSS feeds, 149–151
    cookie settings, 67
    desktop pictures, 359
    getting related terms instantly, 386
    importing bookmarks from, 122
    My Yahoo! Ticker, 152–155
    pop-up windows and, 50
    search bar, 125, 127
    SmartSort tool, 199
    Yahoo! Mobile and, 207
    Yahoo! Toolbar, 47, 52
Internet Information Server (IIS), 403
Internet Message Access Protocol
        (IMAP), 230
intitle: keyword, 7
inurl: keyword, 7
investment-related calculators, 114

investments, tracking, 92–97
invitations
    Yahoo! 360 and, 261, 263, 264
    Yahoo! Calendar, 237, 239
Invitations field (Yahoo! Calendar), 237
IonZoft, Inc., 380
iPods, 411
<item> tag, 412, 436

J

J2ME (Java 2, Micro Edition), 343
Java Developer Kit (JDK), 318
Java language
    creating MIDlets, 343–348
    web services, 317–321
JavaScript
    context menus and, 149
    Flickr badges, 430–432
    getting related terms, 382–387
    keyboard shortcuts, 219
    YME and, 203
    Y!Q library, 417
JDK (Java Developer Kit), 318
job openings, 139
jobs property, 92
JPEG format, 260, 359
.jpg extension, 426

K

Kennedy, Ryan, 317–321
keywords
    adding links, 373–378
    creating TV watch lists, 189
    desktop background searches, 359
    indexes and, 399
    Perl example, 301–302
    quotation marks, 302
    Search Meta Words, 6–7
    searches using, 5, 7
    tags as, 195, 379
    tracking trends, 131
    Yahoo! Video Search, 44–46
Kinja, 122

L

Langreiter, Christian, 36
language parameter, 298
languages
    tracking, 16
    translating, 20–24

Launchcast (Yahoo!), 284
LDIF (Lightweight Directory
        Interchange Format), 244
LEFT function, 108
LEN function, 108
Lenssen, Philipp, 353–357, 373–378
Lerdorf, Rasmus, 367
less-than sign (<), 44
license parameter, 298
licensing, Creative Commons
        and, 37–41
life insurance calculators, 117
Lightweight Directory Interchange
        Format (LDIF), 244
link class (CSS), 130
link count, 86
link: keyword, 6, 332
<link> tag
        RSS format, 395, 415, 436
        photo titles, 433
linkbacks, 332–336
linkdomain: keyword, 6
links
        adding automatically, 373–378
        blogrolls and, 263
        context menus and, 149
        counting, 86–90
        Decliners, 57
        del.icio.us service, 73
        finding to web sites, 332–336
        Flickr community, 292
        garbage characters and, 63
        importing blogrolls, 264–267
        movie showtimes and, 169
        My Favorites, 274
        My Web and, 25
        OPML and, 123
        portal spiders and, 75
        publishing, 128–130
        Save and Share, 201
        saving, 25
        searches and, 2
        Set Alert, 212
        sharing, 253
        Twingine site and, 36
        URL trimming services and, 64
        Yahoo! Mobile, 207
Linux environment
        Password Gorilla, 11
        publishing links, 130
        YPOPs! software, 234
listFolders function, 29

listUrls function, 29
LiveJournal, 422
loans property, 92
Location field (Yahoo! Calendar), 236
logos, 420
lookup module, 341
lookup.py module, 339
lottery property, 92
lottery results, 139
Lotus Organizer, 245
lp variable, 23, 24
Ludicorp, 286
LWP::Simple module
        adding APIs to blogs, 268
        comparing search terms, 389
        displaying messages on sites, 437
        emailing listings, 185
        Flickr feeds, 433
        geocoding and, 247
        graphing markets, 61
        importing listings into Excel, 351
        Mac desktop images, 364
        stock update email, 99
        tracking media trends, 132
        viewing movie lists, 179
        web services and, 300
        Yahoo! API requests and, 315
LWP::UserAgent module, 257

M

m variable, 409
Mac::AppleScript module, 364
Macintosh environment
        Dashboard, 161
        Fire application, 283
        Password Gorilla, 11
        random desktop
                background, 364–366
        uploading photos, 287
        web queries, 102
        Yahoo! Messenger, 277
        YPOPs! software, 234
Macromedia Flash Player, 289
Macromedia Flash plug-in (see Flash
        plug-in)
macros, Yahoo! Mail, 224–228
mag variable, 162
mail (see email)
mail accounts, external
        adding, 230, 231
        editing, 231, 232

mail! shortcut, 10, 217
Mailbox link, 264
Maildir format, 258
mailing lists, 252, 256–258
Make TinyURL! button, 64
Manila, 422
mapping
    contacts, 247–252
    locations, 157–158
    trip itineraries, 195
    work addresses, 251
maps
    Grokker, 328, 329, 331
    plotting points, 392–397
    web services and, 298
Maps API, 299
Maron, Mikel, 247–252
mash-ups, 367–369
mb2md program (Python), 258
mb2md.pl program (Perl), 258
mbox format, 256, 258
McKenzie, Gavin F., 324
McManus, Jeffrey, 72
media RSS, 411–417
<media:adult> tag, 416
<media:category> tag, 413
<media:content> tag, 412, 416
<media:credit> tag, 413
<media:group> tag, 412
<media:player> tag, 413
<media:text> tag, 413
<media:thumbnail> tag, 413
memory games, 369
message boards, 183
message filters, 222–223
messages (see email)
Messenger ID field (Yahoo! Address
        Book), 242
meta keywords, 4, 399
meta tags, 405
metadata, 337, 412
MetaWeblogAPI, 268, 269, 423
Microsoft Excel (see Excel)
Microsoft IIS, 403
Microsoft MSN Messenger, 282
Microsoft Outlook, 244, 245
Microsoft Windows Script, 308, 310
Microsoft XML Parser, 308, 310
MIDlet, 343–348

MIDP (Mobile Information Device
        Profile) specification, 343
<MimeType> tag, 300
minsev variable, 162
minus sign (–), 5, 7
Missing Children Alerts, 213
mobile devices (see cell phones; PDAs;
        Yahoo! Mobile)
Mobile Information Device Profile
        (MIDP) specification, 343
MODE text link, 12
<ModificationDate> tag, 300
modules
    CPAN repository, 269, 294, 300,
        436
    moving, 141–142
    My Yahoo! Ticker and, 153
    overview, 138–141
moods, representing, 275–276
Morris, Sheila, 41
mortgage-related calculators, 116
Movable Type, 422
movies
    finding and rating, 167–174
    showtimes for, 139, 168, 168–170,
        174–177
    viewing lists on cell
        phones, 178–182
    web services and, 295
movies! shortcut, 9, 167
Mozilla, 244
    (see also Firefox browser)
MSN Messenger (Microsoft), 282
music collection, visualizing, 201–206
mutual funds, 92–97, 115
My Favorites link, 274
My Web service
    overview, 25–31
    search results and, 4
    web services and, 296
My Yahoo!
    adding content, 49
    context menus and, 149
    favorite channels, 184
    finding bookmarks, 118
    Flickr and, 432
    navigation bar and, 2
    personalizing, 91, 137–143
    product feeds, 199
    RSS feeds, 4, 149–151, 401

My Yahoo! (*continued*)
  tracking information, 136
  tracking news about Yahoo!, 68
  tracking portfolios, 96
  tracking sites, 143–148
  Yahoo! Bookmarks and, 125
  Yahoo! Finance RSS feed and, 94
My Yahoo! Ticker, 151–155

N

n variable, 20
Nadig, Deepak, 343–348
Name field (Yahoo! Address Book), 242
.name variable, 119
namespaces, 413
navigation bar, 2
Neilsen ratings, 183
Netscape browser
  importing bookmarks from, 123
  LDIF format, 244
  publishing links, 128
NET::SMTP module, 99, 185
NEW! icon, 83
New Web Query dialog box, 102, 103
New Window box, 3, 15
newline character, 248
newPost method, 269, 271
news
  breaking, 213
  entertainment, 168
  health, 213
  monitoring, 91, 135–137
  photo modules, 140
  TV-related, 183
  visualizing topics, 379–382
news! property shortcut, 10
news search (see Yahoo! News)
newspaper icon, 154
newsreaders
  defined, 136
  OPML and, 265
  product feeds, 199
  RSS and, 433
  subscribing to, 4
next! property shortcut, 10
nicknames, 243
Nielsen/Netratings, 398
Nilsen, Asgeir S., 35
Notepad, 217, 309

Notes field
  Yahoo! Address Book, 243
  Yahoo! Calendar, 236
Number::Format module, 389

O

Ogasawara, Todd, 25–31, 163–167,
    207–211
Online Presence Indicator, 408
Open Directory Project (Google), 81,
    88, 89
OPML Link Publisher, 123, 124
OPML (Outline Processor Markup
    Language)
  applications, 123, 124
  blogrolls and, 265, 267
  TagCloud and, 381
opting out (cookies), 66
OR keyword, 5, 7
O'Reilly Media, Inc., 58
Organizr tool (Flickr), 289–290
Outline Processor Markup Language
    (see OPML)
<outline> tag, 267
Outlook Express, 245
Outlook (Microsoft), 244, 245
Oxford Shakespeare, 164

P

package trackers, 139
padlock icon, 12, 13
PageRank (Google), 34
pagers, alerts on, 212
Palm Desktop, 244
Parameters dialog box, 106
parentheses (( )), 6, 112
parse( ) function, 438
Password Gorilla program, 11
Password Safe program, 11
passwords
  cookies and, 13
  Flickr badges and, 430
  managing, 11
  resetting, 11
  in scripts, 265
  server authentication, 403
  weblogs and, 423
  Yahoo! ID and, 11
  Yahoo! Mobile and, 207

Patel, Rikul, 349
PDAs (personal digital assistants)
    ABA format, 244
    content tabs, 281
    vCard and, 336
    web cookies, 207
    Yahoo! Lite, 207
pencil icon, 120
people, finding, 159–160
Perl language
    comparing search terms, 389–392
    CSV files and, 350
    Flickr feeds, 433–434
    programming Yahoo!, 300–302
    random Mac desktop, 364–366
    REST service and, 317
    XSLT stylesheets, 314–316
personal address book (see address
            book)
personal digital assistants (see PDAs)
pets property, 92
Phoenix, Tom, xix
phone books, 155–160
Phone field (Yahoo! Calendar), 237
Phone Numbers field (Yahoo! Address
            Book), 242
photographs, 140
photos
    content tabs, 281
    desktop background, 358
    feeding to web sites, 428–435
    posting to blogs, 421–428
    profiles and, 259
    sharing, 253
    spelling words with images, 353
    storing and sharing, 285–293
    Yahoo! 360 and, 268
photostream (Flickr), 288, 291
PHP language
    adding links automatically, 375
    REST service and, 317
    Web of Letters, 353, 354
    web services and, 302–304
    Yahoo! Buzz Demo, 367
phrases in searches, 5, 7
PICK! icon, 82, 83
Picks of the Day (Yahoo!), 83
Pilgrim, Mark, 31–34
Pillai, Premshree, 73, 321–323, 323–326

pipe
    defined, xvii
    to files, 190
    to text files, 134, 167
pixels
    desktop background, 358, 366
    image sizes and, 426
    spelling words with images, 357
    videos and, 44
plug-ins
    EclipseME, 344
    Flash, 274, 290, 369, 430
    Greasemonkey, 31–34, 218–220
    Quicktime, 164
    TraxStats, 206
    YME and, 203–206
plus sign (+), 49
Pocket PCs, 245
podcasting, 411
polls, 253
POP (Post Office Protocol)
    configuring email clients, 235
    external mail accounts and, 230, 232
    Yahoo! Mail Plus and, 233
    Yahoo! Mobile and, 209
pop-up windows, 50
portal spiders, 74–81
portfolios, 94–97
Post Office Protocol (see POP)
POST request, 377
presence, adding to web sites, 408–411
printing, WML content, 181
privacy
    Acxiom on, 159
    cookies and, 65
    event setting, 241
    Flickr member categories and, 292
    third parties and, 66
    uploaded photos, 287
    web sites and, 402–405
    Yahoo! 360 profiles, 259
    Yahoo! Mail and, 230
    Yahoo! Toolbar, 51–52
product comparison, 196, 199–200
profiles, creating, 259–261
properties
    exclamation point and, 217
    My Yahoo! Ticker and, 155
    for services, 91
    shortcuts for, 9

<pubDate> tag, 436
publishing Yahoo! Bookmarks, 128–130
pYsearch library (Python), 305–307
Python language
    gvcard and, 336, 338
    web services, 305–307

Q

queries
    assembling advanced, 7, 17–20
    definition links, 2
    downloading financial
        data, 102–108
    fine-tuning, 5–7
    link:, 332
    parameters in, 298
    result count, 317
    spelling words with images, 353
    spotting trends in, 55–58
    (see also searches)
query parameter, 298
Quick Add Event form, 239
QuickBuilder tool (Yahoo! Mail), 243
Quicktime plug-in (Apple), 164
quotation marks (" ")
    keywords and, 302
    phrases in, 190
    Python and, 307
    search phrases, 5
quote shortcut, 9

R

ranking
    Google and, 34
    Yahoo! and, 34
ratings
    about businesses, 159, 352, 353
    merchant, 200
    about movies, 173
    Neilsen, 183
real estate property, 92
Really Simple Syndication
    (RSS), 435–439
REBOL (Relative Expression-based
    Object Language), 323–326
reference! shortcut, 163
references, assembling, 163–167
.reg files, 150

Relative Expression-based Object
    Language (REBOL), 323–326
Reminders field (Yahoo! Calendar), 237
Repeating Event field (Yahoo!
    Calendar), 237
requests
    adding links automatically, 377
    daily limits, 297
    LWP::Simple module, 315
    making, 298–299
    Perl and, 364
    REST service, 337
research, 163–167
ResearchBuzz: Yahoo weblog, 71
Resig, John, 162
responses
    Perl and, 364
    REST service, 337
    Ruby script, 322–323
    totalResultsAvailable attribute, 317
    web services and, 299, 300
REST service
    accessing Yahoo! Local Search, 343
    example, 337
    geocoding and, 251
    scripting languages and, 317
    Yahoo! Local, 337
    Yahoo! Web Services and, 295
result count, 2, 317
<Result> tag, 300
Results page, 3, 15
results parameter, 298
<ResultSet> tag, 300, 317
Rich Site Summary (see RSS feed)
Ries, Eric, 336–343
RIGHT function, 108
ringing bell icon, 212
robots
    captcha forms and, 256
    Slurp program, 402, 404–405
robots.txt file, 404, 405
Roger, Ian C., 73
Roget's Thesaurus, 164
RSS auto-discovery, 145
RSS feed
    adding pages to, 28
    adding with right-click, 149–151
    Buzz Log, 57
    Flickr and, 432–434
    grassroot sources, 73–74

RSS feed (*continued*)
  listing sites, 401
  media syndication, 411–417
  messages on sites, 435–439
  monitoring traffic conditions, 162
  My Yahoo! and, 49
  My Yahoo! Ticker, 153
  OPML and, 265
  photostreams, 291
  search results and, 4
  subscribing to movie showtimes, 177
  TagCloud and, 381
  tracking news about Yahoo!, 68
  tracking sites, 143–148
  web services and, 296
  Yahoo! Directory, 83
  Yahoo! employee weblogs, 71–73
  Yahoo! Finance, 94
  Yahoo! information, 68–71
  Yahoo! Shopping, 199
.rss files, 176
RSS readers
  monitoring traffic conditions, 163
  monitoring Yahoo! News, 135–137
  subscribing to movie
     showtimes, 174–177
  web services and, 299
RSS (Really Simple
     Syndication), 435–439
  (see also RSS feed)
Ruby library, 321–323

S

SafeSearch Filter, 15, 16
Save and Share link (Yahoo!
     Shopping), 200–201
Save As dialog box, 105
Save link, 4, 26
savings-related calculators, 114
SAX XML Parser, 324, 326
schedules (see calendars)
school financing calculators, 116
Schwartz, Randal L., xix
scores shortcut, 9
screen resolution, 358
screen scraping
  HTML and, 184
  movie lists on cell phones, 179–181
  movie schedules, 174–177

Perl modules and, 294
personalized TV lists, 184–187
tracking media trends, 131
Yahoo! Reference and, 165
<script> tag, 431
search bars, 125
Search Engine Watch Blog, 71
search engines
  comparing results, 34–37
  Firefox and, 53
  link counts, 86–90
  (see also specific search engines)
Search History, 25, 26
Search Meta Words, 6–7
<SEARCH> tag, 54
Searchblog (John Battelle), 71
searches
  adding search types to
     Firefox, 53–55
  advanced queries, 7, 17–20
  advertiser cookies and, 65–68
  browsing Yahoo! Directory, 81–83
  building specialty, 54
  comparing search engines, 34–37
  comparing terms, 387–392
  creating Yahoo! ID, 10–14
  desktop background, 358, 359
  exporting to spreadsheets, 349–350
  finding hot technologies, 58–62
  finding video clips, 41–46
  fine-tuning queries, 5–7
  getting related terms, 382–387
  grouping results, 327–332
  illustrating web sites, 369–373
  limiting by time, 131
  link:, 332
  link counts, 86–90
  news about Yahoo!, 68–74
  overview, 1–5
  portal spiders and, 74–81
  prefetching results, 31–34
  quick, 51
  reusing content legally, 37–41
  setting preferences, 14–17
  shortcuts for, 7–10
  shortening URLs, 62–65
  spotting trends in, 55–58
  streamlining browsing, 46–52
  tracking Yahoo! additions, 83–86
  translating languages, 20–24

searches (*continued*)
  web services and, 295
  of web sites, 406–407
  in weblogs, 73, 74
  Yahoo! Mobile and, 209
  Yahoo! Shopping, 197
  (see also contextual searches)
searchplugins directory (Firefox), 54
security
  email and, 101
  Yahoo! Finance pages, 97
  Yahoo! ID, 12
  Yahoo! Mobile and, 207
Select Data Source dialog box, 106
semicolon (;), 324
Sent folder, 221
server authentication, 403, 405
services
  adding RSS feeds, 149–151
  alerts, 211–215
  bookmarks, 118–122
  bookmarks in sidebars, 124–127
  building news crawlers, 151–155
  building stock update email, 97–101
  calculators, 112–117
  converting currencies, 108–112
  creating TV watch list, 188–191
  developing trip itineraries, 191–195
  downloading financial
       data, 102–108
  finding and rating movies, 167–174
  importing bookmarks, 122–124
  monitoring commute, 160–163
  monitoring news, 135–137
  movie lists on cell phones, 178–182
  overview, 91
  personalizing My Yahoo!, 137–143
  planning TV viewing, 182–188
  publishing bookmarks, 128–130
  research and fact-checking, 163–167
  shopping online, 196–201
  subscribing to movie
       showtimes, 174–177
  telephone directory, 155–160
  tracking investments, 92–97
  tracking sites, 143–148
  tracking trends, 130–135
  visualizing music
       collection, 201–206
  Yahoo! Mobile, 207–211

sets, photo, 290
Shakespeare, William, 164
shared folders, 25, 27, 29
Sharing Option field (Yahoo!
       Calendar), 237
shopping online, 196–201
  (see also Yahoo! Shopping)
shorl.com, 64
Short Message Service (SMS)
       messages, 158, 211
shortcuts
  keyboard, 218–220
  properties, 9
  saving time with, 7–10
  search results and, 3
  Yahoo! Search forms, 112
Show Tools link (Grokker), 331
showCopyable function, 376
showImage function, 356
showtimes, movie
  finding, 168–170
  subscribing to, 174–177
  web services and, 295
  Yahoo! Movies module, 139, 168
showtimes shortcut, 9
sidebars, bookmarks in, 124–127
Sign Out button, 51
Sign Out link, 13
Silverstein, Jason B., 125
SimpleXML parser, 303, 304
site: keyword
  defined, 45
  opting out of cookies, 66
  overview, 6
  searching sites, 406, 407
siteRestriction tag, 419
Slurp program, 402, 403, 404–405
small business property, 92
Smartphone devices, 208
SmartSort tool (Yahoo! Shopping), 198,
       199
SMS (Short Message Service)
       messages, 158, 211
snowfall, 213
soap operas, 183
SOAP::Lite module, 87, 268
sorting
  with filters, 222–223
  photos, 288–290
spam, 221, 223–224

SpamGuard, 223
spiders, portal, 74–81
sports, alerts and, 214
sports property, 92
sports! property shortcut, 10
spreadsheets, 348–353
SSL, Yahoo! Mail and, 230
start parameter, 298
Startup folder, 363
STDOUT (standard output), 391
stocks
    alerts, 214
    getting quotes, 9, 46
    looking up symbols, 95
    My Yahoo! Ticker and, 154
    price file, 60
    tracking, 92–97
    updates via email, 97–101
    web queries for, 105–106
    Yahoo! Buzz Game, 58
strReqURL variable, 362
<style> tag, 431
stylesheets
    CSS, 357
    XSL, 314
    XSLT, 314–316
    Y!Q, 420
subject variable, 226
<Summary> tag, 300
Sun Java Wireless Toolkit, 344
sunglasses icon, 83
switch-case clause, 356
synchronization, email, 245–246
syndication, 412–417, 433

T

t variable, 409, 410
<table> tag, 431
tag maps, 202, 379
TagCloud, 379–382
tags
    defined, 379
    keywords and, 195
    meta, 405
    photo, 288
    RSS feeds, 291
    vCard, 337
tasks, 239
taxes property, 92
tax-related calculators, 117

Taylor, Alan, 332–336, 369–373
Technorati weblog search, 74
telephone directory, 155–160
television
    creating watch list, 188–191
    planning viewing, 182–188
    schedule for, 139
    web services and, 295
templates
    automating email, 225
    ColdFusion and, 311
    Flickr and, 424
    gvcard, 342
    XSLT stylesheets, 314
    Y!Q search form and, 417
temporary addresses, 224
Term Extraction (Yahoo!), 374
text analysis, 295
text attribute, 124
<textarea> tag, 368, 376
Text::CSV module, 248
text/vnd.wap.wml content type, 181
text/xml content type, 181
text/x-vcard MIME type, 343
theaters (see movies)
themes
    color, 142
    desktop background, 362
Third Party and Affiliate Cookies on
        Yahoo! page, 65
thumbnails
    desktop pictures, 358
    image sizes, 426
    Media RSS and, 413
    search results and, 330
    Yahoo! 360 profiles, 260
Thunderbird email client (Mozilla), 244
ticker symbols, 105–106
tickets property, 92
Time field (Yahoo! Calendar), 236
time in shortcut, 112
TinyURL.com, 64
title attribute, 124, 267
Title field (Yahoo! Calendar), 236
title: keyword, 45
<title> tag
    RSS format, 395, 415, 436
    document titles, 3
    photo titles, 433
    web search results, 300
tld keyword, 44

to variable, 226
toAttribute function, 354
Tobias, Andrew, 92
Top Movers Charts, 56
top-level domain (tld), 44
totalResultsAvailable attribute/tag, 317,
    389
traffic conditions, monitoring, 160–163
trailers, movie, 168
Translate button (Yahoo! Toolbar), 22
translating languages, 20–24
Trash folder, 221, 234
travel plans, 191–195
travel! shortcut, 191
TraxStats, 206
trends
    spotting in queries, 55–58
    technology, 58–62
    tracking, 84, 130–135, 277
Trillian program, 282–285
trip itineraries, 191–195
tt variable, 23
TV Guide, 182
Twingine site, 35, 36
type parameter, 298
TypePad, 268, 422

U

u variable, 409
Udell, Jon, 87
underscore (_), 426
Unix environment, 177
Unofficial Yahoo! Weblog, 70
Uppal, Siddharth, 367
URI::Escape module, 247, 389
url attribute, 124
URL code, 226, 426, 427
url: keyword, 7
<Url> tag, 300
.url variable, 119
URLs
    adding web site presence, 409
    advanced searches, 18–20
    API Endpoint, 272, 423
    context menus and, 149
    Creative Commons license page, 40
    Currency Converter and, 109
    desktop background, 358
    Flickr and, 291, 424–428

    garbage characters, 63
    gvcard and, 338
    hiding portions of web sites, 407
    Java and, 318
    keyboard shortcuts and, 220
    link counts, 86–90
    link: keyword and, 6
    looking up stocks, 60
    monitoring traffic conditions, 162
    movie lists on cell phones, 178, 181
    movie showtimes, 169, 174
    personalized TV listings, 185
    plotting map points, 396
    portal spiders and, 75
    public folders, 27
    search results and, 4
    shortening, 62–65
    sites linking to, 332
    TagCloud and, 381
    translation bookmarklet, 23
    trimming services, 64
    trip itineraries, 191
    web queries and, 102
    Yahoo! Buzz Log, 58
    Yahoo! Calendar, 241
    Yahoo! Finance quote page, 105
    Yahoo! Mail, 225–226, 228
    Yahoo! property shortcuts, 10
    Yahoo! Web Services, 295, 298
    (see also feed URLs)
urltext variable, 23

V

V1 parameter (Yahoo! Search), 298
va search variable, 18, 132
VALUE function, 108
variables
    advanced search, 18–20
    API, 205
    Currency Converter querystring, 109
    monitoring traffic conditions, 162
    translation bookmarklet, 23
    Yahoo! Bookmarks querystring, 119
    Yahoo! Mail URLs, 226
VBScript language
    illustrating web sites, 371
    syndicating media, 414
    web services and, 308–310
vCard standard, 336–343

.vcf file extension, 343
vd search variable, 19
ve search variable, 18
vf search variable, 19, 20
video search! shortcut, 41
videos (see Yahoo! Video)
View Source feature (Firefox), 145
Visual Basic language, 308
VLOOKUP function, 106, 108
vo search variable, 18
void( ) operator, 120
vp search variable, 18
vs search variable, 19

W

wallpaper (see desktop)
Wang, Larry, 206
weather information, 139, 154, 213,
        214
weather property, 92
weather shortcut, 9
Web Beacons, 66
web browsers (see browsers)
Web of Letters, 353–357
web pages
    categories and, 4
    content tabs and, 279
    context menus and, 149
    fromsite keyword, 45
    getting related terms, 382–387
    querying links, 332
    replacing words with
            images, 369–373
    saving copies, 25
    web queries and, 102
    Yahoo! Bookmarks and, 125
    Yahoo! Web Services and, 29
    YME and, 203
Web Query (Excel), 102–108
Web results, 3
web services
    accessing Yahoo! Local, 337
    ColdFusion platform, 311–313
    comparing search terms, 387–392
    creating MIDlets, 343–348
    defined, 294
    finding links to web sites, 332–336
    importing listings into
            Excel, 348–353

Java language and, 317–321
    mash-up images, 367–369
    overview, 295–300
    Perl language and, 300–302
    PHP language and, 302–304
    plotting maps, 392–397
    Python language, 305–307
    random Windows desktop, 358–363
    REBOL and, 323–326
    REST service and, 337
    Ruby library, 321–323
    VBScript language and, 308–310
    XSLT stylesheets and, 314–316
web sites
    adding bookmarks, 118–122
    adding modules from, 141
    blogrolls and, 263
    displaying email, 435–439
    feed URLs, 144
    feeding photos to, 428–435
    finding links, 332–336
    getting listed, 83
    grassroot sources, 73–74
    Grokker maps and, 332
    hiding portions, 402–405
    illustrating, 369–373
    importing lists, 265
    listing, 398–401
    searching, 406–407
    tracking with RSS feeds, 143–148
    Yahoo! employee weblogs, 71–73
    Yahoo! information, 68–71
    Yahoo! Messenger and, 408–411
    Y!Q searches, 419
weblogs
    adding APIs, 268–273
    adding contextual searches, 417–421
    Blogrolling web service, 264
    browsing, 82
    Flickr links, 336
    Flickr photos, 291
    posting photos, 421–428
    profiles and, 259
    searching, 73, 74
    starting, 261–263
    Tagcloud and, 382
    Yahoo! 360 and, 259
    Yahoo! employees, 71–73

webmastering
    adding contextual searches, 417–421
    connecting to Yahoo!
        Messenger, 408–411
    displaying email on sites, 435–439
    feeding photos to web sites, 428–435
    hiding portions of web
        sites, 402–405
    listing web sites, 398–401
    media RSS, 411–417
    posting photos to blogs, 421–428
    searching web sites, 406–407
webSearch function, 298
WebSphere Everyplace Micro
    Environment (WEME), 344
Welcome Tour buttons (Yahoo!
    Toolbar), 47
WEME (WebSphere Everyplace Micro
    Environment), 344
width keyword
    Flickr, 271
    random desktop pictures, 359, 366
    video searches, 44
wildcards, 405
Windows environment
    Intellisync for Yahoo!, 245–246
    monitoring traffic, 162–163
    My Yahoo! Ticker, 152–155
    Password Safe program, 11
    random desktop pictures, 358–363
    REBOL and, 326
    subscribing to movie showtimes, 176
    Trillian program, 283, 284
    uploading photos, 287
    VBScript, 308
    web queries, 102
    Yahoo! Avatars, 274
    Yahoo! Local Search To Excel, 349
    Yahoo! Messenger, 277
    Yahoo! Music Engine, 202
    YPOPs! software, 234, 235
Windows Registry
    content tabs, 278–281
    defined, 126, 150
    YME plug-ins, 205
Wired News, 70
WML (Wireless Markup
    Language), 178, 181
WordPress, 422

words
    avatars and, 276
    excluding in searches, 5
    search shortcuts and, 8
    spelling with images, 353–357
    swapping with images, 369–373
Work Information field (Yahoo! Address
    Book), 242
World Factbook, 164
worldKit application, 247, 251, 252
write command, 391
WSDL file (Google), 87
WWW::Mechanize module
    creating TV watch list, 189
    functionality, 269
    importing blogrolls, 265
    publishing bookmarks, 128
WWW::Yahoo::Login module
    creating TV watch list, 189
    functionality, 269
    importing blogrolls, 265
    publishing bookmarks, 128

X

XML
    adding links automatically, 377
    Buzz Game data, 60
    ColdFusion and, 311
    Flickr and, 432–434
    Java and, 317–321
    JavaScript and, 382
    OPML and, 265
    parsing responses, 299
    REST service and, 251, 295
    RSS feeds and, 144, 145, 174, 435
    SimpleXML parser, 303
    Slurp program, 402
    vCard and, 338
    web services and, 295
    Yahoo! Maps Annotation file, 392
    Yahoo! responses and, 300
    Yahoo! Search Web Services, 314
XML icons, 144, 149
XmlParse function, 311
XMLRPC::Transport::HTTP
    module, 268
XML::RSS module, 433, 436, 438
XML::RSS::SimpleGen module, 175,
    176

XML::Simple module
    comparing search terms, 389
    geocoding and, 247
    importing listings into Excel, 351
    Mac desktop images, 364
    Perl and, 300
XML::XSLT module, 315
XPath, 317–321, 377
XSL (Extensible Stylesheet
        Language), 314
XSLT (XSL Transformations), 314–316

Y

Y! icon, 154
Yahoo!
    acronym, xiii
    CSV format, 244
    mobile site, 282
    tracking additions, 83–86
    tracking news about, 68–74
    web service terms, 296–297
Yahoo! 360
    adding APIs to blogs, 268–273
    alerts, 214
    exploring social networks, 258–264
    importing blogrolls, 264–267
    product blog, 69
Yahoo! Address Book
    adding to, 159, 241–246
    mapping contacts, 247–252
    property shortcut, 10
    Trillian program and, 284
    Yahoo! Mail and, 217
    Yahoo! Mobile and, 209, 210
Yahoo! Advanced Search
    opening form, 218
    overview, 17–20
    query combinations, 7
    Yahoo! News and, 131
    Yahoo! Shopping and, 197
Yahoo! Alerts, 91, 211–215
Yahoo! Auctions, 53, 213
Yahoo! Audio, 295
Yahoo! Auto-Linker, 373–378
Yahoo! Avatars, 274
Yahoo! Bookmarks
    content tabs and, 279, 281
    importing, 25, 122–124
    one-click adding, 118–122
    opening in sidebars, 124–127
    publishing, 128–130

Yahoo! Buzz
    archives, 57
    buzz score and, 60
    content tab, 276
    spotting trends with, 55–58
    Windows Registry and, 278
Yahoo! Buzz Demo, 367
Yahoo! Buzz Game, 58–62
Yahoo! Calculators, 112–117
Yahoo! Calendar
    finding dates, 57
    managing and sharing, 235–241
    property shortcut, 10
    Trillian program and, 284
    Yahoo! Mail and, 217
    Yahoo! Mobile and, 210
    Yahoo! TV and, 188–191
Yahoo! Contextual Web
        Search, 379–382
Yahoo! Creative Commons
        Search, 37–41
Yahoo! Developer Network
    Application ID report, 297
    application list, 327
    tools, 305, 321
    web services list, 295
    Yahoo! and, 296
Yahoo! Directory
    browsing, 81–83
    calculators and, 117
    link counts, 86–90
    page categories, 4
    search links, 2
    site listings, 398–401
Yahoo! Editors
    category title and, 4
    directories and, 82
    listing sites, 401
    search trends, 57
    TV viewing, 182
Yahoo! Education, 10, 163
Yahoo! Finance
    Currency Converter, 108–112
    My Yahoo! Ticker and, 154
    overview, 69, 92–97
    property shortcut, 10
    stock updates, 97, 98
    URL for quote page, 105
    web queries, 103
    Yahoo! Alerts, 212
    Yahoo! Mobile and, 207, 209

Yahoo! First, 244
Yahoo! Games, 10, 209, 284
Yahoo! Group
    archiving messages, 256–258
    categories, 74
    displaying email, 435–439
    overview, 252–256
Yahoo! HotJobs, 139
Yahoo! ID
    accounts in use, 10
    changing email addresses, 211
    contacts and, 242
    Flickr badges and, 430
    friends list, 240
    joining groups, 255
    listing sites, 399
    My Web and, 25
    navigation bar and, 2
    removing accounts, 14
    in scripts, 265
    signing in, 12–13
    signing out, 13–14
    signing up, 10–12
    Trillian program and, 284
    trip itineraries, 192
    weblog limit, 269
    Yahoo! Mobile and, 207
    Yahoo! Toolbar and, 47
Yahoo! Image
    filtering adult content, 15
    Firefox and, 54
    illustrating web sites, 369–373
    mash-up images, 367–369
    random desktop pictures, 358–363
    REBOL and, 323–326
    search links, 2
    spelling words, 353–357
    web services and, 295
Yahoo! Instant Messenger
    Audibles feature, 285
    avatars, 213, 273–276
    functionality, 408–411
    Trillian program and, 284
    Yahoo! Alerts, 91, 212, 213
Yahoo! International Finance Center, 94
Yahoo! Jobs, 69
Yahoo! Language Tools page, 20–22
Yahoo! Lite, 207

Yahoo! Local
    cell phones and, 158
    creating MIDlets, 343–348
    Dashboard widget, 161
    importing listings, 336–343,
        348–353
    Traffic widget, 162
    trimming URLs, 63
    web services and, 295
Yahoo! Local Search To Excel
        program, 349
Yahoo! Local Web Service, 348
Yahoo! Mail
    creating macros, 224–228
    functionality, 48
    keyboard shortcuts, 218–220
    layout, 217–218
    managing, 220–224
    navigation bar and, 2
    nicknames and, 243
    property shortcut, 10
    reading in one place, 228–232
    reading in preferred client, 233–235
    Trillian program and, 284
    Yahoo! Alerts and, 211–212, 213
    Yahoo! Calendar and, 236
    Yahoo! ID and, 10
    Yahoo! Mobile and, 207, 209
Yahoo! Mail Plus, 224, 232, 233
Yahoo! Maps
    Annotation file, 392
    invitations and, 237
    monitoring routes, 160–161
    My Yahoo! Ticker, 155
    plotting points, 392–397
    web services and, 296
Yahoo! Maps Web Services, 392–397
Yahoo! Message Boards, 183
Yahoo! Messenger
    bookmarks and, 125
    connecting sites, 408–411
    content tabs, 276–282
    Yahoo! 360 and, 261
    Yahoo! Mobile and, 209
Yahoo! Mobile
    functionality, 91
    movie lists on cell phones, 181
    movie showtimes and, 169
    overview, 207–211
    search screen, 210
    weblog on, 72

Yahoo! Mobile Mail, 209
Yahoo! Movies
    finding and rating movies, 167–174
    movie showtimes, 139, 174–177
    My Movies tab, 170
    My Yahoo! Ticker and, 155
    properties shortcuts, 9
    videos and, 46
    viewing lists on cell
        phones, 178–182
    Yahoo! Mobile and, 207, 210
Yahoo! Music Engine, 201–206
Yahoo! Network, 259
Yahoo! News
    monitoring with RSS, 135–137
    overview, 68
    photo modules, 140
    property shortcut, 10
    search links, 2
    tracking trends, 130–135
    web services and, 295
    Yahoo! Alerts and, 213
    Yahoo! Buzz Demo, 367
    Yahoo! Contextual Web
        Search, 379–382
    Yahoo! Mobile and, 207, 209
Yahoo! News Tag Soup, 379–382
Yahoo! Next, 10, 70
Yahoo! Notepad, 217
Yahoo! People Search, 159
Yahoo! Photos, 140
Yahoo! Plus premium service, 209
Yahoo! Publisher's Guide to RSS, 401
Yahoo! Reference
    define shortcut, 8
    My Yahoo! Ticker and, 155
    overview, 163–167
    query definition links, 2
Yahoo! Research, 58, 70
Yahoo! Search
    area codes, 9
    calculations, 112
    comparing search terms, 387–392
    developing trip itineraries, 191
    employee weblogs, 73
    filtering adult content, 15
    finding movies, 167
    Google Search and, 34–37
    hiding portions of web
        sites, 402–405
    official weblog, 69
    prefetching results, 31–34

    result components, 2–3
    Ruby library and, 322
    search shortcuts, 7–10
    setting preferences, 14–17
    site listings, 398, 399
    translating results, 21
    V1 parameter, 298
    VBScript and, 308–310
    web services and, 295
    weblog for, 69
    Y! icon and, 154
    Yahoo! Mobile and, 209
Yahoo! Search Web Services
    ColdFusion platform and, 311–313
    comparing search terms, 387
    getting related terms instantly, 386
    Java and, 317–321
    linkbacks, 332–336
    Perl and, 300–302
    PHP and, 302–304
    Python and, 305–307
    Ruby library, 321–323
    tracking media trends, 132
    XSLT stylesheets and, 314–316
Yahoo! Shopping
    overview, 196–201
    search links, 2
    web services and, 295
    Yahoo! Alerts, 212
Yahoo! Small Business, 139
Yahoo! Sports, 10, 207, 209
Yahoo! Toolbar
    feed URLs and, 145
    functionality, 46, 48–51
    installing, 47–48
    My Web and, 25, 27
    one-click bookmarks, 118
    privacy, 51–52
    property shortcuts, 10
    translating pages, 22
Yahoo! Travel, 191–195, 212
Yahoo! TV
    overview, 182–188
    TV schedule, 139
    Yahoo! Calendar and, 188–191
Yahoo! Video
    filtering adult content, 15
    overview, 41–46
    search links, 2
    syndicating media, 412–417
    web services and, 295
Yahoo! Video Web Services, 45

Yahoo! Weather
    Trillian program and, 284
    weather information, 139
    Yahoo! Mobile and, 207, 210
Yahoo! Web Search
    fine-tuning queries, 5–7
    Firefox and, 53
    Grokker service and, 327–332
    opting out of cookies, 66
    Perl example, 301–302
    result components, 3–5
    speed of, 2
    viewing results differently, 4
    web services and, 295, 298
Yahoo! Web Services
    adding pages, 29
    applications and, 327
    background, 294
    ColdFusion platform and, 311–313
    Java language and, 317–321
    JavaScript and, 382
    official weblog, 69
    overview, 295–300
    Perl language and, 300–302
    PHP language and, 302–304
    Python and, 305–307
    REBOL and, 323–326
    Ruby library, 321–323
    weblog for, 69
    XSLT stylesheets and, 314–316

Yahoo! What's New page, 83
yahoo2mbox, 256–258
yahoo.gif file, 54
Yahooligans!, 399
YahooLocalRequest class, 339
YahooParser class, 339
yahoo-ruby API, 321, 322
Yahoo::Search module, 367
Yang, Jerry, xiii, 81
yellow pages property, 92
Yellow Pages service, 336–343
yLinkback bookmark, 335
YME (see Yahoo! Music Engine)
YPOPs! open source software, 233–235
Y!Q, 417–421
yReplacer, 369–373
YSTResultsMax tag, 419

Z

Zawodny, Jeremy, 72, 296
Zeitlin, Vadim, 256
Zip Codes
    Dashboard and, 161
    MIDlet example, 348
    Missing Children Alerts, 213
    movie showtimes, 168, 170, 174
    search shortcut, 9
    TV listings, 182, 183
    weather information, 154, 214

Colophon

Our look is the result of reader comments, our own experimentation, and feedback from distribution channels. Distinctive covers complement our distinctive approach to technical topics, breathing personality and life into potentially dry subjects.

The image on the cover of *Yahoo! Hacks* shows a pair of cowboy boots with spurs. American cowboy boots evolved from Hessians (boots with the familiar V-cut in front, worn by German soldiers who fought in the Revolution), Wellingtons (knee-high British boots), and others. They are treadless, in order for one to quickly slide the forefoot into and out of the stirrup, and have a tall heel that holds the boot in place while one is mounted. The revolving rowel used in modern spurs became popular around the fourteenth century. Earlier spurs (used throughout Europe from the time of the Etruscans, and farther east by Genghis Khan and his support staff) had a single sharp protrusion. Early Native Americans did not use spurs, preferring a sort of quirt (short-handled whip).

Unlike "down at the heel" and "slipshod," the term "well-heeled" originally referred not to footgear but to fowl: in cockfighting, it has long been used to indicate that a bird has sharp spurs (natural weapons on its legs, sometimes augmented artificially). On the American frontier, the term was used to mean one was carrying a gun; later it evolved to mean one was armed with wealth. The phrase "to earn one's spurs" traces back to chivalric tradition, when spurs were awarded in recognition of battlefield or tournament heroics.

Abby Fox was the production editor and proofreader for *Yahoo! Hacks*. Derek Di Matteo was the copyeditor. Lydia Onofrei and Marlowe Shaeffer provided production assistance. Adam Witwer and Claire Cloutier provided quality control. Lucie Haskins wrote the index.

Hanna Dyer designed the cover of this book, based on a series design by Edie Freedman. The cover image is a photograph from Getty Images. Marcia Friedman produced the cover layout with Adobe InDesign CS using Adobe's Helvetica Neue and ITC Garamond fonts.

David Futato designed the interior layout. Keith Fahlgren converted this book from Microsoft Word to FrameMaker 5.5.6 with a format conversion tool created by Erik Ray, Jason McIntosh, Neil Walls, and Mike Sierra that uses Perl and XML technologies. The text font is Linotype Birka; the heading font is Adobe Helvetica Neue Condensed; and the code font is LucasFont's TheSans Mono Condensed. The illustrations that appear in the book were produced by Robert Romano, Jessamyn Read, and Lesley Borash using Macromedia FreeHand MX and Adobe Photoshop CS. Abby Fox wrote this colophon.

Better than e-books

Buy *Yahoo! Hacks* and access the digital
edition FREE on Safari for 45 days.

Go to www.oreilly.com/go/safarienabled
and type in coupon code V8JS-AGTK-JSE6-W4K8-YKUW

Search
thousands of
top tech books

Download
whole chapters

Cut and Paste
code examples

Find
answers fast

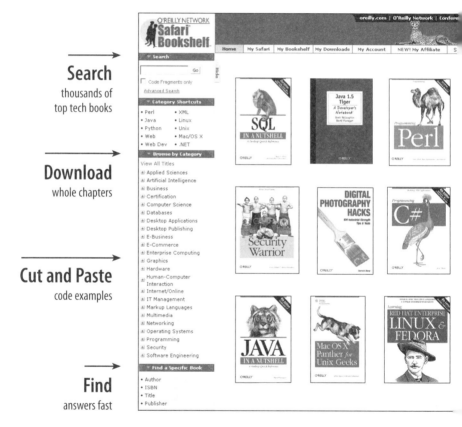

Search Safari! The premier electronic reference
library for programmers and IT professionals.

O'REILLY NETWORK
Safari Bookshelf

Addison
Wesley
Adobe Press

Sun
microsystems
O'REILLY
SAMS

ALPHA
New
Riders

Java
Cisco Press

Microsoft
Press
que

macromedia
PRESS

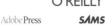

Related Titles from O'Reilly

Web Programming

ActionScript Cookbook

ActionScript for Flash MX: The Definitive Guide, *2nd Edition*

Dynamic HTML: The Definitive Reference, *2nd Edition*

Flash Hacks

Essential PHP Security

Google Hacks, *2nd Edition*

Google Pocket Guide

HTTP: The Definitive Guide

JavaScript & DHTML Cookbook

JavaScript Pocket Reference, *2nd Edition*

JavaScript: The Definitive Guide, *4th Edition*

Learning PHP 5

PayPal Hacks

PHP Cookbook

PHP in a Nutshell

PHP Pocket Reference, *2nd Edition*

PHPUnit Pocket Guide

Programming ColdFusion MX, *2nd Edition*

Programming PHP

Upgrading to PHP 5

Web Database Applications with PHP and MySQL, *2nd Edition*

Webmaster in a Nutshell, *3rd Edition*

Web Authoring and Design

Cascading Style Sheets: The Definitive Guide, *2nd Edition*

CSS Cookbook

CSS Pocket Reference, *2nd Edition*

Dreamweaver MX 2004: The Missing Manual, *2nd Edition*

Essential ActionScript 2.0

Flash Out of the Box

Head First HTML & CSS

HTML & XHTML: The Definitive Guide, *5th Edition*

HTML Pocket Reference, *2nd Edition*

Information Architecture for the World Wide Web, *2nd Edition*

Learning Web Design, *2nd Edition*

Programming Flash Communication Server

Web Design in a Nutshell, *3rd Edition*

Web Site Measurement Hacks

Web Administration

Apache Cookbook

Apache Pocket Reference

Apache: The Definitive Guide, *3rd Edition*

Perl for Web Site Management

Squid: The Definitive Guide

Web Performance Tuning, *2nd Edition*

Our books are available at most retail and online bookstores.

To order direct: 1-800-998-9938 • *order@oreilly.com* • *www.oreilly.com*

Online editions of most O'Reilly titles are available by subscription at *safari.oreilly.com*

Keep in touch with O'Reilly

Download examples from our books

To find example files from a book, go to: *www.oreilly.com/catalog* select the book, and follow the "Examples" link.

Register your O'Reilly books

Register your book at *register.oreilly.com* Why register your books? Once you've registered your O'Reilly books you can:

- Win O'Reilly books, T-shirts or discount coupons in our monthly drawing.
- Get special offers available only to registered O'Reilly customers.
- Get catalogs announcing new books (US and UK only).
- Get email notification of new editions of the O'Reilly books you own.

Join our email lists

Sign up to get topic-specific email announcements of new books and conferences, special offers, and O'Reilly Network technology newsletters at:

elists.oreilly.com

It's easy to customize your free elists subscription so you'll get exactly the O'Reilly news you want.

Get the latest news, tips, and tools

www.oreilly.com

- "Top 100 Sites on the Web"—PC Magazine
- CIO Magazine's Web Business 50 Awards

Our web site contains a library of comprehensive product information (including book excerpts and tables of contents), downloadable software, background articles, interviews with technology leaders, links to relevant sites, book cover art, and more.

Work for O'Reilly

Check out our web site for current employment opportunities:

jobs.oreilly.com

Contact us

O'Reilly Media, Inc.
1005 Gravenstein Hwy North
Sebastopol, CA 95472 USA
Tel: 707-827-7000 or 800-998-9938
    (6am to 5pm PST)
Fax: 707-829-0104

Contact us by email

For answers to problems regarding your order or our products:
order@oreilly.com

To request a copy of our latest catalog:
catalog@oreilly.com

For book content technical questions or corrections: **booktech@oreilly.com**

For educational, library, government, and corporate sales: **corporate@oreilly.com**

To submit new book proposals to our editors and product managers:
proposals@oreilly.com

For information about our international distributors or translation queries:
international@oreilly.com

For information about academic use of O'Reilly books:
adoption@oreilly.com
or visit:
academic.oreilly.com

For a list of our distributors outside of North America check out:
international.oreilly.com/distributors.html

Order a book online

www.oreilly.com/order_new

Our books are available at most retail and online bookstores.
To order direct: 1-800-998-9938 • *order@oreilly.com* • *www.oreilly.com*
Online editions of most O'Reilly titles are available by subscription at *safari.oreilly.com*